EPIGRAPHIA ZEYLANICA

BEING

LITHIC AND OTHER INSCRIPTIONS OF CEYLON

EPIGRAPHIA ZEYLANICA

BEING

LITHIC AND OTHER INSCRIPTIONS OF CEYLON

EDITED AND TRANSLATED BY

DON MARTINO DE ZILVA WICKREMASINGHE

IN THREE VOLUMES
1904-1933

Vol. I
1904 - 1912

GYAN

Published by

GYAN

Gyan Publishing House
5, Ansari Road
Daryaganj, New Delhi-110002
Phone: 011-47034999, 9811692060
E-mail: books@gyanbooks.com

Distribution Network
gyanbooks.com
India, USA, Canada, UK, Australia, France

ISBN : 978-81-212-3351-4 (Set)
ISBN : 978-81-212-4987-4 (PB)
First Published, London, 1912

2nd Impression 2020

Printed at: Gyan Press, Delhi.

ARCHAEOLOGICAL SURVEY OF CEYLON

EPIGRAPHIA ZEYLANICA

BEING

LITHIC AND OTHER INSCRIPTIONS OF CEYLON

EDITED AND TRANSLATED

BY

DON MARTINO DE ZILVA WICKREMASINGHE, Hon. M. A. (Oxon.)

EPIGRAPHIST TO THE CEYLON GOVERNMENT

LECTURER IN TAMIL AND TELUGU IN THE UNIVERSITY OF OXFORD

Vol. I

1904 — 1912

LONDON

PUBLISHED FOR THE GOVERNMENT OF CEYLON BY HENRY FROWDE

OXFORD UNIVERSITY PRESS, AMEN CORNER, E.C.

1912

CONTENTS

LIST OF PLATES

ABBREVIATIONS

A. = Apabhraṁśa.
Abh. = Abhidhānappadīpikā, edited by Waskaḍuwe Subhūti. Colombo, 1865.
A. I. C. = Ancient Inscriptions in Ceylon. By Dr. E. Müller. 2 vols. London, 1883.
Am. = Amāwatura, edited by H. Jayatilaka. Colombo, 1885–86.
AMg. = Ardha-Māgadhī.
Arch. Surv. = Archaeological Survey.
A. S. C. = Archaeological Survey of Ceylon.
A. S. S. I. = Archaeological Survey of Southern India.
A. S. W. I. = Archaeological Survey of Western India.
Bt. = Bell's Text.
C B. R. A. S. = Ceylon Branch of the Royal Asiatic Society.
C. I. I. or Corp. Inscript. Ind. = Corpus Inscriptionum Indicarum.
Comp. Gram. = A Comparative Grammar of the Modern Aryan Languages of India. By John Beames. 3 vols. London, 1872–79.
Dh. = Dhammapada (Fausböll's edition, 1885).
Dv. = Dīpavaṁsa.
Ep. Ind. = Epigraphia Indica.
E. S. = Etymologie des Singhalesischen, von Wilhelm Geiger. München, 1897.
Gram. = Grammar or Grammatik.
Hc. = Hēmacandra.
Ind. Ant. = Indian Antiquary.
J. or Journ. = Journal.
Jay. = H. Jayatilaka's Elu-Akārādiya. Colombo, 1893.
JM. = Jaina-Māhārāṣṭrī. JŚ. = Jaina-Śaurasēnī.
Lit. = literally.
L. S. S. = Litteratur und Sprache der Singhalesen, von Wilhelm Geiger. Strassburg, 1900.
M. = Māhārāṣṭrī. Mg. = Māgadhī.
Mp. = Müller's plate. Mt. = Müller's text.
Mv. = Mahāvaṁsa. Mv. Ṭ. = Mahāvaṁsa Ṭīkā.
M. W. Dict. = Sir Monier Monier-Williams' Sanskrit Dictionary. Oxford, 1899.
Nām. = Nāmāvaliya.
Or. Soc. = Oriental Society.
P. = Pāli. p. = page. par. = paragraph.
Piyum. = Piyummala.
p. p. p. = past participle passive. Pkt. = Prākrit.
R. A. S. = Royal Asiatic Society.
Ruvan. = Ruvanmala.
Ś. = Śaurasēnī.
S. B. E. = Sacred Books of the East, edited by F. Max Müller.
Sinh. = Sinhalese. Skt. = Sanskrit.
T. = George Turnour.
W. = L. C. Wijēsiṇha, translator of the Mahāvaṁsa.
Z. D. M. G. = Zeitschrift der Deutschen Morgenländischen Gesellschaft.

ADDITIONS AND CORRECTIONS

Page 31, text line 9, *for* ඵලු *read* ඵළු

32, text line 26, *for* සාර *read* පෙර

32, text line 33, *for* සබාවසුන් *read* සබාවඩුන්

33, transcript line 26, *for* sāra *read* pere, and *delete* note 15

34, transcript line 33, *for* Sabāvasun *read* Sabāvaḍun

37, lines 8–9, *for* hostile ravagers [or] any barbarians *read vāri* (labourers), *pere-näṭṭiyam* [or] inhabitants of the *dasa-gam* (serf-villages?)

37, note 9, *add* and *pere* possibly from P. *pure*. Compare, however, the forms *perenäṭṭiyam* °*näṭṭu*, °*näṭṭuvam*, and °*näṭu*, below, pp. 53 note 15, 187, 189 note 5, 197, 199, 205, 207.

37, note 10, *add* See, moreover, the remarks on *dasa-gama*, below, pp. 243–244.

38, lines 5–8, *for* Mekāppar Vädārum ...... ceremonies, *read* Mekāppar Vat-kämi Sabāvaḍunnā Raksayim, Mekāppar Valu(vaṇisāsāka)yim and Kaliṅgu Ämbā Kitla-deṭim, [all] of the family of Mekāppar Vädārum Bamba Senevi Lokanāthan and also Kuḍasalā Vat-kām-deṭim of the family of Vaṭarak Saṅgārak-samaṇa

38, note 2, *add* See also below, pp. 193–194.

45, text line 34, *for* ඩිං *read* ඬිං

45, text line 36, *for* කුවුරුදු *read* හවුරුදු

45, text line 45, *for* වියො *read* පියො

48, transcript line 45, *for* viyo *read* piyo

53, note 13, *add* For a fuller explanation, see below, p. 251, note 6.

54, line 18, *for* destitute *read* impartial

54. note 1, *add* For a fuller explanation, see below, p. 251, note 6.

55, note 6, *add* This clause may also be rendered, 'In all these places belonging to Abahaygiri-vehera, [namely] in the image-house, in the dāgaba, in the Maha-bo-ge,' &c.

56. line 17, *for* brought about dissension among *read* practised dissimulation towards

56, note 7, *for* viyo *read* piyo
for viyōga *read* prayōga

57, lines 16–21, *for* A record ...... expiration of [every] year *read* Eight persons from the two seats [or chapters] together with four impartial and four elderly persons delegated, with the concurrence of the monks, by the recipients of *pariveṇas*, shall inquire into [the income and expenditure of] the *pariveṇas*, and making a record [thereof] at the expiration of [every] year, shall read out [the same] before the great congregation of monks.

69, note 14, *add* Cf. *yasa pitusalaka* in Nāsik, No. 10, line 4 (*Ep. Ind.* viii. p. 78).

70, line 13, *for* four *read* six

112, lines 14–15, *for* go repeatedly round *read* watch over

112, note 9, *for* 'having repeatedly gone,' ..... √gam *read* 'having watched over,' from P. *jaggati*, Skt. *jāgṛ*. I am indebted to Mr. D. B. Jayatilaka for this suggestion.

113, line 9, *for* near the 'stone-canoe' *read* north-east of Thūpārāma

113, line 10, *for* This inscription lies near the so-called 'stone-canoe,' a few yards to the east *read* This inscribed slab stands at a distance of a quarter of a mile north-east of the Thūpārāma dāgaba. It has now been re-erected by the Archaeological Survey Department.

115, lines 1–2, *delete* and only a few yards from the spot where the present inscription is

158, text B, line 4, *for* කු *read* තු

159, transcript B, line 4, *for* ku *read* tu

159, *delete* note 1.

161, line 7, *for* great king has granted .... Bamuṇ-kumbara *read* Maharādayan Bamuṇ (Brāhmaṇa) has granted to the dispensary at Tumbarab (Thūpārāma)

PREFACE

AMONGST the early references by Europeans to the existence of lithic records in Ceylon, that of the English captive Robert Knox, in the middle of the seventeenth century, is full of quaint interest. He writes:—

'Here are some *antient writings* engraven upon Rocks which poseth all that see them. There are divers great Rocks in divers parts in *Cande Uda* and in the *Northern* Parts. These Rocks are cut deep with great Letters for the space of some yards, so deep that they may last to the worlds end. No body can read them or make anything of them. I have asked *Malabars, Gentuses* as well as *Chingulays* and *Moors*, but none of them understood them. You walk over some of them. There is an antient temple, *Goddiladenni*[1] in *Yattanour* stands by one place where there are of these letters. They are probably in memorial of something, but of what we must leave to learned men to spend their conjectures[2].'

Since Knox, many have referred to and written upon these inscriptions. Without entering into an enumeration, suffice it to say that the papers which appeared, from time to time, chiefly in the *Ceylon Almanac* and in the *Journal of the Ceylon Branch of the Royal Asiatic Society*, from the pens of Messrs. Armour, Turnour, Hardy, Gogerly, Casie Chitty, De Alwis, Brodie, Rhys Davids, and others, aroused so much interest in Ceylon epigraphy that in 1874 the Government, under the late Sir W. H. Gregory, decided to engage the services of a specialist in the person of the late Dr. P. Goldschmidt to prosecute systematic research in this direction. For two years he worked zealously, exploring in the N. C. and N.W. Provinces, and in the Hambantota

---

[1] Referring to the inscriptions at the Gaḍalādeṇiya Vihāra in Yaṭinuvara, not far from Kandy.

[2] *An Historical Relation of the Island Ceylon in the East-Indies.* By Robert Knox. London, 1681. Fol., pp. 112, 113.

district of the S. Province. From continued exposure to a tropical sun and the malaria of the jungles, he contracted the fever to which he succumbed on May 7, 1877, much regretted as well by those who watched with interest the progress of his well-begun task as by his personal friends. Although he wrote but few reports—probably three which appeared in the *Ceylon Sessional Papers* for 1875 and 1876, and were afterwards reprinted in the *Indian Antiquary*, vols. v. 189 and vi. 318—besides his note on Sinhalese inscriptions contributed to the *C. B. R. A. S. Journal* for 1879, yet he left behind a considerable amount of material for future workers.

His death necessarily caused a break in the continuity of the epigraphical survey of Ceylon. But this was not for long; as, early in 1878, Dr. E. Müller (now Professor of Oriental Philology at the University of Berne) was appointed to carry on the work. He took over Dr. Goldschmidt's papers, and soon after began his investigations in the Hambantota district, the N. W. Province, and other districts where inscriptions were likely to be found. The results of his researches are embodied in his reports to Government (*Sessional Papers* for 1878, 1880, 1881), in his contributions to the *C. B. R. A. S. Journal* for 1880 and 1883, and to the *Indian Antiquary*, vols. ix and xi, and finally in the two volumes entitled *Ancient Inscriptions in Ceylon* (London, 1883), which contain a general account of one hundred and seventy-two inscriptions, with romanized texts, translations, and lithograph plates.

As pioneers, both these scholars have rendered lasting service to the cause of Ceylon epigraphy. But since their time such strides have been made in our knowledge of the ancient records and documents of the island, as well as in the method of treating them for publication, that a new edition of *Ceylon Inscriptions* has become a desideratum. This was specially felt when Mr. H. C. P. Bell, after his appointment as Archaeological Commissioner in 1890, brought out a most interesting and exhaustive report on the archaeology of the Kegalla district (*Ceylon Sessional Papers*, 1893), and still more when, transferred to Anurādhapura and the N. C. Province, he succeeded in discovering a large number of important inscriptions[1].

---

[1] I served as Assistant to the Archaeological Commissioner from 1890–93; and was thus enabled (particularly during Mr. Bell's serious illness in 1892) to aid in the search for lithic records, with considerable success.

On this account Mr. Bell recommended to Government the publication of an epigraphical journal on the lines of the *Epigraphia Indica.* His recommendation was adopted; and I was appointed Epigraphist to the Archaeological Survey in 1899, to work in collaboration with the late B. Guṇasĕkara Mudaliyar, Chief Translator to the Government, by whose death Ceylon has been bereft of a scholar as sound as he was modest, who has done much unostentatiously to elucidate the ancient history and literature of the Sinhalese. In anticipation of the sanction of Government for the publication of this *Epigraphia Zeylanica*, the Archaeological Commissioner had his Head Overseer well trained to take mechanical impressions of inscriptions by a member of the staff of the Epigraphist to the Madras Government, Dr. E. Hultzsch. From these estampages, with the further aid of photographs as well as of eye copies, it was arranged that I should edit the texts for publication.

As to the scrupulous care taken in the preparation of ink-estampages there need not be the slightest doubt. Mr. Bell's own long experience and thoroughness are in themselves a sufficient guarantee. And the method employed is exactly that advocated by the late Dr. Bühler in the Memorandum on the subject which he kindly wrote for my guidance on November 19, 1897, hardly five months before he met with the fatal accident on the Lake of Constance, which deprived us of one of the brightest stars of oriental scholarship.

I give here the Memorandum in full, both because it is probably the last contribution of that distinguished scholar to epigraphical lore, and because it is replete with instructions which must necessarily be followed by every collector of inscriptions.

'The first principle in modern epigraphic research is that all inscriptions should be reproduced by purely mechanical means. All eye copies and tracings have been discarded, and it is no longer considered permissible to whitewash or to paint the letters of inscriptions in black before they are photographed, or to restore by hand doubtful and illegible signs. All such proceedings are misleading, and reproductions which have been prepared in this manner are rejected by all epigraphists as absolutely useless. The materials, which should be placed by the collector before the epigraphists, should give the documents exactly as they are, with all the imperfections which they exhibit in their natural state.

'The only means by which perfectly faithful reproductions can be obtained, are impressions, or estampages, taken according to Dr. Burgess's method (to the exclusion of all pencil rubbings) and photographs. As the photographs only show the surface, not the depth of the strokes, they are inferior to impressions, which besides, if taken properly, give at the back of the paper the letters in relievo. Hence the latter should be taken *always in a number of copies* whenever this is possible. It will, however, do no harm if photographs are taken in addition to the "impressions," as occasionally single letters, or portions of letters, are not caught properly by the paper. Inscriptions with very shallow letters, or such as are situated in inaccessible places, can of course only be photographed. The new telephotographic apparatus should be used for inscriptions on which an ordinary camera cannot be brought to bear.

'Before impressions of stone inscriptions are taken, the stones should be washed with water in order to remove any dirt or dust which may stick in the letters. Copper plates, covered with verdigris, should be cleaned by an immersion in lime juice. The plate should be placed in a shallow bath of white metal, and should be covered by the juice. It may remain immersed, according to the circumstances of the case, for twenty-four hours or more. But it should be cleaned at the end of the immersion, and during it from time to time, with a tooth brush.

'In getting photozincographs or autotypes prepared from impressions or photographs, the greatest caution is necessary to prevent the introduction of any "improvement" by the photographer or the corrector of the proofs.'

In Dr. Bühler's covering letter to me, dated December 1, 1897, he writes further that he 'talked the matter over with Dr. Fleet, who fully agrees' with his views.

The collotype plates which accompany this number of the *Epigraphia Zeylanica* have been prepared by the well-known establishments of Griggs and Sons of Peckham, and of the University Press of Oxford. Thanks to the personal interest and care which Messrs. Griggs and Hart take in the reproduction of inscriptions, I am able to say that these plates represent absolutely faithful facsimiles, on a reduced scale, of the original inscriptions as shown on the estampages taken.

In my account of the inscriptions, I have purposely avoided any generalizations based on insufficient data, but have always kept in view the more useful task of putting before the reader all the material that I had been able to get together bearing on each subject under discussion. For the benefit of those students who are not familiar with the system of transliteration, I have given the texts of some inscriptions in native characters as well.

The system of transliteration adopted here is that approved of by the International Congress of Orientalists in 1894, and followed in the Journal of the Royal Asiatic Society, with such additions and modifications as are necessary to represent Sinhalese and Tamil letters. See Table on p. vii.

In the edition of texts of inscriptions, all doubtful letters, and those that are supplied doubtfully, are enclosed in parentheses, and those which are partially or wholly illegible, but which can be supplied with absolute certainty, are put within square brackets. Those, however, which cannot be supplied are represented by points at the rate of two for each syllable or akṣara.

An asterisk attached to a letter or other sign indicates that that letter or sign was altogether omitted in the original.

A single hyphen is used either to separate words in composition, as far as it is desirable to do so, or at the end of a line, to show that the word is continued in the next line.

A double hyphen is employed to divide words which in the original are joined together by the euphonic rules of *sandhi*, and is limited only to those combinations where a final vowel or consonant blends with the initial vowel or consonant of the following word, so as to form a complex sign. Whenever the phonetic changes are expressed by separate letters, the double hyphen is not used, for example तच्छ्रुत्वा will be transliterated *tac=chrutvā*, whilst तच् छ्रुत्वा (if so found in the original) will be denoted by *tac chrutvā* without the double hyphen.

Corrections of orthographical or other irregularities in the texts are given as footnotes.

In the body of the work I have acknowledged whatever assistance I have received; and I need here only reiterate my indebtedness, not only to those authors whose publications I have consulted, but also to all those who have personally given me the benefit of their scholarship and friendly advice, amongst whom I may be allowed to mention Professors A. A. Macdonell, Cecil Bendall, Dr. J. F. Fleet, Dr. A. F. R. Hoernle, and Messrs. F. H. M. Corbet, R. W. Lee, and J. C. Pembrey. But my specially grateful thanks, and indeed the thanks of all Indologists, are due to the Ceylon Government, and to Mr. Bell, its Archaeological Commissioner, without whose enterprise, as mentioned above, this publication might not have seen the light.

DON MARTINO DE ZILVA WICKREMASINGHE.

INDIAN INSTITUTE, OXFORD,
December, 1903.

SYSTEM OF TRANSLITERATION

अ	අ	அ	a
आ	ආ	ஆ	ā
—	ඇ	—	ä
—	ඈ	—	ǟ
इ	ඉ	இ	i
ई	ඊ or ඊ	ஈ or ஈ	ī
उ	උ	உ	u
ऊ	ඌ	ஊ	ū
ऋ	ඍ	—	ṛ
ॠ	ඎ	—	ṝ
ऌ	ඏ	—	ḷ
ॡ	ඐ	—	ḹ
—	එ	எ	e
ए	ඒ	ஏ	ē
ऐ	ඓ	ஐ	ai
—	ඔ	ஒ	o
ओ	ඕ	ஓ	ō
औ	ඖ	ஔ	au
क	ක	க	ka
ख	ඛ	—	kha
ग	ග	க (medial)	ga
घ	ඝ	—	gha
ङ	ඞ	ங	ṅa
च	ච	ச	ca
छ	ඡ	—	cha
ज	ජ	ஜ, ச	ja
झ	ඣ	—	jha
ञ	ඤ	ஞ	ña
ट	ට	ட (when doubled ட்ட)	ṭa
ठ	ඨ	—	ṭha
ड	ඩ	ட	ḍa
ढ	ඪ	—	ḍha
ण	ණ	ண	ṇa
त	ත	த	ta
थ	ථ	—	tha
द	ද	த (medial)	da
ध	ධ	—	dha
न	න	ந	na
प	ප	ப	pa
फ	ඵ	—	pha
ब	බ	ப (medial)	ba
भ	භ	—	bha
म	ම	ம or ஐ	ma
य	ය	ய	ya
र	ර	ர	ra
ल	ල	ல	la
व	ව	வ	va
—	—	ழ	ḻa
—	—	ள	ḷa
—	—	ற	ṟa
—	—	ன	ṉa
श	ශ	ச	śa
ष	ෂ	ஷ	ṣa
स	ස	ச or ஸ	sa
ह	හ	க or ஹ	ha
ळ	ළ	—	ḷa
ं (anusvāra)	ං	—	ṁ
ँ (anunāsika)	ෆ (ෆ)	—	˘ ˘
ः (visarga)	ඃ	—	ḥ
ऽ (avagraha)	—	—	'

EPIGRAPHIA ZEYLANICA

No. 1. JĒTAVANĀRĀMA SANSKRIT INSCRIPTION

THIS inscription was discovered in 1894, when certain ruins just north of the Kuṭṭam-pokuṇa ('Twin-ponds') in Anurādhapura were being excavated by the Archaeological Survey. The ruins are probably those of a monastery belonging to the so-called **Jētavanārāma** group. Judging from the style of architecture, they may be assigned to a period anterior to the tenth century.

The **granite slab** which contains the inscription measures 4′ 4″ by 3′ 3″. Like most of the important lithic records of the Island, this too seems to have suffered at the hands of treasure-seekers. It is broken into three or four pieces at the bottom, and its surface at the centre is damaged by fire, in consequence of which the last three lines, as well as portions of lines 12 to 28, 35 and 37, are illegible. In other respects the inscription is well preserved. I am editing it from a beautifully clear photograph and two excellent inked impressions on paper, supplied to me by Mr. H. C. P. Bell, the Archaeological Commissioner. As may be seen from the accompanying plate, the inscription consists of forty lines of boldly engraved writing, which, together with a margin of about an inch all round, covers the whole slab. Each line is 3′ 1″ long, and each letter is nearly an inch in size. On either side of the first two lines is carved a conventional form of a lotus-flower[1], hitherto not found in Ceylon inscriptions.

The **characters** call for special remark. They belong to the Northern class of Indian alphabets, and are the first examples discovered so far south as Ceylon[2]. After a careful examination of all known types, I have come to

[1] For similar carvings on the Mathurā Buddhist railing, see Cunningham's *Arch. Survey Reports*, iii. Pl. X.

[2] In his *Ancient Inscriptions in Ceylon* (p. 52) Professor Edward Müller describes an inscription at Demaḷamāna, which seems from his account to be written in this alphabet. Cf. also the characters on the coins of king Parākrama Bāhu, and on the Abhayagiri Copper-plate (pp. 39, 40).

the conclusion that this inscription is written in a variety of the Magadha **Nāgarī** character, which was current early in the ninth century A. D.

The learned monks of Ceylon must have been familiar with this alphabet; for, besides the present inscription, which is itself a proof of this, we find two or three others written by or at the instance of Ceylon monks. The earliest of them is the Bōdh-Gayā inscription of Mahānāman Sthavira, dated the year 269 (A. D. 588–9)[1]. From a glance at the facsimile plate (*Corp. Inscript. Ind.* iii. Pl. XLI A), one can see that its alphabet is of the same class as that here used. Several akṣaras, such as *j*, *m*, *y*, *r*, *l*, *ś*, and *s* are, of course, older in form. In the Aphsaḍ inscription of Ādityasēna (*ibid.* Pl. XXVIII) and in the Sārnāth inscription of Prakaṭāditya (*ibid.* Pl. XLIII c), both of which are assigned to the seventh century, most of these letters are more like those of the present inscription, although distinctly older. We find, moreover, in the Aphsaḍ record (line 12) a sign for the conjunct *rth*, which seems to be a prototype of that given in lines 13, 26, and 33 of the Jētavanārāma inscription. According to Professor Kielhorn, a separate sign for *rth*, developed from the same source, is also to be found in line 13 of the Khālimpur plate of Dharmapāladēva (*Ep. Ind.* iv. p. 243), and in the Kōṭā Buddhist inscription of Sāmanta Dēvadatta of Vikrama saṁvat 847 (?) (*Ind. Ant.* xiv. p. 46). On the other hand, the characters of the Harṣa inscription, A. D. 970 (*Ep. Ind.* ii. No. 8), as compared with those under consideration, are clearly more developed, and present types more or less of a later period (cf. also Ghōsrāwā inscription, *Ind. Ant.* xvii. p. 310, plate). The latest known inscription in this so-called Kuṭila[2] Nāgarī alphabet, written or composed by a Ceylon Buddhist monk, is the one at Buddha-Gayā (or Bōdh-Gayā)[3] recording the dedication of a *gandhakuṭi* for the service of the Buddha, and assigned to the tenth or eleventh century A.D.[4] The name of the monk is given there as Paṇḍita Ratnaśrījñāna Bhikṣu, and he may be the author of the Cāndragōmi-vyākaraṇa-pañjikā and the Śabdārthacintā[5].

Our inscription is in **Sanskrit** prose; and this is most probably the reason

[1] Cf. Mr. Vincent A. Smith's article on this record in *Ind. Ant.* xxxi. pp. 192–7.

[2] See Dr. Fleet's remarks on the Aphsaḍ inscription (*Corp. Inscript. Ind.* iii. p. 201), and those of Professor Bühler on the Dēwal Praśasti (*Ep. Ind.* i. p. 76).

[3] Note the similarity of the akṣaras *ṣ* and *rya* of this inscription to some of the types of the same letters in the present record.

[4] See *Buddha-Gayā*, by Rājēndralāla Mitra, pp. 194–7; *Mahābodhi*, by Sir A. Cunningham, p. 66.

[5] See my *Catalogue of the Sinhalese MSS. in the British Museum*, Introduction, p. xiii.

why it is written in Nāgarī instead of in the then existing Sinhalese characters, which were developed, like those of the Kaḍamba and the Pallava inscriptions, from the southern class of early Indian alphabets.

It is evident from the abrupt beginning of the text (*kaikab-ca* for *ēkaikab-ca*) that we have here only the second portion of the inscription. The first part must have been engraved on a separate slab; for there are no traces of writing on the back of the present stone[1]. As regards **orthography**, the letter *b* is denoted by the sign for *v*[2], which hardly differs from *dh* in conjuncts[3]. The *ṛ* vowel is used for *ri* in *tṛṣṭv-api* (line 1)[2], and frequently in pausā the Anusvāra instead of *m*. The doubling of the consonant both before and after *r*, which is common in Indian inscriptions, is to be found here also, e. g. *tattra* (lines 1 and 2), *prasthārddhaṁ* (line 3), and *nirddhāritēna* (line 18). The conjunct *ṭṭ* is written for *ṭ* as in *kuṭṭumbibhir* (line 5. Cf. *kuṭṭumbikā* in *Ep. Ind.* iii. No. 44, ll. 3, 6). The rules of *sandhi* are not always observed. The **grammar** is in general correct, and the **style** is simple and clear. There are, however, several words either not found in dictionaries or used with peculiar significations. These are:—*Pālikā*, *Pāli*, prescribed quantity or allowance of food, see *Ep. Ind.* i. p. 166, iii. p. 264. *Cīvarikā*, prescribed number of robes. The word *cīvarikā* occurs in one of the Junnar inscriptions, No. 3, line 3 (see *Arch. Surv. of W. India*, iv. p. 93), and in the Nāsik, No. 7, line 2 (*ibid.* p. 102), where it is read as *civarika*. Bühler's translation of it is 'expense for clothes.' See also Nāsik, No. 22 (*ibid.* p. 115); Kanheri, No. 28 (Burgess' *Elura Cave Temples*, p. 85). *Padālāyikā*, *Padālā*, a complaint or a matter of dispute. *Vārika*, probably a person who renders service or holds temple-lands by turns (Sinh. *taṭṭumāru* tenure ?). *Kiri*, a Sinhalese measure of grain[4]. *Parivahaṇa*[5], probably a lay warden or chief concierge of a monastic establishment.

The inscription contains regulations for the guidance of monks and laymen living within the precincts of the Vihāras or in lands belonging to them. These regulations are similar to those of the two inscriptions at Mihintale (*A. I. C.*

---

[1] Search for the other slab has proved fruitless.

[2] For other examples, see *Ep. Ind.* iii. No. 17, iv. No. 11 b.

[3] Compare, for example, *prasthārddhaṁ* in line 3 with *kuṭṭumbibhir-adhiṣṭhitam vihāram* in l. 5.

[4] According to Clough's *Sinh. Dict.* it is 'the ground sufficient to sow four *mānikā* = 64 *lās*.' It is most probably equivalent to Pāli *karīsaṁ* and Skt. *khāri*. According to the *Abhidhānappadīpikā* a *karīsaṁ* = 4 *ammaṇas* (Sinh. *amuṇu*), i. e. 44 (4 × 11) *drōṇas*. The capacity of a *khāri* seems, on the other hand, to vary considerably. Monier Williams fixes it at about three bushels. For further particulars, see Colebrooke's *Essays*, i. pp. 533–7, and Thomas' *Ancient Indian Weights*, p. 26.

[5] Skt. *pari* + √*vah*; cf. Sinh. *pirivahanu* in Mihintale tablets A, line 20 (*A. I. C.* No. 121).

No. 121). They give an insight into the life in, and the administration of monasteries, and show the care that was taken to regulate the conduct of monks and others connected with monastic establishments in the ninth and tenth centuries.

I have ventured to assign this inscription to **the first half of the ninth century** A.D. purely on palaeographic grounds. No date is given in the legible portion of the inscription, and I have as yet not been able to identify any of the villages mentioned in it, or to find any certain reference to this *dhamma-kammam* (Wijēsinha's *Mahāvaṁsa*, p. 25, note) in the chronicles of the Island. The *Mahāvaṁsa*, however, records that King Aggabōdhi VII, who reigned circa A.D. 781–7, issued decrees enforcing discipline among the priesthood, and 'stopped the way of those who set up false cases, by deciding them according to the law' (Ch. xlviii. 71–72).

TEXT[1].

1 [ए*]कैकश्च ग्रामस्थेरः[2] तुष्वपि ग्रामेषु प्रत्येकं प्रत्येकं स्थाप्यः पाचिका तत्र प्रति-
2 दिनं द्विगुणा न चीवरिका विहारे नवकर्म्मकृतोरपि तथा । यत्र ये भिक्षुशालासमाविनाश्चवीरेव देयः ।
3 नियमं । पञ्चोपदंशाः प्रस्थार्द्धं दधि प्रस्थप्रमितेन घृतेन विंशतिः पाचिकाः । त्रिभिर्भिक्षुभिर्महासि-
4 क्षापर्वशालायां द्वाभ्यां ग्रामस्थविराभ्यां सह निवसद्भिर्महासिक्काम् उपल् गोखुम्[3] चीवरनवकर्म्मणे भिक्षु-
5 शांश्च ग्रामान्समन्यमानोऽत्र तत्र तत्र ग्रामभोगैः कुटुम्बिभिरधिष्ठितम्विहारप्रवेश्य वर्षपरिसमाप्तौ तत्र तत्र
6 समवसमायं व्ययं शेषञ्च कर्म्मिभिर्नवकैश्च संघानुज्ञातेषु भिक्षुपूपदर्श्य परिभुक्तपरिवारकैर्यथा सु-
7 खमत्र विहारे विहर्त्तव्यं । ये ये तत्रापरिभुक्तासीतिसत्तुद्रव्यन्देयं सङ्घेनापि[6] यवक्षमेव तद्गृहीत-
8 व्यम् । एवं ऊर्द्धाशापर्वशालायां स्थितैरपि भिक्षुभिरभिनयामे ऊर्द्धाशायां[7] यवपन्नरीखण्डिया-
9 मे च तथैव । चौरापञ्चाययोरपि तथैव । सुनग्रामे पि तथैव भिक्षुभिः पूर्ववदेव कर्त्तव्यम् । तदकुर्वताम्
10 पूर्वोक्त एव दोषः । पञ्जिकास्थविरैरेव पद्राचायिका निरूपणीया । इह देशे[8] चन्द्रविहारोपसम्पन्ना-
11 नामन्यत्र वासवासौ परित्यज्य तत्प्रतिमवविहारकर्म्माकु[र्वता]मेव निवासो नान्येषां[9] । इह द्वीपे पादमात्र-
12 चैत्यवासिनामपि न ग्रासो न वासः । मिथ्याजीविना न च[स्तव्यं ।](स्त्रीपोष)केण न वस्तव्यम् । अन्यत्र मातापि-
13 तृभ्याम् । ग्रामार्थं क्षेत्रार्थं वा ताम्बूलादिकं राजकुल(प्रेषयतापि) [न च]स्तव्यं[10] । चन्द्रविहारसाहाय्यं कुर्वता
14 पि न वस्तव्यम् । मिश्रयादविमुक्तैः स्थविरैरपि(सह ....)[निवस]द्भिर्न वस्तव्यम् । यन्निश्रित्य निवसद्भि-

---

[1] From two inked estampages and a photograph. [2] Read ग्रामस्थविरस्तिष्वपि. [3] Read °खुम्बी°.
[4] Read कुटुम्बि°. [5] Read °ष्ठितं विहा°. [6] Read °नाप्यव°. [7] Read °याम्.
[8] Read देशेऽन्य°. [9] Read °षाम्. [10] Read °व्यम्.

Scale 2'' to 1 foot.

FROM AN INK-IMPRESSION SUPPLIED BY THE ARCHAEOLOGICAL COMMISSIONER, CEYLON. W. GRIGGS, COLLOTYPE.

15 : कृतो दोषस्तमनिवारयता निश्रयदायापि [न वस्तव्यं दो]षं कुर्वतान्तेवासिना। उपसम्पदा-
16 च देशे काषायं परित्यज्य पुनः प्रव्रजितेन न वस्तव्यं। (व्य .... स्व)दारकव्याजेनापि कुर्वतापि न वस्तव्यं
17 किम्पुनः कृषिवाणिज्यादिकम्। यत्किञ्चिल्लोकविरुद्धं य[च्छास]नविरुद्धञ्च कुर्वतापि न वस्तव्यं[1]। अन्यविहारा-
18 न्निर्धारितेन न वस्तव्यम्। प्राप्तकर्मादानमकुर्वता न व[स्तव्यं।] सत्व[2]विघातं कुर्वतापि न वस्तव्यं। सङ्घकार्य-
19 विघाते पि सत्व[2]विघातो न कर्तव्यः। अधिकपा(थेयला)भिनापि तण्डुलादिकं नोत्कर्षयितव्यं। परस्प-
20 रविवादे प्यधर्मवादिना न वस्तव्यं[1]। अननु ....ण........ (पि) न वस्तव्यं[1]। अस्यारामस्य सम्भो-
21 गग्रामादौ येषां भिक्षूणां श्रामणेराणाम्वा[3] ज्ञातयः (सन्ति तैर्यतिभि)रपि न वस्तव्यम्। इहारामे।
22 येषाम्वा[4] आरामे सम्भोगादौ[5] कुटु[6]म्बिभिर्गणकेन क(र्मकारकाणाम् ?) पुत्रादौ नाम क्रियते तैरपि
23 न वस्तव्यं। यस्मिन् ग्रामे क्लृप्तकर्मदण्डांश्च प्रतिनि[वर्तयन्ति] .... पुनस्तेषान्दोषम्विना[7] वारि-
24 कैः कर्मकरैर्वा चेचादि कुटुम्बिभ्यो[6] नापनेयं[8]। एवं सर्वत्र ग्रामेषु (तत्र) स्थाः संघेन कुटुम्बिभिश्च[6] रक्ष-
25 णीयाः। नवकर्मग्रामे चतुरः[9] शिलाकुट्टकाः[10] तक्षकाश्च षटूः[11] ते सर्वे (स्वे) ....
26 कर्मणि निपुणाः[।*] तेषामर्द्धाधिकमेवं किरिचित्रप्रत्येकम्प्रत्येकं जीवितार्थं (देयं) न .... वाट्टि ..
27 कुधान्यवापनाय स्थली चैका प्रत्येकन्देया। एषामेकस्य दत्तप्रमाणं जीवित(दानं का)रकस्य कर्म(कार)-
28 यतो देयम्। तथा द्वितीयस्यापि जीवितदानकाल एव कर्मादिकम्प्रतिनि[रीक्ष्य प]ञ्जिकापुस्तके[12] अभि-
29 निखातस्य तस्य नाम तत्तत्कर्म चाभिलिख्य दातव्यम्। आरामाभ्यन्तरकर्म(कारकैः) पञ्चकौलिकैरेव प-
30 रिच्छिद्य कर्म ग्रहीतव्यम् परिशुध्यैव तैरेव दातव्या। पञ्चदिनाधिकम्मास(द्वयं) कर्मकरणे नियतं। परि-
31 पाट्याकाद्कुर्वताङ्कारकाणाम्वारि[13]काणाङ्कर्मकृताञ्च दोषः। तद्दोषमपरिहरतामकुर्वतामकारय-
32 तां वृत्तिविच्छेदः कार्यः। परिवहणस्यापि[14] अन्तर्वहिश्च रथकुशलस्य पदाणां वर्जम्प्रत्येकं प्रतिग्रा-
33 मं किरिकिरिचिन्दातव्यं। समर्थस्य नान्यस्य। चातुर्महानिकायेषु पञ्चविंशतिः पञ्चविंशतिस्तप-
34 स्विनः[15] तेन शतन्निवासिकानां। चत्वारिंशत्[16] शास्त्राभियुक्तास्तपस्विनः। निकायभेदम्विनापि[17] गृही-
तनिश्रयाः.. ..
35 .... एषु सर्वेषु[18] असभ्यवादिभिरसत्यवादिभिरयुक्तकारिभिरपि न वस्तव्यं। किम्पुनर्लाकुटिकशस्त्रधरकृत-
36 [पस्वि]भिः। येषु निकायेष्वसंपूर्णता तपस्विनां तदन्यनिकायैस्तदाश्रयैश्च स्थातव्यं। तन्निकायतपस्विषु स(ह)
37 .. .. (अप)नेया अन्यनिकायतपस्विनः स्थाप्याश्च तन्निकाया एव ..(स).. .. ..(क) .. क .. न
कर्तव्यः। विहार(पा)-
38 .... भिक्षवः श्रावयितव्याः .... (उ).... (भिक्षुषु) ....
39[19] . . . .
40 . . . .

---

[1] Read °व्यम्. [2] Read सत्त्व. [3] Read °णां वा. [4] Read येषां वारामे. [5] For सम्भोगग्रामादौ. [6] कुटुम्बि°. [7] दोषं विना. [8] °यम्. [9] Read चतुराः. [10] °कुट्टकास्तक्ष°. [11] Probably for पटकः। [12] °केऽभि°. [13] °णां वारि°. [14] °प्यन्तर्ब°. [15] °स्तेन. [16] चत्वारिंशच्छास्त्रा°. [17] °भेदं विनापि. [18] सर्वेष्वस°. [19] These two lines are illegible with the exception of a few letters here and there.

TRANSLATION

[Lines 1, 2] And a single *śrāmaṇēra*[2] shall be stationed in each of all the three villages. There, the allowance[3] of food for each person [shall be] doubled; [but] not that for robes[4]: so likewise [shall it be] in regard to the two doing repairs at the Vihāra (monastery). Whatever place they are attached to, there they themselves shall allow no dilapidation.

[Lines 3–7] According to regulation, five [kinds of] cakes [or curries][5], half a *prastha*[6] of coagulated milk [and] twenty portions (*pālikā*) of ghee [each] measuring a *prastha* [shall be allowed]. The three monks (*bhikṣu*) who live with two novices (*śrāmaṇēra*) in **Lahasikā** monastery, having well looked after [the two villages] **Lahasikā** [and] **Urulgōṇu** and the villages set apart for the renewal of [monks'] robes, having caused the revenue[7] of all these [villages] to be brought into the Vihāra established by the respective householders, and having at the end of [every] year, with the help of accountants and those engaged in work, shown to the monks authorized by the Church (*Saṅgha*) the whole income and expenditure, as well as the balance [in hand], [these three monks] shall live in this Vihāra at their will, together with virtuous attendants. [Lines 7–10] Whoever are dishonest in this place, shall restore whatever property [they have appropriated]. And the *Saṅgha* shall most surely receive

---

[1] In editing and translating this inscription, I have consulted with profit the Sinhalese interpretation of the text made for the Archaeological Commissioner by K. Dhammārāma Thēra, Principal of the Vidyālaṅkāra Parivēṇa, and editor of several important Sanskrit, Pāli, and Sinhalese works.

[2] A term applied to a Buddhist novice prior to his receiving the *upasampadā* ordination. See also Childers' *Pāli Dictionary*, p. 305, *pabbajjā*.

[3] *Pālikā* seems to have the same signification as *Pāli*, 'a measure of capacity, prescribed food, maintenance of a scholar during the period of his studies by his teacher' (M. W. *Dict.*). The latter word seems so far to be found in this sense only in Indian lexicons.

[4] *Civarikā*. See p. 3.

[5] *Upadaṁśa*, 'anything eaten in addition (to excite thirst or appetite), a relish, spice' (M. W. *Dict.*).

[6] *Prasthārdham* may also mean one and a half *prastha*. Cf. Hopkins' remarks on numbers (*Journ. of the American Or. Soc.*, vol. xxiii. pp. 132, 133). *Prastha* is a measure of capacity equal to a Sinhalese *näliya*. See also Hoernle's edition of the *Bower Manuscript*, Calcutta, 1893, Pt. i. p. 13, note 17; *Life and Essays of H. T. Colebrooke*, London, 1873, ii. p. 533 ff.

[7] *Lābha*. Taking *adhiṣṭhitam* as an attribute of *lābham*, this clause can be rendered 'having brought into the Vihāra the profits caused by the respective householders to accrue from all these [villages].'

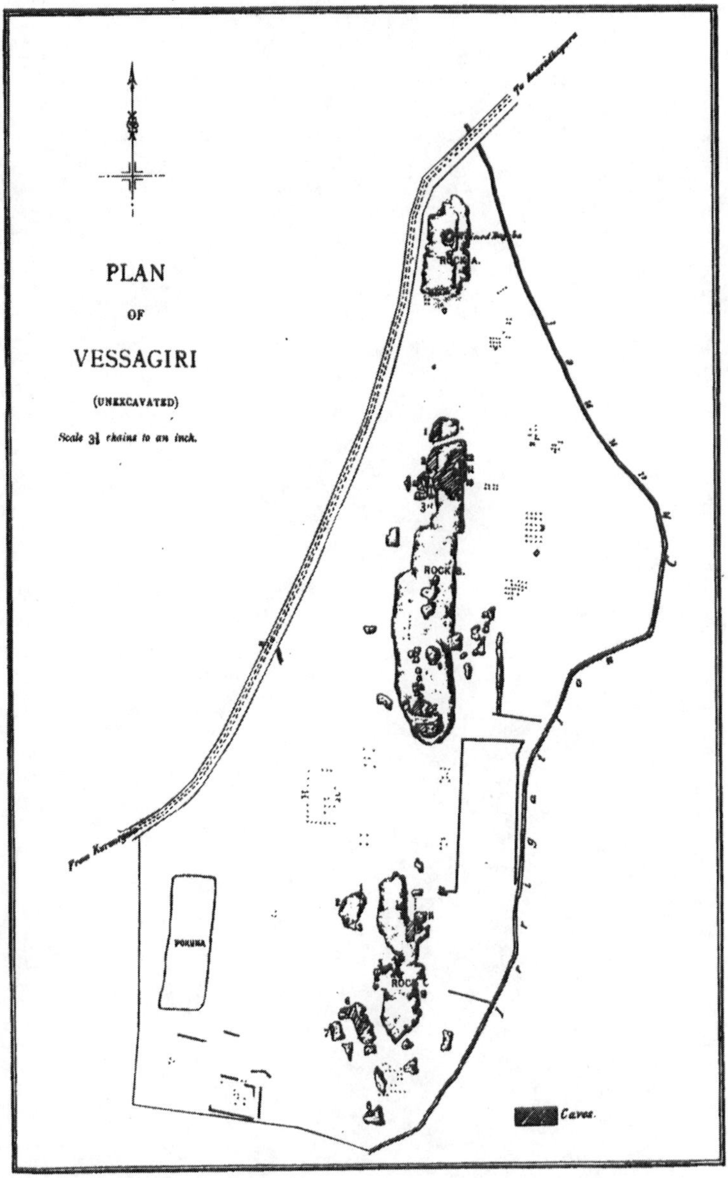
PLAN
OF
VESSAGIRI
(UNEXCAVATED)
Scale 3¾ chains to an inch.
ROCK A.
ROCK B.
ROCK C.
POKUNA
Caves.

it. In this manner, the monks living in **Hunālā** monastery [shall observe] exactly the same [rule] in [respect of the villages] **Ambila-grāma**[1], **Hunālā** and **Ulavannarīkhaṇṭi-grāma.** Exactly the same [shall be the practice] in the two [villages] **Kirā** and **Pallāya.** Likewise in **Sunagrāma**, the monks shall do exactly as aforesaid. To those who do not do that, the above-mentioned culpability [shall attach]. And the matter[2] shall be investigated by the Elders (*Thēra*) themselves who keep the register[3]. [Lines 10–13] [This Vihāra shall, moreover, be] a dwelling-place for such only of those ordained at another Vihāra in this country as have given up the food and raiment of that Vihāra and do not attend to the monastic duties connected therewith; [and] not for others. To those who own[4] even as much as a foot of the soil of this Island, neither food nor raiment [shall be allowed by the monastery]. [This Vihāra] shall not be inhabited by [any] one leading an improper life, or by one who (supports a woman). [The case is] otherwise in regard to [his] mother and father. [Lines 13–15] [This Vihāra] shall not be inhabited (by one who sends) betel-leaves and so forth to the royal household either for the sake of gain or out of regard, or by one who renders assistance to another monastery. It shall also not be inhabited by those who live . . . . . with monks who are not absolved from [the obligation of being under] the protection[5] [of senior monks], or by such a giver of protection (*niśraya*) as does not remove the offence committed by those living with him under his tutelage, or by a pupil who commits an offence. [Lines 15–19] It shall not be inhabited by one who, after taking orders [somewhere else] and after throwing off the yellow robe in this country, has assumed it again, or by one who does . . . . . under the pretext of it being his own child: so much the less [this Vihāra shall be a dwelling-place of those engaged in] agriculture, commerce, and so forth. It shall not be inhabited by one who commits any offence[6] against society or against the Buddhist religion, or by one who has been expelled from another monastery, or by one who does not

---

[1] Sinhalese *Äm̆bul-gama.*

[2] *Padālāyikā* as well as *padālā* in line 32 is not given in Sanskrit Dictionaries. The word *pada* is, however, used in law to mean 'judicial proceeding,' 'matter of dispute,' or 'title of law.'

[3] *Pañjikā*, 'a book in which receipts and expenditure are entered.'

[4] Lit. 'who receive [the profits of].'

[5] *Niśraya* (Pāli *Nissayō*) is the term of apprenticeship which a Buddhist monk must keep before he is permitted by the Buddhist Church to leave his spiritual master and assume full duties as a *bhikkhu.* Cf. Childers' *Pāli Dictionary*, p. 291; *Vinayapiṭaka:—Mahāvagga*, 32–37.

[6] *Lōka-viruddham*, lit. 'that which is at variance with the world'; *Sāsana-viruddham*, 'that which is opposed to the Buddhist religion.'

take up work as it arises, or by one who brings about the destruction of offerings (or meritorious works). Even when the functions of the Order are stayed, a hindrance to offerings shall not be made. And he who receives a large (viaticum) shall not increase the [quantity of] rice and so forth [allowed to him].

[Lines 19–25] In the case of a quarrel also between one [monk] and another, the one who speaks unjustly shall not reside [in this monastery] . . . . . also shall not reside. Moreover [this Vihāra] shall not be inhabited (by those brothers), whether monks (*bhikṣu*) or novices (*śrāmaṇēra*), whose relatives (live) in the villages[1] and so forth belonging to this monastery. It shall not be inhabited also by those [superintendents of work ?], whose sons and so forth are named by the astrologer after the householders of the villages and so forth belonging to their monastery or to the monastery here. If in any village they [i. e. the authorities] cause those [householders] who have undergone lawful punishment [for crimes] to return [to their homes], ... neither the *vārikās*[2] nor those engaged in work shall take possession from [these] householders of their fields, &c., except on account of a fresh offence of theirs. Thus the Order (*Saṅgha*) and the householders shall protect those living everywhere in [these] villages.

[Lines 25–30] [There shall be] clever stone-cutters and skilful carpenters in the village devoted to the work of [temple] renewal. They all . . . . shall be experts in their [respective] work. To each of them shall be given a field of one and a half *kiri*[3] [in sowing extent] for their maintenance . . . . an enclosed piece of ground. And one *hēna* (or a plot of dry land) shall be granted to each of them for the purpose of sowing fine grain. Means of subsistence of the [same] extent [as is] given to one of these, shall be granted to the officer who superintends[4] work. Moreover, when thus conferring maintenance on the latter person, his work and so forth shall [first] be ascertained, and the name of him [thus] settled [with a livelihood], as well as his respective duties, shall be recorded in the register. Those of the five castes who work within the precincts of the monastery shall receive [their] work after it has

[1] *Sambhōga-grāma*, probably Sinhalese *ninda-gama*. For an account of the different kinds of villages according to the system of land tenure in mediaeval Ceylon, see Bell's *Report on the Kégalla District* (Ceylon Sessional Papers, xix, 1892), pp. 115–9. Cf. also Hoernle's translation of the *Uvāsagadasāo*, p. 14, note (25), on *upabhōga* and *paribhōga*.

[2] See above, p. 3.

[3] See above, p. 3.

[4] Lit. 'who causes to do work.'

been apportioned; and they alone shall be answerable for its correctness[1]. The limit [of time] for the completion of work is two months and five days. [Lines 31–34] Blame [shall be attributed] to the superintendents, the *vārikās* and the labourers who do not perform it according to arrangement. Those who do not avoid blame, [and] do not do [the work] or cause it to be done [as arranged], shall be deprived of their share[2]. Further, to the *parivahaṇa*[3] who is efficient in the protection [of the monastery] both inside and outside, there shall be granted, free of dispute[4], a field of one *kiri*[5] [in sowing extent], from each village separately. [This grant shall be made only] to the most efficient [*parivahaṇa*, and] not to another. [There shall reside] twenty-five monks from each of the four great fraternities (*nikāyās*), thus [making] one hundred residents [in all]. [Of these, there shall be] forty monks who are versed in the *Śāstra*[6]. [They shall be] those who have received tutelage[7] void of any sectarian difference . . . . [Lines 35–38] From amongst all these [monks], those whose conversation is coarse, who speak not the truth, and they also who commit wrong acts, shall not dwell [in this Vihāra]; much less monks who carry clubs or weapons [of any kind]. If there be a deficiency[8] [in the number] of monks of any of the sects, this [deficiency] shall be made good by other sects with the sanction of the one [deficient]. From amongst the monks of that sect, ... shall be expelled, and [in their stead] monks from other sects shall be appointed. Just the same sects . . . . shall not be done . . . . The monks shall be informed . . . .

. . . .

---

[1] Lit. 'purity.'

[2] *Vṛtti*, 'share,' see *Ep. Ind.* iii. p. 150.

[3] See above, p. 3.

[4] *Padālā*, see note on *padālāyikā* (p. 7).

[5] See above, p. 3.

[6] Possibly specially signifying the Laws of the Buddhist Church.

[7] *Niśraya.* See above, p. 7, note 5.

[8] Referring to the twenty-five monks from each sect.

No. 2. VESSAGIRI INSCRIPTIONS

VESSAGIRI, or more commonly in Sinhalese Vesagiriya, is the traditional name of a forest-bound cluster of rocks in Anurādhapura, adjoining the highroad to Kuruṇāgala, and about a mile to the south-west of the Sacred Bōdhi-tree. It is surrounded by structural ruins of the monastery which had its cells in the twenty-three caves of two of the three groups of hummock-boulders of gneiss rock that stand not far apart from each other in line north and south[1]. Earlier these rock caves alone served as shelter for hermit

[1] The Archaeological Survey has not yet broken ground at this ancient site. The area is now conserved by the Crown for the sake of its antiquities. The following notes on the rocks and caves thereof, as well as the accompanying plan and photographic illustrations of the site, were furnished to me by the Archaeological Commissioner:—

'**Rock A.** Closely set boulder-rocks, vertical on west, on summit ruins of a breached dāgaba; with pillars at south of rock, where the approach probably was.

'**Rock B. Cave No. 1,** under boulder about 20 feet high, undercut to form shelter, *kaṭāre* the whole way along—in places two—at north end; square mortice holes in cave-face to hold beams for lean-to roof: two inscriptions. **Cave No. 2,** under adjoining boulder 25 feet high, *kaṭāre* whole way —towards north two; rock undercut, less horizontally but more smoothly: two inscriptions. **Cave No. 3,** under rounded boulder standing forward (S.W.) of Nos. 1 and 2 and separated from No. 2 by a wedge-shaped rock slice. The cave is under west and south-west end of the boulder, with single *kaṭāre* which does not extend to north end quite, but runs down south side as well as on west. The rock is 25 feet high, but slopes above cave upwards at an angle of 45 degrees, whereas No. 2 rock runs 8 to 10 feet vertical above cave: one inscription. Adjoining this rock are three or four small boulders, one of which the Public Works Department had blasted before news reached me. **Cave No. 3 a,** a boulder like No. 2, but resting only partially on rock basis at south end, and small boulder (wedge) to west, thus allowing of passage under it between the bottom of boulder and the rock base. The approach to cave No. 3 a is between the wedge rock and rock No. 3 at north-west. The space at back of No. 3 and between it and No. 3 a, with wedge rock at north, where the upper parts of Nos. 3 and 3 a rise towards each other, was clearly once roofed in and converted into a room or rooms. There was a wall on the south, the only open end uniting boulder No. 9 to the small boulders just south of No. 3. A shallowly cut moonstone in the rock base under Cave No. 3 a at the west side, points to an entrance here into the roofed rooms between Nos. 3 and 3 a. The brow of No. 3 a on the west has a beautifully straight horizontal *kaṭāre* with ornamental parallel lines below, nearly a dozen. The west face of No. 3 a rises above *kaṭāre* slightly outwards of the vertical: there is a small wedge rock between No. 3 a and No. 9 on west side. **No. 9,** west face rises at angle of No. 3 a, but has no cave and is unworked. There are no more caves on the west side of Rock B until the south end: remains of brick and tile at the site of the rooms. Immediately behind rock No. 3 a (in fact originally one boulder with it) is **No. 10,** forming part and parcel of No. 3 a. Passing on the rock floor (slippery with bats' dung) under the almost horizontal roof (bottom of No. 3 a and No. 10) one descends between the south-east of No. 10 and the north-east of No. 9, by clearly cut steps (twenty and upwards) on the rock base, to terrace (or terraces)

FROM A PHOTO SUPPLIED BY THE ARCHAEOLOGICAL COMMISSIONER, CEYLON.

monks. The inscriptions are incised on the brows of the caves, just below the *kaṭāraya* or drip-line.

As to the identification of this site with that of Vessagiri Vihāra, stated to have been built by King Dēvānampiya Tissa in the third century B.C.[1], we have only tradition, more or less confirmed by the evidence derived from (1) the probable age of the cave inscriptions, (2) the archaic style of the ruined buildings, and (3) the relative position of the site, in respect

---

at east of Rock B. These terraces had buildings now underground, and there were at least two flights of steps (plain guard stones and balustrades) descending due east from Nos. 9 and 10. Here some damage has been done by stone breakers. The south-east face of No. 10 has *kaṭāre*, and an inscription. The cave is worked and slopes back to the horizontal, where it meets No. 9. The south-east [north-east?] end of No. 10 rests on a small boulder, which, being undercut (with *kaṭāre*) on east face as well, forms another small cave **No. 11** (where brickbats and stones abound) with one inscription. The east face of No. 9 is also cut back at an angle of 45 degrees, but rough: there is one inscription at this cave. **Cave No. 12.**—Rock No. 2 at its back (east) and south-east forms a commodious shelter, almost horizontal and smoothly worked roof. This was likely the Vihāra. The door flags and jamb stones (bottom) are in position. There is an inscription at south-east high up—also a rock-cut (small letters) inscription, shallow on the rock wall at north end of cave No. 12. Beyond cave No. 12 to north the rock runs smooth from summit to ground. The hummock (Rock B) beyond rock No. 9 on to south consists of a line of boulders (as indeed the whole of rock B consists) resting on a long rock base. On east side, this base is smooth and runs up 12 to 15 feet at a steep slope. There are no further caves here until the south end of hummock (Rock B). Towards its south end are three solitary boulders, and at the south end two striking boulders (undercut on most sides deeply) resting like irregular marbles on the top of the base rock which slopes down east, west, and south. Under the most northerly and smallest of the three boulders is a cave **No. 3**, with *kaṭāre* facing east: no inscription. Under the next boulder (sheer on south) is a cave **No. 4**, with *kaṭāre* facing west: one inscription: double *kaṭāre* in part and top-*kaṭāre* continued down south end of roof (as with No. 3): brickbats of ancient room. The north face of third boulder (which stands on south edge of the hummock, Rock B) is also sheer, and separated by 8 to 10 feet from south face of second boulder. Under its west and south-west face, *kaṭāre*-cut cave **No. 5**, but no inscription (notice the rock-cut "sets" as at Sīgiriya to hold wall, all vestige of which has disappeared). About twelve rock-cut steps lead up hummock, Rock B, south end from west. On these are the twin boulders, and after passing between them on the hummock summit, eight more steps lead down to cave **No. 7.** This faces east, and is nearly horizontal at roof with *kaṭāre* and inscription. Cave **No. 6** lies below north-east face of third rock, has *kaṭāre* and letters—also four stone beds on the hummock surface under cave shelter (notice the deep-cut drain 4″ × 2″ deep to turn the rain-water from the beds). On the top of the hummock near the first of the three boulders towards south end are pillars of some ruin. Immediately east of Rock B, 100 yards across the paddy field in private land, are large pillared ruins.

'**Rock C.** This is a cluster of jumbled boulders, very picturesque, with caves here and there in no special order. Two caves have inscriptions; and at one, the stone door frame of the Vihāra (?) is still *in situ*; but all caves are more or less silted up. Note the beautifully cleft vertical rock at south-west corner of Rock C—a real wall of rock. There are structural ruins all round the Rocks A, B, C. Also some in the adjoining paddy fields.'

[1] *Mv.* xx. 15–20.

to the neighbouring Isurumuṇiya ('Issarasamaṇaka') Vihāra, also built by Dēvānampiya Tissa.

According to the *Mahāvaṁsa*[1], 'Vessagiri' received its name from the 500 *Vaiśyās* who lived there in retirement, after they had been ordained by Mahinda Thēra (son of the Indian Emperor Aśōka), who was then promulgating Buddhism in Ceylon. The Isurumuṇiya Vihāra also (it is stated) received its name from 'the eminently pious personages' that sojourned there after their ordination by the same apostle.

The only other reference to Vessagiri in this chronicle is in connexion with King Vaṭṭagāmanī Abhaya or Vaḷagambāhu (*circa* 104–76 B.C.), who 'concealed himself in the Vessagiri forest' after he had been defeated by Tamils in battle. The then abbot of the monastery 'Kutthikkula Mahātissa, meeting him there, presented him with a meal which he had first partly partaken of. The ruler, gratified thereat, dedicated (certain lands) for the support of his fraternity, recording the grant on a *ketaka* leaf (no other writing-materials being procurable)[2].'

Nothing further is known regarding the history of this monastery. That it must have been abandoned many centuries ago, is evident from the state of the ruins and the trees that have since grown over them.

The inscriptions discovered here consist of (1) those on the caves Nos. 1 to 4, 6, 7, and 9 to 12 in Rock B, and Nos. 6 and 8 in Rock C as marked in the accompanying plan, (2) two on Rock B, and (3) those on two slabs now placed in the grounds of the local Museum at Anurādhapura.

i. CAVE INSCRIPTIONS.

The facsimile Plates 5 and 6 show that these records are inscribed in the *Brāhmī lipi* or Mauryan character. As they furnish no historical data, their age can only be fixed, with some probability, by means of the palaeographic and linguistic evidence they afford.

In the study of Ceylon palaeography, two important facts must be borne in mind, namely:—

(1) The most ancient Ceylon inscriptions yet discovered are written in *Brāhmī lipi*; and, as will be shown hereafter, they contain some of the oldest types of that script side by side with the later forms.

---

[2] *Mv.* xxxiii. 50–52.

FROM A PHOTO SUPPLIED BY THE ARCHAEOLOGICAL COMMISSIONER, CEYLON.

(2) Down to the close of the second century A.D., the development of this alphabet, both in regard to the forms of the types and the rate of progress, was to a considerable extent the same as that of India—more especially as that of Western and Southern India. Compare, for example, the Ruvanväli Dāgaba inscription of King Gajabāhu (A.D. 113–35) with some of the inscriptions of about the period of Vāsiṣṭī-putra Puḷumāyi (A.D. 135–63) found at Nāsik, Kārle, and Amarāvatī.

These points of agreement, therefore, not only add weight to the general views already expressed by nearly all the serious students of Sinhalese philology, as to the close affinity of the ancient Sinhalese language to the Pāli dialects either of Western or of Central India [1], but also enable us to form an idea as to the probable age of Ceylon inscriptions down to the second century A.D.

Turning now to our Vessagiri Cave inscriptions and comparing them with those on Tōnigala [2] hitherto attributed to Vaṭṭagāmaṇī Abhaya (B.C. 88[3]–76), as well as with inscriptions of India in the same alphabet prior to the Christian era, we note that there occurs in the present inscriptions a great number of forms of the Brāhmī script, that are undoubtedly earlier than those of Tōnigala.

The letters *k*, *c*, *jh*, *d*, *n*, *p*, *b*, *y*, *r*, and *v*, for instance, closely resemble the forms found in some of the Aśōka edicts; whilst the same characters in the Tōnigala inscriptions are distinctly more advanced and cursive. This is also the case as regards the non-initial vowel signs.

Further, in the Vessagiri records, the dental *s* (𑀲), the palatal *ś* (𑀰), which by the way resembles the type in the Pabhōsa inscription (No. 2) of the second century B.C.[4], as well as the two forms of *m* (ʊ and ʉ)[5], are indiscriminately used; but in the Tōnigala 𑀰 and ʉ are alone represented. The latter is a form of *m* peculiar to Ceylon. It may have been developed from the *m* ʊ with an open 'squarish' top, found in the Śiddāpura edicts of Aśōka and in the inscription on the crystal prism from the Bhaṭṭiprōlu Stūpa [6]. For an intermediate form [7], see Vessagiri Cave, No. 4.

---

[1] Geiger's *Litt. und Spr. der Singhalesen*, pp. 90–93; Franke's *Pāli und Sanskrit*, pp. 127–31. The question to which of the Pāli dialects, the ancient Sinhalese of the cave and rock inscriptions is most related, should, in my opinion, be left open until more reliable material than we at present possess can be had by the publication of more inscriptions and texts.

[2] *A. I. C.* No. 1.

[3] Date of his resumption according to the *Mahāvaṃsa*.

[4] *Ep. Ind.* ii. p. 243.

[5] 𑀰 occurs thirty-eight times, 𑀲 ten times, ʊ nine times, and ʉ ten times.

[6] *Ep. Ind.* ii. p. 324, Plate, and iii. p. 135

[7] See also Cunningham's *Bhilsa Topes*, Plate XXII

The Tōnigala symbol ·|· for the initial *i*, which occurs also in the Diyagama inscription[1] of perhaps a later date, is represented by the advanced form ƒ· in one of the inscriptions of Puḷumāyi (A. D. 135-63) at Kārle[2].

The wavy *ra* of the Girnār and the Śiddāpura edicts of Aśōka recurs in the Vessagiri records (Pl. 5 and 6, Nos. 2, 3, 6 and 7) side by side with the younger straight form found in the Bhaṭṭiprōlu (*circa* 200 B. C.) and in the Nānāghāt (*circa* 150 B. C.) inscriptions; whereas in Tōnigala the latter type alone is used.

The *ya* [ya symbol] of Cave No. 6 (Rock C), like the one of Śiddāpura, edict I, l. 4, clearly indicates that the vertical line and the curve in this particular type of the Mauryan alphabet were written separately, as stated by Bühler[3]. See also Nāsik[4], No. 12.

All these peculiarities prove that the Vessagiri inscriptions cannot on palaeographical grounds be later than those on Tōnigala attributed to Vaṭṭagāmanī Abhaya (B. C. 88-76). They may indeed be earlier by at least three quarters of a century, which would be the period when Buddhism flourished under the auspices of the powerful monarch Duṭṭhagāmanī (B. C. 161-137).

If, however, on further investigation, the Tōnigala inscriptions prove to belong really to Duṭṭhagāmanī (as at first thought by Müller[5]), and not to Vaṭṭagāmanī, the present inscriptions can then be assigned to a period earlier than the latter half of the second century B. C.

In respect of **orthography**, may be pointed out the use of the aspirate *jha* instead of *ja* (Nos. 2 b and 6) as in Tōnigala and Daṁbulla inscriptions[6]. The indiscriminate use of *ś* and *s* and *ṇ* and *n* seems to show not that the engravers were illiterate merely, but also that in ancient days, as at present, the Sinhalese made no appreciable difference in pronunciation between a palatal *ś* and a dental *s*, or a cerebral *ṇ* and a dental *n*. However, the occurrence of these letters, as well as of the aspirates *ṭh*, *bh*[7] and *dh*, and of the combinations *ddha* and *sra* (?), indicates that the Sinhalese must have been acquainted with the Brāhmī alphabet in a form complete enough for writing even Sanskrit[8].

---

[1] *A. I. C.* No. 85. [2] Burgess' *Arch. Surv. W. India*, iv. pp. 81, 113, No. 21, Pl. LIV.

[3] *Indische Palaeographie*, p. 36. [4] *Arch. Surv. W. India*, iv. Pl. LIV.

[5] See *Ceylon Sessional Papers* for 1879, xi, p. 4.

[6] See *A. I. C.* Pl. I, and Rhys Davids' account of the Daṁbulla inscription in *Ind. Ant.* i. pp. 139-41.

Ceylon Sessional Papers for 1880, ii, p. 1, and *A. I. C.* No. 2 text.

[8] Cf. also *Indische Palaeographie*, p. 31, par. 3.

The compound letter  in No. 12 may be read as *sra* or *sṭa*. It may also stand for a badly engraved *ssa* or *sva*. In the latter case the following *va* would be superfluous, unless indeed it is intended to be a substitute for the half-formed *va* in the conjunct. We are unable to say in the absence of other examples, that we have here an *s* with the sign of the *virāma* attached to it[1].

The auspicious symbol  engraved at the end of No. 4 occurs in other Ceylon inscriptions as well as in the Kārle records, at the end of No. 1 and at the beginning of No. 5[2]. For advanced forms of the same, see Kārle, No. 3, Nāsik, No. 1, and Kuḍā, Nos. 17, 25 and 26.

Regarding the **phonology** of our inscriptions, the following points may be observed:—

(1) The shortening of the original long *ā*, as in *agata* = P. *āgata*, *upasika* = P. *upāsikā*.

(2) The de-aspiration of consonants, e.g. *Damarakita* = P. *Dhammarakkhita*, *tera* = P. *thēra*, *bariya* = P. *bhariyā* = Skt. *bhāryā*.

(3) Double consonants are made single, e.g. *puta* = P. *putto* = Skt. *putra*, *Damarakita* = P. *Dhammarakkhita* = Skt. *Dharmarakṣita*, *sagasa* = P. *saṅghassa* = Skt. *saṅghasya*.

(4) The loss of the nasal which forms the first member of a nexus, e.g. *saga* = *saṅgha*.

(5) The change of *s* into *h*, for example the ending of the genitive singular *-ha* = *-sa* = P. *-ssa* = Skt. *-sya*.

As Professor Geiger has already pointed out in his *Litteratur und Sprache der Singhalesen*, these modifications have been carried to the utmost extent in the Sinhalese language. They are, however, not wholly peculiar to Sinhalese[3]. Professor Bühler has noticed most of them in his article on the Jaina inscriptions from Mathurā of the first and second century A. D.[4] Examples of the first change are to be found in Bharhut (Barahut) inscriptions[5], *jataka* for *jātaka*, *digha* for *dīrgha* (cf. Sinh. *diga*), *dēvaya* for *dēvāya*, &c.; in Sāñchi Stūpa inscriptions[6], *danaṁ* for *dānam*, *jamata* for *jāmātā*, *Yasilaya* for *Yasilāya*, &c.; in the Aśōka edicts, and in Māhārāṣṭrī, Ardha-

---

[1] About the *virāma* in Indian inscriptions, see Bühler's *Indische Palaeographie*, pp. 48 and 56.

[2] Burgess' *Arch. Surv. W. India*, iv. Pl. XLVII.

[3] The generally accepted theory that all these peculiarities are 'merely graphic and partly due to negligent spelling' is open to question when applied to Ceylon inscriptions.

[4] *Ep. Ind.* i. p. 373.

[5] Hultzsch's edition in *Z. D. M. G.* xl. pp. 58–80.

[6] Bühler's edition in *Ep. Ind.* ii. No. 7, pp. 87–116.

Māgadhī, Jaina-Māhārāṣṭrī, Jaina-Śaurasēnī, and Apabhraṁśa, these last instances being more or less due to the influence of the accent [1].

Examples of the second occur in Pāli and in AMg. JM. and Ś.[2] In Bharhut inscriptions we find *Asaḍā* for Skt. *Aṣāḍhā*, *Viruḍaka* for *Virūḍhaka*.

The third is a phenomenon very commonly met with in Aśōka and in early Cave inscriptions [3], e.g. *puta* for *putta*, *Utaradatā* for *Uttaradattā* (Kuḍā, No. 1), *Mala* for *Malla* (Junnar, No. 2), *Sata-gabhaṁ* (Junnar, No. 10) for *Satta-gabbhaṁ*, Skt. *sapta-garbhaṁ* (Sinh. *sat-gäba*), *Dhamarakhita* for *Dhamma-rakkhita*.

Instances of the fourth, i.e. the loss of the medial nasal, are *sagha* for *saṅgha* (Pitalkhōrā, No. 2 in Burgess' *Arch. Surv. W. India*, iv. p. 83), *Nadika* for *Nandika* (Kārle, No. 16, *ibid.* p. 91), *Ānada* for *Ānaṁda* (Junnar, No. 2, *ibid.* p. 92), Sinh. *Anada; atevāsino* for *antēvāsinō* (Sāñchi, *Ep. Ind.* ii. p. 397), Sinh. *atväsi*.

The fifth is common enough in the Prākrit dialects and in the modern Aryan vernaculars of India [4].

As to the **grammar** of the present inscriptions, it is to be noticed that the termination *-sa* (P. *-ssa*) is exclusively used in the case of objective genitives, that is to say genitives with dative significations [5]; whilst in other instances *sa* and its secondary form *ha* are indifferently employed. This peculiarity may, however, arise from taking *catudiśa-sagasa dine* as a stereotyped phrase which can be contracted to *catudiśa-sagasa* or simply to *sagasa*. The genitives in *sa* and *ha* are, of course, not limited to Sinhalese. The former occurs in the Aśōka and Cave inscriptions of India, and the latter in Māgadhī and in Apabhraṁśa [6].

An important phenomenon is the omission of the genitive suffix of a word which stands in apposition or in attributive relation to another in the genitive case. According to Professors von Roth and Bühler, instances are not uncommon in the Ṛg-vēda, in Pāṇini's Sūtras, and in the works of the Northern

---

[1] Pischel's *Gram. der Pkt. Spr.*, p. 70.

[2] *Ibid.* p. 154, par. 213, and Müller's *Pāli Grammar*, p. 36.

[3] See also Bühler's remarks on the Pallava grant of Śivaskandavarman (*Ep. Ind.* i. p. 4, par. 6).

[4] See Pischel's *Gram. der Pkt. Spr.*, p. 183, and Beames' *Comp. Gram.* i. pp. 258–60 and 304, par. 80.

[5] 'Dativische Genitive.' See Speyer's *Vedische und Sanskrit-Syntax*, p. 20; Whitney's *Sanskrit Grammar*, p. 99, par. 297.

[6] See Pischel's *Gram. der Pkt. Spr.*, p. 251, par. 366.

Buddhists; while in the modern Aryan vernaculars of India, they are a 'fixed principle'[1]. In such cases, the words in question are generally left in their crude form, as *bariya*[2] (No. 1, line 3, and No. 2 b, line 1), *puta* (Nos. 2 a, 4 and 12), *jhita* (No. 2 b, line 2). But in the Mathurā and in the Sāñchi inscriptions[3], we find examples of the nominative used, instead of the crude form, to represent the genitive. A recurrence of this peculiarity is to be seen in the words *marumakane* and *pute* in No. 7 (Rock B) of our inscriptions.

Finally the words *parumaka*, *jhita* and *marumakane* call for a few remarks. The first seems to be equivalent to the Skt. *paramaka* as suggested by both Dr. Müller and Mons. Boyer[4], although Prof. Geiger assures us that its second half contains the word *mukha*[5]. We know too that the Skt. *pramukha*, Hindī *parmukha*, Pāli *pamukhō* and *pāmokkhō*, Sinhalese *pāmok* also mean 'eminent,' 'chief,' &c. That *parumaka* was a special title, we see from its use in our inscription, Nos. 2 a and 4. In the former, Haruma, the son of Parumaka Palikada, is styled simply *upasaka*, whilst in the latter he is called Parumaka Maha Haruma, having probably received the title after his father's death. In *jhita* (Skt. *duhitṛ*), frequently found in Ceylon Cave inscriptions, we most likely have an old Pāli form in addition to the forms found in Indian inscriptions[6]. The Bengali *jhia* and *jhī* may have been derived from it by the elision of the inter-vocal consonant *t*, although we know of no record of its occurrence in the Indian Prākrit dialects (cf. Beames' *Comp. Gram.* i. p. 192). The known Prākrit forms of this word are AMg. and JM. *dhīyā*, *dhūyā*; Ś. and Mg. *dhīdā*, *dhūdā* and *duhidā*; M. *dhūā*[7] (cf. Sinh. *diyani*, *duva* or *dū*). *Marumakane* (nom. of *marumakana*) in No. 7 (Rock B) seems to be no more than the Tamil word *maru-makaṉ*. Further remarks on the etymology and the signification of this word will appear in a future article.

As to the contents of these cave records, which surpass those of India

---

[1] See *Ep. Ind.* i. p. 375.

[2] *Bariya* (Skt. *bhāryā*) and *jhita* are here crude forms like *jhaya* (*jāyā*) in No. 6 or *bhaya* in Junnar, No. 14 (Burgess' *Arch. Surv. W. India*, iv. p. 95), although all these may stand for nominatives also.

[3] See Bühler's notes in *Ep. Ind.* i. p. 375 and ii. p. 90.

[4] See his interesting article on the Tōnigala inscription in *Journal Asiatique* for Nov.–Dec., 1898.

[5] See p. 39 of his *Litt. u. Spr. der Singhalesen.*

[6] See Franke's *Pāli und Sanskrit*, p. 110.

[7] Pischel's *Gram. der Prk. Spr.*, para. 65, 148, 212, and 392; Hoefer, *De Prakrita Dialecto*, p. 61; and Bartholomae, *Z. D. M. G.* l. p. 693.

in their brevity, it may be noted that in spite of their non-historical character, they present certain points of interest. We see from them the prevalence of the custom (then in vogue in Buddhist India) of dedicating caves as places of shelter to the Buddhist monks as a body, irrespectively of sectarian differences, if they had any at that early period.

Twenty names of persons are mentioned in the inscriptions. They are:—Aṇikaṭa-Śoṇa, Batapala (P. *Bhatta-pāla*?), Cita (Skt. *Citrā*), Damarakita (P. *Dhammarakkhita*), Deva, Haruma, Naga (Skt. *Nāga*), Palikada, Pareta-upasika, Śirikita, Śoṇutara I, Śoṇutara II, Sumana I, Sumana II, Taladara-Naga, Ta- (or Ga-)ṇacadaka-data (°*datta*), Tiśa (P. *Tissā*), Tiśa (P. *Tisso*), Visrava (?), Yahaśini.

Of these, twelve are donors, the remaining eight are either the names of their respective fathers or in the case of two out of the five female donors, those of their husbands. All these personages probably belonged to one family, for it was not likely that the caves which stand practically in the same rock could at that time have been owned by persons other than those of one clan.

This was certainly the case in regard to six of them, namely:—(1) Parumaka Palikada, (2) his wife Cita (*Citrā*), (3) his father-in-law Śirikita, (4) his son Haruma, (5) his daughter-in-law Tiśa (*Tissā*) and (6) his grandson Aṇikaṭa-Śoṇa.

ROCK B. *Cave No. 1.*

1 Damarakita-tera(śa)[1]
2 Agata-anagata[2]-catudiśa-[sa]gaśa[1]
3 Aṇikaṭa-Śoṇa-pitaha bariya [u]paśika[3]-Ti(śa)[1]ya leṇe

The Cave of the female devotee **Tiśa** (*Tissā*), wife of the father of **Aṇikaṭa-Śoṇa**[4], [is dedicated] to **Dhammarakkhita Thēra** [and] to the [Buddhist] priesthood of the four quarters, present and not present.

[1] Read °*sa*.

[2] Cf. *te saṭṭhiṁ vihārē āgatānāgatassa cātuddisassa saṁghassa patiṭṭhāpēsi* (Oldenberg's *Vinaya-piṭaka*, ii. p. 147).

[3] Read °*si*°.

[4] This expression seems to indicate either that Aṇikaṭa-Śoṇa's father had many wives or that he married a second time. It might also indicate a custom (still in vogue) for a wife to speak of her husband as the father of her child, thus avoiding the use of his name as a mark of respect. Traces of this custom are to be found even in England. Aṇikaṭa-Śoṇa may be rendered 'Śōṇa of Aṇikaṭa,' taking Aṇikaṭa as the name of a place.

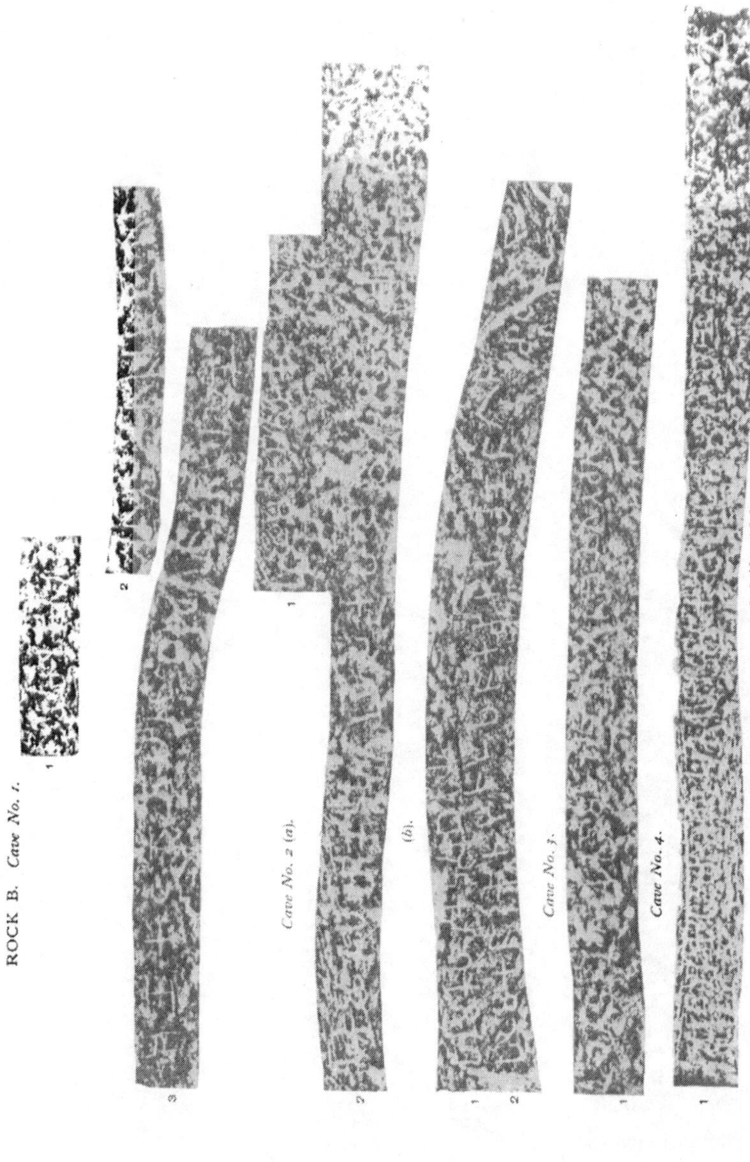

FROM AN INK-IMPRESSION SUPPLIED BY THE ARCHAEOLOGICAL COMMISSIONER, CEYLON

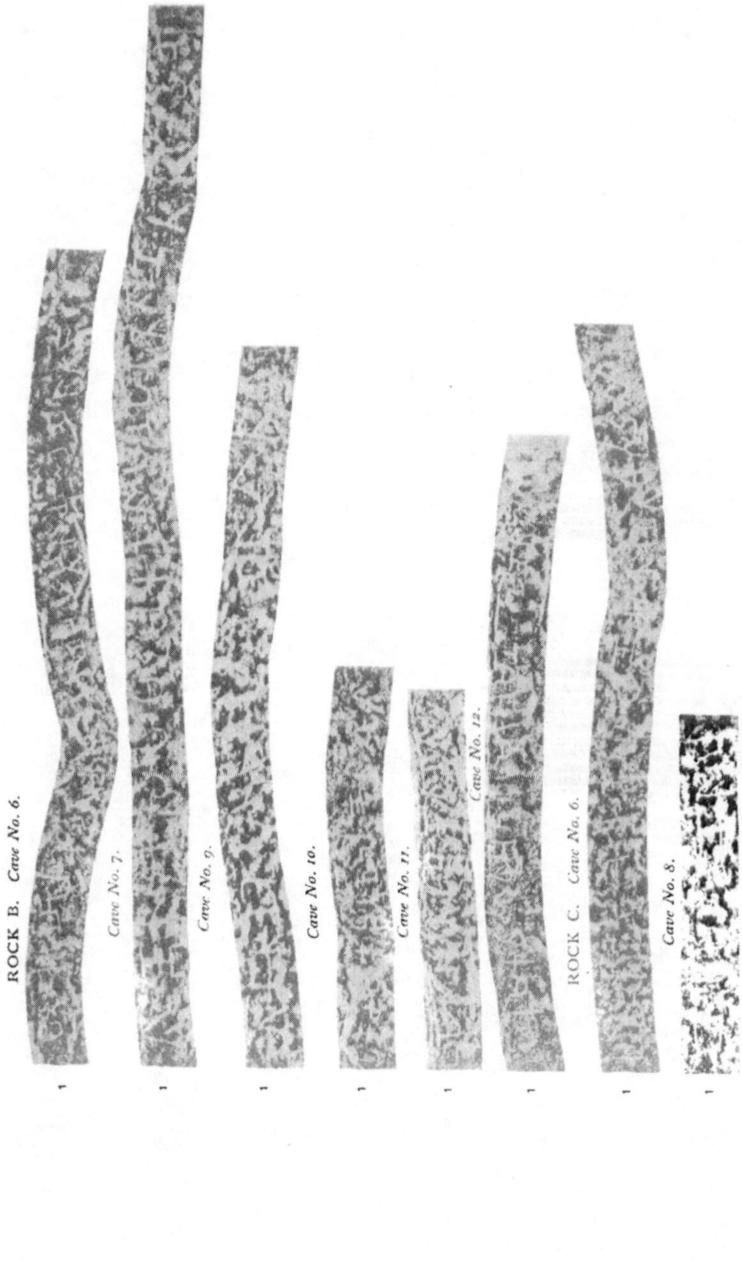

Scale 1⅝ in. to 1 foot

FROM AN INK-IMPRESSION SUPPLIED BY THE ARCHAEOLOGICAL COMMISSIONER, CEYLON

Cave No. 2.

a.

1 Parumaka-Palikada-puta[1]

2 Parumaka-Palikada-puta upasaka-Harumasa leṇe catudisa-śagasa[2]

The Cave of the lay devotee **Haruma**, son of His Eminence **Palikada**, [is dedicated] to the [Buddhist] priesthood of the four quarters.

b.

1 Parumaka-Palikadasa bariya

2 Parumaka-Śirikita-jhita upaśika-Citaya leṇe śagaśa catudiśa[4]

(superscript 3 above "upaśika")

The Cave of the female devotee **Cita** (*Citrā*), daughter of His Eminence **Śiri-kita** (*Śrī-kīrti* ?) and wife of His Eminence **Palikada**, [is dedicated] to the [Buddhist] priesthood of the four quarters.

Cave No. 3.

Taladara-(na)ga(ha[5])puta Devaha leṇe agata-anagata-catudiśa-śagaśa[6]

The Cave of **Deva**, son of **Taladara-Naga**[7], [is given] to the [Buddhist] priesthood of the four quarters, present and not present.

Cave No. 4.

Parumaka-Palikada-puta parumaka-maha-Harumasa leṇe catudisa-śagaśa[6]

The Cave of His Eminence **Haruma**, the great, son of His Eminence **Palikada**, [is dedicated] to the [Buddhist] priesthood of the four quarters.

Cave No. 6.

Parumaka-Palikada-puta Harumaha jhaya[8] Tiśaya leṇe śagaśa[6]

The Cave of **Tiśa** (*Tissā*), wife of **Haruma**, son of His Eminence **Palikada**, [is given] to the [Buddhist] priesthood.

---

[1] This is repeated in line 2. [2] Read *sagasa*. Here *ga* is incised above the line.
[3] Read °*si*°. [4] Read *catudisa-sagasa*. [5] I am not at all sure of this akṣara. [6] Read *sagasa*.
[7] *Taladara* probably for *Tulādhāra* mountain. Cf. *Mv*. xxiii. 89 and xxxv. 30.
[8] Read *jaya* (for *jāyā*).

Cave No. 7.

Śoṇutara-kulaha marumakane Śumanaha[1] pute Śoṇutara(ha) leṇe

The Cave of **Śoṇutara** (*Sōṇuttara*), son of **Sumana** and descendant (?)[2] of the family of **Śoṇutara**, [is given to the Buddhist priesthood.]

Cave No. 9.

Gapati-Naga-puta Tiśaha leṇe śagaśa[3]

The Cave of **Tiśa** (*Tissa*), son of the householder **Naga** (*Nāga*), [is given] to the [Buddhist] priesthood.

Cave No. 10.

Taṇacadakadataha[4] leṇe śagaśa[3]

The Cave of **Taṇacadaka-data** (*°datta*) [is given] to the [Buddhist] priesthood.

Cave No. 11.

Upasika Pa(reta)ya leṇe śagaśa[3]

The Cave of the female devotee **Pareta** [is given] to the [Buddhist] priesthood.

Cave No. 12.

Parumaka-Visrava[5]-puta parumaka-Sumanaha leṇe śagasa[3] ya[6][te ?]

The Cave of His Eminence **Sumana**, son of His Eminence **Visrava**, is dedicated to the [Buddhist] priesthood.

[1] Read *Su°*.

[2] *Marumakaṉ* in Tamil means 'son-in-law' or 'nephew.' *Kulaha marumakane*, 'son-in-law of a family,' is, I understand, quite an idiomatic Indian expression. Cf. the phrase (in Sāñchi i. 73) *tāpasiyānaṁ nusā-Mitāya*, 'of Mitā, daughter-in-law of the Tāpasiyas' (*Ep. Ind.* ii. p. 105), and Bühler's remarks thereon (*ibid.* p. 94). *Manumaraka* (in *A. I. C.* No. 5)=modern Sinh. *munuburā*, 'grandson.'

[3] Read *sagasa*. [4] This may also be read as *Gaṇa°*.

[5] *Visva* (i. e. *vilva*), *vissava* or *vis(ava* may be suggested as alternative readings. See my remarks on p. 15.

[6] This letter occurs in similar position in other cave inscriptions of Ceylon. Perhaps it can be explained as an abbreviation of *yate* (nom. of *yata*, p. p. p. of *yam*, 'to give or bestow').

Scale 1¼" *to* 1 *foot.*

FROM AN INK-IMPRESSION SUPPLIED BY THE ARCHAEOLOGICAL COMMISSIONER CEYLON

ROCK C. *Cave No. 6.*

Yahaśini-(Śamaṇa)ya leṇe agata-anagata-catudiśa-śagaśa[1]

The Cave of **Yahaśini-(Śamaṇa)**[2] [is dedicated] to the [Buddhist] priesthood of the four quarters, present and not present.

Cave No. 8.

Batapalaha leṇe śagaśa[1]

The Cave of **Batapala** (*Bhattapāla?*) [is given] to the [Buddhist] priesthood.

ii. ROCK INSCRIPTIONS.

Two have up to now come to light, both on Rock B.

No. 1.

The first is on the left at the top of the rock-cut steps, west of cave No. 4, and consists of two lines of worn writing, 57 and 34 inches long (cf. Pl. 7). The letters are on the average 3″×4″ in size, and generally resemble those of some of the Kuḍā and the Kārle caves of Western India, but more especially those of the Maharatmale inscription[3]. Hence this inscription may, on palaeographic grounds, be safely assigned to about the close of the second century A. D.

Owing to the indistinctness of the seventh, the eighth, the eleventh, and the eighteenth akṣaras, only a tentative reading can be given. The following transcript is offered from the best ink-impression obtainable :—

1 Sidha - Mahayaha (kani) maha(la)ka
2 Asalayaha (di)ṇi

Hail! the Cell of Mahaya is given to the venerable Asalaya.

At first sight one would read the second letter as *dhā*. It is really *dha*, with the horizontal stroke which we find in Nāsik[4], Nos. 13, 14, and

---

[1] Read *sagasa*.
[2] Skt. *Sramaṇā*.
[3] *A. I. C.* No. 6.
[4] *Arch. Surv. W. India*, iv. Pl. LIII.

in *A. I. C.* Nos. 5 and 7[1], engraved quite separately from *dha*, and which serves as a division between the main text and the auspicious word *sidha* (i. e. *siddham*), here written without *m* or the *anusvāra*[2]. It may be observed *en passant* that none of the earliest Ceylon inscriptions begin with this word, nor is it found similarly used in the Aśōka edicts or in any other pre-Christian record of the same kind. So far as we know, its earliest occurrence is in the cave inscriptions of Western India (second century A. D.), and in an inscription on a slab from Amarāvatī, now in the British Museum. Regarding its meaning, see Bühler's note in the *Ind. Ant.* x. p. 273, Fleet's edition of the Gupta inscriptions (*Corp. Inscript. Ind.* iii), p. 25, note 4, and Bhagwānlāl Indrajī's remarks in Burgess' *Cave Temple Inscriptions*, p. 7.

Mahaya may be a title of a minister of state. Compare *mahayā* in the Mihintale tablets (*A. I. C.* No. 121, l. 2) and in the following slab inscription of Dappula V (line 8).

Kani is equivalent to Skt. *khani* (from root *khan*), 'a cell or cave.'

Diṇi, more commonly written *dini*, with dental *n*, obviously stands for Pkt. *diṇṇī* instead of *diṇṇā* (fem. of *diṇṇa*), agreeing with its subject *kani*. Compare, however, the nominatives *puti* (Skt. *putraḥ*) and *raji* (Skt. *rājā*)[3]. In Jaina-Māhārāṣṭrī and in Ardha-Māgadhī this past passive participle of *dā* is written *diṇṇa*, with cerebral *ṇ* (Pischel's *Gram. der Pkt. Spr.*, par. 566).

No. 2.

The second rock inscription is on the vertical wall facing south-east, to the right of cave No. 12. It contains nine lines of writing, imperfect and too shallowly incised to admit of an estampage being taken.

The letters are smaller than those of No. 1, and probably belong to the period (fourth to ninth centuries) of which records on stone are comparatively few and the script strangely irregular. It is possible that the nine broken lines cover two inscriptions.

---

[1] In Dr. Müller's plate of this inscription the mark in question is not reproduced, although it must be clear on the original stone, judging from the ink-estampage before me.

[2] For other examples of *sidha*, see Kanheri, Nos. 16, 21, 28 (*Arch. Surv. W. India*, v. pp. 80, 83, 84); Kārle, No. 17 (*ibid.* iv. p. 92).

[3] *A. I. C.* Nos. 5, 7, 11; *A. S. C.* A'pura, Report vii, pp. 44, 48.

iii. Slab Inscriptions.

No. 1.

The two inscribed slabs, now lying in the Museum premises at Anurādhapura, are said (probably with truth) to have been discovered at Vessagiriya [1].

The first of these (Pl. 8) contains a well-preserved inscription of King Dappula V (A. D. 940–52 [2]) in twenty-five lines, covering 2⅜′ × 1′ 10″ of the stone.

The **letters** exhibit the genuine type of the alphabet of the period. As to **orthography**, the points that call for notice are—

(1) The retention of the original full nasal in the words *sindä* (P. *chinditvā*, l. 2), *sand* (P. *canda*, l. 7), *vindä* (P. *vinditvā*, l. 8), *saṅg* [3]*-boy* (P. *saṅghabōdhi*, l. 4), all of which are now written with a semi-nasal sign, thereby showing that the original nasal was probably not fully pronounced, even though it appeared in writing. In the modern ligature ඹ *m̐ba*, which is really a modified form of the conjunct ම්බ *mba* in *väjambä* (*vi* + √*jṛmbh*, l. 3), the original *m* is, of course, still preserved, though not always fully articulated [4]. (2) The erroneous interpolation of *n* in *manda* (l. 2) and in *mändi* (l. 20). (3) The use of the *anunāsika* sign in *vīrām̐kurā* (l. 12) instead of the ordinary guttural nasal.

This inscription refers to a grant of 200 *kaḷan̆das* weight of gold to the priests of the **Vīrāṅkurā** [5] monastery, made in the second year of the accession of King **Buddas Abahay Salamevan Dāpuḷa**, son of King **Buddas Siri-Saṅgboy Abahay** and **Dēvā** the sub-queen.

According to the inscription near the stone canopy at Anurādhapura, which has the same phraseology, Buddas Siri-Saṅgboy Abahay's *bisev*, or chief queen, was **Saṅg Banḍay** (Saṅghā Bhanḍikā [6]), and his son by her was

---

[1] They were found by the Archaeological Commission in the Kacceri (?) grounds in 1890.

[2] I adopt for the present Wijēsiṇha's dates as given in his English translation of the *Mahāvaṁsa*.

[3] For earlier forms of this guttural nasal, see Bühler's *Palaeographic Tables*, III. iv. 10 and VII. 12.

[4] Cf. also Geiger's *Litt. u. Spr. der Singhalesen*, pp. 38 and 42, pars. 13 and 17.

[5] A monastery of this name was built at the Abhayagiri temple, and was dedicated to the priests of the Mahāsaṅghika and Thēriya Succession, by Sēna I (A. D. 846–66, W.). See *Mv.* l. 68.

[6] Kassapa V built the Bhanḍikā Parivēṇa at Abhayagiri, probably in memory of his mother Saṅg Banḍay (*ibid.* lii. 59).

Salamevan Abahay. The religious acts of this king, as mentioned in the same inscription, fully agree with those attributed to **Kassapa V**[1] (A. D. 929–39, W.), son of King Sēna II and the chief queen Saṅghā. Further, in an unedited pillar inscription in the Colombo Museum, Kings Kasub (Kassapa) and Abhā Salamevan are called brothers.

These facts, therefore, confirm Mr. Bell's identification of 'Abhā Siri-Saṅgbo' of the Ellewewa inscription or 'Siri-Saṅgboy Abahay' of our inscription with Sēna II. Both **Kassapa V** and his half-brother **Dappula V** evidently adopted the *biruda* or surname 'Abhā Salamevan' or 'Salamevan Abahay,' i. e. 'Silāmēghavaṇṇa Abhaya'[2].

TEXT.

1 මඟුල් සිහසුන් රක් ගල් තල අරා වදන් බෙරසි[නා]
2 නෙත් රුදු වරණින් ඇඹි මතු සිඳැ සි පැරැස්මෙන් වැ(ජ)
3 ම්බැ අනත් අපිරිසෙ සොම් නිමල ගුණ් වතුරෙන් (දි)
4 යල් සනහය් සසුන් අරිඳු ලක්දිව් පොළො මෙහෙස
5 න පරපුරෙන් ශිම් මපුරුම් බුද්දස් සිරිසඟ්බොය් අ
6 බහය් මහරජ්හට් ද, දෙවා රැජ්න කුස්හි ගෙවැ දු
7 නු සැණැහිමෙ යස තෙද් සිරි සඳ්නෙන් ලොව් පහස
8 ය් ඈපා මහයා සිරි විඳැ පිළිවෙළනෙත් රජ්වැ ලොව් ර
9 ක්නා මපුරුම් බුද්දස් අබහය් සලමෙවන් දපුළ ම
10 හරජ්නු සත් ලැගූ දෙවන හවුරුද්හෙයි නිකිත්නි
11 යැ අව දසපස් දවස් මුලහොවෙහෙර් සඟ් වැ
12 ල්ලෙ වත්පුල්ලා උපාසක විරාංකුරා අරමැ මිහස
13 ත් වත්හිමියනට් ලබ් සකර් දෙමිත් දෙසියක් කළ
14 ඳ් රන් දී මෙ රනට් හවුරුදුපතා වසා පවරහ දෙපො
15 හොයැ එක්නට් විසි අඩුල්පතක් දෙනුකොට් ඉසා හ
16 මබු දිගි හමබු ඔනා කොට් ඉසා මෙකුන්මැ ලහා බතට්
17 දුන් සැවක් ඉසා මෙකුන්මෙ හවුරුද් අවසානයෙ
18 හි වසැහින් එක්කෙනෙක්නට් සිවුර් දෙනුකොට් දු
19 න් විස්සක්ඉසා පහයැ බුද්නට් වැට් තෙලට් දු
20 න් දස කලඳක් ඉසා මස්පතා මැඳිමසැ පොහෝ දව
21 ස් වසැහින් එක්කෙනෙක්නට් ඇකෙකැ සතර් හා
22 ඇකැ ගිතෙල් හා දෙනුකොට් දුන් විඳ කලඳක් ඉසා
23 මෙ ගැමැ කවැඩුතු කළ කළමනා කාලයෙහි නොකවැ දී ව
24 ලැකු වත්හිමියන් මෙ අවසැ වාස ලාභයෙහි නො
25 ණිම්ව, යතු ඉසා මෙ කාහිකා මහසඟුන් රැක්කැ යුතු

---

[1] *Mv.* lii. 37 *et seq.*

[2] *A. S. C.* A'pura, Report vii, pp. 44, 45.

Scale $2\frac{1}{4}$'' to 1 foot.

FROM AN INK-IMPRESSION SUPPLIED BY THE ARCHAEOLOGICAL COMMISSIONER, CEYLON. W. GRIGGS, COLLOTYPE

TRANSCRIPT.

1 Magul-sihasun-rak-gal-tala arā vadan-bera-sī-[nā-][1]
2 nen rupu-varaṇan äḍi-manda[2] sindä[3] sī-pärakmen vä(ja)-
3 mbä[4] anat-apirise-somi-nimala-guṇa-vaturen (di-)[5]
4 yaḷ sanahay sasun ariyū Lak-div-poḷo-mehe(sa)
5 na-parapuren himi mapurum-**Buddas-Siri-Saṅg-boy-A-**
6 **bahay-maharaj**-haṭ dā **Devā-rājna**-kushi hevä du-
7 nū-säṇähi-me yasa-ted-hir-sandnen lov pahaya-
8 y āpā-mahayā-siri vindä[6] piḷiveḷanen raj-vä lov ra-
9 knā mapurum-**Buddas-Abahay-Salamevan-Däpuḷa-ma-**
10 **haraj-hu** sat-läṅgū devana-havurudyehi nikinni-
11 yä ava-dasa-pak-davas Mulaso-veher-saṅg-vä-
12 lle Vanpullā[7]-upāsaka-Vīrāṁkurā-aramä maha-sa-
13 ṅg-vat-himiyanaṭ lab-sakar demin de-siyak kaḷa-
14 nd ran dī me ranaṭ havurudu-patā vasā-pavarana[8]-de-po-
15 hoyā eknaṭ visi-avuḷ-patak denu-koṭ isā ha-
16 mbu-dīhi hambu onā[9]-koṭ isā mekun-mä lahā-bataṭ
17 dun-säṭak isā mekun-me havurud-avasānaye-
18 hi vasägin ekkeneknaṭ sivur denu-koṭ du-
19 n-vissak isā pahayä budnaṭ väṭ-telaṭ du-
20 n-dasa-kaḷandak isā mas-patā mändi-masä poho-dava-
21 s vasägin ekkeneknaṭ äkekä sakur hā
22 äkä gitel hā denu-koṭ dun-visi-kaḷandak isā
23 me hämä kaṭäyutu kaḷa-kaḷamanā-kälayehi no-kaṭā dī va-
24 läku-vat-himiyan me avasä väsa-lābhayehi no-
25 himi-vä yanu isā me katikā maha-saṅgun räkkäyutu

---

[1] *Nā* or *naya* or *nay*. Mr. Bell says that none of these words is on the stone. I am, however, inclined to supply one of them, as this reading agrees with a similarly worded inscription near the stone canopy at Anurādhapura, belonging to Kassapa V, half-brother of Dappula V, the donor of the present benefaction.

[2] Read *mada*. [3] Written *sin̆da* in more modern times.

[4] Modern *väjam̆ba*. [5] Or *ji-*. [6] Modern *vin̆da*.

[7] *Saṅg-väl-levan pullā* according to Mudaliyar B. Guṇasēkara.

[8] Read *pavaraṇa*. [9] Read *ònā*.

TRANSLATION.

[Lines 1-11] On the tenth day of the waning moon of the [lunar] month Nikinniya (July-August), in the second year after the [royal] canopy was raised by His Majesty[1] the great King **Buddas Abahay Salamevan Dāpuḷa**[2] who [now] protects the world, having in due course become king after having enjoyed the illustrious positions of governor[3] and chief governor[4]; who illumined[5] the world with the glory and the majesty of the sun and the moon at the very instant[6] of his birth[7], having been conceived[8] in the womb of the sub-queen[9] **Dēvā** and begotten by His Majesty the great King **Buddas Siri-Saṅgboy Abahay**, lord by (right of his) lineal descent from the great lords[10] of the soil of the Island of

---

[1] *Mapurum*, most probably a contraction of *maha-paruma* or *-parumaka* (Skt. *mahā+parama+ka*. See above, p. 17). The form *ma-purmukā* is used as a substitute for *maha-raja* in many inscriptions of the ninth and tenth centuries (see *A. I. C.* 110-15; *A. S. C.* A'pura, Report vii, pp. 44, 59, and 65). The simple word *parumaka* and the forms *parumaya* (*A. I. C.* 42 (*a*)), *purumuka* (*A. I. C.* 67), and probably *purumuvan* (*A. S. C.* A'pura, Report vii, p. 66; *A. I. C.* 120), seem to signify only a title of nobility or veneration, judging from their use in inscriptions. This might be the reason why we find in the present inscription *mapurum* side by side with *maha-raja* as an epithet of Buddhadāsa Śrī Saṅghabōdhi Abhaya as well as of his son. *Mapurum* may also be derived from Pāli *mahā-pārami*, in which case it must be an attribute of *Bud* (i. e. Buddha), and the expression *mapurum Bud-das* would then literally mean 'the servant of the Buddha, endowed with the great *pāramitās* or perfections.'

[2] i. e. Buddhadāsa Abhaya Silāmēghavaṇṇa Dappula.

[3] *Āpā*=*ādipāda*.

[4] *Mahayā*, probably equivalent to *mahapā*, i. e. *mahāpāda*. Compare, however, Dr. Leumann's explanation of this word in his index to the *Aupapātika Sūtra* (Leipzig, 1883). According to him, it may either mean 'with might' or simply 'great.' Hence *āpā mahayā siri vindā* may be rendered 'having enjoyed the great dignity (*mahā-śrī*) of the office of *ādipāda*.'

[5] *Pahayay*=lit. 'having illumined.' Skt. *prabhā*, P. *pabhā*, Pkt. *pahā*.

[6] *Sāṇāhi me*. Here *me* is a particle of emphasis. Cf. *mehun mā* and *mehun me* in lines 16 and 17. *Sāṇā*=P. *khaṇa*, Skt. *kṣaṇa*. Regarding the change of *kṣa* to Avestā *ša* and Pāli and Pkt. *kha* and *cha*, see Pischel's *Gram. der Pkt. Spr.*, pars. 317, 318. Sinh. *sāṇa* may be derived from a form like AMg. *chaṇa*, Tamil சணம் *çaṇam*.

[7] *Dunā*=Skt. *janū*.

[8] *Hevā*, lit. 'having remained.' Cf. the expression *baḍa heva* in Mudaliyar B. Guṇasēkara's glossary to his edition (1893) of the historical portion of the *Pūjāvaliya*, p. xviii.

[9] *Rājna*=Skt. *rājñī*, P. *rājinī*, Sinh. *rājāna*, wife of a king other than the crowned queen (see Baṭuwantuḍāve's edition of the *Ruvanmala*, p. 39, v. 256).

[10] *Mehesana*. Mr. Bell and Mudaliyar B. Guṇasēkara take this word to be a modification of Mahāsēna, the Great Sēna, thereby appearing to refer it either to the last king of the Mahāvaṁsa, who reigned A. D. 277-304 (W.'s date), or to Sēna I (A. D. 846-66). According to this explanation, the phrase *lakdiv-poḷo mehesana parapuren himi*, which occurs also in the inscription of Kassapa V,

Lankā, who [i.e. Siri-Saṅgboy Abahay] promoted the [Buddhist] religion, having comforted [1] the people with showers [2] of [his] boundless, all-embracing [3], gentle and pure qualities; and who flourished with the prowess of a lion, having ascended his auspicious lion-throne which was like unto a rock of safety, and having exhausted the ichor-like pride of his elephant-like enemies with [his] words which were like unto the terrific roar [4] of a lion.

---

near the stone canopy at Anurādhapura, can be rendered rather loosely 'lord of the soil of the Island of Laṅkā by (right of his) lineal descent from Mahāsēna.' In other lithic records of the same period (i.e. the tenth century) containing this phrase, we find *poḷo-yon* (*A. I. C.* 116, 120, 122) and *poḷonava-yon* substituted for *poḷo-mehesana* of our inscription. In the Devanagala record of Parākramabāhu I, A.D. 1164–97 (*A. S. C.* Kegalle Report, p. 75), we read *poḷo-yohon*, and in that of Nissaṅka Malla (A.D. 1198–1207) at Dambulla (*A. I. C.* 143) *poḷo-yon*, whilst his inscription on the Polonnaruva-galpota (*A. I. C.* 148) has *taman yona parapuren himi*. With these facts before us, I am inclined to derive *mehesana* of the present inscription from Skt. *mahēśāna* (*mahā*+*īśāna*), 'great ruler.' The words *yon yohon* and *yona* of the other records are probably derivatives of *īśāna* (through a Prākrit form) without *mahā*, but in combination with *poḷo*, which accounts for the insertion of *y*.

[1] *Sanahay* (from Skt. √*snih*), 'having comforted, or conciliated.' It may also be connected with Skt. √*snā*, used here as a transitive verb, 'having bathed.' Cf. *sanahā* in the Sinhalese poem, *Kāvyaśēkhara*, ix. 67, where it is used intransitively.

[2] *Vatura* is used here in the sense of 'continuous flow or shower of water.' This is really its original meaning, and only as such is it found in its more archaic form *vaturu* in Nissaṅka Malla's inscription (*A. I. C.* 148, l. 9), in the *Ruvanmala* and the *Piyummala* (see Baṭuwantuḍāve's edition of 1892, pp. 21, 81, and 90), and in Jayatilaka's *Elu-akārādi*, p. 37. Clough's *Sinhalese Dictionary* gives both the forms *vaturu* and *vatura*, translating the former by 'flood, flow of water, squall, rainy cloud' (see also *Piyummala* for this last meaning), and the latter by 'water,' while Jayatilaka's edition (1888) of the *Nāmāvaliya* has only the form *vatura* as a synonym of *ōga* (P. *ōgha*), 'flood.' As to the etymology of this word, there have been differences of opinion. See contributions on the subject in *J. C. B. R. A. S.* for 1867–70, 1879, 1883, and *J. R. A. S.* for 1898, pp. 198, 367–9. James de Alwis derives it from Skt. *vāri*, Dr. Goldschmidt from *vātula*, Professor Geiger and Mudaliyar B. Guṇasēkara from *vistara*, 'extensive,' through P. and Pkt. *vitthara* (see the former's *Etymologie des Singhalesischen*, Munich, 1897, p. 78, also his *Litt. u. Spr. der Singhalesen*, Strassburg, 1901, pp. 32 and 36). Mr. Ferguson in his last note on the subject (*J. R. A. S.* 1901, p. 119) seems to adhere to this derivation. I would rather connect *vatura* with the Sanskrit word *vartarūka* (Hēmacandra's *Anēkārthasaṅgraha*, iv. 31), through a Prākrit form **vattarūa* and Sinhalese **vataru* and *vaturu* (cf. Sinh. *katura* = Skt. *kartarī*). *Vartarūka*, moreover, means 'a whirlpool, an eddy;' it is also the name of a river. Compare, in this connexion, Skt. *ā-varta*, 'whirlpool,' and *ā-vartaka*, 'whirlpool,' name of a form of cloud personified.

[3] *Apiriss* = Skt. *apariśēṣa*.

[4] *Bera-si-[nā]-nen* = Skt. *bhairava-siṁha-nādēna*. See my remarks on the text. *Nen* in l. 2 is the ending of the auxiliary case as it is in lines 7 and 8 (see also Alwis' *Sidat-saṅgarā*, pp. 31–3). As for the simile employed here, compare the expression *Manōsilātalē sīhanādaṁ nadantō taruṇasīhō viya . . . . . . madhura-dhamma-kathaṁ kathēsi* (*Jātaka*, i. p. 95).

[Lines 11–15] [His said Majesty Dāpuḷa], bestowing gifts and honour on the great body of monks who are the directors of religious rites in the **Vīrāṅkurā** monastery of the lay-devotee Vanpullā [1] and who belong to the fraternity of monks of the **Mulaso-vihāra**, granted [2] them 200 *kaḷaňdas* [3] [weight] of gold [with instructions:—] that out of this gold, a bowl of twenty cakes shall be supplied to one [monk] every year on the two *upōsatha* days at the end of the season of 'retreat' (*vassa*); [Ll. 16–19] that gruel be poured into the gruel vessel; that out of this same [sum], sixty [*kaḷaňdas*] shall be assigned for 'ticket-rice' [4]; that twenty [*kaḷaňdas*] be granted for the purpose of giving robes at the end of the year to one of those [monks] in [receipt of permanent board and] residence [5]; [Ll. 19–22] that ten *kaḷaňdas* be given to him who sleeps in the temple for lamp-oil; that twenty *kaḷaňdas* be set apart for the purpose of providing one of those [monks] in [receipt of permanent board and] residence [5] with one

---

[1] If the reading *Mulaso-veher-sang-väl-levan pullā* is adopted, the translation would run: '[His said Majesty Dāpuḷa], inspiring with joy the laity attached to the Mulaso-vehera fraternity and bestowing gifts and honour on the great body of monks who are the directors of religious rites in the Upāsaka-Vīrāṅkurā monastery, granted them 200 *kaḷaňdas* of gold,' &c.

[2] Lit. 'having granted.'

[3] *Kaḷaňda* (Tamil கழஞ்சு), jewellers' and apothecaries' weight. Rhys Davids, following Subhūti's translation of Moggallāna's table in his *Abhidhānappadīpikā* (ed. 1865, p. 67), makes it equivalent to a *dharaṇa*, i.e. twenty *māṣakas* (see his *Ancient Coins and Measures of Ceylon*, p. 14). Taking the average weight of a *māṣaka* as 3·62 grs. (Thomas' *Ancient Indian Weights*, p. 11), a *kaḷaňda* will weigh 72·4 grs. of gold. According to the *Kaṇakka-Sāram*, as quoted at p. 47 of Elliot's *Coins of Southern India*, as well as according to several Sinhalese vocabularies, a *kaḷaňda* is the weight of twenty *mañjāḍi* (Sinh. *madaṭa* or *mārā*, seed of the *Adenanthera pavonina*), and as each *mañjāḍi* weighs about 4 grs. (Watts' *Dict. of Ec. Products of India*, p. 108), a *kalaňda* will come up to 80 grs. In Tinnevelly a *kaḷaňda* weighs between 60 and 70 grs. (Elliot's *Coins of S. I.*, p. 52). Clough, on the other hand, makes it '$\frac{1}{12}$ of an ounce,' i.e. 40 grs.

[4] *Lahā-bat* = Pāli *salāka-bhattam*. For particulars regarding the distribution of tickets, see *Samantapāsādikā*, commentary on *Cullavagga*, vi. 21 (1).

[5] *Vasaga*. Neither the etymology nor the meaning of this word is very clear. Of the several Sanskrit and Pāli words with which it can well be connected, the following only need be mentioned as more or less bearing upon what seems to be the purport of the present passage:—(1) P. *vassagga* (Skt. *varṣa*+*agra*). See Dickson's note in *J. C. B. R. A. S.* 1884, p. 200, and Chalmers' translation of it by 'seniority' in *Jātaka*, i. p. 21. In the Sinhalese version of *Jātaka*, no. 5, and in the *Samantapāsādikā* (*Cullavagga*, vi. 11), *agga* is explained by *koṭṭhāsa* (*Abh.* 843) and *ṭhānam* respectively, whilst Rhys Davids gives it the subsidiary meaning 'number' in his translation of the same Vinaya text (*S. B. E.* xx. p. 202). But as *agra* also means 'a measure of food given as alms,' the Sinhalese *vasog*, if derived from *vassagga*, may convey the idea of a certain fixed quantity of food granted for the *vassa* season, and *vasaga*, a person in receipt of such alms. (2) P. *vassagga*

[gold] *aka* [1] worth of jaggery and one of ghee every month on the *upōsatha* day in the middle of the month; [Ll. 23–25] that those directors of religious rites who shall prevent the performance of any of these duties at the time when they ought to be performed, shall leave the monastery, not being entitled to live there nor to receive its emoluments. This regulation is to be observed by the great body of monks.

No. 2.

The second slab, measuring 5′2″ × 2′11″, has two separate inscriptions of Mahinda IV (975–91 A.D. [2]), one engraved on each of the broad faces.

Both these records refer to benefactions made to the clergy of the monastery **Bo-Upulvan-Kasub-giri Vehera,** the first one on the 10th day of the waxing moon of the month of Binara (Sept.–Oct.), in the 9th year of his reign, and the other on the 5th day of the waxing moon in the month of Durutu (Jan.–Feb.) of the following year.

A.

The inscription upon side A (Pl. 9), in thirty-seven well cut lines, covers 4′7″ × 2′7″ of the prepared surface. The **letters** represent the usual

equivalent to Skt. *varṣāgāra*, 'a house for the season of retreat.' (3) P. *vāsagga* (Skt. *vāsāgāra*), 'a cell or sleeping apartment' (*Abh.* 214).

In the Mihintale inscription (*A. I. C.* 121), *vasag* like *lahäg* (P. *salākagga*) occurs several times in such passages as (a) *gilanvä lahäg iya no yahana himiyanaṭ vedun kiyū sändä vasag diyä yutu* (A. ll. 11–12), 'to the monks who are unable to come to the rice-distribution-hall or "check-room" (*salākagga*) on account of illness, a *vasag* shall be given, when recommended by physicians'; (b) *me veherä väsä vanavaḷä kiyana bik-saṅg-himiyanaṭ kaṇḍin piṇḍin vasag pasak* (A. ll. 12–13), 'five *vasags* with (?) food and clothing [shall be assigned] to the monks who reside in this Vihāra and recite the *Vinayapiṭaka*'; [similarly seven *vasags* to the monks reciting the *Suttapiṭaka* and twelve *vasags* to those reading the *Abhidharmapiṭaka*;] (c) *maṅgul jeṭak-haṭ ek-kiriyak isä Damiyen vasagak isä* (B. l. 6), 'one *kiriya* [extent of land] and a *vasag* from Damiya [shall be assigned] to a manager of festivals'; (d) *me veherhi bik-saṅg-himiyanaṭ vasägin sivur sähä* (B. ll. 15–16); (e) *näkätiyak-haṭ de-kiriyak isä Damiyen vasagak isä*, 'two *kiriyas* [extent of land] and a *vasag* from Damiya to an astrologer.'

These examples of the use of *vasag* in connexion with allowances, not only to monks but also to laymen, make me inclined to connect our word more with *vāsagga* than with *vassagga*, and to believe that it means not merely a 'cell' but a 'permanent residence with fixed board' or in a wider sense 'a house with land adjoining it for one's maintenance.' As a *bahuvrihi* compound, *vasaga* may further mean 'the receiver of such board and lodging.'

If, however, *vasägin* is taken to mean here Skt. *varṣāgreṇa*, the expression *vasägin ekkenekhaṭ sivur denukoṭ* may be rendered 'for the purpose of granting robes (*cīvara*) to one [monk] according to seniority.'

[1] *Aka* (P. *akkhō*)=the weight of 2½ *māṣakas* or twenty grains of rice in the husk (*vīhi*). See the *Abhidhānappadīpikā*, 479 and 893.

[2] This is Wijēsiṅha's date. Turnour makes it 997–1013 A.D.

type of the period. Their average size is $\frac{1}{8}''$. A comparison of them with the letters of the foregoing inscription of Dappula V (940–52 A.D.[1]) will convey some idea of the nature and degree of the development of the script in the course of about forty-two years. This is especially noticeable in the letters *a*, *i*, *ṭ*, *m*, and *r*.

As to **orthography**, we see in the words *ambaraṇin* (l. 1), *maṅga* (l. 4), and *munduna* (l. 17) a repetition of the erroneous interpolation of the nasal to which attention has been drawn above.

In identifying **Siri-Saṅgbo Abhā Mihindu** of our inscription with **Mahinda IV**, I have followed Dr. Goldschmidt (*A. I. C.*, pp. 54, 55). My chief reason for doing so is because the inscription records with pardonable exaggeration that 'Mahinda brought all the wealth of India to his feet by means of the valour of his Commander-in-Chief, **Sēna**,' thereby evidently referring to the successful campaign led by the latter against a Cōla king named Vallabha (probably the great Rāja Rāja), as related in the Mahāvaṁsa (Ch. liv. 12–16). The **date** of the inscription being the ninth year of the reign of Mahinda, the invasion in question must have taken place before that year. Moreover the reference in the same chronicle (Ch. liv. 28) to this king setting up inscribed stones containing his edicts is more or less confirmed by the wording of lines 30–32[2].

Regarding the officials mentioned, the Sinhalese chronicles are silent, or record them in different, unrecognizable form. The names, however, of some of them appear in other inscriptions dealing with religious benefactions of the period. The Padaviya[3] and Kongollewa[4] pillars, probably of Kassapa IV (A.D. 912–29), as well as those at Buddhannehela[5] and at Äṭavīragollewa[6] of Dappula V, mention the name Mekāppar Vädārum as that of one of the ministers present when these royal orders were promulgated. The names Rak-(or Arak-)samaṇanvarā and Kuḍasalā, on the other hand, appear amongst those of the personages who took part in setting up the inscriptions at Mahākalattewa and Iṅginimiṭiya[7], probably of Kassapa IV, as well as those at Ellewewa, Raṁbewa[8], and Buddhannehela belonging to Dappula V. In

---

[1] Turnour, A.D. 964–74.

[2] Mr. Bell confirms the identification, and mentions other slab inscriptions of this king, e.g. at Kahaṭagasdigiliya, Vēvälkäṭiya, Raṁbewa.

[3] *A. S. C.* A'pura, Report vii, p. 61.

[4] *A. I. C.* 112.

[5] *A. I. C.* 117.

[6] *A. S. C.* A'pura, Report vii, p. 65.

[7] *Ibid.* 110 and 113.

[8] *A. S. C.* A'pura, Report vii, pp. 45, 59, and 65.

the absence of more historical material, it is, of course, impossible to say with any certainty that these persons were identical with their namesakes in our inscriptions, especially in view of the possibility of a son or a pupil bearing the name of his father or his teacher.

Evidently the chief object of the present edict was to provide in perpetuity a definite supply of water from **Tissā** tank for the purpose of irrigating and cultivating the lands adjoining the royal monastery **Isuramenu Bo-Upulvan-Kasubgiri**-rad-maha-vehera or as it would be called in Pāli Issara-samaṇa-Bōdhi-Uppalavaṇṇā-Kassapa-giri-rāja-mahā-vihāra. Judging from the name, this Vihāra seems to be the one built by Kassapa I the parricide (A. D. 479–97). The Mahāvaṁsa says that 'he repaired the Issarasamaṇārāma, and by buying and making gifts of more lands for its support, he gave unto it more substance than it had possessed at any former time. And he had two daughters, the one named Bōdhi and the other Uppalavaṇṇā. And he called this Vihāra after their names and his own[1].'

This inscription, if its original site was really at Vessagiri, shows, therefore, that at this period the Vessagiri buildings &c. most probably formed, with the neighbouring rock temple now known as Isurumuṇiya, part of an extensive monastery, which from its proximity to Tissā tank was doubtless the Kasubgiri-vehera of Kassapa I.

TEXT.

1 සවසති සිරිබර් සැහැ කුල කොත් ගුණ අම්බරණින්[2] සැ
2 දී ලක්පොළො මෙහෙසනාව් තලා පින් බඹු[3] දසරදඹම් සතර
3 සඟවත් නො ඉක්මෑ දනුමුවා සැපැත් සිල්මුවා සුහිනුවණුමුවා මො
4 ක් මඟ[4] තුමහට් එකත්සරුකොට් ලොගී කුළුණින් මිඟත්වෑ සියල් දන
5 ත් මත් අරිසු තුමා පියෙදු සෙන් සෙනෙවි ඒක්මෙන් මූළුදමිබිදිවිහි ස
6 විසිරූ තුමා පාමිලි කළ සිරි සඟබො අභා මිහිඳු මහරජ්හු සත්
7 ලැගූ හවවන හවුරුද්යෙහි බිනෙර සඳ් පෙරෙ අඩ මස්හි දස ප
8 ක් දවස් නහරහි සිරිය දකුණ් දෙසෙහි පිහිටි මහමෙව්නා තී
9 සරම රද්මහවෙහෙර්හි ආවූ අනුබුදු මහමිහිඳු මහහිමියන්
10 විසින් පිනොයා සසුන් වැඩ ලොවැඩහි යෙදු රකුස්පිරිහා පැන්තිසැ
11 උවහිසා පිහිටි ඉසුරමෙණු බොඋපුල්වන් කසුබ්ගිරි රද්මහවෙ

---

[1] Wijēsiṇha's translation of *Mv.* xxxix. 10 to 12.

[2] අබරණින් [3] බදු [4] මග

12 ගෙහර්ගි වසන මහසඟ්වත්ගිම්ගහට කෙතපල නුලබව(නුවව
13 ස්) පෙරෙ තුමා මිමිති මගරදුන් පැවැත්වූ කිසැ දිගෙහි වීයවූල් මහගෙ
14 වසාසකාගි මගසඟ්වත්ගිම්යන් පාමොක් මෙ වෙහෙර්ගි සඟු
15 ත් වදතින් අසා මෙ දිගෙත් කාරෙත[1] වෙහෙර අවට ඵස්සිග සූ
16 සාලිස් කිරි එක් පගක් කුමබුරව් දැන වවැකින් බොකොල්ගසැ ර
17 ද් සොරො පෙරෙමැ සතර රියනක් දියට් ගිඅූවූ දිය කටැ පගණ් මූසු[2]
18 හ පැනෙනතාක් ඛහක් නැගිවැ දිය පවත්වනු ඉසා මෙසෙ පඬත්වන දි
19 ය රන්මසු උයන ඉසා කෙල ගෙය ඉසා උයන් තෙග ඉසා මහගෙල් තෙය
20 ඇතුළුවැ මෙතුවාක් තැනට් හා වෙහෙර අවට්ැ පෙරෙ කි කුමබුරව් පවත්වනු
21 ඉසා (නොසෙ) දිය කොලොමබ් ඇළැ ඛගා බැහැරව් දිය පවත්වැ සඟ් නොපිජ්ග
22 නු ඉසා දිය(දෙ)නාල්ගි බුනැල් කැමි යෙන්[3] වැජැරමින් වෙහෙරින්[4] උත්කොවයට් ග
23 ත්නා පිළි නොගත්නා ඉසා වෙහෙරැ කැබැලි ගත්නා (අවසියැ) සත්ගා ඇතුළ(කො
24 ට) හොසිත් ඵ තෙරැ මෙ තෙරැ වෙහෙර අවටැ කැබැලි නොගත්නා ඉසා වෙ
හෙර අවටැ අ
25 වූ තාක් තනට් දෙරුවැනැ දෙකම්තැන් වැසසන් වැදූ අකුල් නොකරනු[5] ඉසා
26 වැරිසැර නා(ණ්ට්) යම් දසගම් නොවද්නා ඉසා මෙ වෙහෙර අවටැ බද් කෙත් වතු(ව්)
27 දැන වවැකින් දිය තබා සිගිනැපි වපුර(නු)[5] මිසැ බුන්ඇැපි නොවපු
28 රනු[5] ඉසා මෙකි වැවසථා ඉක්මැ වෙහෙර අවටැ කුමබුරව් දෙන දිය
29 ඛගස්කොට් කෙත් වත් නැසුවනට් අ(ය)සම(නාර)දෑලෙන් තබා දෙ
30 නුකොට් මෙ වැවසථා නොඉක්මැ මගුල් මහ උයන්තැම් රද්කොල්
31 සම්දරුවන් (වැටෙනු)ව්වස් සනිවගත්කල මෙ වැවසථා පහණ හි
32 ඥුවත්නට් වදළ එක්තැන්සම්යෙන් (අඩු) මෙකාප්පර් වැදූරුම් බ
33 ඹ සෙනෙව් ලොකනාථස්වරැ මෙකාප්පර් (වත්කැම්සබාවසුන්
34 නා) රක්සසිම් ඉසා මෙකාප්පර් වදූ(වණ්සැසාක)සිම් ඉසා ස
35 ලිගු ඇමබැ කිත්ලදෙම්ම් ඉසා වමරක් සගාරක්ස
36 මණ්වරැ කුඛසලා වත්කැම් දෙවිච් ඇතුළුවැ අප
37 මෙයිතුවාක් දෙනාවිසින් මෙ වැවසථා තබනුලදි

TRANSCRIPT.

1 Svasti siri-bar-Sähä[6]-kula-kot guṇa-ambaraṇin[7] sä-
2 di Lak-poḷo-mehesanaṭ talā-ṭik-bandu[8] dasa-rad-dham satara-
3 saṅg-vat no ikmä danu-muvā säpät-sili-muvā sugi-nuvaṇu-muvā mo-

---

[1] ණ [2] මූදුන [3] කැමිඋයන්? [4] වෙහෙර් ඇත්කොවයට්? [5] ණු

[6] This may also be read *Sägā*, but compare *Sähāmuni*=*Śākya-muni* (*Piyummala*, p. 4), *Sähā-sī*=*Śākya-siṁha* (*Jay.*, p. 44), and *Sähā-rajahu* (*Am.*, ch. iii. pp. 27, 28).

[7] Read *abaraṇin*. [8] In modern Sinh. *bañdu*.

Scale 1¼" to 1 foot.

FROM AN INK-IMPRESSION SUPPLIED BY THE ARCHAEOLOGICAL COMMISSIONER, CEYLON. W. GRIGGS, COLLOTYPE.

Anurādhapura:—Abhayagiri Copper-plate.

Scale full-size 10¾ *by* 1¼''.

FROM AN INK-IMPRESSION SUPPLIED BY THE ARCHAEOLOGICAL COMMISSIONER, CEYLON.

W. GRIGGS. PHOTO-LITH.

4 k-maṅga[1] tumahaṭ ekatsaru-koṭ lohi kuluṇin mahat-vä siyal-dana-
5 n man ariyū tumā piyedū **Sen-senevi**-vikmen muḷu Damb-dịvhi sa-
6 v-isir(ā) tumā pāmili kaḷa **Siri-Saṅgbo Abhā Mihindu** maharaj-hu sat-
7 läṅgū nava-vana havurudyehi Binera-sand pere aḍa-mashi dasa-pa-
8 k-davas nagarahi siṭiya dakuṇ-desehi pihiṭi **Mahamevnā Ti-**
9 **saram**-rad-maha-veherhi ävū **Anubudu Maha-Mihindu**-maha-himiyan-
10 visin vinoyā sasun-väḍa lo-väḍahi yedū rakus-pirihā-päntisā
11 uvanisā pihiṭi **Isuramenu Bo-Upulvan-Kasub-giri**-rad-maha-ve-
12 herhi vasana maha-saṅg-vat-himiyanaṭ keta-pala sulabava(nu-vava-
13 s) pere tumā mimiti maharadun pävätvū **Tisā** diyehi viyavūl **Maha-me-**
14 **vnā-nakāhi** mahasaṅg-vat-himiyan pāmok me veherhi saṅgu-
15 n vadanin asā me diyen kārena[2] vehera avaṭa eksiya-sū-[3]
16 sālis kiri ek payak kumburaṭ[4] dāna-vavākin **Moholnaṅgā**[5] ra-
17 d-soro pereṭā satara riyanak diyaṭ hinduvū diyakaṭā[6] pahaṇ mundu-[7]
18 na (pä)nenatāk ḍahak nātivā diya pavatvanu isā mese pavatvana di-
19 ya ran-masu-uyana isā kela-geya isā uyan-teya isā mahanel-teya[8]
20 ätuḷuvā metuvāk tänaṭ hā vehera avaṭā pere kī kumburaṭ pavatvanu
21 isā (nose) diya **Kolomb** äḷä bahā bähäraṭ diya pavatvā saṅg no piriha-
22 nu[9] isā diya(de)nālhi mundal kämiyen[10] vajāramin[11] veherin[12] utkovayaṭ ga-
23 nnā piḷi no gannā isā veherā käbäli gannā (aṭasīyā)[13] sat hā ätuḷu(ko-
24 ṭ)[14] hoyin e terā me terā vehera avaṭā käbäli no gannā isā vehera avaṭā ā-
25 vū tāk tanaṭ deruvānā dekamtān vässan vädā ākul no karanu[9] isā
26 väri sāra[15] nā(ṣṭi) yam dasa-gam no vadnā isā me vehera avaṭā bad-ket-vatu(ṭ)
27 dāna-vavākin diya tabā sihin-äṭi vapura(nu)[9] misā muṅg-äṭi no vapu-
28 ranu[9] isā me kī vävasthā ikmā vehera avaṭā kumburaṭ dena diya
29 ḍahak-koṭ ket vat näsuvanaṭ a(ya)sama(nāra)dolen tabā de-
30 nu koṭ me vävasthā no ikmā maṅgul-maha-uyan-kämi rad-kol-
31 sam-daruvan[16] väṭenu-vavas[17] saniṭ.han[18]-kaḷa me vävasthā-pahaṇa hi-

---

[1] Read *maga*. [2] °*ṇa*. [3] Mr. Bell reads °*sa*-. [4] Mr. Bell reads *kumbur padāna*.
[5] B. reads °*ṅgā*. [6] B. reads °*kaṭā*. [7] Read *mudana*. [8] B. reads -*keya*.
[9] °*ṇu*. [10] *kämisen* or *kämi uyan* may be suggested as an alternative reading.
[11] According to the eye-copy *vadāraman*. [12] This may also be read *veher ätkovayaṭ*.
[13] B. reads *avadhiya*. [14] *ätuḷuvarun* may be suggested as an alternative reading.
[15] B. reads *pere*. I am not quite sure of my reading. [16] -*duruvan*, according to one estampage.
[17] This may also be read *pävenuṭavas*. The last three akṣaras are evidently the same as those in *sulabavanuṭa*-(or °*va*-)*vas* at the end of line 12. *Vas* is a postposition (now obsolete) used mostly with verbal nouns. Like *piṇisa*, it means 'for the purpose of' (Mendis Guṇasēkara's *Sinh. Gram.*, §§ 108, 208, and 309). The akṣara preceding *vas* may be *ṭa*, the dative suffix, which Geiger derives from a form **aṭṭhaṁ* (P. *atthaṁ*). See his *Litt. u. Spr. d. Singh.*, p. 62.
[18] B. reads *saniṭahan*.

82 nduvannaṭ vadāḷa ektän-samiyen (ävū) mekäppar **Vädārum Ba-**
83 **mba** senevi **Lōkanāthanvarā** mekäppar **Vatkämi Sabāvasun-**
84 **nā Raksayim** isā mekäppar **Valu(vaṇisāsāka)yim** [1] isā **Ka-**
85 **liṅgu Ämbā Kitla**[2]**-deṭim** isā **Vaṭarak Saṅgā-rak-sa-**
86 **maṇanvarā Kuḍasalā** [3] vatkäm-deṭim ätuḷuvā apa
87 meyituvāk denāvisin me vävasthā tabanu-ladi

TRANSLATION.

[Lines 1–8] Hail! On the tenth day of the first half of the (lunar) month Binara[4], in the ninth year since the elevation of the canopy of state by the great king **Siri-Saṅgbo Abhā Mihindu**[5], pinnacle of the illustrious Śākya race; who is decked with the ornaments of virtuous qualities; who is like unto a Tilaka mark[6] [of adornment] of the great lords[7] of the soil of Laṅkā; who has not transgressed[8] [the rules pertaining to] the ten regal virtues[9] and the four 'elements of popularity'[10]; who has secured for himself the way to Nirvāṇa, which consists in charity[11], in accomplished virtues[12], and in righteous conduct[13]; who has won[14] the hearts of all men by being great in his compassion for the world, and who has brought to his feet all the

---

[1] B. reads *Valupāṇisāsālayim*. [2] B. reads *Kital*.

[3] *Kuṇḍasalā* according to one estampage.

[4] Sept.–October; probably derived from the nakṣatra *Bharaṇi*.

[5] =*Śrī Saṅghabōdhi Abhaya Mahinda*.

[6] *Talā-ṭik*=Skt. *tilaka* (Pkt. *tilaa*)+*ṭīkā*. Cf. *Rāja-ṭīkā*, 'mark of colour put on the forehead of a king,' Haughton's *Bengālī Dict.*, p. 2387 a.

[7] See above, p. 26, note 10. [8] *No ikmā*, literally 'not having transgressed.'

[9] *Dasa-rad-dham*=Skt. *daśa-rāja-dharma*. For particulars, see index to the printed edition of the *Sinh. Mv.*, p. 354, and also Childers' *Pāli Dict.* under *rājadhammā*. Cf. also *Mv.* lii. 43, 44.

[10] *Satara-sang-vat*=Skt. *catussaṅgrahavastu*. Cf. *Sinh. Mv.*, pp. 351 and 373; Childers' *Pāli Dict.*, p. 447 a.

[11] *Danu-muvā*=Skt. *dāna-maya*. Cf. *ran-muvā* (in *Amāvatura*, ch. ii. p. 8, *Sinh. Mv.* xlix. 77, l. 71); *piḷimiṇi-muvā* (in *Amāvatura*, ch. iii. p. 21).

[12] *Sāpät-sili-muvā*=Pāli *sampatta-sīla-mayō*. Cf. *sampanna-sīlō* in *Dh.* 11.

[13] *Sugi-nuvaṇu-muvā*= Skt. *sugati-nayana-maya*. *Sugi* may also be connected with *svarga*. Cf. Sinh. *sugi-mok-maga* (*Am.*, ch. i. p. 1), *sugi-sapuva* (*Am.*, ch. iv. p. 34). Cf. also Sinh. *dugī*, *dugiya* equivalent to Skt. *durgata*. *Nuvaṇu* commonly means 'wisdom.' If the words *danu-muvā*, &c., are taken as attributes of Siri-Saṅgbo, the translation would run, 'who is full of (lit. made of) charity, of accomplished virtues, and of righteous conduct (or heavenly wisdom); who has [thereby] secured for himself the way to salvation.'

[14] *Ariyā*=Pkt. *ārāhiya*, Skt. *ārādhita*.

riches of the whole of Daṁbadiva[1] by means of the valour of his (favourite ?) Commander-in-Chief, **Sēna**.

[Ll. 8–15] [His Majesty] heard[2] concerning the dispute[3] in respect of the water of the **Tissā** tank, which his royal ancestors[4] formerly supplied[5], in order that the produce of fields might be easily obtained[6] by the steward[7] of the clergy (Mahāsaṅgha) resident in the royal monastery **Isuramenu Bo-Upulvan-Kasub-giri**, which was established for the sake of[8] the thirty-five out of the circle of Rākṣasas[9], whom the eminent spiritual lord **Anubudu Maha-Mihindu** employed in the interests of the Buddhist religion and the world, and which belongs[10] to the royal monastery **Tissārāma** in **Mahamevnā** (Mahāmēghavaṇṇa), situated in the south side of the city. [His Majesty having thus heard of the dispute] by word of mouth from the monks of this [Kasub-giri] Vihāra, headed[11] by the steward of the clergy of the Mahamevnā fraternity, [Ll. 30–32] gave orders[12] to set up this

---

[1] =*Jambudvīpa*, here meant for South India only.

[2] Lit. 'having heard.'

[3] *Viyavūl* (Skt. *vyākula*), lit. 'confusion.'

[4] *Mimiti* = *mīmutu* in modern Sinhalese: *tumā mimiti maharadun* may also be rendered 'his royal great-grandfather.'

[5] *Pāvātvū*, p. p. p. of *pavatvanavā*, causative of *pavatinavā*, from Skt. *pra* + √*vṛt*. Cf. *lōhita-nadiṁ pavattetvā*, 'having set flowing a river of blood,' in *Dhammapadaṭṭhakathā* (Colombo edition, p. 179).

[6] Cf. *āvāsaṁ katvā sulabha-paccayaṁ* (*Mv.* xlviii. 1): Pāli *sulabha-paccayō*=Sinh. *sulaba-pasa*.

[7] *Vat-himiyan* may be derived either from Skt. *vastu-svāmin*, 'lord of property,' or *vṛtta-svāmin*, 'director of religious observances.' This epithet may also be applied to a king. See Buddhannehela inscription *A. S. C.* A'pura, Report vii, p. 65.

[8] *Uvanisā*=*upanisā*. See Childers' *Pāli Dict.*, p. 529 b. This word may also be a derivative of *upanissāya*, in which case *uvanisā pihiṭi* should be translated 'situated near.'

[9] The reading *rakus-pirihā-pāntisā* not being very clear, I cannot be sure of my translation. *Rakus*=P. *rakkhasō*, Skt. *rākṣasa*; *pirihā* probably from P. *parisā*, Skt. *pariṣad*; and *pāntisā* may be equivalent to P. *pañca-tiṁsa*.

[10] *Āvū*. I have taken this word as an attribute of *Bo-Upulvan-Kasub-giri* (line 11). It can, of course, qualify *Anubudu*, in which case the translation will run, 'whom the eminent spiritual lord, Anubudu Maha-Mihindu, of the royal monastery Mahamevnā Tissārāma, employed.' Compare, however, the expressions *me kumburhi āvū Asunbada-vatta*, *mahimā āvū ge-bim piṭi-bim*, and the like in the Buddhannehela inscription referred to above.

[11] *Pāmok*=Skt. *pramukha*. Cf. *raja budu-pāmok mahasaṅganaṭa dan dī*, 'the king having given alms to the eminent monks with Buddha at their head' (*Amāvatura*, ch. iii. p. 25). The same idea is expressed by '*Buddhapamukhassa bhikkhu-saṅghassa dānaṁ datvā*' (*Dhammapadaṭṭhakathā*, p. 49).

[12] *Vadāḷa*. For the sake of clearness, I have translated this word as a finite verb, although it is only the p. p. p. of *vadāraṇavā*. The expression *vadāḷa ektān-samiyen*, which occurs also in other tenth-century inscriptions, seems to signify 'in accordance with the mandate delivered.' *Ek-tān*= Skt. *ēka-sthāna*, 'one or the same place'; *samiyen*=Skt. *samayēna*, 'by (or in accordance with) the reso-

slab-edict[1], which was indited[2] in order that lords of royal[3] blood who are officials of royal parks[4] shall, without transgression, observe these [following] regulations[5]:—

[Ll. 15–18] The fields around the Vihāra, in sowing extent 144 *kiri*[6] and one *paya*[7], cultivated by means of this water [of the Tissā tank] shall be supplied with water [from the same tank] through the medium of a distributing tank[8], [the flow of water being continued] without interruption, until the top of the aqueduct-stone[9] [pillar], set up in front of the **Moholnaṅga** royal sluice at [a depth of] 4 cubits of water, appears [above water].

[Ll. 18–20] The water thus set flowing shall be directed to the above-mentioned fields around the monastery, as well as to the gold-fish park[10], to the nursery[11], to the pond[12] in the park, and to the lotus pond[12].

[Ll. 21, 22] The monks shall not be made to lose[13] by leading the .... water to **Kolomb** canal[14] and [thereby] letting the water flow out.

---

lution or order.' Cf. the passages—(a) *Kasub Sirisaṅgbo mapurmukā soḷosvanne ... vajāḷeyin eklān-samiyen ā Mekāpar Vādārum* (Padaviya pillar of Kassapa IV (912–29 A.D.), *A. S. C.* A'pura, Report vii, p. 61). (b) *Pere ki-tāk samdaruvan eksevā vadāḷa samiyen* (Ellewewa inscription of Dappula V (940–52 A.D.), *ibid.* pp. 45, 46). (c) *Vat-himiyanvahanse vadāḷa eklān-samiyen me samvatā pahaṇa hindvanu ladī* (Buddhannehela pillar, *ibid.* p. 65). (d) *Bhuvaneka Bāhu ... vadāḷa mehevarin me abhayadāna śilā-lēkhanaya lī bhavaṭa ... Vikramasiṁha adhikāramha* (Dedigama inscription of A. D. 1478, *A. S. C.* Kegalle Report, p. 84). Here *mehevarin* is used in place of *samiyen*.

[1] *Vāvasthā-pahaṇa* = Skt. *vyavasthā-pāṣāṇa*.

[2] *Saniṭ.hun-kaḷa* = modern Sinh. *saniṭuhan-kaḷa*, p. p. p. of *saniṭuhan-karaṇavā*, 'to distinguish, to notice, to indite, to compose, to fix the mind.' See Clough's *Sinh. Dict.*, p. 658 b. P. *sanniṭṭhānaṁ*.

[3] *Rad-kol-sam-daruvan* = Skt. *rāja-kula-svāmi-dārakāṇām*, lit. 'of the children (or descendants) of lords of royal dynasty.'

[4] *Maṅgul-maha-uyan-kāmi* = Skt. *maṅgala-mahā-udyāna-karmin*.

[5] Cf. *Mv.* liv. 28.

[6] See above, p. 3, note 4.

[7] *Paya*, probably from Skt. *pāda*, 'a quarter,' i.e. an *ammaṇa* or a quarter of a *kiri*. Cf. *A. I. C.* 121 b, Rhys Davids' *Ancient Coins and Measures of Ceylon*, pp. 18–20, and *Navanāmāvaliya* (ed. 1872), p. 26. *Paya* is also a derivative of P. *patio*, Skt. *pātra*. Cf. *gana-ran-payak kiri-batin purā*, 'having filled a solid gold bowl with milk-rice'; *kasun paya*, 'gold bowl' (*Am.*, ch. ii. p. 16).

[8] *Dāna-varā* = Skt. P. *dāna-vāpi*, 'a tank or reservoir for the distribution of water.'

[9] *Diya-kaṭā pahaṇ*, lit. 'the stone at the outlet of the water.'

[10] *Ran-masu-uyana* = Skt. *hiranya-matsya-udyāna* (*masu* = *matsya*, see *Piyummala*, p. 24). *Masu* may also be equivalent to Skt. *māṣaka*, name of a coin: hence *ran-masu-uyana* may be rendered 'the park of gold māṣakas.'

[11] *Kela-geya*, 'sprout-house' (*Jay.*, p. 13). It may also mean 'a sporting-house,' in which case one would expect *keli* (from √*kēl*) rather than *kela*.

[12] *Teya*, probably equivalent to Skt. *taṭāka*.

[13] *Pirihaṇu* = Skt. *parihāṇa*.

[14] *Āḷa*, 'a rivulet or canal.'

[Ll. 22, 23] Clothes[1] which are taken from the Vihāra for [use at] the *utkovaya*[2] by order of the principal[3] officials[4] at (Diyadenāl?) shall not be appropriated.

[Ll. 23, 24] By including the eight hundred and seven who participate in Vihāra allotments[5], no allotments [of lands] round the Vihāra on either bank[6] of the stream shall be taken.

[Ll. 24–26] Inhabitants holding two kinds of services[7] shall not enter[8] the grounds round the Vihāra and cause confusion; nor shall hostile ravagers[9] [or] any barbarians[10] enter [therein].

[Ll. 26–28] By leading the water from a distributing tank to fields and gardens adjoining the Vihāra all round, *sihināṭi*[11] paddy shall be raised[12], but not *muṅgäṭi*[13] grain.

---

[1] *Piḷi.* See Geiger's *Etymol. des Singh.*, Nos. 876, 877.

[2] This may probably be a mistake for *utsavaya* (Skt. *utsava*), 'a festival,' because the Mihintale inscription of this same king Mahinda IV (*A. I. C.* 121 b, lines 8 and 12) also refers to clothes used at festivals.

[3] *Mundal*=Tamil முதல்.

[4] *Kämiyen* (for °*yan*) or *kämi-sen*, 'employees or officials.' In support of the reading *kämi uyan*, see *uyan-kämi*, 'officials of the royal park,' in line 30.

[5] *Kābäli.* The exact meaning of this word is not clear. In modern Sinhalese, *kābäli* or *kābali* is the plural of *kābella*, a piece or slice of land or of anything else: e. g. *vel-kābella*, 'a piece of paddy land'; *li-kābella*, 'a chip of wood.' According to the *Nāmāvaliya* and Jayatilaka's *Elu-akārādiya*, Sinh. *kābali* means 'half' or 'half-moon.' Clough gives the same meaning to *kābili*, but not to *kābali*. Cf. also *kābali-karaṇavā*, 'to reduce to pieces'; *kābilitta*, 'a fragment of an earthen vessel.' Mr. Bell says that *kābili damanavā* is used by the Veddas for 'eat.' In inscriptions we find the word used as follows:—*vattehi kābäli*, 'allotments or divisions of the garden' (*A. S. C.* A'pura, Report vii, p. 65); *sa-kiriyehi kābäli*, 'shares in the six *kiriya* (P. *karīsa*) extent of land' (loc. cit.); *veher kābäli*, 'allotments in connexion with the monastery' (loc. cit.); *kābili pirivahannā*, 'the warden of allotments' (*A. I. C.* 114 A, line 3, B, line 1), as distinct from *kābili-deṭun* (*ibid.* B, line 1) or *kābili-jeṭak* (*A. I. C.* 121 B, line 48), 'the chief (P. *jeṭṭhō* or *jeṭṭhakō*) of the allottees.' Cf. *kābiḷi dolos janak-haṭa* (*ibid.* line 49), 'to twelve persons from among the allottees or participators.' *Kābiḷi* is 'a labourer' according to Mudaliyar Guṇasēkara.

[6] Lit. 'on this bank, on that bank.'

[7] *Deruvānā dekamitān vässan.* The text here being rather doubtful, I cannot be quite certain of the above rendering. Compare, however, *dekamitān deruvan* in Padaviya pillar (*A. S. C.* A'pura, Report vii, p. 61).

[8] Lit. 'having entered.' [9] *Näṭṭi*, probably a corruption of either *nāṣṭrā* or *nāṣṭika*.

[10] *Dasa-gam*=Skt. *dāsa*, 'fiend, barbarian, slave' + *grāma*, 'village, community, race.' According to Jayatilaka *dasa* = Skt. *diśā*. If so, *dasa-gum* = Skt. *diśā-gama*, 'he who goes in all directions, a vagrant.'

[11] *Sihin-äṭi*=Skt. *sūkṣma* + *asthi*, P. *sukhuma* + *aṭṭhi*, Pkt. *saṇha* + *aṭṭhi*, modern Sinh. *hīn-äṭi* or *hīn-āṭi* 'a variety of *oryza sativa*' (Clough).

[12] Lit. 'sown.' [13] A sort of small green grain used for food, *phaseolus mungo* (Leguminosae).

[Ll. 28–30] Upon those who shall have destroyed the fields and gardens by transgressing these said regulations and obstructing the water supplied to the fields round the Vihāra, shall be laid[1] . . . . . .

[Ll. 32–37] By Order, we all of us, who have come together, [namely] Mekāppar[2] **Vädārum**, General **Bamba, Lōkanāthanvarä**, Mekāppar[2] **Vatkämi Sabāvasunnā Raksayim**, Mekāppar[2] **Valu(vaṇisäsākayim)**, **Kaliṅgu Ämbā Kitla-deṭim, Vaṭarak Saṅga Araksamaṇanvarä**, and **Kuḍasalā** master of religious ceremonies, have established these regulations.

B.

The inscription on this side is only partially legible. It seems to have originally covered about 1′·9″ × 4′·2″ of the surface; although there are no traces of writing after the middle of the fourteenth line. See Plate 10.

The first eight lines are boldly carved; but the letters in the next six are so faint that only a tentative reading can be given of many of them. In size the letters are slightly larger than those of inscription A: their form is the same.

The king styled here **Siri-Saṅgbo** was evidently **Mahinda IV**; for the above inscription (A) shows that that title was one of his *birudas*.

TEXT.	TRANSCRIPT.
1 සිරිසංබො මපුර්මුකා දසැව	1 **Siri-Sambo**[3] mapurmukā dasä va-
2 න්නෙ දුරුත්තෙ පුර විසෙණි දව	2 nne Durutte pura viseṇi dava-
3 ස් බොඋපුල්වන්කසුබ්ගි	3 s **Bo-Upulvan-Kasub-gi-**
4 රි රද්මහවෙහෙරින් විදුරඹමු	4 ri-rad-maha-veherin **Vidurambamu**
5 දෙසියක් කළඳ් රන් දී ගත් ව	5 desiyak kaḷand ran dī gat va-
6 සැගැ කණ්ඩ පිණ්ඩ හා මුවරියෙ	6 sägä kaṇḍa piṇḍa hā muvariye
7 ආවූ මාගෙ ගොංගයන් පමණු	7 āvū māge goṅgayan pamaṇu-
8 ව හා මෙ අවසැ පරිගණිත(ස)	8 va hā me avasä parigaṇita(sa)
9 (.. න . . . . . . මූ) සඟ්නට් නැ(තු ද)	9 (.. na . . . . . . mū) saṅgnaṭ nä(tuda)
10 මෙ වසග දෙනු ඉසා වෙහෙරි	10 me vasaga denu isā veheri-
11 න් (බෙහෙද් ගෙට)දුන් . . . . වත්	11 n (behed-geṭa) dun . . . . vat-
12 ත ඉසා (බෙහෙද් වරෙයන්)දෙ	12 ta isā (behed-vareyan[4]) de-
13 (දන්)හට් පහණ්ගමු(කුබ)	13 (dan)haṭ **Pahaṇgamu**(kuba)
14 (රැ) .. කිරියක්ඉසා	14 (rä) .. kiriyak isā . . . . .

---

[1] I cannot make out the meaning of *ayasamandradoḷn*.

[2] Tamil மெய்காப்பர், 'body-guard.' See *A. S. C.* A'pura, Report vii, p. 60, note 2.

[3] Read *Saṅg-bo*.

[4] *Vāriyan* may be suggested as an alternative reading.

Anurādhapura :—Vessagiri Slab, No. 2. Side B.

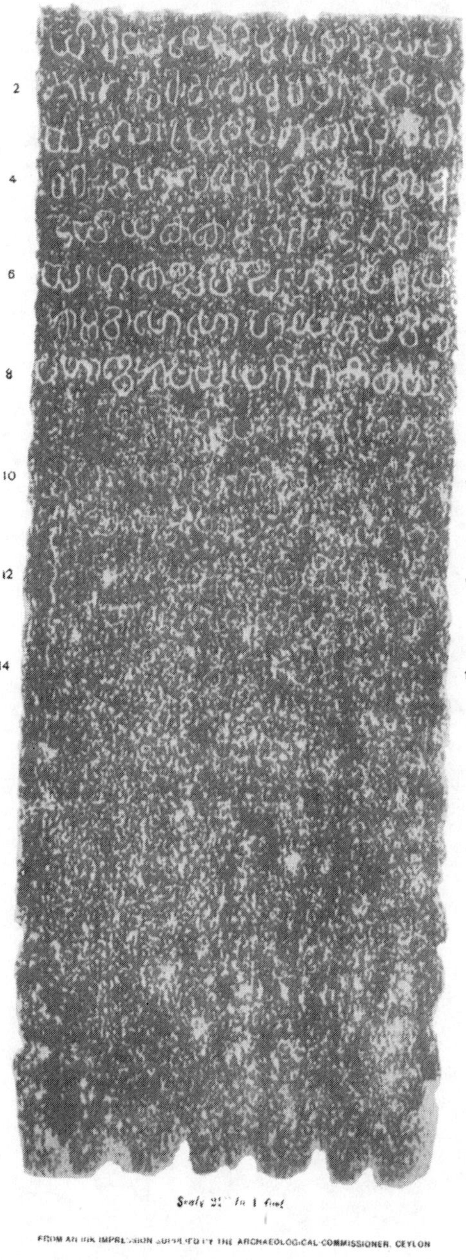

Scale $2\frac{1}{4}$" to 1 foot

FROM AN INK IMPRESSION SUPPLIED BY THE ARCHAEOLOGICAL COMMISSIONER, CEYLON

W. GRIGGS COLLOTYPE

TRANSLATION.

On the fifth day[1] of the waxing moon [of the lunar month] of Durutu[2], in the 10th year [of the reign] of **His Majesty**[3] **Siri-Saṅg-bo**[4], [it was enacted that] if the food and clothing[5] appertaining to the *vasaga* which **Vidurambamu** had obtained from the royal monastery **Bo-Upulvan-Kasub-giri** by paying 200 *kaḷañdas*[6] [weight] of gold, and also if the gift of my cattle[7] belonging to Muvariya[8] were not [set apart] for the monks of ascertained . . . . in this residence, [then] this *vasaga* should be bestowed [upon them]. The . . . . garden given (to the dispensary[9]) and . . . . *kiri*[10] [sowing extent of land] from the paddy fields at **Pahaṇ-gama**[11] [given] to the two (medical attendants) . . . .

No. 3. ABHAYAGIRI COPPER-PLATE INSCRIPTION

THIS rectangular copper-plate ($10\frac{1}{4}'' \times 1\frac{1}{2}''$) was unearthed in 1893 at the ruins of the Abhayagiri Vihāra in Anurādhapura. It is probably a votive offering of a Buddhist pilgrim, and is inscribed with the following mixed Sanskrit ślōka in the North Indian **Nāgarī character** of about the second half of the tenth century A. D.[12] The letters are about $\frac{1}{4}''$ in size, and are in two lines $6\frac{1}{2}''$ and $5\frac{1}{2}''$ long respectively (Plate 11). The engraving is bold and clear except in places where the plate is chipped. The fourth, fifth, seventh

---

[1] *Viseṇi* (probably from Skt. *viṣāṇa*). According to Clough, *viseniya*=fifth day, day after the new or full moon.

[2] January-February. [3] *Mapurmukā*. See above, p. 26, note 1. [4] Skt. *Śrī Saṅghabōdhi*.

[5] *Vasāgā kaṇḍa piṇḍa*=literally 'fragments (of cloth) and lumps (of food) of the *vasaga* or maintenance.' *Kaṇḍa* (Skt. *khaṇḍa*, modern Sinh. *kaḍa*) seems here to have the same signification as *cīvara*, 'rags of a religious (esp. Buddhist or Jain) monk' (M.W. *Dict.*, p. 399). Skt. *piṇḍa* and its Sinh. derivative *piḍa* are both used in the modern vernacular. Regarding *vasaga*, see above, p. 28, note 5.

[6] See above, p. 28, note 3.

[7] *Goṅgayan*. I am not sure that this can be taken as the plural of *gon-geya*, which means 'a yoke of oxen.' [8] I cannot make out the meaning of this word.

[9] *Behed-ge* = Skt. *bhēṣaja-gṛha*, 'house of medicine.'

[10] See above, p. 3, note 4. [11] Skt. *Pāṣāṇa-grāma*.

[12] Cf. the Khajurāho record No. 2 of A. D. 953-4 (*Ep. Ind.* i. No. 19); the Harṣa stone inscription of August 8, A. D. 970 (*ibid.* ii. No. 8); and the Badāl pillar inscription of the time of Nārāyaṇa-pāla (*ibid.* No. 10).

and eighth akṣaras of the first line are peculiar forms; the thirteenth of the same line and the last five of the second are not very legible.

TEXT.

1 सत्थि प(ञ्चा)[1]सय(व)ना[:] सन्ति पारा(ञ्ञ)वञ्चना । माता

सत्थि

2 पिता तलिक्खन्ति दातवे (दमयि)क्क(मं) ।

TRANSLATION.

Hail! The mother [and] the father are they who keep off the five desires; they are beyond having illusions regarding the self. They write this [with a view] to offering up (a course of mortification?).

REMARKS.

Pañca is wrongly written here with dental *n*, although the correct form is to be found further on in the line. The compound *pañcāśa* probably stands for *pañcāśā*, with final short *a* for the sake of the metre. *Pañcāśa* may also mean 'five expectations' or 'five meals' (cf. *dur-āśa*, *sāyam-āśa*, &c.). *Yavanāḥ* is from √*yu*, 'to separate, to keep aloof.' Compare the term *vantāso*, 'one who has renounced all desires.'

Pārānyavañcanā may be suggested as an alternative reading.

Mātā-pitā stands either for *mātā-pitaraḥ* (plural instead of dual) or for *mātā pitā ca* (mother and father), *ca* being omitted very likely for the sake of the metre. In the modern Āryan vernaculars, however, *mātā-pitā* is not an uncommon term for parents. It is always used with a plural verb, just as the Sinh. *mav-piyō*.

Talikkhanti is most probably intended for *tal-likhanti*, *l* being elided to make the fifth syllable of the line short, as it should be in a ślōka. Mr. Barnett of the British Museum suggests that *likkhanti* may be the peculiar Pāli form for *likhanti*, found in *likkhitvā*, *likkhissaṁ*, &c. at p. 15 of the Burmese edition of the *Paritta*, Rangoon, 1877.

Dātavē is the Vedic infinitive, often found in Pāli, but not in inscriptions of the tenth century, so far as I can remember.

The reading as well as the signification of the last word is very doubtful. *Darśayikkarmaṁ* or *Damayikkarmaṁ* may be suggested as an alternative reading.

---

[1] Dr. Hoernle, who has kindly examined the plate, also thinks that the fourth akṣara is *nca*, and not *nka*.

No. 4. ANURĀDHAPURA: SLAB-INSCRIPTION OF KASSAPA V[1]

(circa A. D. 929–39)

THIS inscribed slab was unearthed some twenty years ago, when the ruins round the so-called 'stone canopy' in the Jētavanārāma area, about one mile and a half north of the Sacred Bōdhi-tree at Anurādhapura, were partially excavated. It is in excellent preservation, and contains fifty-six lines of clear writing, covering 3′ 3″ by 5′ 4″ of the smoothed surface of a slab[2]. The edges of the slab are marked by a neatly moulded framing. Two other inscribed slabs, plain, lie near. Their records both belong to Mahinda IV (A. D. 975–91), but are much weather-worn in places.

The **characters** of Kassapa's inscription show very little variation from the type employed in the Vessagiri slab-inscription No. 1, which was set up about six years only after the present stone. The letter *l*, however, has its circular stroke made fuller here than in the Vessagiri record.

As to **orthography**, we find, as usual, (1) the retention of the original full nasal in the words *sindä* (l. 1) and *väḷandūvan* (l. 27); (2) the wrong insertion of *n* as in *manda* (l. 1), *mäṇḍä* (l. 5), and *mändä* (l. 37); (3) the interchange of *d* and *j* as *bad* (l. 15) and *baj* (ll. 17 and 40), *pahaḷavan-ud* and *ovn-uj* (l. 24), *bud* (ll. 9 and 10) and *buj* (l. 26), *varaj* and *varad* (l. 20); (4) the change of Skt. *vyākhyāna* to Sinh. *viyak-han*, වියක්හන් (ll. 11–12), the original aspirate *kh* being represented by the two letters *k* and *h*[3]; (5) the ending *ay* of the gerund of some verbs, which in the later writings is represented by *ā* or *a*, as *aray* (l. 1) for *arā* (in the Vessagiri slab), *karay* (l. 6) for *kara* (in mod. Sinh.), *pujay* (l. 7) for *pudā* (mod. Sinh.); similarly *poḷov* (l. 2) for mod. *poḷo* or *poḷō*, *apirisey* (l. 2) for *apirise* (Vess. slab, l. 3), *meyvan* (l. 5) for *mevan* (Skt. *mēghavarṇa*).

The **language** of the inscription agrees in its phraseology and general style with that of the Vessagiri slab of Dappula V (A. D. 940–52) referred to above, the first three lines of the former being the same as the first five of the latter, word for word[4].

---

[1] The inscription is edited from particulars and estampages furnished by the Archaeological Commissioner. I am further indebted to the late B. Guṇasēkara Mudaliyar, Chief Translator to the Ceylon Government, for much valuable aid in the elucidation of several doubtful passages.

[2] Plate 12. [3] For other examples, see Geiger's *Litt. u. Spr. der Singh.*, § 18. 2. [4] See above, p. 25.

Its **content** is full of historical interest, recording, as it does, some of the important religious acts of king **Salameyvan Abahay** (Silāmēghavaṇṇa Abhaya, in Pāli). This king, as already pointed out at p. 24, was **Kassapa V**, who, according to the *Mahāvaṁsa*, reigned for ten years (A. D. 929-39, W.). There is not the slightest doubt as to the correctness of this identification. The *Mahāvaṁsa* and the inscription agree in asserting that he was the son of Saṅghā, that she was a twice-anointed queen [1], spouse of Buddas Siri-Saṅgboy Abahay or Sēna II; that Kassapa was given the title of *Yuvarāja* (heir-apparent) soon after his birth (*Mv.* li. 12; Inscr. l. 4); that when king, he enforced the rules of discipline amongst the priesthood; that he had the Maricavaṭṭi Vihāra rebuilt (*Mv.* lii. 45; Inscr. l. 6); that he expounded the Abhidhamma and had it written on plates of gold (*Mv.* lii. 49-50; Inscr. ll. 10-11), and that he caused the erection of the Silāmēgha-pabbata Vihāra at the Abhayagiri (*Mv.* lii. 58; Inscr. l. 13). This last event took place in the sixth year of Kassapa's reign (i.e. about A. D. 936); and the present inscription was set up in order to record the benefactions conferred on it, and to promulgate the elaborate regulations enacted by him in connexion with monastic duties and administration of temple property.

Kassapa V, moreover, built the *Saṅghasēna-Ārāma* and *Kassapa-rāja-Vihāra* (l. 6). The *Mahāvaṁsa*, however, gives the credit of the erection of the former to his mother, queen Saṅghā (li. 86), and that of the latter—provided it was identical with the Kassapa-Rājaka Vihāra mentioned at chap. l. 81—to Sēna I (A. D. 846-66, W.).

The *Pūjāvaliya* ascribes the building of the Kapārā Piriveṇa, probably the one mentioned in the present inscription (l. 13), to Kassapa IV (A.D. 912-29, W.). Possibly, Kappūra Parivēṇa (Sinh. Kapuru Piriveṇa), as given in the *Mahāvaṁsa* (xlv. 29, xlvi. 21, l. 77), is its more correct name.

On perusing the monastic rules embodied in the present inscription, one cannot but notice the care with which they were drawn up with a view to securing the independence, the exalted prestige, and above all the purity of the Buddhist Church. No kind of corruption was tolerated in the management of temple property; no slackness in the observance of religious ceremonies. No monk of questionable character was allowed to remain in the

[1] This princess was raised to the rank of a queen, first by Sēna I, when she was married to prince Sēna, then sub-king (*Mv.* l. 58), and for the second time by her husband on his accession to the throne as Sēna II (*ibid.* li. 6). This train of identification was first followed out by Mr. H. C. P. Bell, Archaeological Commissioner (*A. S. C.* Report vii, p. 66. note 3).

Vihāra; nor was any one allowed to enter the Order unless he knew (probably by heart) at least four sections (*bhāṇavāra*) of the *Paritta* (l. 38).

The reference to the *Paritta*, commonly called *Pirit-pota*, is very interesting, for it shows that early in the tenth century A.D. this compilation must have contained at least four *bhāṇavāras*.

TEXT.

1 මඟුල් සිනහුන් රක් ගල් තල අරය් වජන් බෙරසිනස්නෙන් රුපු වරණින් ඇබ
මඬ[1] සිඳැ සි පැරැක්මෙන්

2 වැජැඹැ අනත් අපිරිසෙය් සොමි නිමල ගුණ චතුරෙයින් ජියළ් සනහය් සහුන්
අරිහු ලක්දිව් පොලොව් මෙහෙ

3 සන පරපුරෙන් හිමි මපුරුම් බුද්දස් **සිරි සඟ්බොය් අබහය්** මහරජ්හට් ජා **සඟ්**
බිඩිය් අප බිසෙව්

4 රැජ්නැණියන් කුස්හි ගෙවැ දුනු සැණැහි මෙ පුවරජ් බිසෙව් සිරි පැමැණැ යස
තෙජ් ගිර් සඳ්නෙන් ලොව් පහ

5 යය් සිය වික්මෙන් සතුරන් මැඩැ[2] පල නිමල කිත් චතුරෙන් ලොවත් පතුළ් දෙ
බිසෙවැ ජා **සලමෙය්වන් අබ**

6 **හය්** මහරජ්පුතාර් **ඔපිසිවිපි සඟ්සෙන්අරම් කසුබරජ් මහවෙහෙර්** කරය් අරි පත්
සියන් වසවය් හුලබ්

7 සතර් පසයෙන් පුජය් සහුන් කොත් හුවය් ඇතිනකර[3] මඟුල් මහවෙයැ දකුණ්
දෙර් අසන්හි රජ්වෙද්හල්

8 කරය් රොව් බිය සමය් පොදෙනහුලු පුලුබාහිලුයෙන් කොත් කම් හුලබ් කොට
සිරි ලක් ලොහුර්වය් සාබිය නි

9 වය් රට් සොයය් සැත් බිය නෙර නන් ජැසින් නත්සෙය් බුදු බඳ් කරය් සිසල්
ඉසිරයෙන් පුජය් දු සැණෙ

10 න් බුද්රුවන් අරියය් ධමුරුවන් තවරිසෙයෙහින් පුජනෙම් හො යන අදහස්
පුරය් අභිධම් දෙසුන් කසුන්

11 පත් අරවය් මහ පුජැ කොට් සහුන් සිවවම් යන සිත් දෙළ්නෙන් ඇජර පය
හවුයෙහි එ ගෙ ධම්දෙසුන් වියස්

12 හත් කල සිය බස්නෙන් බුද් ගුණ වැනු රිවි අන්වයෙන් බට් සැහැකුල කොත්
ඛතා රජ්කුලට් නලාටිස් අප පුරුමු

13 වො තුමන් සයිලැඟු සවන ගවුරුදුයෙහි **අබහය්ගිරි[4] වෙහෙර කපාරමුලට**
සලමෙයිවන් සමු කරය් සහුන්

14 වසවය් සතර පස හුලබ්කොට් මෙමෙ නකය් අබදි අවසට් මෙ සිරිත් තැබැවුනු
අබහය් ගිරි[4] වෙහෙරිනි

[1] මද [2] මැඩැ [3] ඇතිනගර (?) [4] ගිරි

15 ඉසා **ගෙයෙ ගිරි**[1] **වෙහෙර්හි** ඉසා බද් තුවාක් **ඇත් වෙහෙර** ගම්කිමට ඉසා මෙගිමෙ අබැදි තුවක් වෙහෙර්ගි ඉසා

16 **රජ්මහවෙහෙර්හි** ඉසා **පිරිවෙන්හි** ඉසා **පියන්ගල්හි** ඉසා **මෙහෙණිවර්හි** ඉසා සඟ් සතු පුගුල් සතු ලාභ

17 යෙහි ඉසා බජ් තුවාස් ගම්කිමට රජ්කොල් කැමියන් වැදූ වැරියන් ගැල් ගොන් මිවුන් නොගන්නා ඉසා ගස්කො

18 ළ් නොකපනු ඉසා මෙලාට්සි නොවද්නා ඉසා මිනී කොටූ කෙනෙකුන් ඇත ගමට වැදූ ඔවුන් මැ ඉල්ලයමුත් සෙසු

19 එහි නොපහල් සෙසු කුඩිනට් අතියා නොකරනු ඉසා දෙදෙ හවුරුද්දෙන් ගොස් රජ්කොල් සම් දරුවන් රට් ඉල්ලා

20 (පස්) මහා සාවද්දූ වරජ් ඉල්ලන්මුත් සෙසු වරද් නො ඉල්ලනු ඉසා පෙරෙ කැමියන් ගම් දත්නාසෙ දඩ්ගෙනැ

21 පැට්වූ වරදට් වටාලා දඩ නොගන්නා ඉසා **ඇත්වෙහෙර** ගම්කිමින් ගත් ගැමැ දඩ **ඇත්වෙහෙර** කම් න

22 වාමට් දෙනු ඉසා පෙරෙ නොවන් විරි තැනට් පෙරෙ නාට්ටියම් නොවද්නා ඉසා රට් පවවන්නට් ගිය රජ්කොල්

23 සම්දරුවන් ගත් දඩැ ගිහිරියක්[2] ඇත සම්දරුවන් දඩ නායකයන් ගිඤැ විචාර කොට් හැරියැ යුතුවක්

24 හර්නා ඉසා මිනී කොටා සඟුන් වන් තැනට් වන් කෙනෙකුන් ඇත එහි පගලවනුද් ඔව්නුප් විචාරකොට් දමඹ්

25 දුව් යවන්නට් හර්නා ඉසා සෙසු බියෙන් වන් කෙනෙකුන් ඇත ගෙ දඩ නො ගන්නා ඉසා දෙස් නොයවනු ඉ

26 සා රජ්කොලෙන් බගා බූජ් සස්නෙහි අනුසසැ බැඳැ දුන් පමණු උදහසැ නො ගන්නා ඉසා කැමිකම් කළවුන් ග

27 ම් පාව්ට වැළඹූවන් සඟුන් කරා වන විචාරකොට් ගත යුතු ණයක් ගනුත් මුත් සෙසු නිගා[3] නොකරනු ඉසා සඟු

28 න් වාසකරන අවසැ රදෙලෙන් යවාදිගි මිනිස්නට් නවා තැන් නොගෙනැ දෙනු ඉසා සන්කළ අවස් පුගුල් නොකර

29 නු ඉසා අපිළිසරණ වත් ගිමියන් ඉසා ලාභ ලදුවන් ඉසා අවස් ලදුවන් ඉසා කළහ යන වරදක් අතපූවා

30 ත් මුළැ සඟුන් ගිඤැ නිමවනු ඉසා සඟුන්විසින් නො නිමත් සම්දරුවන් හා මූල්වැ විචාරකොට් නිමවා පත් පත්

31 සෙයින් දඬුවම් කරනු ඉසා සඟුන් හමබු අමා කරන විවාදයක් ඇත සම්දරුවන් යවා සඟුන් සමාගි

32 හ කොට් හම්බු ගන්වන් මුත් බලකරින් හමබු නො ගන්වනු ඉසා මෙ කී දූසින් එකකුද් රදෙල් නො යෙ

33 ද්මෙන් කළ කෙනෙකුන් ඇත කළවුන් මෙහෙයින් පහකරනු ඉසා රදෙල් යෙද් මෙන් කළ එය්කැරුණ් වෙහෙරට්

---

[1] ගිරි [2] ගිගිරියක් [3] නිගා

34 රජ්කොලෙන් පසලක් දී හමබු ගන්පිනු ඉසා සඟුන් සිඩාත්ත පියා බැහැර්
වැඩියු[න්] පෙරෙ සිරිත් දඬ දී ග

35 මබු ගන්වනු ඉසා අබහයගිරි[1] වෙහෙර පිළිම ගෙහි ඉසා දළඹුග් ඉසා මිගංඩා
ගෙයි ඉසා රුවන් පහාගි ඉ

36 සා බත්ගෙයි ඉසා ඇතුල්කොට් මෙතුවාක්හැත් දෙමුළු සැගැ තන්හ් ස අවසින්
ඉල්ලා හවුරුදු නිමියතැ ලෙකම්

37 කොට් මහසන් මැණැ[2] අස්වනු ඉසා සෙණිහි ද් දෙමුළු සැගැ තනින් ඉල්ලා
හවු[රු]දු නිමියතැ ලෙකම්කොට් මහසැගැ

38 අස්වනු ඉසා මහණ් කරත් පිරිත් සතර් බණ්වර් පිණිස්දුවත් මහණ්කරනු ඉසා
මහණ්වත්නවුන් අතින් යම්

39 කවරි වතක් නොගන්නා ඉසා ගතුවන් දුනුවන් එ අවසැ නොවසවනු ඉසා එක්
අවසැ නැයන් සතර්දෙනකු නො ව

40 සවනු ඉසා දෙමුළු බත්තුවාක් අවසට් දායකයන් කළ නියත පමණින් වත් සිරිත්
නො ඉක්මැ වසැගින් සඟුන්

41 එල්වනු ඉසා අවස් දත්නාසෙ පිණිස්වා පෙල් හදුළ වත්ගිම්යන් නො වසැගිනිප්
උනු තැනාට් එල්වනු ඉසා (ව)

42 ද්දි තනට් වතැ කියෙන ගිම්යන් ගන්නා ඉසා නො සමන්වැ වසන පමණින් වඩා
වත් සිරින් ඉක්මැ වත් වත්ගිම්

43 යනුප් එයට් පසවූ වත්ගිම්යනුප් එ අවසැ නොවසවනු ඉසා උදහසින් දම්බිදි යැවූ
වත්ගිම්යනුද්

44 අවස වනින් පහකළ වත්ගිම්යනුද් ඔවුන් පහකළ අවසට් වටාලං නො වැද්දුදෙනු
ඉසා ඔවුන් නෙනැ

45 වද්නාට් විනෙයා කළ වත්ගිම්යනුද් එ අවස්හි නො වසවනු ඉසා කර්වල් හලැ බද්
ගොත් අන්නට් දුන් කැම්

46 යනුද් තුමනට් ගත් කැම්යනුද් මෙහෙයින් පහකරනු ඉසා ඇත්වෙහෙර බද්
තුවාත්[3] ගම් කිමින් තුමනට්

47 දුන් දසකැර මුත් වැසර් පැත් පමණු නො ගන්නා ඉසා ගොවිකම් නො කරනු
ඉසා මහනෙත්පා මහදූ දෙ අ

48 වසවද් මෙ සිරිත් කරනු ඉසා මෙහිද් සෙසු අවසැද් උනුපොවා මහණ් නො
කරනු ඉසා මහකපාර සිරිවෙනැ[4]

49 පිරිවෙන් ලදුවනට් පිඬපසයට් එක් දවසකට් අඹුණස් සාල් ඉසා සතර් අකස් රන්
ඉසා හවුරුදු නිම්

50 යත 'සිවුර් මිලැයට් රන් දහසක් ඉසා මෙහෙකරුවනට් වැලිගමු දෙ පයල ඉසා
මෙහි බද් මිනිසුන් මෙහෙ

51 යට් ඉසා පිරිවෙන් ලද්දන් තමනට් පිරිකැපු මෙ පසමුස් පිරිවෙනැ[4] ඇතුළ් බැහැ:
යම් කවරි පසයක් තු

52 මහට් පිරිබොකළ සඟුන් සම්දරුවන් ගිනැ විචාරකොට් අවිසින් පහකරනු ඉසා
පිරිවෙන් ලද්දන් තමනට්

---

[1] ගිරි [2] මැදූ [3] ක් [4] ණැ

53 පිරිකැප්පු වතින් මූන් ඉතිරිතුවාක් දූසින් සඟුන් දසන් වටා කම් නවාම් පුජ සිතුවම් කොට් වැඩියාස් ඇත නම් ග

54 න්නා ඉසා අභිපූස්ත බත්[1] හිමිසුරන් පෙරෙ පිරිත් සෙ වටනු ඉසා පිරිවෙන් ලද්දන් සඟුන් සැමැඟින් දක්වා

55 දුන් අපිළිසරණ සතර් දෙනකු හා ගොරෙකුන් සතර දෙනකු අතුළ්වැ දෙ අසනින් අව් දෙනකු පිරිවෙන් ඉල්ලා

56 හවුරුදු නිමියතැ ලෙකම් කොට් මහසඟැ අස්වනු ඉසා

TRANSCRIPT.

1 Maňgul-sihasun-rak-gal-tala aray[2] vajan-bera-sīnaynen[3] rupu-varaṇan äḍi-manda[4] sindä sī-päräkmen

2 väjämbä anat-apirisey-[5] somi-nimala-guṇa-vaturen jiyaḷ sanahay sasun ariyū Lakdiv-poḷov-[6]mehe-

3 sana-parapuren himī mapurum **Buddas Siri-Saňgboy Abahay** maharaj-haṭ jā **Saňg-Baňḍay** apa bisev-

4 räjnäṇiyan kushi hevä dunū-säṇähi me yuva-raj bisev-siri pämäṇä yasa-tej-[7]hir-sand-nen lov paha-

5 -yay siya-vikmen saturan mäňḍä[8] paḷa-nimala-kit-vaturen lov-at-patuḷ de-bisevä jā **Salameyvan Aba-**

6 **hay** maharaj-yutär **Mirisiviṭi Saňgsen-aram Kasub-raj-maha-veher** karay arī pan-sīyan vasavay sulab-

7 satar-pasayen pujay sasun-kot huvay äti-nakarä[9] Maňgul-maha-veyä dakuṇ-dor-asanhi raj-ved-hal

8 karay rov-biya samay Podonavulu-Puluňḍāvuluyen ket-kam sulab-koṭ siri-Lak ḷondurvay sā-biya ni-

9 -vay raṭ-soyay sät-biya nerä nan-jäyin nan-sey Bud-band karay siyal isiräyen pujay dā-säṇe-

10 -n Bud-ruvan ariyay Dhamu-ruvan kavari-seyekin pujanemi ho yana adahas puray Abhidham-desun kasun-

---

[1] වින් (?)
[2] Written *arā* in the Vessagiri slab, line 1 (above, p. 25).
[3] Cf. above, p. 25, note 1.
[4] Read *mada*.
[5] Written *apirise* in Vess. slab, line 3 (above, p. 25).
[6] Written *poḷo* in Vess. slab, line 4 (p. 25).
[7] *Ted*, ibid. line 7.
[8] Read *mäḍä*.
[9] Probably for *ät-nagarā*.

Scale 1⅜ in. to 1 foot.

11 -pat aravay maha-pujä koṭ sasun siṭvamī yana sit doḷnen äjara-paya hamuyehi e me dham-desun viyak-

12 -han kaḷa siya-basnen Bud-guṇa vänū rivi-anvayen baṭ Sähä-kula-kot Okā raj-kulaṭ talā-ṭik apa purumu-

13 -vo tuman sat läṅgū savana havuruduyehi **Abahay-girī**[1]**-veherā Kapārā-muḷaṭ Salameyvan-pavu** karay saṅgun

14 vasavay satara-pasa sulab-koṭ me me nakay abadi avasaṭ me sirit täbävūhu **Abahay-girī**[1]**-veherhi**

15 isā **Sey-girī**[1]**-veherhi** isā bad-tuvāk **Ät-veherā** gam-bimaṭ isā mehi-me abädituvak veherhi isā

16 raj-maha-veherhi isā pirivenhi isā **Piyangalhi** isā meheṇivarhi isā saṅg-satu pugul-satu lābha-

17 -yehi isā baj-tuvāk gam-bimaṭ raj-kol-kämiyan vädä väriyan gäl gon mīvun no gannā isā gas-ko-

18 -ḷ no kapanu isā melāṭsī no vadnā isā minī-keṭū kenekun äta gamaṭ vädä ovun mä illat-mut sesu

19 ehi no pahaḷ sesu kuḍīnaṭ aniyā no karanu isā dede havurudden gos raj-kol-sam-daruvan raṭ illā

20 (pas) mahā sävaddä-[2]varaj illat-mut sesu varad no illanu isā pere kämiyan gam dannāse daṇḍ genä

21 päṭvū varadaṭ vaṭālā daṇḍ no gannā isā **Ät-veherā** gam-bimin gat hämä daṇḍ **Ät-veherā** kam na-

22 vāmaṭ denu isā pere no van viri tänaṭ pere näṭṭiyam no vadnā isā raṭ paṭavannaṭ giya raj-kol-

23 sam-daruvan gat daṇḍä giṅgiriyak[3] äta sam-daruvan daṇḍa-nāyakayan hindä vicāra-koṭ häriyä yutuvak

24 harnā isā minī koṭā saṅgun van tänaṭ van kenekun äta ehi pahaḷavan-ud ovn-uj vicāra-koṭ Damb-

25 -div yavannaṭ harnā isā sesu biyen van kenekun äta ge-daṇḍ no gannā isā des no yavanu i-

26 -sā raj-kolen bahā Buj-sasnehi anusasā bändā dun pamaṇu udahasā no gannā isā kämi kam kaḷavun ga-

27 -m päṭṭa väḷandūvan saṅgun karā vana vicāra-koṭ gata yutu ṇayak ganut mut sesu niṅgā[4] no karanu isā saṅgu-

28 n vāsa-karana avasā radolen yav-ädihi minisnaṭ navätän no genä denu isā saṅg kaḷa avas pugul no kara-

---

[1] Read *giri*. [2] Skt. *sāvadya*. [3] Read *gigiriyak*. [4] Read *nigā*.

29 -nu isā apiḷisaraṇa vat-himiyan isā lābha laduvan isā avas laduvan isā kaḷaha yana varadak ata-puvā-

30 -t muḷā saṅgun hindā nimavanu isā saṅgunvisin no nimat sam-daruvan hā muḷvā vicāra-koṭ nimavā pat-pat-

31 -seyin daṅḍuvam karanu isā saṅgun hambu āmā karana vivādayak äta sam-daruvan yavā saṅgun samā-hi-

32 -ta koṭ hambu ganvat-mut balakarin hambu no ganvanu isā me kī däyin ekak-ud radol no ye-

33 -dmen kaḷa kenekun äta kaḷavun meheyin paha-karanu isā radol yedmen kaḷa eykäruṇ veheraṭ

34 raj-kolen payalak dī hambu ganvanu isā saṅgun siddhānta piyā bähär väḍiya[n] pere sirit daṅḍ dī ha-

35 -mbu ganvanu isā **Abahay-girī**[1]**-veherā** piḷima-gehi isā dāgab-hi isā maha-bo-gehi isā ruvan-pahāhi i-

36 -sā bat-gehi isā ātuḷ-koṭ me tuvāk tän de-muḷā säṅgä-tanin sa-avasin illā havurudu nimiyatā lekam-

37 koṭ maha-saṅg mändā[2] asvanu isā **Se-giri**-d de-muḷā säṅgä-tanin illā havu-[ru]du nimiyatā lekam koṭ maha-säṅgā

38 asvanu isā mahaṇ-karat pirit satar baṇvar piṇis-vūvan mahaṇ-karanu isā mahaṇ-vannavun atin yam-

39 kavari-vatak no gannā isā gatuvan dunuvan e avasā no vasavanu isā ek avasā nāyan satar-denaku no va-

40 -savanu isā de-muḷā baj-tuvāk avasaṭ dāyakayan kaḷa niyata pamaṇin vat sirit no ikmā vasāgin saṅgun

41 eḷvanu isā avas dannā-se piṇis-vā peḷ hadāḷa vat-himiyan no vasāgin-ij unu-tänaṭ eḷvanu isā (va-)

42 -ddī-tanaṭ vatā kiyena himiyan gannā isā no samaṅg-vā vasana pamaṇin vaḍā vat-sirit ikmā van vat-himi-

43 yan-uj eyaṭ pasavū vat-himiyan-uj e avasā no vasavanu isā udahasin Damb-dī yävū vat-himiyan-ud

44 avasa-vatin paha-kaḷa vat-himiyan-ud ovun paha-kaḷa avasaṭ vaṭālā no väddā denu isā ovun genā

45 vadnāṭ viyo-kaḷa vat-himiyan-ud e avashi no vasavanu isā Karvaḷ-halā bad gon annaṭ dun kämi-

---

[1] Read *giri*.

[2] Read *mädā*.

46 yan-ud tumanaṭ gat kämiyan-ud meheyin paha-karanu isā **Ät-veherā** bad-tuvät[1] gam-bimin tumanaṭ

47 dun dasakärä-mut väsar pät pamaṇu no gannā isā govī-kam no karanu isā **Mahanet-pā Vahadū** de-a-

48 -vasaṭa-d me sirit karanu isā mehi-d sesu avasä-d unupovā mahaṇ no karanu isā **Maha-Kapārā-pirivenā**[2]

49 piriven laduvanaṭ piṇḍ-pasayaṭ ek davasakaṭ amuṇak sāl isā satar akak ran isā havurudu himi-

50 -yata sivur-milāyaṭ ran dahasak isā mehekaruvanaṭ Väligamu de-payala isā mehi bad minisun mehe-

51 -yaṭ isā piriven laddan tamanaṭ pirikäpū me pasa-mut pirivenā[2] ätuḷ bähäri yam kavari pasayak tu-

52 -manaṭ piribo-kaḷa saṅgun sam-daruvan hindā vicārakoṭ avasin paha-karanu isā piriven laddan tamanaṭ

53 pirikäpū vatin mut itiri-tuvāk däyin saṅgun dasan vaṭā kam-navām puja situvam koṭ väḍīyāḳ äta gam ga-

54 nnā isā abhiyukta batī[3] himīsuran pere sirit-se vaṭanu isā piriven laddan saṅgun sämäṅgin dakvā

55 dun apiḷisaraṇa satar denaku hā gorokun satara denaku atuḷvā de asanin aṭ denaku piriven illā

56 havurudu nimiyatā lekam koṭ mahasaṅgā asvanu isā

TRANSLATION.

[Lines 1–6] The great king[4] **Salameyvan Abahay**[5] was conceived[6] in the womb of our anointed queen[7] **Saṅg-Baṇḍay**, being born[8] unto his Majesty[9]

---

[1] Read *tuvāk*. [2] Read *pirivenā*. [3] Probably for *vat-himīsuran*.

[4] *Maha-raj-yulār* (line 6). The etymology of *yulār*, which seems to be an honorific suffix, is not quite clear. Probably, it is composed of *yula* (p.p.p. of √*yu*) and *ār*, an epicene pluralizing particle in Tamil, added to nouns often honorifically, as *Tāy-ār* (*tāy* mother). According to this derivation, *Maha-raj-yula* + *ār* must be equivalent to Skt. *Mahā-rājya-yuta* with Tamil *ār*, signifying 'he who is possessed of the dignity of a great king (cf. *śrī-yuta*).' *Yulār* is quite clear on the stone, as may be seen from the accompanying facsimile plate.

[5] i.e. Skt. *Silāmēghavarṇa Abhaya*.

[6] *Hevā* (line 4), lit. 'having reposed.' See above, p. 26, note 8. This is evidently the gerund of *hovinavā* or *hōnavā*, a derivative of Skt. √*svap* (*svapiti*, Ved. *svápati* = Pāli *supati*, Pkt. *suvai*, *sovai*, and *suyai*). See also *E. S.* No. 1657. Clough's Dict. gives *heva* as the gerund of the causative *hovanavā*.

[7] *Bisev rājnā* = Skt. *abhiṣēka* + *rājñī*, 'anointed queen' as distinct from the other wives of the king, who bore the simple title *rājñī*, and of whom one was *Dēvā*. See above, p. 26, note 9. Regarding the form *rājnāṇiyan*, see Geiger's *Litt. und Spr. der Singh.*, § 37, c.

[8] *Jā* = Skt. *jāta*, Pkt. *jāa*, Sinh. *jā* and *dā*. [9] *Māpurum*. See above, p. 26, note 1.

Buddas Siri-Saṅgboy Abahay[1] Maharaj, lord by (right of) lineal descent from the great lords[2] of the soil[3] of the Island of Laṅkā; who promoted[4] the (Buddhist) religion, having comforted[5] the people with showers[6] of (his) boundless, all-embracing[7], gentle and pure qualities; and who flourished[8] with the prowess of a lion[9], having ascended[10] his auspicious lion-throne[11] which was like unto a rock of safety[12], and having exhausted[13] the ichor-like pride[14] of his elephant-like enemies[15] with [his] words which were like unto the terrific roar of a lion[16].

[His Majesty] born of the twice-anointed queen[17], received[18] at the very instant of his birth[19] the auspicious unction of *yuva-rāja*[20] (heir-apparent) and illumined[21] the world with the glory and the majesty of the sun and the moon. With his own valour[22], he subdued[23] enemies; and with the waters[24]

---

[1] i.e. *Buddhadāsa Śrī Saṅghabōdhi Abhaya Mahārāja.*

[2] *Mehesana.* See above, p. 26, note 10. [3] *Poḷov.* See *E. S.* No. 933.

[4] *Ariyū* (l. 2). See p. 34, note 14. In the above translation this word is rendered as an equivalent of either Skt. *ārādhya* or *ārādhitavān.* But it can also be taken as a past passive participle qualifying *Lak-div*, in which case the phrase *sasun ariyū Lak-div* must be translated 'the Island of Laṅkā blest by the Buddhist religion.'

[5] *Sanahay.* See above, p. 27, note 1, and *J. R. A. S.* for 1905, p. 185.

[6] *Vaturen.* See above, p. 27, note 2.

[7] *Apirisey.* Ibid., note 3, where it is spelt *apirise.*

[8] *Vājāmbā*, lit. 'having flourished.' Skt. *vijṛmbhya.* [9] *Si-pārākmen*=Skt. *siṁha-parākrameṇa.*

[10] *Aray*, spelt *arā* on the Vessagiri slab (above, p. 25), is equivalent to Skt. *āruhya*, P. *āruyha*, Pkt. *āruhia*, Tamil *ēṟi* (gerund of *ēṟugiṟēṉ*).

[11] *Sihasun*=P. *sihāsana.* [12] *Rak-gal-tala*=Skt. *ārakṣa-giri-tala.*

[13] *Sindā* (modern *siňda*)=AMg. *chindiya*, Ś'. °*chindia* (Pischel's *Pkt. Gram.* § 591), P. *chinditvā.* Cf. Tamil *ċidāi* and *ċēdi.*

[14] *Äḍi-mada*=Skt. *āṭōpa* (Pkt. *āḍōva*)+*mada.* In modern Sinh. *eḍi.* Cf. Tamil *eḍu* and *eṟu* (எறு).

[15] *Rupu-varaṇan*=Skt. *ripu-vāraṇānām.* For the casus obliquus of the plural, see Geiger's *L. S. S.* § 34, iv.

[16] *Bera-si-naynen.* See above, pp. 25 and 27, notes 1 and 4 respectively.

[17] *Debisevā-jā* (line 5)=Pāli *dvayābhisēkā-jāto*, an epithet of this king, Kassapa V. See *Mv.* lii. 37, and the colophon of the *Dampiyā-aṭuvā-gäṭapada* as well as Wijēsiṇha's note at p. 78 of his translation of the *Mahāvaṁsa.*

[18] *Pāmāṇā* (line 4), modern Sinh. *pämiṇa*, 'having attained.' See also *E. S.* No. 942.

[19] *Dunū-sāṇāhi-me.* See above, p. 26, notes 6 and 7.

[20] *Yuvaraj-bisev-siri* (line 4)=Skt. *Yuvarājābhiṣēkaśrī.*

[21] *Pahayay*, lit. 'having illumined.' See above, p. 26, note 5.

[22] *Siya-vikmen*=Pāli *saka-vikkameṇa.* For the change of *saka* into *siya*, see Geiger's *L. S. S.* § 11, 2.

[23] *Māňḍā* for *māḍā*, 'having subdued'=Skt. *-mṛdya*, through Pkt. *maḍḍiya* or *maḍḍia* (cf. *Hc.* ii. 36 and iv. 126, where *maḍḍai*=P. *maddati*, Skt. *mardati*).

[24] *Vaturen.* Instrumental case of *vatura.* See above, p. 27, note 2.

of the unsullied fame [thus] wide-spread, he [anointed] the hands[1] and feet of his people.

[Ll. 6–12] He [re-]built[2] the **Mirisiviṭi**[3] [vehera], the **Saṅgsen-aram**[4] and the **Kasub-raj-maha-veher**[5], caused[6] five hundred monks[7] to reside, and honouring[8] [them] with gifts[9] of the four priestly requisites, raised[10] the standard[11] of the religion. By establishing[12] royal medical halls near the Southern Gate of the auspicious high-street[13] in the inner city[14] he allayed[15] the fear of disease. By affording facilities for the cultivation of fields by means of [the tanks] Podonavulu and Puluṇḍāvulu, he caused [this] illustrious Laṅkā to prosper[16], [and thus] dispelled[17] the fear of famine[18]. By inspecting[19] the country, he removed[20] the fear of enemies[21]. In various ways[22] he made converts to Buddhism from divers nationalities, [and] made offerings out of all his wealth.

---

[1] *Lov-at-paṭuḷ*=Skt. *lōka-hasta-pādatala*, unless we take *paṭuḷ* to be a derivative of Skt. *pratilya*. 'having anointed,' or more probably of *pratuṣṭa* (p.p.p. of *pra+tuṣ*), P. *paṭuṭṭho*. In colloquial Sinhalese *paṭula* (pl. *paṭul*) means 'sole of the foot.' Compare the expression *nimala-guṇa-vaturen jiyaḷ sanahay*, in line 2.

[2] *Karay*=mod. Sinh. *karā* or *kara*, 'having done'; Pāli *kariya*; Pkt. *karia* and *kari*; Modern Hindi *kar(a)* or *kar ke*. This form of the gerund is apt, at first sight, to be confounded with the third person, singular present, *karayi*, P. *karoti*, Pkt. *karaï*.

[3] *Maricavaṭṭi-vihāra*. See *Mv*. lii. 45.

[4] *Saṅghasēna-ārāma*. See *Mv*. li. 86. [5] *Kassapa-rāja-mahā-vihāra*.

[6] *Vasavay*=modern Sinh. *vasavā*, 'having caused to reside.' Pāli *vasāpetvā*. For the gerund in *ā* of Sinh. verbs, see Geiger's *L. S. S.* § 56, 2.

[7] *Arī*=P. *ariyā*, 'saints or holy persons' (from Skt. *ārya*).

[8] *Pujay*=modern Sinh. *pudā*, P. *pūjayitvā*. Cf. *L. S. S.* § 56, 2.

[9] *Sulab-satar-pasayen*=P. *sulabha-catupaccayēna*, 'with the four requisites [made] easy to be obtained.' For the etymology of *satara*, see *E. S.* No. 1593.

[10] *Huvay* or *huvā*=modern Sinh. *usuvā* or *osavā*, 'having raised.' P. *ussāpetvā*. See also *E. S.* No. 205.

[11] *Kot* is here used in the sense of Pāli *ketu*, 'banner or flag.' Cf. the phrase *dhammaketuṁ ussāpēti*. See also *E. S.* No. 396. [12] Lit. 'having made.'

[13] *Veyā*, loc. of *vī*, *vehe*=Skt. *vīthi* or *vīthī*, Pkt. *vihī* (cf. *Gauḍavaho*, 663, 1188), *vīhiya* (*ya*=*ka*).

[14] *Äti-nakarā* is treated for the present as a derivative of Skt. *antar-nagara*. Cf. Sinh. *ätuḷ-nagara* or *-nuvara*.

[15] *Samay*, 'having allayed' (from Skt. √*śam*).

[16] *Ḷondurvay*. The etymology or the exact meaning of this word is not quite clear to me.

[17] *Nivay*, 'having extinguished,' Skt. *nirvāya*.

[18] *Sā*=Skt. *psā*, 'hunger,' or *psāta*, P. *chāta*, 'hungry' (just as P. *chaṇa*=Sinh. *saṇa*). Geiger, however, derives it from Skt. *kṣaya*. See *E. S.* No. 1469. *Biya*=Skt. *bhiyā* or *bhiyas*.

[19] *Soyay*=modern Sinh. *soyā*, 'having examined,' from Skt. √*śudh* in causative, *śōdhayati*, P. *sōdhēti*. Tamil *śōdikkirēṉ*, 'I examine.'

[20] *Nerā*, 'having removed'=Skt. *nirhṛtya*, P. *nīharitvā*. [21] *Sāt-biya*=Skt. *śatru-bhiyas* (or *-bhiyā*).

[22] *Nan-soy*=P. *nānā-chāyā*.

By [celebrating] relic-festivals [1], he honoured [2] the Buddha-gem [3]. In fulfilment [4] of the resolution [5] [appearing in his words] 'how [6] shall I honour the Dhamma-gem,' he caused the Abhidhamma discourses to be transcribed [7] on plates of gold [and therewith] made a great offering. Yearning in his heart to establish the Buddhist religion [8], he preached [9] that same Dhamma in the presence of [his] esteemed teacher, and extolled the virtues of the Buddha in his own language.

[Ll. 12–14] Our Sovereign Lord [10], [who has done all these acts and] who is [like unto] a *tilaka* mark [11] [of adornment] of the Okkāka [12] royal dynasty pinnacle [13] of the Śākya [14] race that was descended from the Solar line, built [15], in the sixth year after the elevation of his royal canopy [16], the monastery **Salameyvanpavu** [17] for the **Kapārā** fraternity at the **Abhayagiri-vihāra** and caused [18] monks to take up their residence in it. [His Majesty, moreover] made the four priestly requisites [19] easily procurable and enacted these [following] regulations [20] for the monasteries [21] connected [22] with this fraternity.

[Ll. 15–20] [Touching] the villages and lands of **Ätvehera** [23] appertaining to **Abahay-giri** [24]**-vehera** and **Sey-giri-vehera** [25], as well as all the villages and lands belonging to the Vihāras attached to these same [establishments] and

---

[1] *Dā-sāṇen*=P. *dhātu-chaṇēna.*

[2] *Ariyay*, 'having honoured.' Probably from Skt. *ārādh.* See above, p. 34, note 14, p. 50, note 4, and *E. S.* No. 75. It may also be connected with Skt. *ārya* (Pāli *ariyo*) from √*ṛ*. Cf. *namasya* (denom. of *namas*).

[3] The three gems (Pāli *ti-ratana* or *ratanattaya*, Sinh. *te-* (or *tuṇu-*)*ruvan*) of Buddhism are the Buddha, *Bud-* (or *Budu-*)*ruvan*; the Law, *Dam-* (or *Damu-*)*ruvan*; and the Clergy, *Saṅg* (or *saṅgu-ruvan*).

[4] *Puray*, 'having fulfilled,' P. *pūriya, pūretvā.*

[5] *Adahas*=P. *ajjhāsaya.*

[6] *Kavari-seyekin. Kavari* (more commonly *kavara*)=Skt. *katara.* For the etymology of *sey* or *sī*, see p. 51, note 22, and *E. S.* No. 1567.

[7] *A:ravay* (lit. 'having caused to mount') is the causative of *aray* (p. 50, note 10). *Kasun-pat aravay*=Skt. *kāñcana-pattram ārōpya.*

[8] *Sasun siṭvami yana sit-doḷnen*, lit. with the heart's longing 'I will establish the religion.'

[9] *Dham-desun-viyak|han-kaḷa*=Skt. *Dharma-dēśanā-vyākhyāna-kṛta.*

[10] *Apa purumuvo.* See above, p. 26, note 1.

[11] *Talā-ṭik.* See above, p. 34, note 6.

[12] *Okā*=P. *Okkāko*, Skt. *Ikṣvāku.*

[13] *Kot*, see above, p. 51, note 11.

[14] *Sākā-kula.* See above, p. 32, note 6.

[15] *Karay*, lit. 'having made.' See above, p. 51, note 2.

[16] *Sat läṅgū.* See Vessagiri slab-inscriptions, Nos. 1 and 2 (pp. 25 and 33). Cf. also *chattaṃ laṅghēsi*, 'he raised the royal umbrella' (*Mv.* xxxvii. 50).

[17] Pāli *Silāmēghavaṇṇa-pabbata.*

[18] *Vasavay*, lit. 'having caused to reside.'

[19] *Satara pasa*=P. *cattāro paccayā.*

[20] *Sirit*=P. *cāritta.*

[21] *Avasa*=P. *āvāsa*, 'a monk's dwelling.'

[22] *Abadi* (*abādi* in l. 15)=Skt. *ābaddha*, probably through a form *ābaddhika.*

[23] P. *Hatthi-vihāra.*

[24] *Abhaya-giri-vihāra.*

[25] P. *Cētiya-giri-vihāra*; Pkt. *ceie-.*

also those [belonging to] Raj-maha-vehera [1], the Pariveṇas, the Piyangal [1] monastery, the nunneries [2] and [finally] those villages and lands connected with the incomes accruing to the clergy in common [3] or to individual [4] monks—into none of these shall employés [5] of the royal family enter [6] and take away [therefrom] the farm labourers [7], carts [8], oxen and buffaloes [9], or cut down trees and shrubs [therein]; savages [10] also shall not enter. If there be any murderers [in a village, the king's employés or officials] may enter [that] village and demand them only, but no wrong [11] shall be done to other villagers who have not abetted [12] [the murderers]. At the expiration of every two years, princes of the royal family may, in claiming the country [13], demand [the surrender of] perpetrators of the five great offences, but they shall not demand other offenders.

[Ll. 20–25] If fines have already been levied by former officials in the manner known to the village, no fines shall be levied again for the offences [with which the villagers were] charged. All the fines levied on lands and villages [14] appertaining to **Ätvehera** shall be expended on repairs to works in **Ätvehera.** The former (villagers?) [15] shall not occupy [16] the places they have not occupied [16] before. If there be a dispute [17] concerning

[1] P. *Rāja-mahā-vihāra.* According to the *Pūjāvaliya* a Piyagal-piriveṇa was established by king Siri-Saṅgabo, i.e. Aggabōdhi IV (A.D. 673–89).

[2] *Meheṇivara*=Skt. *śramaṇī-gṛha*, P. *samaṇī-ghara.* See also *E. S.* No. 1072.

[3] *Saṅg-satu*=P. *saṅgha-santaka.* [4] *Pugul-satu*=P. *puggala-santaka.*

[5] *Kāmiya*=P. *kammika.* [6] *Vädä*, 'having entered,' from Skt. √*vraj*. See *E. S.* No. 1281.

[7] *Vāriyan.* The meaning of this word is not clear. Müller takes it to mean 'enemies,' evidently connecting it with the Skt. *vairin* or *vārakin* (*A. I. C.* 110 C, 113 C, 117 C, 120 B), while Mudaliyar Guṇasēkara renders it 'by force' (see also *E. S.* No. 1388). I am inclined to treat it, for the present at least, as a Sinhalese form of the word *vārika* (from √ *vṛ*) occurring in the Jētavanārāma Sanskrit inscription (see above, pp. 3, 5, and 9). Tamil *vārak-kuḍi* means 'a cultivator of the soil' (Winslow).

[8] *Gāl*, plural of *gāḷa*, probably connected with Skt. *śakaṭikā*, or *śakaṭa*, pronounced in Tamil *śagaḍa*.

[9] *Mīvun*, from Skt. *mahiṣa.* See *E. S.* No. 1100.

[10] *Melāṭsī.* This does not look like a Sinhalese word. The above is Mudaliyar Guṇasēkara's rendering of it, probably taking it as a corrupt form of Skt. *mlēccha.* [11] *Aniyā*=Skt. *a-nyāya.*

[12] *Pahaḷ* (in lines 19 and 24), probably an older form of *vahal* (Skt. *upakāra*). The etymology is not clear, but see *E. S.* Nos. 1323–24 and 832.

[13] *Raṭ*=P. *raṭṭhaṁ*, 'country, land,' referring probably to the Government share or tax on land.

[14] *Gam-bim* (Skt. *grāma-bhūmi*) may also mean 'lands of the villages.'

[15] I do not quite understand the sentence *pere novan-viri-lānaṭ pere nāṭṭiyam no vadnā isā.* The above translation is offered tentatively. The word *nāṭṭiyam* is there taken as an equivalent of Tamil *nāṭṭār.* Mudaliyar Guṇasēkara renders it 'dancers,' evidently connecting it with Skt. *nāṭya.* It may, also, be a derivative of Skt. *nāṣṭika.* In Tamil, *nāṭṭiyam* means 'design, aim,' and *nāṭṭa* (inf. of *nāṭṭugiṟēṉ, nāṭṭiṉēṉ*) 'to establish (law).' *No-van-viri* may probably be a compound, like *nu-duṭu-virū* (Skt. *na dṛṣṭa-pūrva*). [16] lit. 'enter' and 'entered.'

[17] *Giṅgiri* (more correctly *gigiri*), modern Sinh. *gugura-ṇavā* (pret. *giguruvā*), 'to thunder, make a loud noise,' from Skt. *ghurghura.* Cf. also Skt. *gharghara.*

the fines levied by princes of the royal family who had gone out to govern[1] the country, [then these] princes and judges shall sit and investigate [the matter] and shall, thereafter, remit whatever [fine] ought to be remitted. If there be any who, after committing murder, have taken refuge in the premises occupied by the Saṅgha, these [murderers] and their abettors shall be tried and sentenced to be exiled to Daṁbdiv[2]. If, however, there be any who have taken refuge [in temple premises] from other [causes of] fear, no fines on account of lodging[3] shall be exacted from them nor shall they be exiled.

[Ll. 26–31] [Officials] shall not take away in anger the gifts granted [to the Church] in full reliance on the efficacy of the Buddhist religion though with prejudice to the royal family. When artificers and holders of village leases[4] take refuge with the monks, any debts[5] that should be recovered [from them] shall be recovered after investigation, but no other [kind of] coercion[6] shall be employed. Lodgings[7] shall not be provided for men sent by royal order in cells wherein monks reside. Cells made over to the community of monks[8] shall not be converted into personal[9] property. If an act of misconduct, such as a tumultuous dispute[10], arise[11] amongst destitute (?)[12] masters of religious ceremonies[13], recipients of benefits [from temple property, or] among those who have received cells [to live in], the monks of the [Kapārā ?] Muḷa [fraternity[14]] shall sit [in council] and settle [the dispute]; if the monks cannot settle it, they shall hold a conference[15] with the princes, and, due investigation being made, shall decide [the case] and impose punishment according to merit.

---

[1] Or 'to impose taxes.' This seems to be the signification here of *paḷavannaḷ*. In modern Sinh. *paḷavanavā* means 'to load.' The phrase *raḷ paḷavannaḷ giya raj-kol-sam-daruvan gat daṇḍā* can also be rendered, 'concerning the fines levied on [those] princes of royal families who had undergone banishment from the country.'

[2] Skt. *Jambudvīpa*, 'India.'

[3] *Ge-daṇḍ*, probably equivalent to Skt. *gṛha-daṇḍa*. See also Mihintale Inscription A, l. 37.

[4] *Pāḷḷa*, or *paḷḷa*, a grant usually inscribed on copper-plate or on stone. Here it means probably 'a lease.' See Mihintale Inscription A, l. 46. Compare also Tamil *pāḍu*, and the expression *taṉ pāḍḍilē pōga*, 'to attend to one's business.'

[5] *Ṇaya*=Skt. *ṛṇa*.

[6] *Nigā*=Skt. *nigraha*, P. *niggaha*.

[7] *Navā-tän* (l. 28)=Skt. *nirṛtta-sthāna*. P. *nivattaṭṭhānam* (cf. *Mv.* xv. 10).

[8] *Saṅg-kaḷa-aras*=P. *saṅghika-kata-āvāsa*.

[9] *Pugul*=P. *puggalika*.

[10] *Kaḷaha*=Skt. *kōlāhala*, 'uproar.'

[11] *Atapumit*, from Skt. *hasta+pravṛt*.

[12] *Apiḷisaraṇa*=P. *a-paṭisaraṇa*. According to Clough's Dict. *piḷisaraṇa* means 'help, favour, patronage.' Cf., however, its use in line 55.

[13] *Vat-himi*. See above, p. 35, note 7.

[14] See above, line 13.

[15] *Mul-vä*, lit. 'having assembled.' Cf. *muḷu-dī* (*Amāvatura*, ch. ii. p. 5).

[Ll. 31–35] If there be a dispute in respect of the monks' refusal (?) of gruel[1], the princes shall be sent to reconcile the monks and induce them to partake of the gruel, but no compulsion shall be exercised to make them accept it. If there be any one who has done any one of these things without royal order, he shall be dismissed from the service. To the Eykäruṇ[2] monastery, which was built by royal order, there shall be granted a *payala*[3] [of rice ?] from the royal household, [and thus] gruel shall be provided [for the monks]. Those who have gone away, disregarding[4] the rules ordained by the priesthood, shall pay the customary fines and so provide for the partaking of gruel.

[Ll. 35–40] In all these places, [namely] in the image house[5] at **Abahay-giri-vehera**[6], in the dāgaba, in the Maha-bo-ge[7], in the Ruvan-pahā[8], in the refectory, a record shall be kept [of income and expenditure, all details] having been obtained from the six monasteries and from the places belonging to the monks[9] of the two fraternities [or chapters]. This record shall be written up and read out[10] at the end of [every] year before the assembly of senior monks.

At **Segiri**[11], too, a record shall be kept, based on information obtained from the places belonging to the monks[9] of the two chapters; and this, also, shall be written up and read out at the end of the year before the assembly of elders. If any are to be admitted to the order[12] they shall be those familiar[13] (?) with the four sections [*bhāṇavāra*] of the *Paritta*. Nothing whatever shall be received from those entering the order. The recipients [of such gifts] and donors [thereof] shall not be lodged in the same cell: nor shall four relatives be lodged in one [and the same] cell.

---

[1] *Hambu*=P. *ācāma*, according to Müller (*A. I. C.* p. 211).

[2] I do not know the meaning of this word. If *kaḷa* is taken in combination with *eykäruṇ*, the passage *radol yedmen kaḷa eykäruṇ veheraṭ rajkolen payalak dī hambu gamvanu isā* can be rendered, '[but] those . . . who have done [the same] by royal order shall grant to the Vihāra a *payala* [of rice] from the royal household, and thus provide gruel [for the monks].'

[3] *Payala*, probably same as modern *päla*, a measure of capacity equal to one-fourth of an *amuṇa* (P. *ammaṇa*) or *paya* (above, p. 36, note 7), that is about 1¾ bushel. It is also used as in line 50 to signify the extent of land on which this quantity of paddy is sown.

[4] *Piyā*=P. *pahāya*. Cf. the expression *ataṭa pat nivan-sāpa piyā* in *Amāvatura*, ch. i (p. 1 of the printed edition).

[5] *Piḷima-gē*=Skt. *pratimā-gṛha*, Pkt. *paḍimā-gāha*.

[6] i. e. *Abhayagiri-vihāra*.

[7] i. e. the building enclosing the Sacred Bōdhi-tree.

[8] P. *Ratana-pāsāda*.

[9] *Sāṅgātanin*, from P. *saṅghikaṭṭhānam*.

[10] *Asvanu*, causative of *asanu*, 'hear,' probably from Skt. *ā-śru*.

[11] P. *Cētiyagiri*.

[12] *Mahaṇ-karaṭ*, from Pāli *samaṇa-karoti*, 'to make one a *śramaṇa*,' i.e. to invest him with the yellow robe.

[13] *Piṇis*, probably from Skt. *pra-ṇi-śri*.

[Ll. 40–45] Without transgressing the customary observances, the monks shall be served[1] with *vasags*[2] according to the scale prescribed by the givers [of contributions] to those cells which are attached to the two fraternities. But those religious preceptors who have committed to memory the Pāli [canonical texts], after having been instructed[3] conformably to the known practice of the cells, shall be served[1] at the places where they reside, though not with *vasags*[4].

There shall be admitted such monks as shall, at need, discourse on religious duties[5]. Monks who have entered [the order] contrary to the customs and observances, and who, moreover, live not in harmony [with other monks]—these preceptors of religious ceremonies, as well as those preceptors who countenanced[6] such procedure, shall not be lodged in the same cell [or *āvāsa*]. Those religious preceptors who have been deported to Daṁbadiva [India] by the [king's] wrath, as well as those who have been dismissed from monastic duties, shall not be allowed to enter again the *āvāsa* from which they had been expelled. Those preceptors also, who, by admitting them, have brought about dissension[7] among the inmates, shall not be lodged in the same *āvāsa*.

[Ll. 45–50] The officials[8] who have given to others the cattle belonging to the Karvaḷ stall[9], as well as those who have taken the same for themselves, shall be dismissed from the service. No gifts of land on the tank-side shall be accepted save only the tenth part granted out of the villages and the lands[10] belonging to **Ätvehera**. No agricultural labour shall be performed. The same law shall be observed also at the two *āvāsas*, Mahanet-pā[11] and Vahadū. Neither here nor in the other *āvāsas* shall youths[12] of tender

[1] *Eḷvanu*. I am not sure of the meaning or the etymology of this word.

[2] *Vasāgin* may be rendered here 'at the end of the *vassa* season' or 'according to seniority,' but see above, p. 28, note 5.

[3] *Piṇis-vā*. See p. 55, note 13.

[4] *No vasāgin-ij* may also be rendered, 'and [or though] not according to seniority.' See note 2.

[5] The meaning of *vaddūlanaḷ valā kiyena* in lines 41–42 is not clear. The above rendering is offered tentatively.

[6] *Pasavū* = Skt. *pārśva-bhūta*.

[7] *Viyo-kaḷa* = Skt. *viyōga-kṛta*.

[8] *Kämiya* = Skt. *karmika*, 'worker.' In *Piyummala* (p. 50) the word *käm* is used as a synonym of *līkam*, *liyana*, and *lipi* in the sense of 'clerk' or 'secretary.'

[9] *Hala* = Skt. *śāla*.

[10] *Gam-bimin* may also be rendered, 'out of the lands of the village.'

[11] i.e. *Mahānētra-prāsāda*.

[12] *Unu-povā* (l. 48). I do not quite understand this expression. The above is Mudaliyar Guṇasēkara's rendering, evidently connecting it with Skt. *ūna* + *pōtaka* (cf. Sinh. *pov* or *povu*, Skt. *pōta*, 'a young animal').

age be received into the order. One *amuṇa*[1] of raw rice and four *akas*[2] of gold a day [shall be granted] to those who have received lodgings at the Maha-Kapārā-piriveṇa for their maintenance[3]. At the expiration of every year, 1000 [*akas*] of gold [shall be given] to [meet] the expenses of their robes; the two *payalas*[4] [sowing-extent of land] in Väligamu for their servants and the men thereof as serfs.

[Ll. 51–56] Monks who have appropriated for themselves any article (*pasaya*, P. *paccayo*) whatever that is inside or outside the [Kapārā-]piriveṇa, except those requisites (*pasaya*) assigned to them as recipients of cells [for their maintenance] shall be expelled from the cells, after due investigation has been made thereof by the nobles. Except out of the share allotted to the recipients of cells, villages shall be acquired only when there is a surplus [in temple revenue] after defraying the expenses connected with temple decorations[5], offerings, repairs[6], and the wages[7] of monks' servants.

The appointed masters of religious ceremonies shall act according to former customs. A record shall be kept [of income and expenditure] by means of information obtained[8] from the cells inhabited by the eight persons from the two seats (?) and by the four destitute and the four decrepit persons who have been introduced, with the concurrence of the monks, by the recipients of cells, and [this record] shall be written up and read out before the community of elders at the expiration of [every] year.

---

[1] P. *ammaṇam*=about five or six bushels. See above, p. 55, note 3.

[2] See above, p. 29, note 1.

[3] *Piṇḍ-pasaya*=P. *piṇḍa-paccayo*.

[4] See above, p. 55, note 3.

[5] *Situvam*=P. *cittakamma*, 'painting.'

[6] *Kam-navām*, lit. 'renewal of work.'

[7] *Vaṭā*, probably from Skt. *vartaka*. Cf. also Skt. *bhāṭaka*.

[8] *Illā*. In modern Sinhalese *illanavā* means 'to ask, solicit.' Pret. *illuvā*; ger. *illā*; verbal noun *illīma*, 'petition.' Its real signification here, as well as in lines 18–20, 36 and 37, is not quite clear, and it is difficult to say whether it is etymologically connected with one of the Skt. roots *iṣ*, 'to desire,' or *īḍ* (*īl*), 'to praise, implore.' Cf. Tamil *kēḷ*.

No. 5. MAHA-RATMALE ROCK-INSCRIPTION (circa A.D. 135–41)

ABOUT two and a half miles south-west of Anurādhapura, not far from the main road to Kurunegala, there is an old tank, now abandoned, called Ratmala-väva. Close by are ruins of an ancient site and an inscription engraved on a large slab-rock, 48 by 54 feet, in four lines, covering a surface of 11′ 10″ by 2′ 6″. The letters are clearly cut, and are about three to four inches in size, not taking into account the long strokes of *a*, *k*, and *r*. As a result, probably, of fires made on it by treasure-seekers, three akṣaras of the first line, five of the second, six of the third, and four of the fourth are obliterated (see Plate 13 *a*).

This inscription was examined both by Goldschmidt and Müller[1].

As both these scholars have already stated, the Brāhmī characters in which the inscription is written belong to the second century A. D., i.e. to the latter half of it, to be more precise. Their type closely resembles that of the period of king Puḷumāyi found in Kaṇheri, Kārle, and other cave-inscriptions of Western India[2].

As to the grammar of the inscription, we see (*a*) the nominative singular in *-e* (*maharajẹ*), as in AMg., Mg., and in the Aśoka edicts; (*b*) the genitive singular in *-ha* (*rajaha*), as explained above at p. 16; (*c*) the genitive plural in *-āna* (Skt. *-ānām*), common enough as *āṇa* in M., AMg., JM., JŚ.[3]; and (*d*) the locative singular in *-hi* (*viharahi*), which, according to Geiger[4], should be *-ahi*, as it is derived from P. *-amhi* by the loss of the nasal. This explanation would, perhaps, be better understood if we regard Skt. *-smin* (not *-asmin*) as the pronominal case-ending of the locative singular. *-Smin* becomes P. *-mhi* as well as *-si*, according to Kaccāyana; M., JM., JŚ. *-mmi*; AMg. *-ṁsi*, *-ṁmi* and *-mmi*; dialectic Mg. *-hiṁ* (through *-ssiṁ*), A. *-hi*[5]; Aśoka edicts *-mhi* (Girnār) and *-si* (Khālsī and Dhauli). The transition from these to the

---

[1] See Goldschmidt's 'Report on the Inscriptions in the North-Central Province' (*Ceylon Sessional Papers*, ix. 1875, p. 3); and Müller's *Ancient Inscriptions in Ceylon* No. 6, pp. 27, 73, and 109): transcript, English translation, notes, and lithograph plate.

[2] For Ceylon inscriptions besides the present one, written more or less in this alphabet, see the Vessagiri rock record above, page 21, and *A. I. C.* Nos. 2 to 20.

[3] See Pischel's *Gram. der Pkt.-Spr.* p. 257, § 370.

[4] *L. S. S.* p. 60, § 38.

[5] Pischel's *Gram. der Pkt.-Spr.* § 366ᵃ.

Sinhalese *-hi* is quite an easy and a most natural step. It is, therefore, not quite accurate to treat it as a derivative direct from the Pāli ending *-amhi*.

Kaṭu is, according to all authorities, a derivative of the Sanskrit *kṛtvā*. The gerund in *-tu* is one of the distinguishing features of the Shāhbāzgarhi, Khālsī, Dhauli, and Dehlī edicts of Aśoka. The word *kaṭu* itself occurs in *Dh.* ii. l. 7[1].

Dine is equivalent to P. *dinno* (p.p.p. of √*dā*), used here as an active aorist, agreeing with its subject *Naka-maharaje*. This active use of the passive past participle has already been correctly explained by Childers[2] and M. Boyer[3].

In the scanty **historical** element of the inscription, we see the names of three kings:—(1) Devānapiya Tisa-maharaja, (2) Devānapiya Puṭikaṇa Gamiṇi Abhaya-maharaja, and (3) Devānapiya Naka-maharaja. These sovereigns Goldschmidt and Müller have correctly identified with (1) Vaṅkanāsika Tissa, (2) Gaja-bāhu I, and (3) Mahallaka Nāga of the *Mahāvaṁsa*. The third was, according to the inscription, a *marumakaṇakan*, i.e. a grandson (or son-in-law[4], or nephew) of the first. The words indicating the relationship of the second to the third are unfortunately obliterated, but they have been supplied with some certainty in the text from Gajabāhu's inscriptions at Ruvanväli dāgaba and elsewhere (*A. I. C.* Nos. 5, 10, 11 B, and 12). These records distinctly state that the second was a son of the first. Therefore the third must have stood in the relation of a son or a nephew or a brother-in-law to the second. The Ceylon chronicles, while admitting that Gajabāhu was the son of Vaṅkanāsika Tissa, differ totally as regards the relationship of Gajabāhu's successor Mahallaka Nāga. The *Mahāvaṁsa* (Colombo edition, 1883, ch. xxxv. v. 123) makes him the *sasurō* or father-in-law of Gajabāhu[5]; the *Rājāvaliya* and the *Pūjāvaliya* call him the *suhuru-baḍu*[6]. Possibly the reading *sasurō* in the Colombo edition of the *Mahāvaṁsa* is

---

[1] *A. S. S. I.* vol. i. p. 128.

[2] *J. R. A. S.* n. s. viii. pp. 151–3.

[3] *Journal Asiatique*, Nov.–Dec., 1898.

[4] See above, p. 20, note 2.

[5] To which the *Mahāvaṁsa Ṭīkā* adds that he was a *Sēnāpati* or Commander under Gajabāhu (*Gajabāhu-raññō Sēnāpati Mahallakō Nāgō*). See p. 480 of the Colombo edition of 1895.

[6] 'Brother-in-law,' according to Mudaliyar Guṇasēkara's rendering. Ranesinghe derives *suhuru-baḍu* from Skt. *śvaśura*, 'father-in-law,' and *bhāṇḍa*, 'treasure' (see his Glossary to the Sinhalese *Ummaggajātaka*). Geiger, however, correctly gives *sahōdara* as the Skt. equivalent of *suhuru* (*E. S.* No. 1553).

inaccurate, and should really be some other word like it derived from Skt. *svasrīya*, 'sister's son.' If this be the case, there would be complete agreement between the *Mahāvaṁsa* and the inscription, because Gajabāhu's sister's son would naturally be a grandson of Vaṅkanāsika Tissa. If, on the other hand, *marumakan* really means here 'son-in-law' or 'nephew' as it does in Tamil, then Mahallaka Nāga must have been either 'a brother-in-law' or 'a cousin' of Gajabāhu. And this would point to the correctness of the reading *suhuru-baḍu* in the Sinhalese works mentioned above.

These facts, coupled with the information contained in the inscription at Situlpav-vihāra (*A. I. C.* No. 16), furnish the following historical data:—

(1) King Vasabha, called in inscriptions *Vasaba* or *Vahaba*, and in Sinhalese records *Vähäp*, a descendant of the Lambakaṇṇa or Lämiṇi race, reigned for forty-four years (A. D. 66–110, T. and W.). The story of his assumption of regal power, of his marriage with *Mettā*, the wife of his uncle, the general in whose service he was before he became king, and of his many religious acts, is narrated in detail in the *Mahāvaṁsa*[1] (ch. xxxv. 59–100).

(2) Vaṅkanāsika[2] Tissa, named in inscriptions Devānapiya Tisa-maharaja, or simply Tisa-maharaja, in the *Pūjāvaliya* Vaknähä Tissa, and in the *Rājāvaliya* Vannäsi-nambapa, Sīn Kasubu or Sīna-nambapa[3], was, according to all authorities, the son of Vasabha. The *Mahāvaṁsa* (xxxv. 111–14) adds that his queen was *Mahāmattā*, daughter of king Subha, and agrees with the Sinhalese chronicles as to the length of his reign, viz. three years (A. D. 110–13, T. and W.).

(3) Gajabāhuka Gāminī[4], called in inscriptions Gayabāhu Gamiṇi Abaya or Devānapiya Gamiṇi Abhaya, or simply Gamiṇi Aba, son of the preceding king, reigned for twenty-two years[5] according to Pāli and Sinhalese authorities,

---

[1] It is, perhaps, of sufficient interest to bring to notice the following important passage from the *Mahāvaṁsa Ṭīkā*, which should be added to those already adduced by Snyder and Geiger (*Dīpavaṁsa und Mahāvaṁsa*, p. 35), in determining the date of the compilation of that work. The *Mahāvaṁsa Ṭīkā* (p. 476) comments on *Mv.* xxxv. 87:—*Issarasamaṇakē idhā ti, idha Anurādhapura-santikē pubbaröhi vēna pākaṭabhūtē Issarasamaṇa-saṁkhātē Kacchapa-giri-vihārē sō Vasabhō jēva upōsathāgāraṁ kārēsī ti atthō*, 'the meaning of "here at Issarasamaṇaka" is that here in the vicinity of Anurādhapura, at Kacchapagiri-vihāra, known by tradition as Issarasamaṇa, that [king] Vasabha also built an *upōsatha* hall.' Now this *Kacchapagiri-vihāra* (Sinh. *Kasub-giri-vehera*), which was formerly known as *Issarasamaṇa-vihāra* (Sinh. *Isuramuṇu-vehera*), was evidently the one built by Kassapa I, the parricide (A. D. 479–97), and mentioned in the Vessagiri slab-inscription, No. 2. See above, p. 31.

[2] *-nāsika*, *Mv. Ṭ.* p. 477. [3] See Mudaliyar Guṇasēkara's edition (1899), p. 38.

[4] Gāmanī, both in the *Mahāvaṁsa* and in its *Ṭīkā*.

[5] Turnour's translation of *bāvīsa-vassāni* by 'twelve years' is wrong.

except the *Rājāvaliya*, which allots him twenty-four years (circa A. D. 113–35 or 137). Regarding the events of this king's rule, the *Mahāvaṁsa* mentions only his benefactions to the Buddhist Church, and makes no reference whatever to his invasion of the Soḷī or Chōla country in South India, related in detail both in the *Pūjāvaliya* and in the *Rājāvaliya*.

(4) Mahallaka Nāga, called in the present inscription Devānapiya Nakamaharaja, and in Sinhalese historical works Mahaḷumānā, reigned for six years (circa A.D. 135–41). According to the *Mahāvaṁsa* he built seven vihāras[1].

The chronicles make no mention of his gift to the priesthood of gruel, rice and cloths recorded in the inscription. It appears from the Mihintale inscription (*A. I. C.* No. 20, line 12) that Vihirabijaka was a large village, probably the same as *Vihīrabija* mentioned in *Mv.* xvii. 59, and in Galkōvila inscription (*A. I. C.* No. 98, line 3), and that Muṭigutika was a hamlet within its bounds, with a tank and very likely a vihāra also.

(5) Bhātika Tissa or Bhātiya Tissa was, from all records, the son and successor of Mahallaka Nāga. He is stated to have reigned twenty-four years (circa A. D. 141–65). For an account of his religious acts see *Mv.* xxxvi. 1–5.

(6) Kaniṭṭha Tissa, his younger brother, succeeded him and reigned twenty-eight years according to the *Mahāvaṁsa*, or eighteen years according to the *Pūjāvaliya* (A. D. 165–83 or 193). The *Rājāvaliya* omits this king altogether.

In re-editing the present inscription, I have used several estampages supplied by the Archaeological Commissioner. With these I have collated Müller's text (Mt.) and plate (Mp.), and I give below as foot-notes the various readings found in them.

TRANSCRIPT.

1 Sidhaṁ[2] Devānapiya[3] Ti[sa-maha]-rajaha maru-makaṇakane[4] Devāṇapiya[5] pu(ṭi)kaṇa[6] Gamiṇi[7]

---

[1] Namely: 'in the eastward, the Pējalaka; in the southward, the Kōṭipabbata; in the westward, the Udakapāsāṇa; in the isle of Nāgadīpa, the Sālipabbata; at Bījagāma, the Tēnavēli (Cānavēla in *Mv. T.*); in the Rōhaṇa division, the Tobbalanāgapabbata and Girihālika-vihāra in the interior country.'

[2] Mt. *sidha*. The *anusvāra* is quite legible on the ink-impressions before me.

[3] Or *-piye*, Mp. *devānipiya*. [4] Mt. *marumanaka*; Mp. *maranaṇaka*. [5] Mp. *buvānapiya*.

[6] Mt. *putaka[na]*; Mp. *puḍaka* .. [7] Mt. *Gāmini*; Mp. *Gamiṇi*.

2 Abhaya-maharaja[ha pute[1] Devā]napiya[2] Naka-maharaje[3] Vihirabijakahi[4] Muṭigutika[5]

3 saha Parivataka .. .. viharahi bhiku-sagaha visiti hamāṇana(ya)[6] yāku[7] ca bata ca

4 vasavasika[8]-hāṭika (ca) .. .. (na) kaṭu dine (uti)rika[9] .. .. ra (pa)ṭa vānaka kaṭu dine

TRANSLATION.

Hail! The great king Naka, beloved [of the gods, son (?) of] the great king Pu(ṭi)kaṇa Gamiṇi Abhaya, beloved of the gods, [and] grandson[10] of the great king Tisa, beloved of the gods, having caused [to prepare] gruel, boiled rice and undergarments for (presentation at) the Vassa[11] ceremony, granted [the same] for the benefit of twenty monks (*śramaṇa*) of the community of *bhikṣus* at Vihirabijaka and at Muṭigutika and Parivataka . . . . Buddhist monasteries. [His Majesty, moreover] granted outer garments . . . . . having had them woven in silk [for the purpose].

REMARKS.

Sidhaṁ stands for *Siddhaṁ*. See above, page 22.

Devānapiya [or *-piye*]. There is no trace of an *anusvāra* either above or, as in the Aśoka edicts, immediately after the akṣara *na*. In the Paḍariā (or Paḍēria) edict from the Nepal Tarāi this title has the same spelling as here[12]. In Shāhbāzgaṛhi and Mansērā it is spelt *devanaṁpriya* and *devanapriya*, while in all other Aśoka edicts we find the form *devānaṁpiya* (or *-priya*), with the exception of that of Siddāpura, where the spelling *devāṇaṁpiya*[13] with a cerebral *ṇ* is used. Its Sanskrit equivalent is *dēvānāṁ priya*, Pāli *dēvānaṁ-piya*, Sinh. *devana-* or *deveni-pā*. The form *dēvāṇuppiya* occurring in the Jain canonical works *Upāsakadaśā-sūtra* and *Aupapātika-*

---

[1] Mt. gives only two akṣaras, *dē* and *vā*, but the blank space in Mp. has room for five or six.
[2] Or *-piye*, Mp. *devānipiya*.
[3] Mp. °*raja*.
[4] Mt. °*ha*; Mp. *vihira*°.
[5] Mt. *muḷa*; Mp. *muḍagulaka*.
[6] Mt. *pāmana naye*; Mp. *hamāṇanaye*.
[7] Mp. *yaka* .. *pata*.
[8] Mt. *vasāvasikahaṭa kaṭe pa* .. ..; Mp. *vasa(va)sika-hāṭika* .. ..
[9] Mt. *utirika* .. .. *rahaṭa*; Mp. *utirika* .. .. *ra(ha)ṭa*.
[10] Or 'son-in-law' or 'nephew.' See above, p. 20, note 2.
[11] For explanation, see remarks below.
[12] See Bühler's edition (*Epigraphia Indica*, v. No. 1).
[13] See *ibid.*, iii. No. 22.

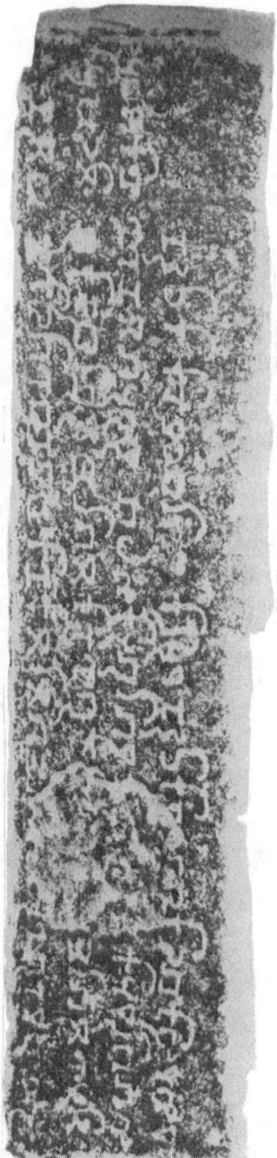

(*a*) Maha-Ratmale:—Rock-Inscription.

(*b*) Perumäiyan-kuḷam:—Rock-Inscription.

Scale $\frac{3}{4}$ in. to 1 foot.

sūtra is treated by Bhagwānlāl Indrajī, Leumann, Bühler, Jacobi, and others as a Prākrit corruption of *dēvānām-priya*[1]. Hoernle, on the other hand, rejects this explanation and takes it to be a regular derivative of Skt. *dēva* + *anupriya*, 'agreeable to the dēvas[2].' The term *Dēvānaṁ piya*, as has already been pointed out by these scholars, was used as a royal title not only by Aśoka, but also by his predecessors and by his grandson Daśaratha. It was also used in Ceylon by the Great Tissa, who reigned, according to Turnour, from 307–267 B.C., by Gamiṇi Abaya (probably Vaṭṭagāmanī Abhaya, circa 88–76 B.C.), mentioned in the inscriptions on Tōnigala, and at Gallena Vihāra and Daṁbulla-vihāra, and also by the three sovereigns named in the present record. In view of these facts, Mr. Vincent A. Smith, the latest writer on the subject, thinks that 'the rendering by the conventional phrase "His Majesty" or "His Sacred Majesty" is a more faithful representation of the real meaning of *dēvānaṁpiya* than the verbal translation "beloved of the gods" or "dear to the gods".'

Marumakaṇakane is either a clerical mistake for *marumakane*, which occurs in the Vessagiri cave-inscriptions (above, pp. 17 and 20), or a compound of *marumakaṇa* and Skt. *kana*, probably meaning 'the younger (brother) of the grandson[3].' The form *manumaraka* occurs in inscriptions of king Gajabāhu[4], the predecessor of king Naka (i.e. Nāga) of our record. Hence it appears that both these forms were in use in the second century A.D., and that from the latter must have been derived the modern word *munuburā*, 'grandson,' and *minibiri*, 'granddaughter[5].'

Puṭikaṇa. The meaning of this word is not at all clear. From Müller's rendering of the phrase *devānapiya puṭikaṇa*[6] *Gamiṇi Abhaya-maharaja* by 'the younger son of the great king Gāmini Abhaya,' it appears that he has taken *puṭi kaṇa* as composed of Skt. *putra* and *kana*. A comparison, however,

---

[1] See *Ind. Ant.* x (1881), p. 108; Leumann's edition (1883) of the *Aupapātika-sūtra*, Pt. I, index, p. 126; Notes by Senart and V. A. Smith in *Ind. Ant.* xx (1891), p. 231; xxxii (1903), pp. 265–7; *J. R. A. S.* for 1901, pp. 485, 577, and 930, and Jacobi's glossary to his edition of the *Kalpa-sūtra*, p. 149.

[2] See Hoernle's translation of the *Upāsakadaśā-sūtra*, notes 215, 255, 257, and Appendix III, p. 31.

[3] Cf. also the names *Agimitra-ṇaka* and *Mahādēva-ṇaka* in Kārle inscriptions and *Nāka-ṇaka* on Kaṇheri Cave, No. 2, where *ṇaka* seems to be an honorific addition (Burgess' *Cave Inscriptions*, p. 29, and *A. S. W. I.* v. p. 75). Possibly in *ṇakane* (the last portion of *marumaka-ṇakane*) we see this same ending used in the nominative singular.

[4] See *A. I. C.* Nos. 5, 10, and 61.

[5] See also Geiger's *Etym. des Singh.*, p. 65, under *manumaraka*.

[6] *putaka*[*na*] in his text.

of the construction of similar phrases in other inscriptions makes it quite obvious that this interpretation is inadmissible. The words expressing the relationship should come after *Abhaya-maharaja*, where there is a lacuna, as indicated in the text given above. The word *puṭikaṇa*, moreover, occurs in the Mihintale inscription of the same period (*A. I. C.* No. 20), where also it comes immediately before the name *Gamini*, as though it were an epithet of that king.

Naka stands for *Nāga*, just as Pāli *chakala* for Skt. *chagala*[1]; *Kōṇākamana* (Nigliva) for Kōṇāgamana, *Makā* (Kālsi) and *Maka* (Shāhbāzgaṛhi) for the Greek Magas[2]. With these forms compare the Tamil rule that intervocal surds such as *k*, *t*, *p* are pronounced flat as their equivalent sonants *g*, *d*, *b*; that is to say, an original sonant, e.g. *g*, when occurring between vowels is represented in Tamil by *k*, as there is no separate letter for *g*; thus *nāga* is written in Tamil *nāka*, though pronounced *nāga*. Hence *yāku* in line 3 must have been pronounced like its Pāli original *yāgu*. In Apabhraṁśa also original *k*, *t*, *p*, when intervocal, are pronounced as well as written *g*, *d*, *b*. The same is often the case in respect of *k* in AMg., JM., M., Mg., and JŚ.[3]

Regarding the phonology of the words *vihara*, P. *vihāra*; *bhiku*, P. *bhikkhu*; *saga*, P. *saṅgha*; *bata*, P. *bhatta*, all in line 3, see above, p. 15.

Hamāṇanaya. Müller's text gives *pāmana naye*, but *h* is clear on his plate and on the estampages before me. There is, therefore, no doubt that it stands for the dative plural of *hamaṇa* (P. *samaṇa*), which, as Goldschmidt and others have already pointed out, is formed by the addition of *arthāya* or *arthaṁ* to the genitive. We find it in the Habaraṇa inscription, where it is spelt *hamaṇaṇaṭaya* according to Müller's text (*A. I. C.* No. 61, line 8), or *hamāṇanaṭaya* according to Goldschmidt's (*C. B. R. A. S. Journal*, vi. 1879, p. 5). The former is, of course, the more correct form, although the latter is most likely what is on the stone[4], judging from the erroneous spelling in the present inscription. The Sanskrit equivalent would be *śramaṇānām arthāya*, P. *samaṇānaṁ atthāya*, AMg. and JM. *samaṇāṇa(ṁ) aṭṭhāya* or *aṭṭhāe*. From this Pāli or Prākrit basis we get the Sinhalese *hamaṇānaṭaya* or *hamaṇāṇaṭaya*, *hamaṇanaṭaya*, *hamaṇanaṭa*, then by metathesis *mahaṇanaṭa*

---

[1] Gray's *Indo-Iranian Phonology*, p. 57.   [2] Bühler on the Nigliva edict of Aśoka (*Ep. Ind.* v. p. 6).

[3] Pischel's *Gram. der Prk.-Spr.*, §§ 192 and 202.

[4] Mr. H. C. P. Bell, Archaeological Commissioner, who has examined this record on the extensive stretch of flat rock near the Buddhist Temple at Habaraṇa, says 'the letters on the rock, as eye-copied, appear to be—𑀳 𑀫𑀡𑀦 𑀝𑀬 which should read *hamāṇanaṭaya*.'

and modern *mahaṇunṭa*. The first of these forms is evidently what was intended to be used in the inscription. The omission of the akṣara *ṭa* and the lengthening of the syllable *ma* instead of *ṇa* must have been due to the carelessness or ignorance of the engraver.

Vasavasika-hāṭika, P. *vassāvāsika-sāṭikā*. In the *Dhammapadaṭṭhakathā* we find *vassāvāsika-sāṭaka*[1] (not °*sāṭikā*), which the author of the *Dampiyā-aṭuvā-gäṭapada* has rendered into Sinhalese by the words *vasvisi-piḷiyun*[2], and Dhammasēna in his *Saddharmaratnāvali* has explained it as 'a waist-cloth' (*ina-kaḍa*[3]), presented to a monk at the expiration of the *Vassa* or period of 'retreat.' Compare also *śaṇa-śāṭikā* and *śaṇa-śaṭi*, 'hemp-cloth' (Cowell's *Divyāvadāna*, p. 83, l. 22, and p. 463, l. 8); *jala-sāṭikā*, *udaka-sāṭikā*, 'bathing dress' (*Mv.* xv. 157, *Mv. Ṭ.* p. 253, *Mahāvagga* VIII. xv. 15), and *vassika-sāṭikā*, which Rhys Davids and Oldenberg describe as 'a garment for the rainy season, limited in size to six spans by two and a half—that is, just enough to go round the loins from the waist half down to the knee' (*S. B. E.* xvii, *Vinaya Texts*, p. 212, note 2, and p. 225, note). Moreover, the use of the word *śāṭaka* in the *Kathāsaritsāgara* (ch. liv. verse 105) shows clearly that it means a cloth wrapped round the loins in the manner still prevalent in some parts of India, Burma, Ceylon, and Java.

Utirika or *utarika* is most probably equivalent to a Skt. form *uttarika*, meaning 'upper' or 'superior.' Cf. *uttarīyaka*, 'an outer garment.'

Vānaka, from Skt. √*vē*, 'to weave': *vāna*, 'act of weaving.'

---

[1] The passage in which it occurs runs:—Sō Bhāgineyya-Saṁgharakkhitō nāma hutvā vayappattō thērass'ēva santikē pabbajitvā laddhūpasampadō aññatarasmiṁ gāmakārāmē vassaṁ upagantvā ēkaṁ sattahatthaṁ ēkaṁ aṭṭhahatthan ti dvē vassāvāsikasāṭakē [vassavāsika° in Fausböll's text, p. 198] labhitvā, &c., 'having become [known] by the name of Bhāgineyya Saṅgharakkhita, and being of age, he took orders under the thēra himself and [in due course] received the ordination. [Thereafter] on spending a season of *vassa* at a certain village monastery, he received two *vassāvāsika-sāṭaka* [clothes], one seven cubits and the other eight cubits [long].' See p. 151 of the Colombo edition of 1886.

[2] See p. 73, l. 2, of the edition of 1891.

[3] Bhāgineyya-Saṁgharakṣita kumārayō yayi prasiddhava, mahaṇavūmanā vayasaṭa pämiṇa mayila-nuvan-vahansē kerehi-ma mahaṇava, visi-havurudda pirennāma mālupävidiva, ektarā gameka vasväsa *vas-antayehi vasvāsika-lābha valayen* sat-riyan *ina-kaḍak* hā aṭa-riyan *ina-kaḍak* hā ladin, &c., 'he became known as prince Bhāgineyya Saṅgharakṣita, and arriving at the proper age for taking orders, entered the order under his reverend uncle himself. Then when he had passed twenty years [as a novice] he was [duly] ordained and spent the season of *vassa* out at a certain village. At the end of the *vassa* season, as a reward for holding the *vassa*, he received an *ina-kaḍa*, "waist-cloth," seven cubits [long] and another eight cubits [long].' See p. 302 of Vēragamabaṇḍa's edition. For an account of this work, see pp. 11–19 of the *Catalogue of Sinhalese Manuscripts* in the British Museum.

No. 6. PERUMĀIYAṈ-KUḶAM ROCK-INSCRIPTION

(circa A.D. 66–110)

PERIMIYANKULAM, more correctly either *Perumāiyaṉ-kuḷam*, 'the tank of the great personage,' or *Perumāiyāṉa-kuḷam*, 'the great tank,' is the Tamil name by which an abandoned tank, with a bund of about half a mile long, is known. Situated on the path to Galkaḍawala, it is 1⅛ miles north of the Sacred Bōdhi-tree at Anurādhapura and about half a mile north of the so-called Laṅkārāma dāgaba.

Müller[1] rightly describes the inscription as 'on a flat rock by the side of a hollowed-out cave. There are many stone pillars near the place, which is north-west of the Laṅkārāmaya. The inscription is on the whole very well preserved.' He adds, 'there are several clerical errors.'

The inscription consists of four lines covering a smoothed surface of about 8′ by 1′ 8″. Each letter is about 2″ in size. The *maṅgala* word *siddham* is engraved on the margin, a horizontal stroke separating it from the text, as is often the case also in Indian inscriptions[2]. Between the second and third lines is interlineated the word *dakapati*, omitted from the second line as indicated by means of a double pair of dots arranged vertically[3]. See Plate 13 *b*.

The **characters** belong to the same alphabet as those of the Maha-Ratmale inscription of king Mahallaka Nāga (A.D. 135–41), but the type is older by at least fifty years, the curves at the ends of *a*, *ka*, *ra*, and of medial vowels *i* in *di*, *pi*, *hi*, and *u* in *ṭu* and *pu*, being very much more developed in the Maha-Ratmale record. On these and other palaeographic grounds I would place the date of the present inscription between A.D. 50 and 120. This, as it happens, nearly agrees with the period A.D. 66–110 assigned, on the authority of the *Mahāvaṁsa*, to the reign of **Vahaba** or **Vasabha**, the king mentioned in the inscription.

---

[1] *A. I. C.* p. 27, Periyankulama [*sic*].

[2] See also Vessagiri rock-inscription, No. 1, above, p. 21.

[3] See Bühler's *Indische Palaeographie*, pp. 85–6, for information on the method of marking corrections in Indian inscriptions.

In regard to **orthography**, I fail to see the 'several clerical errors' referred to by Müller, except the use of the dental *n* for the cerebral in the word *karanaka* (lines 1 and 3).

The **grammar** is quite simple. The nominative *puti* (l. 2) is used for the genitive. See above, pp. 16–17, for an explanation of this peculiarity. We see the locative in *e* in *atane* (l. 1), while *karisehi* and *amaratanehi* are probably double locatives, namely in *e*+*hi*. This seems apparent from the forms of the locative *viharahi*, *vihare*, *viharehi*, *veherhi*, *veherä*, *vihārē*, and *vihārehi* found in lithic records, and other writings ancient and modern. Compare, however, Geiger's explanation of this locative ending in his *L.S.S.* § 38, and my remarks thereon (above, p. 58).

The inscription notifies a gift[1] of revenue, derived from water-supply, to a thēra named Majibuka (or -bika) for looking after certain dilapidated buildings at Patanagala, or in other words for expenses connected with their repair and general up-keep. As to who this thēra was, the Sinhalese chronicles give no information whatever. He can hardly be identical with the one mentioned in the inscription at Periyakaḍu Vihāra[2] in the N.-W. Province.

King **Vasabha** (Sinh. Vahaba or Vähäp), in whose reign the gift was made, ruled for forty-four years (A.D. 66–110, T. and W.). He belonged to the Lambakaṇṇa or Lämiṇi clan, and before he became king was in the service of a maternal uncle who was a chief in command of the troops under the usurper Subha. The cause of his flight to Rōhaṇa, his subsequent return at the head of a powerful army to attack the capital, and his success in obtaining the sovereignty after a severe conflict in which his uncle fell and the usurper Subha was put to death, all this is narrated in detail in the *Mahāvaṁsa* (ch. xxxv. vv. 59–100). His religious acts are many. Every third year he conferred on priests the sacerdotal garments in addition to offerings of milk, rice, &c. He kept up an illumination of lamps at the Cētiya mountain, the Thūpārāma, the Mahāthūpa, and at the Bōdhi-house. On the Cittala mountain (Sinh. Situl-pavu) he had ten thūpas built, and had dilapidated edifices repaired throughout the island. 'Delighted with the thēra resident at Valliyēra vihāra, he built for him the great Valligotta

[1] For a similar gift granted to the bhikkhus of the bhadāyaniya fraternity by Siri Puḷumāyi Vāsiṭhiputa (circa A.D. 137), see Nāsik, Ksh. 19 (*Ep. Ind.* viii. p. 65).

[2] *A. I. C.* No. 8.

vihāra. He built also the Anurā vihāra near Mahāgāma, on which he bestowed eight thousand karisas' extent of land in Heligāma. Having constructed the Mucela vihāra at Tissavaḍḍhamānaka, he conferred thereon the moiety of the waters of the Alisāra canal. He made a covering of tiles for the thūpa at Galambatittha and the upōsatha hall also; and to supply oil and wicks for it, he formed the Sahassakarīsa[1] tank, and dedicated it thereto. At the Kumbhigallaka vihāra he built an "upōsatha" hall; as also at the Issarasamaṇaka vihāra[2]; and this monarch constructed also the roof over the Thūpārāma here (at Anurādhapura). At the Mahāvihāra he built a range of pariveṇas, facing the west, and repaired the Catusāla hall which had become dilapidated. He caused also exquisite images to be formed of the four Buddhas, as well as an edifice (to contain them) near the delightful Bōdhi-tree.

'The consort of this monarch constructed a beautiful thūpa, to which she gave the name of Vutta, as well as an elegant roof, or house, over it. Having completed the roof over the Thūpārāma, this monarch, at the festival held on that occasion, distributed great alms; unto the bhikkhus who were in process of being instructed in the word of Buddha, the four sacerdotal requisites; and to the bhikkhus who expounded the scriptures, clarified butter and curds; at the four gates of the city he distributed alms to mendicants, and medicinal drugs to priests afflicted with disease. He formed also the following eleven tanks[3]:—The Mayetti, Rājuppala, Kōlambagāma, Mahānikavitti, two called Mahāgāma, Kēhāḷa (near Mahātittha), Kelivāsa, Cambuṭṭhi, Vātamaṅgana, and Abhivaḍḍhamāna. For the extension of cultivation he formed twelve canals of irrigation; and for the further protection of the capital, he raised the rampart round it (to eighteen cubits). He built also guard-houses at the four gates, and a great palace (for himself). Having laid out the park he kept swans in it, and built many ponds for them in the city, into which he caused water to be conducted by means of aqueducts.'

---

[1] Cf. Tihalaka-karisa in the present inscription. Karisa (P. *karīsa*) is a measure of capacity equal to four ammaṇas.

[2] See above, p. 60, note 1.

[3] According to the *Rājāvaliya* the tanks were: Nitupatpāna, Kebagalureru, Mānikavāṭi, Kālaṇikolonna, Kalivāsama, Maṅgunna, Alavaḍunna, Radupalla, Kaḷusiḷubala, Makulla, Vaḍunna, and Abivaḍunna. According to the *Pūjāvaliya* they were: Nitupatpāna, Koḷomgalu, Rērumānākāṭi, Kāḷikoḷom, Nākāḷivasā, Maguṇu-āla. Vaḍunnā. Ratupula, Kaḷusimbaḷa, Makuḷumunguṇu, and Akvaḍunnā. In the *Dīpavaṃsa* they are named: Mayanti, Rājuppala, Vaha, Kolamba, Mahānikkhavaṭṭi, Mahārametti, Kehāla, Kāli, Jambuṭi, Cāthamaṅgana, and Abhivaḍḍhamānaka.

TRANSCRIPT[1].

1 Siddham[2] - Vahaba-maharaji ni[3] .. adasana[4] patanagala[5] hiya jiṇa paṭisatariya kama[6] karanaka koṭu Tiragama atane hiya (ti)halakakarisehi[7]

2 Palinakaraka-vaviya: ma tera Majibuka[8] dini ~ baḍa-kariya Batakayaha puti[9] : dakapati

Ayisayiha[10] (na)vaka(ri)yaha[11] patanagala hi(ya)[12]

3 jiṇa paṭisatariya kama karanakā koṭu Amaratanehi Ketavalikavaviya dakapati tumaha pita-sataka koṭasa (hatipati[13] yākuhaṭe) Majibika dini

4 satana nime dakapati yasa-koṭasahi caka[14] koṭasa patisavaṇu[15] bera paharavaya[16] dini ~

---

[1] Müller's transcript (*A. I. C.* No. 7) runs as follows:—Siddham. Wahaba maharajino . . . ga sudasana patanagalihi ya . . . jinapalisatariya kama karanā karoṭu tiragama atanahi yaṇi halanaka . . . yeha (2) halinaka rukawawiya ima tera Majibaka dini . . . . . baḍa kariya bajikayaha puti ayasaya puta caka kaha patanagalihi (3) dakapata (4) jina palisataraya kama karaṇa karoṭu Amaraterahi keta calikawawiya dakapati tumaha patisatara koṭu sahana patiya nahati Majiba mana (5) ataṇani ma dakapatiyasa koṭu sahi caka koṭu sapatisāwana bera paharawasa dini.

[2] There is no *virāma* sign attached to the final *m*, unless the curved vertical stroke under *m* is meant for it. In Ṛṣabhadatta's inscription (Nāsik No. 5) also, the *m* in *siddham* is without the *virāma* sign, but it is incised below the line as if to indicate that it is final and devoid of the inherent vowel *a*. In some of the fragments of the Buddhist canon discovered at Idykutśari in Chinese Turkestan, the *virāma* is indicated by a point (single or double) above the letter. See Pischel's interesting article in *Sitzungsberichte der Kgl. Preuss. Ak. der Wiss.* July 28, 1904 (p. 1138). Modern Tamil also uses a dot or a small circle, as the *virāma* sign, though in MSS., both ancient and modern, it is very frequently omitted, just as in the word *siddham*. In Bhaṭṭiprolu inscriptions, the consonants have no inherent *a*. See Bühler's *Indische Palaeographie*, p. 16, 'Das system der Drāviḍī.'

[3] The symbol after *ni* on the ink-impression (Pl. 13*b*) looks like that of a numeral—a badly formed five or eight; Mp. *rajina . . . ga*.

[4] I prefer this reading to that of *sudasana* (Skt. *sudarśana*), because the initial akṣara of this word resembles the initial *a* in *ayisayiha* (l. 2), and in *amaratanehi* (l. 3), and differs more or less from the type of *s* found in the present record.

[5] Mp. *gali*.

[6] Not in Mp.

[7] Mp. *tihalanaka · yeha*.

[8] Mp. °*baka*.

[9] Mp. *puni*.

[10] Mp. *ayasaya*(*ha*).

[11] Mp. *tareka*(*ya*)*ha*.

[12] Mp. °*galihi*.

[13] Possibly, *utapati yāku*; Mp. *utapatiyana hati majibinana*.

[14] Possibly, *yasa koṭasa hevaka koṭasa*.

[15] Mp. °*savaṇa*.

[16] Mp. °*rasa*.

TRANSLATION[1].

Hail! The great king Vahaba granted the revenue (derived) from the water of Palinakaraka tank in Tihalaka-karisa, situated in the locality of Tiragama, unto the thēra Majibuka, by reason of the function of looking after the dilapidated (buildings) situated at (his) place of sojourn, Patanagala[2].

The revenue (derived) from the water of Ketavalika tank at Amaratana is (also) given to Majibika, by reason of the function of looking after the dilapidated (buildings) at Patanagala belonging to the architect Ayisayi, son of Batakaya, keeper of the (royal) store. The share belonging to his (i.e. king Vahaba's) own father (and) the revenue (accruing) from elephants (are also given) for the sake of gruel[3].

The revenue (accruing) from water within the precincts of his own place (as well as) four shares out of Yasa's shares[2] are dedicated by beat of drum (which proclaims royal) assent.

REMARKS.

Vahaba-maharaji ni. In our present imperfect knowledge of the phraseology of Sinhalese inscriptions of this period, it is not safe to take this as a locative absolute, equivalent to *Vahabē rājini*, 'when Vahaba has been king (for so many years)[4],' just as *Kanhē rājini* in Nāsik No. 1[5], or to regard it merely as *Vahaba-mahārājñī*, 'the queen consort of Vahaba.' I, therefore, take *Vahaba-maharaji* as a nominative and subject of *dini*[6] and the akṣara *ni* as the first syllable of the following word.

Adasana admits of several derivations. If it stand in attributive relation to Patanagala, it may be an equivalent of Pāli *adassana* in the sense of 'not visible' or 'neglecting,' just as *sudassana*, 'beautiful.' It may also be

---

[1] Müller's translation:—'Hail! the great king Wasabha . . . at Patanangala, having restored the decayed buildings, at Thiragāma . . . . . he gave the Rukkhawawiya to the thera Majjhima . . . . having made the son of Bajika and the son of Ayasa six karshāpaṇas (?) at Patanagala, having seen, having restored the decayed buildings at the field of the thera Amara, the Calika tank, having seen, having restored for himself . . . . . Majjhima . . . . . having made six (?) together with a water strainer . . . . . he gave it.'

[2] See remarks below for an alternative rendering of this sentence.

[3] This sentence may also be translated 'the revenue (derived) from elephants in his (i.e. king Vahaba's) own father's share (is also given) for the sake of gruel.'

[4] The illegible symbol on the stone probably representing the number of years.

[5] *A. S. W. I.* iv. p. 98.

[6] See above, pp. 22 and 59.

a derivative of Skt. *adhyāsana* (Pāli *ajjhāsana*), 'the act of sitting down upon,' 'that on which one sits, a seat,' or 'dwelling-place,' and if we read the indistinct akṣara as *ha*, we get *Vahaba-maharajiniha adasana*, which may mean 'the residence of the queen consort of Vahaba.' In this case the translation of the first sentence would run, 'Hail! The revenue (derived) from the water . . . was granted to this thēra Majibuka, by reason of the function of looking after the dilapidated (buildings) situated at Patanagala, the dwelling-place of the queen consort of Vahaba.'

Patanagala, Skt. *prārthanā-giri* (P. *patthanā-giri*), 'rock of supplication.' Sinh. *gala* (Tamil *kal*) means 'rock.'

Hiya, probably from Skt. *hita* (p. p. p. of *dhā*), 'situated,' 'lying,' or 'established.' Boyer connects it with Skt. *heya*, 'to be abandoned[1]'; but in the Piyummala[2], the participial noun *hiyanu* is given as a synonym for *pihiṭu*, 'established' (Skt. *pra* + √*sthā*), *tubu*, 'placed' (Skt. *sthāpita*), *huu*, 'been' or 'seated,' *hiňduvu* (Skt. √*sad*, *sīdati*) and *sat*.

Jiṇa paṭisatariya kama = P. *jiṇṇa-paṭisanthārika-kammaṁ*, 'the work of looking after the dilapidated (buildings).' In the *Mahāvaṁsa*, the word *paṭisaṅkharaṇaṁ* is used in connexion with the restoration of ruins, e.g. *Kātabbaṁ jiṇṇakāvāsa-paṭisaṅkharaṇaṁ tathā*, 'the restoration of dilapidated edifices should also be done' (ch. xxxv. 75); *āvāsē jiṇṇē ca paṭisaṅkharī*, 'and he (i.e. king Vasabha) repaired dilapidated monasteries' (*ibid*. v. 81). But in Nasik No. 19, we find *leṇasa paṭisatharane*, and Senart's rendering of it is 'for the care of the cave[3].'

Karanaka koḷu, Skt. *kāraṇakaṁ kṛtvā*, 'having made (it) a reason,' i.e. 'by reason of'; same as modern Sinhalese *karaṇakoṭa* or *karaṇakoṭa geṇa*, which is now used more or less as a 'post-position' to express the auxiliary or instrumental case.

Atane, possibly equivalent to Skt. *āsthānē*, 'in the locality.'

Dakapati has already been interpreted in various ways. According to Goldschmidt[4], *pati* means 'after,' and *daka pati*, 'after having seen,' probably connecting it with the modern word *dakinavā*, 'to see' (*däka*, 'having seen'). Müller and Franke[5] take *dakapati* to be a gerund, *pati* being the ending

[1] *Journal Asiatique*, Nov.–Dec., 1898.

[2] Colombo edition of 1872, p. 68.

[3] See his notes on this passage in *Ep. Ind.* viii. pp. 64, 67, and 69. Cf. also Goldschmidt's notes in *J. C. B. R. A. S.* 1879, p. 12.

[4] *J. C. B. R. A. S.* 1879, p. 10.

[5] Franke's *Päli und Sanskrit*, p. 129.

equivalent to Skt. *tvā* (Girnār *tpā*), while Boyer derives it from *dakṣaṃ prati*, 'according to skill' (i.e. 'skilfully')[1].

This word occurs in other inscriptions also, e.g.:

(*a*) *Dakapati bikusagaha aṭaya catari paceni paribujanaka koṭu dine*, 'having caused the enjoyment of the four requisites, the *dakapati* was given[2] to the community of monks' (*A. I. C.* No. 5, l. 4).

(*b*) *Dakapata* (?) *sakalasamata dini*, 'the *dakapata* which was approved by all was given' (*ibid.* No. 16, l. 5).

(*c*) *Sama satara vavisara dakapati kaṇaya badipila Bamanogiriya vihara bikasagahaṭa caka pacayaṭa dine*[3] (*ibid.* No. 97, ll. 3–4).

From these passages and from those in the present inscription, we see that we must regard *dakapati* as a noun. As such it admits of three derivations[4], namely, from Skt. *dakṣa-pati*, 'lord of faculties,' *udaka-pati*, 'lord of waters,' and *udaka-prāpti* (P. *daka-patti*), 'profit accrued from water.' Of these, the last is, I think, our word, not only because it suits the context, but also because the very expression actually occurs in the *Mahāvaṃsa* (ch. xxxv. 48), as follows:—

Tassa raññō mahēsī ca taṅ gāmē pattiṃ attanō ı
tass'ēvā-dā vihārassa Damiḷā Dēvī ti vissutā ıı

'And the consort of the king, celebrated under the appellation of Damiḷā Dēvī, dedicated the profit accruing to her from the village (Maṇikāra) to the same vihāra.'

In explanation of the phrase *taṅ gāmē pattiṃ attanō*, the Ṭīkā[5] adds *tasmiṃ Maṇikāra-gāmē attanō daka-pattiṃ*, 'her own "water-revenue" of the village Maṇikāra.' There is, therefore, no doubt that *dakapatti* here and *dakapati* in inscriptions both refer to the revenue derived from water, probably

---

[1] *Journal Asiatique*, Nov.–Dec., 1898.

[2] *Dine* can also be used in the sense of an active aorist, as the modern *dunnā*, 'he gave.' See above, p. 59.

[3] This is not worth translating, as the text is not certain.

[4] It might perhaps be worth drawing attention to the close resemblance of the akṣara *da* to the cerebral *ḷa*, which at first sight might suggest the reading *ḷakapati*, written erroneously for *laka-pati* (Skt. *laṅkā-pati*), 'lord of Laṅkā.'

[5] See p. 471 of the Colombo edition of 1895.

some sort of irrigation-tax. For the technical meaning of *patti* as applied to the acquisition of merits, see Childers' *Dictionary*, s. v., and Senart's note in *Ep. Ind.* viii. p. 64.

Ma, 'this.' See Geiger's *Litt. und Spr. der Singh.*, p. 67, § 48.

Tera = P. *Thērō.*

Majibuka, probably a corrupt form of *Majima-biku*, P. *Majjhima-bhikkhu*, compare *Maji-bika* in l. 3.

Dini (from *dinna*), see above, pp. 22 and 59. If *Vahaba-maharaji* is the subject, then we must take *dini* as a masculine nominative used in the sense of an active aorist like the modern *duni*, 'he gave [1].' Otherwise we must regard it as a feminine agreeing with its subject *daka-pati* and used in the usual passive meaning: 'the revenue (derived) from water was given.'

Baḍa-kariya and *nava-kariya* point to forms *Bhāṇḍa-kārika* (or *karika*) and *nava-kārika.* The former seems to signify 'the manager of royal property' or 'treasurer,' probably a synonym of *bhāṇḍāgārika*; the latter 'an architect' or a *nava-karma-kāraka*, 'one who looks after repairs of buildings,' &c.

Puti, nominative instead of the genitive. See above, p. 17.

Tumaha, genitive of *tuma*, P. *ātumā.* Cf. also *tumō* in Fausböll's *Sutta-Nipāta*, p. 170.

Pita-sataka-koṭasa (possibly *piṭu°*), P. *pitu santakō koṭṭhāsō*, 'the share belonging to the father.' Cf. *pitu sataka* in Nāsik No. 10, l. 4 [2].

Hati-pati, probably P. *hatthi-patti*, 'revenue (derived) from elephants.'

Yāku = P. *yāgu.* See above, p. 64. Regarding the dative termination *haṭe* or *haṭa*, see *A. I. C.* p. 10.

Satana-nime. I am not sure of the meaning of this compound. *Nima* in modern Sinhalese means 'end, boundary, circumference of a wheel.' Whether it represents here the loc. of *nimitta* ('on account of') or not, it is difficult to say. *Satana* can stand for Skt. *sva-sthāna*, 'his own place,' or *santāna*, 'lineage, race,' or it can be a genitive plural equivalent to P. *sattānam* [3], 'of all beings,' or Skt. *śrāntānām*, 'of the afflicted or hungry [4].'

---

[1] See also Boyer's remarks in *Journal Asiatique*, Nov.–Dec., 1898.

[2] *Ep. Ind.* viii. p. 78.

[3] Cf. the expression *sava satānaṁ hita sukhāya* in Jaggayyapeta inscription (*A. S. S. I.* p. 110).

[4] On the other hand, if we take *satananime* as consisting of *sata + nāni* and *me*, we get quite a different translation of this last sentence. *Sata + ṅani* may be equivalent to P. *sata + ñāni*, Skt. *smṛta + jñānī*, 'the thoughtful and wise (king),' *dini*, 'gave,' *me daka-pati*, 'this water-revenue.' &c.

Yasa-koṭasa may also mean 'share bestowed by royal ſavour.'

Patisavaṇu, Skt. *pratiśravaṇa*, 'assenting to.'

Paharavaya. I take this to be a gerund equivalent to modern *paharavā*, 'having caused to strike,' from the causative of *paharaṇavā*, P. *paharati*, Skt. *praharati.* This meaning is now obsolete. See Clough's *Sinhalese Dictionary*, s.v.

No. 7. THE TWO TABLETS OF MAHINDA IV AT MIHINTALE

OF all the countless lithic records of Ceylon, none, I believe, has attracted so much attention as these tablets. This is due partly to the interesting account which they give of the administration and inner life of a well-endowed Buddhist monastery; but more especially to the striking position which the tablets occupy on the sacred hill so frequently visited by pilgrims and sightseers.

There have been many accounts, topographical and other, of Mihintale. The most recent are those found in books by Messrs. S. M. Burrows and H. W. Cave [1].

Mihintalā Kanda rises abruptly to the height of about a thousand feet from the low plain, at a distance of eight miles east of Anurādhapura. It is traditionally identified with **Missaka-pabbata,** called afterwards **Cētiya-pabbata** [2] (Sinh. *Seygiri* or *Sāgiri*), on the **Ambatthala** [3] summit of which the missionary prince Mahinda is stated to have made his permanent residence during his life-time in Ceylon (*circa* 253–205 B.C.) [4]. Although no inscription has yet come to light which distinctly confirms this identification, the tradition can be accepted as true, especially as this is the only hill within easy reach of Anurādhapura, the ancient capital to which Mahinda repaired daily to preach the Buddhist doctrine.

---

[1] For other accounts, more or less accurate, see Geiger's *Ceylon: Reiseerinnerungen*, p. 204; Forbes' *Eleven Years in Ceylon*, vol. i. pp. 382–7; Pridham's *Ceylon*, vol. ii. pp. 535–7. In his article on the inscription of Parākrama Bāhu I (*J.R.A.S.* vii. 8), Prof. Rhys Davids speaks of a book called *Mihintale Varṇṇanāva*, which gives a history of the principal buildings on the mountain. I do not know this work, and it is not mentioned in any of the existing catalogues.

[2] Ṭhapēsi dhātuyō sabbā thērō tatth'ēva pabbatē | Missakaṁ pabbataṁ tasmā āhu Cētiyapabbataṁ ‖ (*Mv.* xvii. 23.) 'The thēra deposited all these relics there, on that mountain; from that circumstance the "Missaka" mountain obtained the name of the "Cētiya"' (Turnour).

[3] See *Mv.* xiii. 20.

[4] Apa budun pirinivi de-siya-sa-tis-vana Dharmāśōka raja-haṭa aṭaḷos-vana havurudu Devanapātissa raja-haṭa paḷamu-vana havurudu Poson pura pasaḷos-vaka Mihintalāvaṭa vāḍa chāyā-sampanna mi-aṁba-gasak mula vū Aṁbatalā nam galatala sat-denā-vahansē piḷiveḷin vāḍa hunsēka (*Pūjāvaliya*, ch. xxxiv). '[Mahinda and other thēras] alighted on Mihintalāva—in the 236th year of the Buddhist era, which corresponded with the eighteenth year of king Dharmāśōka's accession to the throne and with the first year of Devanapé Tissa's reign—on the 15th day of the bright fortnight of Poson (May–June). All the seven rested in order on the summit of the rock Aṁbatalā, which is at the foot of a fragrant umbrageous mango tree' (Mudaliyar Guṇasēkara's translation). Aśōka ascended the throne in 272 B.C., but was crowned only in 269. The Buddhist missionaries were dispatched before the year 256 B.C. See V. A. Smith's *Early History of India*, pp. 137 and 164.

There is, of course, no doubt that **Mihintalā** and **Sāgiri** are Sinhalese synonyms for **Missaka-pabbata** or **Cētiya-pabbata,** for we find them so used by Mayūrapāda Thēra[1] early in the fourteenth century A.D. Besides, the word *Mihintalā* itself is most probably a derivative of *Mahinda-thala*[2] just as *Amba-talā* is of *Ambatthala.* The question we have to settle is the identity of Mihintalā or Seygiri with the hill now known by this name. The manner of reference to Seygiri-vehera in the present record seems to point to the contrary, unless, of course, there were more than one vihāra on the hill. That this was really the case we shall see when we come to discuss the history of the buildings.

The ascent to the mountain is by an ancient stairway[3] said to consist of 1840 steps, formed of long granite slabs to a width of about twenty feet, and is arranged in four flights one above the other on the western slope, which is the least steep. To the left of the third set of steps, up the hill, are two granite slabs, each measuring seven feet high by four wide and two thick, and standing upright near a ruined site, the so-called Bhōjana-sālā, or refectory.

These slabs bear on their faces the inscription of Mahinda IV in two equal sections, each having fifty-eight lines. The average length of each line is 3 ft. 7 in. and the size of each letter is about $\frac{7}{8}$ of an inch.

The **characters** represent generally the type of the Sinhalese alphabet of the late tenth and early eleventh centuries. In their roundness and regularity, they approach very closely, as Goldschmidt[4] has already noticed, the forms of the modern Sinhalese alphabet. The letters *a* and *r*, however, differ from the type found in the Vessagiri inscription[5] of Mahinda IV. They resemble that employed in the inscriptions of his predecessors Kassapa V (A.D. 929–39) and Dappula V (A.D. 940–52)[5].

Regarding the **orthography** and the **language** Goldschmidt[6] says, 'it will be observed that the language employed in these (tenth-century) inscriptions, though by no means devoid of adopted Saṃskṛt and Pāli words (*tatsamas*), still puts them into a Siṃhalese shape. It is curious even to notice here the difference between the Saṃskṛt words used in the inscription of the apā

---

[1] See above, p. 75, note 4.

[2] Cf., however, *Mahinda-taṭa-vāpi* (Sinh. *Mihin-taḷa-väva*), so called from the statue of Mahinda Thēra on the bund of the tank (*Mv.* xlii. 29).

[3] Supposed to be the work of king Mahādāṭhika Mahānāga (*circa* A.D. 9 to 21), though no statement to that effect is to be found in the Sinhalese chronicles.

[4] See his report in *Ceylon Sessional Papers*, xi, 1876.

[5] Cf. plates 8, 9, and 12, above.

[6] *Ceylon Sess. Papers*, xi, 1876, p. 10.

Mihinda at Mayilagastoṭa and in the inscription at Mihintala of the same person as king Siri Saṅgboy Abahay. In the Mayilagastoṭa inscription we find still *rad* (Skt. *rājau*), *rædna* (Skt. *rājñi*); in short, the sounds foreign to the Siṃhalese of those days are changed into genuine Siṃhalese sounds. In the Mihintala inscription these words already approach the Saṃskṛt form closer, and the tendency of transporting back, as it were, genuine Siṃhalese words into their Saṃskṛt originals is already growing into fashion; thus, Saṃskṛt and Pāli *jana* ("person") is constantly used for Siṃhalese *dena*; *raj*, *ræjna* have supplanted *rad*, *rædna*; and there are such uncouth words as *samajæya* ("born") for Saṃskṛt and Pāli *samjāta*, *sasænda* ("having united") from Pāli *saṃsandeti*, and the like. King Mahindo was also fond of words redolent of antiquity, as *sey* ("as"), *Sey-giri* (Caitya-giri, Mihintala), the younger forms of which, *se* and *Sægiri*, occur already in inscriptions undoubtedly more ancient.' Müller also says that 'the language employed in the inscription is older than that which was spoken at the time of king Mahindo[1].'

An examination of the records of the period does not altogether bear out these remarks. It is true that some old forms, such as *abahay* (l. 1), *sey* (l. 3), *sey-giri* (l. 4), *karay* (l. 5), *nimavay* (l. 10), have crept into the inscription; but this is not surprising because of the fact that the regulations embodied in it were, as stated in slab A, line 6, founded on earlier monastic laws. Besides, these forms could not have been obsolete at the time, for they occur in other tenth-century inscriptions, often side by side with their younger equivalents[2]. *Rad* and *rädna* are forms younger than *raj* and *räjna*[3], just as *vadan* and *ted* are younger than *vajan* and *tej*[4]; and the occurrence of these, I venture to think, is not due to the Sanskritising tendencies then prevailing, as Goldschmidt

---

[1] See *Journal C.B.R.A.S.* 1880, p. 6.

[2] In the Padaviya pillar-inscription of Kassapa IV (*circa* 912–29 A.D.), *abhay* and *abhā*, *raj*, *bo*, *vajāḷeyin*, and *vadāḷeyin*. (See *A. S. C.* Report vii, p. 61.) On the Nāmbākaḍa pillar of Kassapa V (929–39 A.D.), *abhahay* and *abhā*, *raj*, *räjnā*, *bo* (*ibid.* p. 67). In a slab-inscription of this king, near the Stone-canopy at Anurādhapura (above, p. 43), *abahay*, *raj*, *räjnā*, *sey*, *se*, *boy*, *bo*, *jā*, *karay*, *pujay*, *aray*, *abhidham*, *ājara*, *nakay*, *bad*, *baj*, *varaj*, *varad*, *bud*, *buj*. On the Vessagiri slab (above, p. 24) of Dappula V (940–52 A.D.), *abahay*, *raj*, *rājna*, *se*, *boy*, *dā*, *arā*. On the Älleväva pillar of this king (*A. S. C.* Report vii, p. 45), *abhā*, *rad*, *bo*. On the Mayilagastoṭa pillar of Mahinda IV (*A. I. C.* 120), which was set up before he became king (A.D. 975–91), *abhā*, *rad*, *rädna*, *dā*, *nakā*. On the Vessagiri slab (above, p. 31) of the ninth year of this king's reign, *abhā*, *raj*, *rad*, *nakā*. In the present inscription of the sixteenth year of his reign, *abahay*, *raj*, *rājna*, *sey*, *se*, *boy*, *bo*, *karay*, *bad*, *jeṭu*, *janā*, *jivel*, *varaja*, *nakā*.

[3] See Geiger's *Litt. und Spr. der Singhalesen*, § 23 (2–3).

[4] See above, pp. 24 and 43.

seems to suppose. These facts, as well as grammatical forms, such as the ablative in *keren*, the instrumental in *visin*, the passive verb with *labanu*, show that the language of the present inscription is on the whole in keeping with the style of similar records of the period. It has, moreover, many points of agreement with the language of the *Dampiyā-aṭuvā-gäṭapada* attributed to Kassapa V. In this work is found a complex variety of old and young forms of words used indiscriminately. That the written language of the tenth century differed more or less in style and phraseology from that spoken, there is not the slightest doubt. We get glimpses of this fact from inscriptions and even from Kassapa's work; and we know that it is so at the present day.

It is unnecessary to dwell upon the misstatements regarding the **date** and the **author** of this inscription made at a time when the study of Ceylon epigraphy was still in its infancy. The first trained epigraphist, Dr. P. Goldschmidt, appointed in 1874 to make a systematic examination of the lithic records of the island, was soon able on palaeographic grounds to fix its correct age and, furthermore, to identify its author, **Siri Saṅgboy Abahay**, with **Mahinda IV**[1] (A.D. 975–91, W.; 997–1013, T.). This he did with the aid of the partly-effaced pillar-inscription at Mayilagastoṭa[2], by identifying the names *Abhā Salamevan maharad* and *Gon biso rädna*, the parents of *āpā Mihinda*, with the names *Abahay Salamevan maharaj* and *Dev-Gon bisev rājna* given in the present tablets as those of the parents of *Siri Saṅgboy Abahay maharaj*.

Goldschmidt's identification rests on—

(1) The absolute similarity of the names of the parents.

(2) The fact that Mihinda was an *āpā*, and that Siri Saṅgboy Abahay too was an *āpā* before he became king.

(3) The fact that the language and the form of characters employed in the two inscriptions belong to the tenth and beginning of the eleventh century A.D.

(4) The statement in the *Mahāvaṁsa* (ch. liv. 1) that Mahinda IV, who reigned about the close of this period, was at first an *āpā* (*ādipāda*), and that he set up inscribed slabs for the protection of temple property (*ibid.* 28).

---

[1] See *Ceylon Sessional Papers*, xi, 1876, pp. 7–10.

[2] A village in the Hambantoṭa District, South Ceylon. The inscription was discovered by Mr. J. H. Dawson, the irrigation officer of the place. The text given in *A.I.C.* (No. 120) is not at all satisfactory.

These do not positively prove that *Mahinda* of the *Mahāvaṁsa* was the same person as *Mihinda āpā* and *Siri Saṅgboy Abahay maharaja* of the inscriptions, or that the father of the latter, namely *Abahay* or *Abhā Salamevan maharaj* was identical with *Abhā Salamevan* of Äṭavīragolläva (*A. I. C.* 117), or *Abhā Salamevan Dāpuḷu* as he is called in Ällevāva inscription (l.c. 116; *A.S.C.* Report vii, p. 45). But every fresh material bearing on the point that has since come to light tends to show the correctness of Goldschmidt's conclusions, which were supported by Müller, his successor.

The Vessagiri slab [1] No. 2 gives us the full title of king **Mahinda** as **Siri Saṅgbo Abhā Mihindu** (P. *Siri Saṅghabōdhi Abhaya Mahinda*); and the reference therein to the Indian campaign led by his commander-in-chief Sēna, conclusively confirms his identity with **Mahinda IV** of the *Mahāvaṁsa*, as explained above at page 30. But definite proof is still wanting regarding the identity of his father, the great king **Abhā** or **Abahay Salamevan**, with his namesake in the inscriptions at Ällevāva, and Äṭavīragolläva [2] who was no other than **Dappula V**, half-brother of Kassapa V and son of Sena II by his sub-queen Dēvā [3].

Touching the dates of Ceylon kings of this period, the labours of Professor Kielhorn in South Indian chronology furnish us with a landmark of some importance.

In the Tanjore inscription [4] of the sixth year of the reign of king **Parakēsarivarman** *alias* **Rājēndra Cōḷadēva I**, reference is made to his successful invasion of Ceylon and to his capture of the Pāṇḍyan crown, which had been left in the charge of the king of Ceylon. Kielhorn's computation places Cōḷadēva's accession to the throne between Nov. 26, 1011 and July 7, 1012 A.D. [5] Therefore he must have invaded Ceylon before 1018 A.D., and probably after 1015; because there is no reference to the event in his inscription of the fourth year of his reign [6] or in any previous ones. Now, according to the *Mahāvaṁsa*, it was in the reign of Dappula V that the Pāṇḍyan king 'left his crown and other apparel [7]' in Ceylon. About twenty-four years later, in the reign of Udaya III, who was 'a drunkard and a sluggard to boot,' king Cōḷa, obviously

---

[1] See above, pp. 29-38.

[2] *A. I. C.* Nos. 116, 117.

[3] See above, pp. 23, 24; *A. S. C.* Report vii, pp. 44, 45.

[4] See Hultzsch's *South Indian Inscriptions*, vol. ii. No. 9.

[5] *Ep. Ind.* vol. vii. p. 7.

[6] *South Ind. Inscr.* vol. iii. No. 54.

[7] Paṇḍu-rāj' ettha vāsēna kammaṁ natthī-ti cintiya ı ṭhapetvā makuṭā-dini gatō Kērala-santikaṁ ıı (*Mv.* liii. 9.)

Rājēndra Cōḷa Dēva I, invaded Ceylon and regained the crown[1]. Udaya's rule lasted eight years, and that of Sēna IV, his successor, three years. Then Mahinda IV ascended the throne. Thus the number of years that must have elapsed between the Cōḷa invasion (A. D. 1015–18) and Mahinda's accession could not have been more than eleven or less than four, that is to say **the date** of the latter event must fall between A. D. 1019 and 1029. But Turnour's table gives A. D. 997 and that of Wijēsiṇha A. D. 975 as the year of Mahinda's accession.

Again, the Manimaṅgalam inscription of Dec. 3, A.D. 1046, mentions the names of four Ceylon kings, Vikrama-bāhu, Vikrama-Pāṇḍya, Vīra-Śalāmēgaṉ and Śrīvallabha Madanarāja, whom the Cōḷa king, Rājādhirāja I, had conquered. And these have been identified[2] with Vikrama-bāhu, Vikrama Pāṇḍu, Jagatipāla and Parākrama Pāṇḍu mentioned in the fifty-sixth chapter of the *Mahāvaṁsa.* Their struggles lasted from A. D. 1059–71 according to Turnour. But greater reliance should be placed on the date of the Manimaṅgalam inscription; hence it is reasonable to conclude that the eleven Ceylon kings from Udaya III down to Parākrama (Nos. 111 to 121 in Wijēsiṇha's table) must have reigned between A.D. 1015 and 1046, that is within a period of only thirty-one years and not eighty-five or ninety-five as calculated by Turnour and Wijēsiṇha respectively.

The **contents** of the present inscription are as usual devoid of historical matter, yet they give a true picture of a properly constituted Buddhist monastery of the beginning of the eleventh century A. D., which in many respects bears an interesting comparison with similar institutions of mediaeval Europe[3]. We may, moreover, infer from the reference to the temple of the goddess Miṇināl[4], that already at this period the worship of local divinities had become engrafted in the popular ritual of Buddhism, as is the case at present in Ceylon and elsewhere.

The name of the vihāra which forms the subject of the record is not given. That it must have stood quite near Ät-vehera (P. *Hatthi-vihāra*) is obvious from the fact that the monks were enjoined to go to the refectory of this monastery for their morning meal[5]. Further, Kassapa V's inscription near the 'stone canopy' in Anurādhapura[6], states that both Seygirivehera (P. *Cētiyagiri-vihāra*) and Ät-vehera then belonged to the Kapārāmuḷa fraternity of Abhayagiri-vihāra, and the *Mahāvaṁsa*[7] also records that Dhātusēna (A.D. 463–79) rebuilt the

---

[1] *Mv.* liii. 44.

[2] See Hultzsch's *South Ind. Inscr.* vol. iii. No. 28.

[3] Cf., for example, the duties assigned to some of the 'obedientiaries' and paid servants as explained in Abbot Gasquet's interesting work on *English Monastic Life.*

[4] Slab A, lines 33, 34.

[5] Slab A, lines 10, 11.

[6] Above, No. 4, lines 13–16.

[7] See ch. xxxviii. 75, 76.

Ambatthala-vihāra and conferred it on the Dhammaruci sect of Abhayagiri-vihāra, who dwelt in it since the time of Mahāsēna[1]. Still more, the order[2] that the Abhayagiri monks should be represented on the managing committee of the present vihāra makes it clear that this monastery also belonged to the Kapārāmuḷa chapter. But regarding the situation of the Seygiri-vehera, and its distance from Ät-vehera, the inscriptions are silent. However, the many references to the Cētiyagiri-vihāra in the Sinhalese and Pāli chronicles leave us in no doubt as to its having been the principal monastery on the Cētiya-pabbata or Mihintale. It could not have been a different temple named after the Cētiya mountain.

The *Mahāvaṁsa* records that Dēvānampiya Tissa (*circa* 307–267 B.C., W., more correctly 253–213 B.C.) planted a Bōdhi-tree at the Cētiya-pabbata-ārāma[3], and completed the repairs [of buildings] at this mountain. Mahinda Thēra died there in the eighth year of the reign of Uttiya (267–257 B.C., W., or 213–203 B.C.). Lajji Tissa (119–109 B.C., W.) encased with stone the *cētiya* at the Cētiyagiri-vihāra[4]. Kālakaṇṇi Tissa (42–20 B.C.) erected a great *upōsatha* hall with a stone thūpa in front of it. He planted also a Bōdhi-tree on the mountain[5]. Bhātikābhaya (20 B.C.–A.D. 9) had provisions constantly given on tickets[6] to the thousand priests resident at the Cētiya mountain[7]. His younger brother, Mahādāṭhika Mahānāga (A.D. 9–21), erected a great thūpa on Ambatthala, and constructing four entrances and a street all round the mountain, held a great festival, which became known as the 'Giribhaṇḍa' festival[8]. Kanijānu Tissa (A.D. 30–3) settled a case that had arisen in the *upōsatha* hall[9] of the Cētiyagiri-vihāra, and 'forcibly seizing the sixty wicked priests who were engaged in a conspiracy against the king, imprisoned them in the Kaṇīra cave, in the Cētiya mountain[10].' Vasabha (A.D. 66–110) kept up an illumination of a thousand lamps at the mountain[11]. Kaniṭṭha Tissa (A.D. 165–93) built a *cētiya-ghara* at Ambatthala[12] which was

---

[1] See also *Nikāyasaṅgraha* (printed edition), p. 14.

[2] In the present inscription, slab A, lines 20–23.

[3] *Mv.* xix. 61.

[4] *Ibid.* xxxiii. 25.

[5] *Ibid.* xxxiv. 30, 31.

[6] *Salāka-vaṭṭa-bhattam.* Cf. *lahag* (P. *salākagga*), 'check-room' of the Ät-vehera, to which the monks had to go to receive tickets for their food (slab A, line 10).

[7] *Mv.* xxxiv. 64.

[8] *Mv.* xxxiv. 71–81.

[9] Probably the one built by Kālakaṇṇi Tissa.

[10] *Mv.* xxxv. 10, 11. See also the *Ṭīkā*, according to which the name of the cave is Karinda.

[11] l.c. 80.

[12] *Ibid.* xxxvi. 9.

afterwards repaired by Goṭhābhaya[1] (A.D. 254–67). This king's son, Jeṭṭha Tissa (A.D. 267–77), granted the Kāḷamattika tank for the use of the Cētiyagiri-vihāra[2]. Sirimēghavaṇṇa (A.D. 304–32) had a golden image of Mahinda Thēra made, and held a great festival, carrying the statue in procession from Ambatthala to his capital Anurādhapura[3]. Aggabōdhi I (A.D. 564–98) 'built a bath at the Abhayagiri-vihāra and another at the Cētiyagiri, which he called Nāgasoṇḍī ('the elephant's pool'), and supplied it with a continual stream of water, and in due course he built the tank Mahindataṭavāpi, and ordained that the statue of the thēra (Mahinda) should be carried in procession from the bund thereof[4].' Aggabōdhi III (A.D. 624–40) dedicated the village Ambillapadara to the Cētiyagiri[5]. Aggabōdhi V (A.D. 726–32) 'spent six and twenty thousand *suvaṇṇa* in repairing the dilapidated structures at the Cētiya-pabbata[6].' Sēnā, the queen of Dappula II (A.D. 807–12), 'built the Kaṇṭaka Cētiya at the Cētiya-pabbata, as also the rock-temple Jayasēna, which she gave to the country priests, together with the village Mahummāra. She built also a second convent, called Silāmēgha, for the use of the sisterhood, and provided the sisters of the (old) Silāmēgha with all the necessaries of conventual life. Those villages also which had passed to aliens in former times she redeemed by payment in money, and restored them to the selfsame vihāra. She caused the branches of all the great trees at the Cētiya-pabbata to be cut down, and made offerings of flags and banners of divers colours to be hung thereon. She repaired the terraced house on the eastern vihāra and brought back to fruitfulness the unfruitful village Ussāna-viṭṭhi that belonged to it. She also restored the Giribhaṇḍa[7] vihāra that had gone to decay and set apart villages for the support of the priests who dwelt therein[8].' Sēna II (A.D. 866–901) established a hospital at Cētiyagiri[9]. Ilaṅga Sēna, the commander-in-chief of the army of Kassapa IV (A.D. 912–29)[10], built the Hadayuṇha-parivēṇa at the Cētiya-pabbata and dedicated it to the Dhammarucika brethren[11].

---

[1] *Mv.* xxxvi. 106.

[2] l.c. 130.

[3] *Mv.* (Pt. II) chap. xxxvii. 16–41. Another statue of this Buddhist missionary was set up by Dhātusēna. See *Mv.* xxxviii. 58.

[4] *Ibid.* xlii. 28, 29.

[5] *Ibid.* xliv. 122.

[6] *Ibid.* xlviii. 7, 8.

[7] Cf. the reference above to a Giribhaṇḍa festival.

[8] *Mv.* xlix. 23–29.

[9] *Ibid.* li. 74.

[10] *Ibid.* lii. 18.

[11] That is, the Abhayagiri fraternity. See above, p. 81. For an account of this Dhammaruci sect, and their establishment at Abhayagiri in the 454th year after the demise of the Buddha, which was the fifteenth year of the reign of Vaṭṭagāmani Abhaya (*circa* 104–76 B.C.), see my edition of the *Nikāyasaṅgraha*, pp. 11–13.

Such are the notices in the *Mahāvaṁsa* of buildings and festivals on the Cētiya mountain. In none of them is there any allusion whatever to Ät-vehera, and this is greatly to be regretted, as it is just the information most needed to settle definitely the question of the identity of the present Mihintale hill with the Cētiyagiri or Cētiya-pabbata of yore. For the present, however, we must accept the traditional identification, as it is supported by (*a*) the etymology of the name Mihintalā, and its use as another name of Sāgiri or Cētiyagiri in the fourteenth century A.D.; (*b*) the fact that it is the only hill near Anurādhapura; (*c*) the existence of numerous ruins and inscriptions upon it, which attest its ancient importance as a sacred place of Buddhist worship; and (*d*) Fâ Hien's authentic statement that 'forty *le* to the east of the Abhayagiri-vihâra there is a hill, with a vihâra on it, called the Chaitya, where there may be 2,000 monks. Among them there is a Śramaṇa of great virtue, named Dharma-gupta [1], honoured and looked up to by all the kingdom. He has lived for more than forty years in an apartment of stone [2].'

The first portion (A) of the inscription gives the rules and regulations of the monastery. They are more or less similar to those in the Jētavanārāma Sanskrit inscription and in that of Kassapa V, near the 'stone canopy' at Anurādhapura [3].

The second part (B) deals with the emoluments of servants. It will be seen from this that no service whatever was exacted without paying for it either in money or in the shape of grants of land or food-stuff. The expression *damiyen vasagak* which occurs repeatedly in the text cannot mean 'a farm from Damiya' as rendered both by Müller and Guṇasēkara, because of the fact that some of the servants received *vasag* in addition to grants of land, whilst others were allowed only the latter, with or without a daily supply of raw rice. I think, therefore, that this phrase refers to a certain 'measured quantity of provisions' (*vasaga*) [4] from the common store or almonry of the monastery, in which case *damiya* may possibly be a derivative of Pāli *dhammikaṁ*, 'that which belongs to *dhamma*,' that is 'the practice of virtue,' a formation similar to *saṅghikaṁ*, 'that which belongs to the Buddhist clergy.'

The full text of the inscription was for the first time published by Müller in

---

[1] Dharma-kôti, according to Beal's translation in his *Buddhist Records of the Western World*, vol. i. p. lxxvi. The reference is probably to Mahā Dhammakathī, the translator of the Suttas of the Piṭakattaya into Sinhalese in the reign of Buddhadāsa (*circa* A.D. 341–70, W.). See *Mv.* xxxvii. 125.

[2] Legge's translation of *The Travels of Fâ-Hien*, p. 107.

[3] See above, Nos. 1 and 4.

[4] See above, p. 28, note 5.

the *C.B.R.A.S.* Journal for 1880, and afterwards as No. 121 in *A.I.C.* Before him, Goldschmidt printed the first nine lines of A in his report on inscriptions in *Ceylon Sessional Papers*, No. xi of 1876, and De Alwis quoted, in his *Sidatsaṅgarā* (pp. xxxvi and cxlvii), two extracts[1] as specimens of ancient Sinhalese prose.

In the preparation of the present edition of the text from the ink-estampages supplied by the Archaeological Commissioner, I have made full use of (*a*) Müller's plates[2] and transcripts, (*b*) a manuscript copy of the text made by the late B. Guṇasēkara Mudaliyar, and (*c*) another on palm leaves with an anonymous paraphrase or *sanne*. This edition has, moreover, been carefully checked, letter by letter, with its original on the slabs at Mihintale, by the Archaeological Commissioner (Mr. H. C. P. Bell) personally.

The translation now presented to the reader has been made with great care. In this task I have consulted with profit (*a*) Armour's translation of the whole inscription, published first in the *Ceylon Almanac* for 1834, afterwards in Forbes' *Eleven Years in Ceylon* (vol. ii. pp. 334–43); (*b*) Goldschmidt's and De Alwis' translations of the extracts referred to above; (*c*) the anonymous *sanne*, and (*d*) the translation with notes made by the late Mudaliyar Guṇasēkara when connected with the Archaeological Survey. Wherever my translation differs from them, I have duly noted their respective renderings in the footnotes; but not in cases of obvious mistakes due to faulty readings of the text or otherwise.

TEXT.

Slab A.

1 සිරිබර් කැත කුල කොත් ඔකාවස් රජ්පරපුරෙන් බට කැතලසබ අබිසෙස්ලද මෙවන් මහර

2 ජ්හට එමෙ කුලෙන් සමජ්ජය් දෙවගොණ් බිසෙව රැජ්න කුසැ ඉපැදැ ඇපා මහයා සිරි විඳැ පිළිවෙළැ

3 සෙය් රජ්වැ තුමා සිරින් ලක්දිව් පහගමින් සිවැ සිරි සඟ්බොය් අබහය් මහරජ්හු තුමං සත්

4 ලැඟු සොංළොස් වන හවුරුදුයෙහි වප් සඳ් පුන් මස්හි දස පක් දවස් සෙන්හිඳ[3] වෙහෙරහි ඉසා ඇ

---

[1] Lines 1–17 of A.

[2] These are not very accurate.

[3] සිරි

5 අභය්ගිපි[1] වෙහෙර්හි ඉසා වසන මහබික්සඟ්ගිමියන් මගසෙන්වා කරය් තුමා බෑ වත්ගිමිය

6 න් සෙය්ගිපි[1] වෙහෙර්හි පෙරෙ තුබූ සිරිත් නිජ අභය් ගිපි[1] වෙහෙර්හි සිරිත් නිජ රුස්වා ගෙනෑ මෙ වෙ

7 හෙරව මෙ සිරිත් තුබූව වට් හිමියන්හා සසැඳෑ මෙ වෙහෙරැ වසන මහබික්සඟ් ගිමියනව් ඉසා

8 කැමියනව් ඉසා දස්නව් ඉසා කවැයුතු ඉසා ලබනු දියැයුතු සෙ ඉසා විවරුණෙන් එක් සෙ කොට මෙ

9 සිරිත් තබන ලදි මෙ වෙහෙර්හි වසන බික්සඟ්ගිමියන්විසින් බිලී පසොස්සල්හි නැඟී සිදු අර

10 ස් මෙනෙහිකොට දුගිව් කිසැ නිමවය් සිකකරණීම කියූ සෙයින් සිවුර් හැඳෑ පෙරෙවැ ඇත්වෙහෙරැ ලහා

11 ග් අවුද් මෙත් පිරිත් කොට බැසැ හමුබුබන් ගතැයුතු ගිලන්වැ ලහාග් ඉසැ නො සගන ගිමියනව් වෙදුන්

12 කියූ සැඳෑ වසග් දියැයුතු මෙ වෙහෙරැ වැසැ වනවලා කියන බික්සඟ්ගිමියනව් කඩින් පිඩින් වස

13 ග් පසස් ඉසා සුතන්වලා කියන බික්සඟ්ගිමියනව් වසග් සතක් ඉසා හිදම්වලා කියන බික්

14 සඟ්ගිමියනව් වසග් දෙළොසක් ඉසා දියැයුතු ඉසා දෑගබයන් පිරිකපා සඟ්නව් දෙනු කළ පස

15 නො පිරිගෙලා දියැ යුතු මෙ වෙහෙරැ අවූ තුවාක් අවසැ බද් ගම්හිම වෙහි මෙ පසක් දි නිබද්වැ වැසැ වල

16 දුත් මුත් බදවස් හා එක්කුසවැ නො වැළැඳියැ යුතු සඟ්සැමැහින් කැමියනව් වජාරත් දගවූත්

17 මුත් පුගුල්වැ නො වැජැරියැ යුතු නො දූහැවියැ යුතු මෙ වෙහෙරැ වසන බික්සඟ් ගිමියන් ඇත්වෙහෙරැ

18 බද් තුවාක් තන්හි කුමබුර් අරුඹ ඇය් කවරු පරියාහෙන් නො වැළැඳියැ යුතු තුමන් පිළිබදුන්විසි

19 න් ඇත්වෙහෙරැ අබැදිතාක් තන්හි ඉසිරැ නො කවැ දියැ යුතු මෙ සිරිත් ඉකුත් ගිමියන් මෙ වෙහෙර්හි

20 නො විපියැ යුතු නකා බලන ගිමියන් ඉසා වෙහෙර් පිරිවහනුවා ඉසා නියම්ජෙටු ඉසා ආකැමියා ඉසා

21 පසක්කැමියා ඉසා වෙහෙර්ලෙයා ඉසා කරඹලෙයා ඉසා කරබූ අත්සබූ ඇතුළ්වැ මෙ තුවාක් ජනා අභ

22 ගය්ගිපි[1] නකය්හි දෙබුළින් සාහනුවට වැඩි සඳුන් සැමැහින් ඇත්වෙහෙර්හි හිඳෑ කම්තැන්කොට ඇ

23 තුළ් බැහැරි අයවිය ඇය් කම් කවැයුතු ඇතුළ් බැහැරි අයවියෙහි පුත් කැමියන් හෑසූවාක් දෙනුව

---

[1] ගිරි

24 ව තිසි තුඞින් ඇපැ ගෙනැ කම්තැන් සැමැකින් තිබියැයුතු මෙ වෙහෙර් වසඟ කැමියන් පිළිබඳුන් තිසිද්

25 හොත් වෙහෙයැ නො තිබියැයුතු තැර්ගැයුතු කැමියන් ලෙකම් කරණ්වූ දුගස් ගෙනැ ගැරියැයුතු මුඤුකර

26 මූ කම්තැන් කැමියන් හසින් ගස්කොට දුගෙ කැමියන් පසැකින් දුගෙහි තිබ්ගැ යුතු මෙ වෙහෙර්හි යුත්

27 කැමියන්කෙරෙත් වෙහෙරට කැමිත් අනොබ ගිය කෙනෙකුන් මුත් තනැ සිටි කැමි යන් කෙරෙන් වට් ඔනා තැ

28 නැ ඉසා සැල් ගන්නා තැනැ ඉසා පෙරෙවරු හම්බු බත් සාහන තැනැ ඉසා තුන් ජනකුකෙරෙත් නො උතුවැ ප

29 සැකැ සිටියැ යුතු ඇත්වෙහෙර් දුගෙ පිළිබඳ් කවරිවතකුද් පිරුළ් නොදියැ යුතු කැමියන් විකිණිජ්

30 නො ගතැ යුතු මෙහෙයැ බඳ් මිනිසුන් කැමියන් තුමනට මෙහෙ නො ගතැ යුතු අනොබ මෙහෙයට නො දියැ යුතු

31 කතුමහසැගෙහි කම්නාවාමට දම්ගම්යෙන් දුන් පගල ඇත්වෙහෙර් කැමියන් බලා ගෙනැ දුගැබ්හි

32 කම්නාවාම් කැරැවියැ යුතු කිර්බඩ්පවු දුගැබ්හි අරකට ඇල්ගම්යෙන් දුන් දෙකිරිය දි අරස්

33 කැරැවියැ යුතු දුගෙහි ඉසා මඟුල්මහසලපිළිමගෙහි ඉසා මහබොය්ගෙහි ඉසා සසිඳැ ඉසා මිණිනා

34 ල් දෙව්දුන් ගෙහි ඉසා කතුමහසැගෙහි ඉසා කිර්බඩ්පවු දුගැබ්හි ඉසා උඩගලැ යටගලැ ඇත්වෙ

35 හෙර් පිළිබඳ් දුනැබ්හි ඉසා මෙතුවාක් තන්හි පිජ්නිවත් ඉසා ඇත්වෙහෙයින් රන් එස්සියක් කළ

36 න් ඉසා වී දස යහළක් ඉසා මෙතුවාක් ගෙනැ හවුරුදුපතා මෙ වෙහෙර්හි දුගබ් ඇය් හැමැ තන්හි කම්

37 නාවාම් කැරැවියැ යුතු දුගෙ පිළිමගෙහි බඳ් ගුණැ කරණැ ඒද ගැම්හි දුම්මලස්සමුන් ගෙදඬ කොදඬ

38 කැරැ පෙරෙළිවර් බැලු වෙහෙරට ගතැයුතු කිර්බඩ පවුගෙහි ගසගැසියෙන් තුනින් එකක් ඉසා මෙ

39 හි සඟ්වැල්ලෙහි ගෙතුලී ඉසා මණ්ඩුවැසර ඉසා ලකිණ්යපවුගෙහි උඩැයි යටැයි දෙවැසර ඉසා මෙහි ස

40 ග්වැල්ල ඉසා පහනැම්ල් වට්හි කිම් ඉසා පොරෙණ්දෙණි පොකුණ් වටැ කිම් ඉසා මෙ තුවාක් තන්හි ලබනු

41 වෙහෙරට ගතැයුතු වෙහෙර් දසුන් හා කැමියන්මුත් වෙහෙර් කිමැ හුන් කුඩින් ගෙන් කිම් ගොවස් නිසිසෙ

42 සින් වෙහෙරට ගතැයුතු කහසන්වැ ගත් රවසට නො අනුරූ කියවිකිය ඇය් කම් කරනුවන පණිවා

43 කරනුවන ගල්වටැ නො විසියැ දියැයුතු සුදසුන් වත් වෙහෙරවිලින් කැමියන් නො ගතැයුතු මෙ වෙහෙ

44 ර. බද් තුවාක් ගම්කිම් කැරැයෙහි බැඳැ සලසත් මුත් පාවිට නො දියැයුතු තුග් දෘ වර් මුත් පොහො මඟු

45 ල් ඈය් සෙසු වර් නො ගතැයුතු කැමියන් වෙහෙර්දසුන් ජිවෙල්කොව් දුනුවක්මුත් ඈත්වෙහෙර. බද් තුවා

46 ස් තැග්හි උකස් පමණු පාවිට කැර. කුඹුර් අරුබ් ඈය් නො වැළැඳියැ යුතු වෙ හෙරව් කැමින් ගිය කැ

47 මියන් හස්කරුවන් දෙන පෙරෙ සිරිත් කිලි සාල් මුත් රටින් වැටුම් නො ගතැයුතු කුඩින්ගෙන් පඬු

48 ර් නො ගතැයුතු මෙකුන්ගෙන් ගෙහොත් ගෙනැ කැමියන් තුමනව් ගොවිකම් නො කැර.වියැයුතු හස්කරු පර

49 පුරෙන් වැවෙන කැර. කුඹුර් ගනා වැපියැ හෙත් මුත් හැර. නො ගතැයුතු වතු පැතව් වැදූ අනියා නො·කවැයුතු

50 ගස්කොල් නො කැපියැයුතු වෙ වෙහෙර. අවු තුවාක් ගම්කිම්හි තලග් මිවත් ඈය් පලරුක් කම්තැන් සැ

51 මැඟින් දුනමුත් නො කැපියැ දියැයුතු කුඩින් කල වරජක් ඈත ගම් සිරිත් දඬ කිර කිරූ දඬ මිණැ ඈකැ

52 අවවැ සොළොස් රියන් ගැමබුර. රියන් කබුල් බැගින් ගෙනැ වැව් මෙහෙ කැර. වියැ යුතු නො කල කිරූ දඬ ග

53 තැයුතු මෙ වෙහෙර. අවුතුවාක් ගම්කිම්හි ලබනුවනව් ජිවෙල් කොව් දුනුවක් මුත් තුබුතාක් තත්හි

54 කම්තැන් සැමැඟින් පසක් වනසෙයින් අකල තුවාත් පස්පොත්හි ලියැවියැ යුතු මහපා වටව් ඉසා

55 ලබනුවනව් ඉසා කම්නවාමව් ඉසා දවස්පතා වියවුතුවාක් පස්පොත්හි ලියවා . කම්තැන් සැ

56 මැඟින් අත්වතු කරය්[1] සත් ඔතමනවුන් සනින් පටවය් මුඅුකරවුයෙහි තබා මස් මස්පතා මෙ

57 අත්වතු පලා එක් අත්වතු කොව් හවුරුදුයෙහි දෙළොස් අත්වතුයෙන් හවුරුදු අවසන්හි ලෙකම්

58 කරය්[1] සන්මැඳැ ජන්වා නිමැවියැයුතු මෙ සිරිත් ඉකුත් කැමියන් ගෙදඬ[2] ගෙනැ මෙහෙයින් හැරියැ යුතු

Slab B.

1 නකා බලන ගිම්යනව් දවස් පතා සාල් එක් නැළියක් ඉසා වසන් බණැ රන් එක් කලඤ් සතර් අක

2 ස් ඉසා පවරුණ් බණැ ද් මෙතෙස් මෙ ඉසා නියම් ජවක්නව් ජිවෙල් පස් කිරියක් ඉසා දවස් පතා සාල්

---

[1] කරය්

[2] ගෙදඬ according to Mr. Silva.

3 එක් හැළියක් ඉසා හවුරුදුවකාට සෙතුවම්ව චල් මිලැ පසළොස් කළඳක් ඉසා ආකැමියා ඉසා වෙහෙ

4 ර් ලෙයා ඉසා කරඬ ලෙයා ඉසා කරබු අත්සබු ඉසා පසක් කැමියා ඉසා එක්හට පස් කිරී බැගින් ඉසා

5 පිරිවහනු වතකැමියක්හට එක් කිරී දෙ පයක් ඉසා සාල් දෙ අඬම්නාළ් ඉසා සැරි.පින් ගත්නක්හ

6 ට දෙ පයක් ඉසා සාල් එකඬමනාක් ඉසා මඟුල් පෙවස්හට එක් කිරියක් ඉසා දම්ගෙණ් වසගක් ඉසා

7 හවුරුදුවකාට සෙතුවම්ව චල් මිලැ තුන් කළඳ් දෙ අකක් ඉසා වත්පිසාකැමියක් හට එක් කිරියක්

8 ඉසා දම්ගෙන් වසගක් ඉසා සොම්නස් මහබො මඟුලෙහි පිළියට එක් කළඳක් ඉසා මැට් පතක්හට

9 එක් පයක් ඉසා සාල් දෙ පතක් ඉසා පිවස්සමක්නට ඉසා රජ්ගෙ උපැනි කැමිය ක්හට ඉසා එක්න

10 ට එක් කිරී දෙ පා බැගින් ඉසා එක්නට දෙ අඬමනා බැගින් සාල් ඉසා බළ කැමියක්හට දෙ පයක් ඉසා

11 සාල් එකඬමනා දෙ පතක් ඉසා පියන්ගල් පෙරෙවැළියක්හට දෙ පයක් ඉසා දම්ගෙණ් වසගක් ඉසා

12 රුවනසුන් මහබො මඟුලෙහි පිළියට එක් කළඳක් ඉසා මුවු පෙරෙවැළියක්හට දෙ පයක් ඉසා දම්ගෙ

13 ණ් වසගක් ඉසා ඇළිනාවක්හට දෙ පයක් ඉසා සාල් එකඬමනා එක් පතක් ඉසා ඇළි එකළොසක් ඉසා

14 එක්නට දෙ පා බැගින් ඉසා දම්ගෙණ් එක් බැගින් වසග් ඉසා විචිනා වැරි සතරක් ඉසා එක්නට එක

15 ඬමනා බැගින් සාල් ඉසා එක්නට පිංවෙල් දෙ පා බැගින් ඉසා මෙ වෙහෙර්හි මිත්සන්නිමියනට වසැගි

16 ත් සිවුර් සාහා එක්කෙනෙක්නට ලද්දු සිවුර් සාහනකැමියන් බෙද, නතැපුනු ඉසා වෙහෙර් අත්සම් දෙ ජ

17 නක්හට එක්නට දෙ පා බැගින් ඉසා සාල් එකඬමනා එක් පත් බැගින් ඉසා කොට රැකිනාවක්හට දෙ ප

18 යක් ඉසා සාල් එකඬමනා දෙ පතක් ඉසා කොට රැකියක්හට දෙ පයක් ඉසා සාල් එකඬමනාක් ඉසා ජෙ

19 වමවට එක් පයක් ඉසා සාල් එකඬමනා දෙ පතක් ඉසා බත්ගෙ ලැදියට එක් පයක් ඉසා සාල් එකඬ

20 මනා දෙ පතක් ඉසා මීඹ වැජැර්මක්හට දෙ පයක් ඉසා වඩුම්ඬ සුවිසි.ජනකු ඉසා එක්නට එක් පා බැ

21 ගින් ඉසා හවුරුදුවකාට පිළිවරට එක්නට එක් කළඳ් බැගින් ඉසා සන්වැලි උපැනි කැමියක්හට

22 එක් කිරියක් ඉසා සාල් එකඬමනාක් ඉසා පිසන සලසින් දෙළොස් ජනක්හු ඉසා එක්නට කළොළඟැ

23 මින් එක් කිරී දෙ පා බැගින් ඉසා සලාජෙවක්හට් සාල් එකඬමනා එක් පතක් ඉසා දර් නහා බත් පක් ස

24 ලයක්හට් සාල් තුනඬමනාක් ඉසා ගෙනා පිසෑ දර් නැහු සලයක්හට් ඉසා ගමන්වර් ගිය සලයක්හ

25 ට් ඉසා එක්නට් සාල් දෙ අඬමනා බැගින් ඉසා නැගු දරු බත් පක් සලයක්හට් සාල් එකඬමනාක් ඉසා

26 පහාවැසිජෙවක්හට් දෙ පයක් ඉසා සාල් එකඬමනා එක් පතක් ඉසා පහාවැසි එකළොසක් ඉසා එක්

27 නට් දෙ පා බැගින් ඉසා එක්නට් සාල් එකඬමනා බැගින් ඉසා දවස් පතා ගලා පසක් දෙන කුඹල් පස්

28 ජනක්හට් එක්නට් එක් කිරී බැගින් ඉසා මස් මස් පතා පා දසයක් හා කුමඬු දසයක් දෙන පාකුඹලක්

29 හට් දෙ කිරියක් ඉසා සාල් දෙ අඬමනාක් ඉසා මසකට් පැරුගැනක් දෙන පැරු ගැන් දියක්හට් එක් කි

30 රී දෙ පයක් ඉසා වෙදක්හට් දෙතිසැසෙණෙග් නියපැළියාක් ඉසා දම්ගෙණ් වසගක් ඉසා පුහුඬා වෙදක්

31 හට් දෙ පයක් ඉසා දම්ගෙණ් වසගක් ඉසා මඬොවුවක්හට් එක් කිරී දෙපයක් ඉසා දම්ගෙණ් වසගක්

32 ඉසා නැකැතියක්හට් දෙ කිරියක් ඉසා දම්ගෙණ් වසගක් ඉසා නැවියක්හට් එක් කිර්යක් ඉසා දම්ගෙ

33 ණ් වසගක් ඉසා දෑගෙ අත්සමක්හට් ඉසා ගණිජෙටුවක්නට් ඉසා කරඬලෙයක්හට් ඉසා වර්ජෙටු තු

34 න් ජනක්හට් ඉසා මෙක්නට් ජිවෙල් කරඬෑගම ඉසා වරු දුම්මලස්සම්නට් දම්ගෙණ් වසග් සතර

35 ක් ඉසා දෑගෙහි වැව් තෙලට් මෙ ගැමින් පයලක් ඉසා දෑගෙහි හෙල්මල් ඔහා මල්වර් ඟද ජනක්හට් මෙ ගැමි

36 න් දෙ කිරියක් ඉසා දම්ගෙණ් එක් බැගින් වසග් ඉසා මසකට් එක් සිය විසි බැගින් මල් දෙන මහතෙල්

37 ගොවුවක්හට් සපුගම්ගෙණ් දෙ කිරියක් ඉසා සිත්තරක්හට් දෙ කිරියක් ඉසා දෑගෙ රක්නා රවලදුව

38 ක්හට් සාල් එක්නැළියක් ඉසා මහබුදුන්ගෙහි දුම්මලස්සම් ස ජනක්හට් ඉසා බණ්වජාරන දම්

39 නට් ඉසා ඇදුරදම්නට් ඉසා දමින් ස ජනක්හට් ඉසා මෙක්නට් ගුකෑගම ඉසා මහබුදුන්ගෙහි මල්

40 වරක්හට් මෙ ගැමින් දෙ පයක් ඉසා දම්ගෙණ් වසගක් ඉසා මෙ ගැමැ දුම්මලස්සම් නට් දම්ගෙණ් දෙ ව

41 සගක් ඉසා මඟුල්මහසලපිළිමගෙහි පූණ් කැමියක්හට් ඉසා කමස්සමක්හට් ඉසා එක්නට් දෙ පා

42 බැගින් ඉසා එක්නට් එකඬමනා දෙ පත් බැගින් සාල් ඉසා දෑගෙහි බුද්ධිසොවට් තෙල් ගන්නා එක් පොවාක්

43 ඉසා දිග පරගහ එක් තුළුලක් ඉසා පිළිවගෙගිද් මෙතෙත්මෙ ඉසා කම්තැත් ලෙදරුවක්හවි එක් කිරි

44 දෙ පයක් ඉසා සාල් දෙ අඬමනාක් ඉසා වඩු මහඇඳුරක්හවි බොඬවෙහෙර සෙණාය ඉසා ඇඳුරවඩු දෙ ජ

45 නක්හවි ඉසා සිරවඩු අට ජනක්හවි ඉසා උළුවඩු දෙ ජනක්හවි ඉසා මෙක්නාවි වඩුදෙවෑගම ඉසා ක

46 වුවඩු දෙ ජනක්හු ඉසා එක්නාවි එක් කිරි බැගින් ඉසා මිණීර් මහඇඳුර් දෙ ජනක්හු ඉසා එක්නාවි තු

47 න් කිරි බැගින් ඉසා කම්බුර් දෙ ජනක්හු ඉසා එක්නාවි එක් කිරි බැගින්. ඉසා සුනුබොළ්නාවි සුසුබොළ් දෙවෑ

48 ගම ඉසා ගැල්ලන් ස ජනක්හු ඉසා මෙක්නාවි දුනුමුගම ඉසා කම්නාවැමෑ කැබිළි ජෙටක්හවි එක් කිරි

49 යක් ඉසා සාල් එකඬමනා එක් පතක් ඉසා කැබිළි දෙළොස් ජනක්හවි එකඬමනා බැගින් සාල් ඉසා මෙක්

50 නාවි ජීවෙල් දෙ පා බැගින් ඉසා නවගුණ මහසෑයෙහි ඉසා නැමෙව්ය මහසෑයෙහි ඉසා ඇමඩුදු දගැඹිහි ඉසා

51 සෑගොවුවන් තුන් ජනක්හවි එක්නාවි දෙ පා බැගින් ඉසා මෙ වෙහෙර උඬගලෑ යටගලෑ ඈත්වෙහෙර පිළිබ

52 ද් දගබ් ඈද් හැමැසෑ දගෑ රක්නානාවි දම්සෙන් එක් බැගින් වසග් දියෑ යුතු ඉසා දගෙහි ඉසා පිළිමගෙ

53 හි ඉසා බත්ගෙහි ඉසා මෙහෙකරන මිනිසුන් ඉසා පිළී ඉසා පොරෙනා කසු ඉසා හිස්කොළ් ඉසා අපුලන රද

54 වුන් දෙ ජනක්හු ඉසා මෙක්නාවි මඟුලැමෑ තුන් කිරිය ඉසා මෙ වෙහෙර. බද්තුවාක් ගම්කිම්හි මන් මහට

55 ර් කුලී මෙලාවිසි මෙ වෙහෙරවි මෙ නිසඳකොට ගතැයුතු ඉසා මන්ගිව පියගිව නොවද්නා කොට ඉසා කණෑවැමෑ

56 දිය වන් තාක්තන්හි පෙරෙ දෙමෙල් කලෑ පෙරෙ සිරිත් දිය බෙදුම් මෙ වෙ හෙරවි ගෙ ගතැයුතු ඉසා මෙ වෙහෙර්හි

57 බද්තුවාක් ගම්කිම් කවරෑ පරියායෙන් උකස් පමණු නො දියැයුතු ඉසා ගතුවන් රනෑ නො හිම්කොට වෙහෙ

58 රවි මෙ නවතා ගතැයුතු ඉසා දුනුවන් දෙස් යවනු කොට මෙ නියැමින් තුඹු මෙ සිරිත් නො ඉක්මෑ වැටියැයුතු

Tablets of Mahinda IV at Mihintale.

Slab A.

Scale 1⅜ inches to 1 foot.

From an ink-impression supplied by the Archaeological Commissioner, Ceylon.

TRANSCRIPT.

Slab A.

1 Siri-bar Käta-kula-kot Okā-vas raj-parapuren baṭ Käta-usab **Abahay Sala--mevan**-mahara-

2 -j-haṭ eme kulen samajāy **Dev-Gon-bisev-räjna** kusä ipädä āpā mahayā siri vindä piḷiveḷä-

3 -sey raj-vä tumā sirin Lak-div pahayamin siṭä **Siri Saṅg-boy Abahay--**maharaj-hu tumā sat-

4 -läṅgū soḷos-vana havuruduyehi Vap-sand pun-mas-hi dasa-pak davas **Sey--girī[1]-veherhi** isā **A-**

5 **-bahay-girī[1]-veherhi** isā vasana maha-bik-saṅg-himiyan maha-sen-vā karay tumā bā vat-himiya-

6 -n **Seygirī[1]-veherhi** pere tubū sirit nija **Abahay-girī[1]-veherhi** sirit nija rus-vā genā me ve-

7 -heraṭ me sirit tubuva vaṭī nisiyan-hā sasändä me veherä vasana maha-bik--saṅg-himiyanaṭ isā

8 kämiyanaṭ isā dasnaṭ isā kaṭä-yutu isā labanu-diyä-yutu-se isā vivaruṇen ek-se koṭ me

9 sirit tabana ladi me veherhi vasana bik-saṅg-himiyan-visin bilī-pasos-salhi näṅgī siyu ara-

10 -k ṃenehi-koṭ dähiṭ-kisā nimavay **Sikakaraṇīhi** kiyū seyin sivur händä perevä **Ätveherä** lahā-

11 -g avud met pirit koṭ bäsä hambu-bat gatä yutu gilan-vä lahāg iyä no yahana himiyanaṭ vedun

12 kiyū sändä vasag diyä yutu me veherä väsä Vanavaḷā kiyana bik-saṅg--himiyanaṭ kaṇḍin piṇḍin vasa-

13 -g pasak isā Suṭat-vaḷā kiyana bik-saṅg-himiyanaṭ vasag satak isā Bidam--vaḷā kiyana bik-

14 -saṅg-himiyanaṭ vasag doḷosak isā diyä yutu isā dāyakayan pirikapā saṅgnaṭ denu kaḷa pasa

15 no piriheḷā diyä yutu me veherä āvū tuvāk avasä bad gambim mehi-me pasak dī nibad-vä väsä vaḷa-

16 -ndat-mut bad-avas hā ek-kusavä[2] no väḷändiyä yutu saṅg-sämäṅgin kämi--yanaṭ vajārat dahavut-

---

[1] Read *giri*.

[2] Mt. *ekkasavā*.

17 -mut pugul-vä no väjäriyä yutu no dähävīyä[1] yutu me veherä vasana bik- -saṅg-himiyan **Ät-veherä**

18 bad tuvāk tanhi kumbur arub āy[2] kavaru pariyāyen no väḷändiyä yutu tuman piḷibadun-visi-

19 -n **Ät-veherä** abädiṭāk tanhi isirä no kaṭä diyä yutu me sirit ikut himiyan me veherhi

20 no visiyä yutu nakā balana himiyan isā veher-pirivahanuvā isā niyam-jeṭu isā ā-kämiyā isā

21 pasak-kämiyā isā veher-leyā isā karaṇḍ-leyā isā karaṇḍu at-samu ätuḷ-vä me tuvāk janā **Aba-**

22 **-hay-giri**[3]**-nakayhi** demuḷin sāhanuvaṭ väḍi saṅgun sämäṅgin **Ätveherhi** hindä kam-tän koṭ ä-

23 -tuḷ bähäri aya-viya āy kam kaṭä yutu ätuḷ bähäri aya-viyehi yut kämiyan näsūvāk denuva-

24 -ṭ nisi kuḍīn äpä genä kam-tän sämäṅgin tibiyä yutu me veherä vasana himiyan piḷibadun nisid-

25 -hot meheyä no tibiyä yutu häriyä yutu kämiyan lekam karāṇavū[4] däyak genä häriyä yutu mundu-kara-

26 -ṇḍu kam-tän kämiyan hasin has-koṭ däge kämiyan pasäkin dā-gehi tibiyä yutu me veherhi yut

27 kämiyan-keren veheraṭ kämin anoba-giya kenekun-mut tanä[5] siṭi kämiyan- -keren vaṭ onā tä-

28 -nä isā sāl gannā tänä isā perevaru hambu-bat sāhana tänä isā tun janaku- -keren no unuvä pa-

29 -säkä siṭiyä yutu **Ät-veher-däge** piḷibad kavari vatakud pirūḷ no diyä yutu kämiyan vikiṇīj

30 no gatä yutu meheyä bad minisun kämiyan tumanaṭ mehe no gatä yutu anoba meheyaṭ no diyä yutu

31 **Katu-maha-säyehi** kam-navāmaṭ **Dam-gamiyen** dun payala **Ät-veher** kämiyan balā genä dägäb-hi

32 kam-navām käräviyä yutu **Kirbaṇḍ-pavu**-dägäb-hi arakaṭ **Äḷgamiyen** dun de-kiriya dī arak

33 käräviyä yutu **Dāgehi** isā **Maṅgul-maha-sala-piḷima-gehi** isā **Maha-boy-** **-gehi** isā **Nayindä** isā **Miṇinā-**

[1] Mt. *dähīpiyā*. [2] Mt. *äy*. [3] Read *giri*. [4] Mt. *karunavū*. [5] Mt. *kanā*.

34 **-l-dev-dūn-gehi** isā **Katumahasāyehi** isā **Kirbaňḍpavu-dāgäb-hi** isā **Uḍgalä Yaṭgalä Ätve-**

35 **-her** piḷibad dāgäb-hi isā me tuvāk tanhi pijnī-vat isā **Ätveherin** ran ek-siyak kaḷa-

36 -nd isā vī dasa yahaḷak isā me tuvāk genä havurudu patā me veherhi dāgab āy hämä-tanhi kam-

37 -navām käräviyä yutu dāge piḷima-gehi bad **Gutä Karandä** de gämhi dum--malassamun ge-daňḍ ko-daňḍ

38 kärä pereḷivar bäḷä veheraṭ gatä yutu **Kirbaňḍ-pavuyehi** gasagäsiyen tunin ekak isā me-

39 -hi Saňg-vällehi ge-kulī isā **Maṇu-vāsara** isā **Ḷahiṇiya-pavuyehi** uḍäsi yaṭäsi de vāsara isā mehi Sa-

40 -ňg-välla isā **Pahanā-vil** vaṭ-hi bim isā **Porodeni** pokuṇ[1] vaṭä bim isā me tuvāk tanhi labanu

41 veheraṭ gatä yutu veher dasun hā kämiyan-mut veher bimä hun kuḍīngen bim sovas nisi se-

42 -yin veheraṭ gatä yutu kahasan-vä gat vesaṭ no aṇurū[2] kiya-vikiya āy kam karanuvana paṇīvā

43 karanuvana gal-vaṭä no visiyä diyä yutu sudasun vat veheraṭ-mut kämiyan no gatä yutu me vehe-

44 -rä bad tuvāk gam bim käräyehi bändä salasat-mut päṭṭa no diyä yutu tun dā-var-mut poho maňgu-

45 -l āy sesu-var no gatä yutu kämiyan veher dasun jivel koṭ dunuvak-mut **Ätveherä** bad tuvā-

46 -k tanhi ukas pamaṇu päṭṭa kärä kumbur arub āy no väḷändiyä yutu veheraṭ kämin giya kä-

47 -miyan has-karuvan dena pere sirit bili-sāl-mut raṭin väṭum no gatä yutu kuḍīngen paňḍu-

48 -r no gatä yutu mekungen ge-gon genä kämiyan tumanaṭ govī-kam no käräviyä yutu has-karu para-

49 -puren väṭena kärä kumbur no väṭiyä het-mut härä no gatä yutu vatu--pätaṭ vädä aniyä no kaṭä yutu

50 gas-koḷ no käpiyä yutu me veherä āvū tuvāk gam-bim-hi talan mīvan āy palaruk kam-tän-sä-

---

[1] Mt. *pokuṇi*. [2] Mt. *anuru*.

51 -mäñgin duna-mut no käpiyä diyä yutu kuḍīn kaḷa varajak äta gam sirit daṇḍ kirā kirū daṇḍ **Minä** äkä
52 avaṭä soḷos riyan gämburä riyan kabuḷ bägin genä väv mehe käräviyä yutu no kaḷa kirū daṇḍ ga-
53 -tä yutu me veherä ävū tuvāk gam-bim-hi labanuvanaṭ jivel koṭ dunuvak-mut tubū-tāk tanhi
54 kam-tän-sämäñgin pasak vana seyin ā-kaḷa tuvāk pas-pot-hi liyäviyä yutu maha-pā-vaṭaṭ isā
55 labanuvanaṭ isā kam-navāmaṭ isā davas-patā viyavū tuvāk pas-pot-hi liyavā kam-tän-sä-
56 -mäñgin atvatu karāy[1] san-otamana-vun sanin paṭavay[2] mundu-karaṇḍuyehi tabā mas mas patā me
57 atvatu paḷā ek atvatu koṭ havuruduyehi doḷos atvatuyen havurudu avasanhi lekam
58 karāy[1] sañg-mändä[3] janvā nimäviyä yutu me sirit ikut kämiyan ge-daṇḍ[4] genä meheyin häriyä yutu

Slab B.

1 Nakā balana himiyanaṭ davas patā sāl ek näḷiyak isā vasan baṇā ran ek kaḷand satar aka-
2 -k isā pavaruṇ baṇā-d[5] metek-me isā niyam jeṭak-haṭ jivel pas kiriyak isā davas patā sāl
3 ek näḷiyak isā havuruduvakaṭ setuvamaṭ mal milä pasaḷos kaḷandak isā ā-kämiyā isā vehe-
4 -r-leyā isā karaṇḍ-leyā isā karaṇḍu-at-samu isā pasak-kämiyā isā eknaṭ pas kirī bägin isā
5 pirivahanu-vata[6]-kämiyak-haṭ ek kirī de payak isā sāl de aḍ-manāk isā säräyin gannak-ha-
6 -ṭ de payak isā sāl ek aḍ-manāk isā mañgul jeṭak-haṭ ek kiriyak isā **Damiyen** vasagak isā
7 havuruduvakaṭ setuvamaṭ mal milä tun kaḷand de akak isā vatsikā kämiyak-haṭ ek kiriyak
8 isā **Damiyen** vasagak isā somnas maha-bo mañgulehi piḷiyaṭ ek kaḷandak isā mäṭi patak-haṭ

---

[1] Read *karay*. [2] Mt. *vaṭavay*; Mp. *paṭavay*. [3] Read *mädā*.
[4] According to Mr. Silva, *ge-daḍ*. [5] Mt. *bāṇäd*. [6] Mt. *vaṭ*.

9 ek payak isā sāl de patak isā piṭassamak-haṭ isā raj-ge upāni[1] kämiyak-haṭ isā ekna-

10 -ṭ ek kirī de pā bägin isā eknaṭ de aḍmanā bägin sāl isā oḷ-kämiyak-haṭ de payak isā

11 sāl ek aḍ-manā de patak isā **Piyan-gal** pere-väḷiyak-haṭ de payak isā **Damiyen** vasagak isā

12 ruvan-asun-maha-bo-maṅgulehi piḷiyaṭ ek kaḷandak isā **Pavu** pere-väḷiyak-haṭ de payak isā **Damiye-**

13 **-n** vasagak isā äḷināvak-haṭ de payak isā sāl ek aḍ-manā ek patak isā äḷi ekaḷosak isā

14 eknaṭ de pā bägin isā **Damiyen** ek bägin vasag isā vaṭnā väri satarak isā eknaṭ ek a-

15 -ḍ-manā bägin sāl isā eknaṭ jivel de pā bägin isā me veherhi bik-saṅg-himiyanaṭ vasägi-

16 -n sivur sāhā ek-keneknaṭ ladu sivur sāhana kämiyan bedā gatā yutu isā veher atsam de ja-

17 -nak-haṭ eknaṭ de pā bägin isā sāl ek aḍ-manā ek pat bägin isā koṭa-räki-nāvak-haṭ de pa-

18 -yak isā sāl ek aḍ-manā de patak isā koṭa-räkiyak-haṭ de payak isā sāl ek aḍ-manāk isā je-

19 -ṭ-mavaṭ ek payak isā sāl ek aḍ-manā de patak isā bat-ge-lädiyaṭ ek payak isā sāl ek aḍ-

20 -manā de patak isā miṇḍi[2] väjārmak-haṭ de payak isā vaṭ miṇḍi[2] sū-visi janaku isā eknaṭ ek pā bä-

21 -gin isā havuruduvakaṭ piḷīvaraṭ eknaṭ ek kaḷand bägin isā Saṅg-väli[3] upāni kämiyak-haṭ

22 ek kiriyak isā sāl ek aḍ-manāk isā pisana salayin doḷos janak-hu isā eknaṭ **Taloḷa-gä-**

23 **-min** ek kirī de pā bägin isā salā jeṭak-haṭ sāl ek aḍ-manā ek patak isā dar naṅgā bat pak sa-

24 -layak-haṭ sāl tun aḍ-manāk isā no pisā dar näṅgū salayak-haṭ isā gamanvar giya salayak-ha-

25 -ṭ isā eknaṭ sāl de aḍ-manā bägin isā näṅgū darā bat pak salayak-haṭ sāl ek aḍ-manāk isā

26 pahā-väsi-jeṭak-haṭ de payak isā sāl ek aḍ-manā ek patak isā pahā-väsi ekaḷosak isā ek-

[1] Mt. *upāni.* [2] Mt. *miṇḍi.* [3] Mt. *saṅg-vali.*

27 -naṭ de pā bägin isā eknaṭ sāl ek aḍ-manā bägin isā davas patā yalā pasak dena kumbal pas

28 janak-haṭ eknaṭ ek kirī bägin isā mas mas patā pā dasayak hā kumbu dasayak dena pā-kumbalak-

29 -haṭ de kiriyak isā sāl de aḍ-manāk[1] isā masakaṭ pärähänak dena pärähän dīyak-haṭ ek ki-

30 -rī de payak isā vedak-haṭ **Detisäseṇen** niya päḷiyāk isā **Damiyen** vasagak isā puhuṇḍā vedak-

31 -haṭ de payak isā **Damiyen** vasagak isā maṇḍovuvak-haṭ ek kirī de payak isā **Damiyen** vasagak

32 isā näkätiyak-haṭ de kiriyak isā **Damiyen** vasagak isā näviyak[2]-haṭ ek kiriyak isā **Damiye-**

33 **-n** vasagak isā dāge atsamak-haṭ isā gaṇa-jeṭuvak-haṭ isā karaṇḍ-leyak-haṭ isā var-jeṭu tu-

34 -n janak-haṭ isā meknaṭ jivel **Karandägama** isā varä dummalassamnaṭ **Damiyen** vasag satara-

35 -k isā dāgehi väṭ telaṭ me gämin payalak isā dāgehi heḷ-mal onā malvar de janak-haṭ me gämi-

36 -n de kiriyák isā **Damiyen** ek bägin vasag isā masakaṭ ek-siya-visi bägin mal dena maha-nel-

37 -govuvak-haṭ **Sapugamiyen** de kiriyak isā sittarak-haṭ de kiriyak isā dāge raknā raṭ laduva-

38 -k-haṭ sāl ek näḷiyak isā maha-budun-gehi dummalassam sa janak-haṭ isā baṇ-vajārana damī-

39 -naṭ isā ädura damīnaṭ isā damīn sa janak-haṭ isā mek-naṭ **Gutägama**[3] isā maha-budun-gehi mal-

40 -varak-haṭ me gämin de payak isā **Damiyen** vasagak isā me gämä dum-malassamnaṭ **Damiyen** de va-

41 -sagak isā Maṅgul-maha-sala-piḷima-gehi[4] pūṇā kämiyak-haṭ isā kam-assamak-haṭ isā eknaṭ de pā

42 bägin isā eknaṭ ek aḍ-manā de pat bägin sāl isā dā-gehi bud[5]-bisovaṭ tel gannā ek poṭāk

43 isā diya parahana ek tuḷulak isā piḷima-gehi-d metek-me isā kam-tän-ledaru-vak-haṭ ek kirī

---

[1] Mt. *aḍmanak.* [2] Mt. *näpiyak-haṭ.* [3] Mt. *-gam.*
[4] Mt. *-gähi.* [5] Mt. *budi.*

44 de payak isā sāl de aḍ-manāk isā vaḍu-maha-ädurak-haṭ **Boṇḍ-vehera**[1] seṇāya isā ädura-vaḍu de ja-

45 -nak-haṭ isā sir-vaḍu aṭ janak-haṭ isā uḷu-vaḍu de janak-haṭ isā meknaṭ **Vaḍu-devâgama**[2] isā ka-

46 -ṭu-vaḍu de janak-hu isā eknaṭ ek kirī bägin isā miṇīr-maha-ädur de janak-hu isā eknaṭ tu-

47 -n kirī bägin isā kambur de janak-hu isā eknaṭ ek kirī bägin isā sunu-boḷnaṭ **Sunuboḷ-devâ-**

48 **-gama** isā gällan sa janak-hu isā meknaṭ **Dunumu-gama** isā kam-navâmä käbiḷi-jeṭak-haṭ ek kiri-

49 -yak isā sāl ek aḍ-manā ek patak isā käbiḷi doḷos janak-haṭ ek aḍ-manā bägin sāl isā mek-

50 -naṭ jivel de pā bägin isā **Navaguṇa-maha-sâyehi** isā[3] **Näṭeviya-maha--sâyehi**[4] isā **Ämbulu-dāgäb-hi** isā

51 sā-govuvan tun janak-haṭ eknaṭ de pā bägin isā me veherä uḍ-galā yaṭ-galā **Ätvehera** piḷiba-

52 -d dāgab äy hämändä dägä raknānaṭ **Damiyen** ek bägin vasag diyä yutu isā dā-gehi isā piḷima-ge-

53 -hi isā bat-gehi isā mehe-karana minisun isā piḷī isā poronā kasu isā his-koḷ isā apulana rada-

54 -vun de janak-hu isā meknaṭ **Mañgulävä** tun kiriya isā me veherä bad-tuvāk gam-bim-hi mañg maha-va-[5]

55 -r kulī melāṭsī me veheraṭ me ninda koṭ gatä yutu isā mañg-giva piya-giva no vadnā koṭ isā **Kaṇâ-vävä**

56 diya van tāk tanhi pere Demeḷ kalä pere sirit diya bedum me veheraṭ me gatä yutu isā me veherhi

57 bad tuvāk gam bim kavaru pariyāyen ukas pamaṇu no diyä yutu isā gatuvan ranä no himi koṭ vehe-

58 -raṭ me navatā gatä yutu isā dunuvan des yavanu koṭ me niyämin tubū me sirit no ikmä väṭiyä yutu

---

[1] Mt. *veherä*. [2] Mt. *-gam*. [3] Mt. *isa*.
[4] Mt. *mahasāyēhi*. [5] Mt. *vaha-var*.

TRANSLATION[1].

Slab A.

[Lines 1–5] On the 10th day of the waxing moon, in the [lunar] month of *Vap*[2], in the sixteenth year after the elevation of his regal canopy, the great king **Siri Saṅgboy Abahay**[3], who was born unto the great king **Abahay Salamevan**[4], an eminent Kṣatriya, being descended from the royal line of the Okkāka dynasty, which is the pinnacle of the illustrious Kṣatriya race, having been conceived in the womb of the anointed queen **Dev Gon** of equal birth in the same [Kṣatriya] race—who enjoyed the dignities of Governor and Chief Governor[5], and who, having in due course become king, has been illumining[6] the Island of Laṅkā with his majestic effulgence—convened[7] an assembly of the great community of monks resident in **Sey-giri-vehera**[8] and **Abahay-giri-vehera**[9].

[Ll. 5–9][10] [At this assembly, His Majesty] conferred[11] with competent persons as to the expediency of selecting[12] such of the [monastic] rules as

---

[1] For the meaning and etymology of separate words in the text, see the glossary at the end of the volume.

[2] 'The sowing month,' Sept.–Oct. (fr. Skt. √ *vap*), nearly corresponding with the solar month, *Kanyā*, Tamil *Puraṭṭāśi*.

[3] Skt. *Śrī Saṅghabōdhi Abhaya*.

[4] Skt. *Abhaya Śilāmēghavarṇa*.

[5] *Āpā mahayā siri vindā*, as in the Vessagiri slab, l. 8. See above, pp. 25, and 26, note 4.

[6] *Pahayamin siṭā*. Here *siṭā*, gerund (past) of *siṭinavā* (√ *sthā*) is used with the present adverbial participle *pahayamin* (*pra* + √ *bhā*) to express continued action (cf. Apté's *Skt. Composition*, p. 124, and Geiger's *L. S. S.* § 63).

[7] *Maha-sen-vā karay*, lit. 'having caused the becoming of a great assembly.' For the gerund *karay*, see above, p. 51, note 2. The suffix *vā* seems to me to be a derivative of √ *bhū*, but see Geiger's *L. S. S.* §§ 64 and 65.

[8] P. *Cētiya-giri-vihāra*.

[9] P. *Abhaya-giri-vihāra*.

[10] This passage can also be rendered, '[At this assembly, His Majesty] selected such of the [monastic] rules as pleased him out of those [in force] at his own Abahay-giri-vehera . . . . and after conferring with competent persons, as to the expediency of establishing these rules at this vihāra also, he enacted the [following] regulations with comments [thereon] so as to render them uniform in respect of the great community of monks resident in this vihāra, as well as in respect of the employés, the serfs, [their respective] duties, and the receipts and disbursements.'

[11] *Sasāndā*, 'having consulted'; Skt. **saṁsyandya* for *saṁsyadya* (through P. *saṁsandati*).

[12] *Nija rus-vā genā*, 'having taken those which were pleasing to himself'; but Mudaliyar Guṇasēkara translates 'having approved of.' I take *rus-vā* as composed of *rus* (Skt. *ruc*) and the suffix *vā*, a verbal noun (probably connected with Skt. *bhū*), here in the accusative case, being governed by *genā*; same construction as *maha-sen-vā karay* in l. 5. I do not think *rusvā* is a direct derivative of *rucitvā*. Cf. also Childers' Notes in *J. R. A. S.* viii. pp. 146 et seq.

pleased him out of those [in force] at his own **Abahay-giri-vehera** and out of those formerly instituted at **Sey-giri-vehera** by his brother, the master of religious ceremonies[1], and of establishing the same at this vihāra also.

[Thus] in respect of the great community of monks living in this vihāra, as well as in respect of the employés, the serfs, [their respective] duties, and the receipts and disbursements, His Majesty passed these [following] regulations, rendering[2] them explicit by means of comments.

[Ll. 9–15] The monks residing in this vihāra shall rise at the time of early dawn and shall meditate on the four protective formulas[3], and having finished cleansing the teeth[4], shall put on and cover themselves with their [yellow] robes as prescribed in the *Sikakaraṇī*[5]. They shall [then] go to the 'check-room' of **Ät-vehera**, and exercising a spirit of benevolence and reciting

---

[1] *Vat-himiyan.* See above, p. 35, note 7.

[2] *Vivaruṇen ek-se koṭ.* Mudaliyar Guṇasēkara translates, 'making them alike by enactments.' It seems to me, however, that *ek-se* (prob. Skt. *ēkacchāyā*) is here used in the sense of 'one shade (of meaning),' that is, 'unambiguous,' or 'quite plain.'

[3] These exercises are:—(1) Meditating on the virtues of the Buddha; (2) Wishing unto all beings deliverance from the misery of existence; (3) Reflecting on the impurity of the substances which constitute the corporeal frame; (4) Contemplation of death (*Ceylon Almanac*, 1834). See also Hardy's *Eastern Monachism*, pp. 28, 243–252, and Rhys Davids' Introduction to his edition of the *Yogāvacara's Manual.*

[4] *Dähiṭ-kisā*, P. *danta-kaṭṭha-kiccaṁ*, lit. 'tooth-stick-duty.'

[5] In the Nevill Collection of Ceylon MSS., now in the British Museum, there is a MS. (ff. 9) of a short commentary in Sinhalese on the *Sēkhiyā Dhammā* section of the *Pātimokkha*, bearing the title *Sikhakaraṇī* for P. *Sikkhā karaṇīyā.* Evidently this is the treatise referred to here. It begins:—*mehi* Sikhakaraṇīya *nam kavarayat sakhevin kiyanem. Avaṭa nätlā koṭa sivuru haňdīnam dukuḷā vē. Vaḍu aňgulen aṭaňgulak daṇa-maňḍalen bahā vamat pasā hasunkan labā ek keḷavarekin no elvā avaṭa ätlā koṭa häňda yutlēyi. Avaṭa äti koṭa haňdanā säda vārada avaṭa nätivūva varaja näti. Avaṭa nätlā koṭa sivuru porovīnam dukuḷā vē. Ätpiṭalī govū seyin de keḷavara sama-koṭa vam atin pal piṭu bahā lā ek keḷavarakin no elvā avaṭa äti koṭa peraviya yutlēyi*, 'here I shall state briefly what the *Sikhakaraṇīya* is:—

'If the *cīvara* (under-garment) is worn so that it may not go completely round [the loins], this will be a *dukkaṭa* offence [requiring confession and absolution]. It must be worn so that it may reach eight finger-breadths in carpenter's measure below the knee-cap, being wrapped completely round (the waist) from the left side, without letting one end hang down [more than the other?]. If when putting on the (under-)*cīvara* in order that it may pass right round [the loins], should it, by mistake, happen not to fit completely round [the waist], this will not be [reckoned] a fault.

'If the *cīvara* (outer robe) is put on so that it may not cover (the body) completely round, this will be a *dukkaṭa* offence. The (outer) *cīvara* must be wrapped round by making both its ends equal, just as an (elephant)-keeper on his elephant. Then with the left hand it must be drawn over the back downwards, thereby covering (the body) completely without letting one end hang down [more than the other?].'

Cf. also *Pātimokkha* ix. (*J. R. A. S.* viii. pp. 62–130; *S. B. E.* xiii. pp. 59–67, xvii. p. 212, note 2).

paritta[1] formulas shall descend [into the refectory] and receive gruel and boiled rice.

To the monks who are unable to attend the 'check-room' through illness, shall be granted a *vasag*[2] each, when recommended by the physicians.

To the monks who reside in this vihāra and read[3] the **Vinaya-piṭaka,** shall be assigned five *vasag*[4] of food and raiment; to the monks who read the **Sutta-piṭaka,** seven *vasag*; and to the monks who read the **Abhidhamma-piṭaka,** twelve *vasag*.

The necessaries [of life] assigned to monks by lay patrons[5] after due calculation shall be given without causing any omission thereof[6].

[Ll. 15–20] Those that reside permanently and grant the necessary things [for the maintenance of monks] here, shall enjoy[7] the lands and villages attached to all the *āvāsa* [monks' residences] connected with this vihāra, but they shall not enjoy the same conjointly[8] with the *āvāsa* so attached[9].

Orders shall be issued to employés and employés shall be dismissed only by the monks in council; no orders shall be issued or any servant be dismissed by individuals acting alone.

The monks residing in this vihāra shall by no means possess the fields, orchards, &c., in any place belonging to **Ät-vehera.**

---

[1] Evidently stanzas from the *Piril-pota*. Cf. reference to this compilation in the Slab-inscription of Kassapa V (No. 4, l. 38) above, p. 43.

[2] See above, p. 28, n. 5.

[3] *Kiyana*, in the sense of 'reading aloud and explaining to an audience.'

[4] Mudaliyar Guṇasēkara translates, 'five cells with food and raiment.' He adds, however, in a note, that the word *vasag* 'admits of two renderings, (1) residence or cell of a monk, (2) *pingo* load of boiled rice and curry'; but compare note 5 on p. 28. Müller takes it to mean 'a farm' (*A. I. C.* p. 115), and De Alwis 'a meal' (*Sidatsañgarā*, Introd. p. 149).

[5] *Dāyakayan*, lit. 'donors,' a term still applied in Ceylon especially to those who contribute to the maintenance of a Buddhist monastery.

[6] De Alwis' translation runs:—'Donations made unto the priests shall be applied in accordance with the intention of the donors, and without misappropriation.' Compare also Armour's and Müller's renderings.

[7] *Vaḷandat-mut*, lit. 'except that they make use of.' Cf. P. *valañjēti*.

[8] *Ek-kusa-vā* (P. *ēka-kucchi-hutvā*) may also mean 'inclusive of.'

[9] Mudaliyar Guṇasēkara's rendering of this passage is:—'They shall make use of the villages and lands attached to all the monasteries which belong to this vehera, living there permanently and giving articles (fit to be given) for services rendered to this vehera, but they shall not make use of them by intruding on a monastery so attached.' Cf. also the translations by Müller and others, which differ from this considerably.

They shall not allow their dependants to exercise supremacy over any place connected with **Ät-vehera.**

Monks that infringe these regulations shall not live in this vihāra.

[Ll. 20–25] The monk[1] who looks after the **Nakā**[2], the lay warden[3] of the vihāra, the administrator of rules[4], the steward[5], the almoner[6], the clerk of the vihāra, the registrar[7] of caskets, including the keeper of caskets[8]—all these persons shall hold sessions in the **Ät-vehera** in company with the monks from the two fraternities[9] at **Abhayagiri,** who have come to assist [them in their deliberations]. They shall then fix places of business and shall attend to duties connected with receipts and disbursements, &c., both inside and outside [the vihāra].

For the purpose of compensating for whatever may be destroyed by those engaged in matters relating to receipts and disbursements, both inside and

---

[1] Lit. 'monks,' but the plural is, I think, used here merely *honoris causa.* Müller's and Armour's translations of lines 20–30 differ materially from Guṇasēkara's and my renderings.

[2] P. *nikāya,* 'fraternity of monks,' applied also sometimes to 'a monastic establishment with its *dāgaba* and *āvāsa.*' See also the second portion of this inscription (l. 1).

[3] *Pirivahanuvā.* See above, p. 3, and note 5. 'The warden or superintendent of the vihāra,' according to Dr. Müller and Mudaliyar Guṇasēkara.

[4] *Niyam-jeṭu* admits of two derivations, namely, Skt. *nigama-jyēṣṭha,* 'the chief over a market town'; and *niyama-jyēṣṭha,* 'the pre-eminent in law.' Müller, adhering to the former, renders it 'the eldest of the villages,' while the Mudaliyar translates it 'duly appointed overseers.' My rendering is based on the technical use of the words *niyama* and *jeṭu* in Ceylon inscriptions. In the Jētavanārāma Sanskrit inscription (l. 4), above, p. 4, the word *niyama* means undoubtedly 'fixed regulation.' For the use of *jeṭu* or *jeṭa,* compare the compounds *niyam-jeṭak* (l. 2), *maṅgul-jeṭak* (l. 6), and *kābiḷi-jeṭak* (l. 48) in the present record, second part.

[5] *Ā-kāmiyā* = P. *ādi-kammika,* 'the principal workman.' See also below, second part, l. 3.

[6] *Pasak-kāmiyā,* P. *paccaya-kammika,* 'the officer connected with the supplying of necessary articles.' Compare, however, the expression *kāmiyan pasākin* in l. 26 and the note thereon.

[7] *Karaṇḍ-leyā* = P. *karaṇḍa-likhaka.*

[8] *Karaṇḍu-atsamu.* I am not quite sure of my interpretation. Müller derives *at-samu* from Skt. *hasta* + √ *śam,* and gives it the meaning 'receiver of revenue.' Mudaliyar Guṇasēkara renders it 'the sealing of caskets,' probably connecting it with *at-sana* (P. *hattha-saññā*), 'signature.' But *samu* is more likely a derivative of P. *sammuti,* 'permission.' Compare *samu-denavā,* 'to grant permission'; also the phrase *hasin has-koṭ,* 'having stamped with the seal,' below, in line 26.

[9] *Abahaygirī-nakayhi de-muḷin sāhanuvaṭ vāḍi saṅgun sämäṅgin.* The Mudaliyar's rendering of this passage is:—'With the monks who come to accept alms from the two Piriveṇas in the Abhayagiri Nikāya.' Possibly one of these two orders at Abhayagiri Vihāra was the Kapārā-muḷa, the subject of the inscription of Kassapa V at Anurādhapura (see above, pp. 41–57). *Sāhanu* means also 'the acceptance of alms'; cf. *bat sāhana tänä* in l. 28 (p. 102, note 9).

outside [the vihāra], security shall be taken from suitable householders and be deposited at the [respective] places of business[1].

If any of the dependants of the monks of this vihāra are appointed[2], they shall not be retained in service but be dismissed. Employés shall be dismissed after recovery of what has been entered [in their name] in the register.

[Ll. 25–30] Caskets furnished with locks shall be deposited in the 'relic-house'[3] in the presence[4] of the officials of the 'relic-house,' with the seal[5] of the officials[6] at the place of business[7] duly stamped on them.

Apart from the case of any one of the officials of this vihāra going, not far, on vihāra service, there shall [always] be in attendance not less than three persons from amongst those employed at [each of the following places, namely] the pay-office[8], the place where raw rice is received, and at the place where, in the forenoon, boiled rice and gruel are accepted[9] [by monks].

Nothing whatever belonging to the 'relic-house' of **Ät-vehera** shall be lent out[10], or be purchased if offered for sale[11] by the officials.

---

[1] The Mudaliyar translates, 'They shall take as bail, and appoint with the workmen, retainers who are able to compensate for what was destroyed by the workmen.'

[2] *Nisid-hot.* The Mudaliyar translates this by 'prohibited'; but I think it should be connected with Skt. *ni-ṣad*, not *ni-ṣidh.*

[3] *Dāge* = P. *dhātu-gēha*, a house where reliquaries are deposited, generally built near the dāgaba of the monastery within the inner quadrangle.

[4] *Pasäkin*, instr. of *pasäk* = P. *paccakkha* (or rather **paccakkhi*) = Skt. *praty-akṣa.* The Mudaliyar translates *kämiyan pasäkin* 'by the side of the workmen,' evidently deriving *pasa* from P. *passa.*

[5] *Hasin*, instrumental case of *has* (*Ruvanmala*, 553), modern *as*, 'a seal.' Cf. *as obanavā*, 'to stamp with a seal.'

[6] *Kämiyan*, lit. 'of the workmen.'

[7] *Kam-tän*, Skt. *karma-sthāna*, means here either 'the manufactory' or 'an assay office.'

[8] *Vaṭ-onā-tänā*, 'at the place where wages are paid in kind.' The Mudaliyar makes this compound equivalent to modern Sinhalese *väṭup ōnā tāna. Vaṭ* is a derivative of Skt. *vṛtta*, P. *vaṭṭa*, and is different from *väṭ* (above, p. 25, l. 19) which is derived from P. *vaṭṭi. Onā* may be connected with Skt. *avana* + *ka* (from √ *av*) rather than with *avanāya* (*ava* + √ *nī*). It is, I think, the same as the modern word *ōnā* (sometimes written *ōṇā*).

[9] *Sāhana*, from √ *sah.* In polite language, when a monk accepts food, one says in Sinhalese, 'he endures or permits [the offering of] food.'

[10] *Pirūḷ.* This and the word *piruvaṭa* or *pirivaṭa*, commonly applied to cloths lent by a '*dhobey*' or washer-man, seem both to be derivatives of Skt. *pari* + √ *vṛt.* Cf. P. *pārivaṭṭakaṁ.*

[11] *Vikiṇij.* I have tentatively treated this as a form of the conditional mood of the Sinhalese verb *vikuṇanavā*, P. *vikkiṇāti*, M. *vikkiṇat.* The Mudaliyar gives two possible interpretations of this passage, namely, (1) 'nor shall anything be taken, if the servants sell'; (2) 'nor shall anything be purchased from the servants.'

[Ll. 30-33] The officials shall not exact services for themselves from the men engaged for [vihāra] service; nor shall such men be allowed out on other service in the neighbourhood.

The officials at **Ät-vehera** shall look after the *payala*[1] [of land] granted from **Damgamiya** for the purpose of [executing] repairs at **Katu-maha-sāya**[2], and [with the income thereof] shall cause the works of the [said] dāgäba to be renovated.

They shall cause the taking care of **Kiribaňḍ-pavu**[3] dāgäba by granting the two *kiriya*[4] [of land] set apart for the purpose from **Āḷ-gamiya.**

[Ll. 33-37] The 'relic-house,' the house containing the auspicious colossal stone-image[5] [of the Buddha], the house at the great Bōdhi-tree, [the shrine] **Nayinda**[6], the house of the goddess[7] **Miṇinal**, the [afore-mentioned] **Katu-maha-sāya**, the **Kiribaňḍ-pavu** dāgäba and the dāgäbas on the upper rock[8] and on the lower rock[9] belonging to **Ät-vehera**:—the offerings made at all these places, as well as 100 *kaḷaňd*[10] [weight] of gold and 10 *yahala*[11] of paddy from **Ät-vehera**—all these shall be utilized and [by means of them] the repairs at the dāgäbas and at all other places within [the precincts of] this vihāra shall be executed every year.

[Ll. 37-41] The share [due] out of the fines[12] *ge-daňḍ* and *ko-daňḍ* [levied]

---

[1] See above, p. 55, note 3.

[2] *Sāya* = P. *cētiya*. See also *E. S.* No. 1587.

[3] *Pavu* = P. *pabbata*, 'rock.'

[4] *Kiriya* or *kirī*. See above, p. 3, note 4.

[5] *Maňgul-maha-sala-piḷima-gṛhi* = P. *maṅgala-mahā-silā-paṭimā-gēhamhi*.

[6] Probably equivalent to Skt. *nāgēndra*, P. *nāginda*, 'Nāga or snake king.'

[7] *Dev-dū*. Cf. P. *dēva-puttō*, Sinh. *dev-put*, 'a male deity,' and *dēva-dhitā* (or *-duhitā*), Sinh. *dev-dū*, 'a female deity.'

[8] *Uḍ-galā*.

[9] *Yaḷ-galā*.

[10] See above, p. 28, note 3.

[11] *Yahala*, modern *yāla* = a score, i.e. 20 *amuṇa* (P. *ammaṇa*) of grain or 20 head of cattle (Armour). According to Subhūti, a *yāla* is equivalent to 20 *khāri* (i.e. one *vāhō* or *sakaṭō*, 'cart-load'). See *Abh.* 484. Cf., also, above, pp. 3, note 4, and 55, note 3, and Rhys Davids, *Coins and Measures of Ceylon*, § 34.

[12] The meaning of this passage is somewhat obscure. The present translation is offered tentatively. The Mudaliyar's rendering is, 'brooms for removing faded flowers and house-timber shall be collected in the two villages Gutā and Karandā belonging to the relic-house and the image-house, and the former timber utilized for a strong vihāra.'

In the phrase *gedaňḍ kodaňḍ kärā* he treats *kärā* as a gerund. If it is so, it should be spelt either *karay* as in l. 5, or *koṭ* as in l. 8. I take it as a derivative of *kārikā*, used here technically to mean 'a fixed rate,' such as 'a tithe.' Cf. *kärāyehi* in l. 44, and *dasa-kärā*, 'tenth part,' in the inscription of Kassapa V (l. 47) above, p. 49.

Ge-daňḍ (Skt. *gṛha-daṇḍa?*) and *ko-daňḍ* (prob. for *ku-daṇḍa*, 'minor fines') seem to me to be the names of two kinds of fines. See above, p. 54, n. 3. In Skt. and P. *kō-daṇḍa* means 'a bow.' In Sinhalese *kō* = Skt. *kōpa*. In Tamil *kō* means 'a king.'

on *dummalassamun*[1] in the villages **Gutâ** and **Karandâ** belonging [respectively] to the 'relic-house' and to the 'image-house,' as well as the wages[2] of those [servants] who are refractory[3] shall be appropriated by the vihāra.

One-third of [the produce of] trees and plants on **Kirbaṇḍ-pavu,** the house rent of the *saṅg-välla*[4] here, the tank **Manuvâsara,** the two tanks in the upper-side and in the lower-side of **Ḷahiṇiya-pavu** (the Swallow-rock) together with the *saṅg-välla*[4] thereof, the land around the pond **Pahanâ-vil** and the land around the pond **Porodeni-pokuṇa**—the income derived from all these places shall be appropriated by the vihāra.

[Ll. 41–45] From the householders who live on the vihāra lands, ground rent shall be levied in a fitting manner on behalf of the vihāra, but not from the vihāra serfs and employés.

Those who having put on yellow [robes] commit acts inconsistent with the dress they have assumed—acts such as buying, selling, &c., taking away animal life, shall not be permitted to dwell around the mount.

The property of well-conducted serfs[5] shall not be appropriated by the employés except for the [use of the] vihāra.

All the villages and lands belonging to this vihāra shall be administered

---

[1] I am not at all clear as to the meaning of this word. The Mudaliyar's interpretation is *dummal*, 'faded or bad flowers,' and *as-samun*, 'brooms for putting to a corner.' *Dum-mal* may also mean 'incense and flowers.' Müller translates *assamun* by 'those who supply.' None of these meanings seems to suit the context either here or in lines 34, 38, 40, and 41 of the second portion of this record. Tentatively I take *assam* as composed of *as* + *kam* (Skt. *aṁśa* + *karman*) and meaning 'distributing or apportioning.' Cf. *vissam* = *vis* + *kam* (Skt. *viśva* + *karman*) given in the *Sidatsaṅgarā* as an example of *perarū* (*pūrva-rūpa*), 'assimilation.' Thus *maha-budun-gehi dummal-assam sa-janak-haṭ* (B. l. 38) would mean 'to six persons who distribute incense and flowers in the temple containing the colossal image of the Buddha'; *me gämä dum-mal-assamnaṭ* (l. 40), 'to those in this village who distribute (as their duty) incense and flowers' [in the temple]; *kam-assamak-haṭ* (l. 41), 'to one who apportions work.'

[2] *Bäḷā* (spelt *bäla* in Clough's *Dict.*), 'hire.' Cf. *bäḷa-meke*, 'work done for wages'; Skt. *bhāṭa*.

[3] *Pereḷivar* = *perḷi-karu*, 'those who quarrel,' 'rebels.' Cf. *at-varu* for *at-karu* (Skt. *hasta-kāra*, 'manufacturer'); *sit-varu* for *sit-karu* (Skt. *citra-kāra*), 'painter,' quoted in the *Sidatsaṅgarā*, ch. ii. *Pereḷi* or *peraḷi* (*peraḷanavā*, 'to upset') must, I think, be connected with Skt. *pari* + √*vṛt*.

[4] This is obviously not a proper name. From the context it seems that it must refer to some sort of ground, probably a sandy plain near a tank or river specially set apart for the use of the community of monks (*saṅgha* + Sinh. *välla*, a sandy shore). Cf. *Mulaso-veher-sangvälle Vanpullā upāsaka* in Vessagiri slab-inscription, l. 11 (above, p. 25). This should have been translated 'the lay-devotee Vanpullā of the *saṅgvälla* of Mulaso-vihāra.'

[5] *Su-dasun* admits of two meanings, namely, (1) P. *su-dassana*, 'good-looking'; (2) *su* + *dasun*, 'well-conducted serfs'; *dasun* being the pl. of *das* (Skt. *dāsa*). Cf. *veher-dasun* in lines 41 and 45.

upon deeds[1] of lease, but no [absolute] transfers[2] [of the same] shall be executed.

Excepting the three days 'service by turn[3]' no other 'service by turn' such as [that at] *upōsatha* festival shall be exacted.

[Ll. 45–50] Unless it be a property given as 'a living'[4] to the employés and the serfs of the vihāra, no paddy fields, orchards, &c., in any place belonging to **Āt-vehera** shall be held by them on mortgages or as gifts or on leases[5].

Officials who have gone out on vihāra service[6] shall not receive means of subsistence[7] from the inhabitants of the country, except the contribution of raw rice[8] given by the cultivators[9] in accordance with former custom[10].

They shall not accept presents from tenants[11], nor shall the officials take yokes of oxen[12] from these [tenants] and have their own fields cultivated.

The leasehold fields which are held by cultivators in hereditary succession shall not be taken away unless they are not so held.

No trespass shall be committed on the gardens[13] and thereby injustice be done.

Trees and shrubs shall not be cut down.

[Ll. 50–54] In none of the villages and lands belonging to this vihāra

---

[1] *Kārāyehi* (loc. of *kārā*, in l. 38), 'in rental'; *bāndā* (P. *bandhitvā*), 'having tied.' See above, p. 103, note 12.

[2] *Pāṭṭa* or *paṭṭa*, a deed inscribed on copper-plate or on stone. In this connexion, probably a final transfer of land. According to Tamil and Indian usage in general, it means 'a deed of lease.' Cf. *paṭṭādār*, 'a lease-holder.' See also above, p. 54, note 4.

[3] *Var* = Skt. *vāra*, evidently used here in the sense of 'service by turn.' Cf. *vārika* in the Jētavanārāma Skt. Inscription, l. 31 (above, pp. 3, 5, and 9), and *vāriyan* in the Slab-inscription of Kassapa V, l. 17 (above, pp. 47, 53, note 7).

[4] *Jivel* or *divel*, 'lands granted to persons for their maintenance in consideration of certain services rendered or offices held by them.' See also *Ruvanmala*, 364, and *Nāmāvaliya*, 209.

[5] *Pāṭṭa-kārā*. See above, notes 1 and 2.

[6] *Veheraṭ kāmin*. See also above, l. 27.

[7] *Vāṭum* = Skt. *vṛttam*. See above, p. 102, note 8; also p. 57, note 3.

[8] *Bili-sāl*, lit. 'tribute-rice.' *Bili* = Skt. P. Pkt. *bali*. See *E. S.* No. 993.

[9] *Has-karuvan*. See *Piyummala*, p. 56, and *E. S.* No. 100.

[10] The Mudaliyar's rendering of this passage runs:—'Except the raw rice which, according to former custom, is given to the vehera by workmen gone on business or by the signers, no victuals shall be received from the (other) inhabitants of the country.'

[11] *Kuḍī* = Skt. P. *kuṭi*, Tamil *kuḍi*, in the sense of 'householder' or 'tenant,' both here and in lines 24 and 41.

[12] *Ge-gon* = *gon-gē* or *gon-geya*, Skt. *gō-yuga*.

[13] *Vatu pāṭaṭ*, modern *vatu-pelaṭa*, 'range of gardens'; *pela* = P. *panti*, Skt. *paṅkti*.

shall *talipot*[1], *mī*[2], and other fruit-bearing trees be allowed to be felled except by permission and consent of [the officials at] the place of business[3].

If any fault be committed by tenants[4], a fine shall be assessed[5] according to village custom, and in lieu of the assessed fine, they shall be made to perform tank-work by undertaking portions[6] [of work] 16 cubits in circumference and one cubit in depth at the side[7] of **Minā** [tank]. If this be not done, the assessed fine shall be levied.

Except that which is given[8] as means of subsistence for the collectors[9] of revenue of the villages and lands belonging to this vihāra, all [other] affairs transacted[10] bona fide[11] with the concurrence of [officials at] all the respective places of business[12] shall be entered[13] in the register[14].

[Ll. 54–58] Whatever is spent[15] daily on the maintenance of the *Maka-pā*[16], on revenue-collectors[17] and on the renovation of works shall be entered in the register. [From the particulars contained therein] a statement of accounts[18]

---

[1] *Talan*, the corypha palm.

[2] The wild sapota tree (*Bassia longifolia*), the wood of which is used for timber, and the seeds yield the oil (Clough).

[3] *Kam-tān*. The Mudaliyar renders this word by 'tenants,' but compare its use in lines 22 and 24.

[4] See note 11, p. 105.

[5] *Kirā*, ger. of *kiranavā*, 'to weigh.'

[6] *Kabuḷ*, apparently another form of *kābāli*. See above, p. 37, note 5.

[7] *Ākā*, loc. of *āka*, Skt. *aṅka*.

[8] *Jivel koṭ dunuvak*, lit. 'that which is given by making it a means of subsistence.' See also above, line 45 (p. 105, note 4).

[9] *Labanu-vanaṭ*, lit. 'to receivers.'

[10] *Ā-kaḷa*, Skt. = *ākṛta*.

[11] *Pasak vana seyin*, lit. 'in a manner apparent (to all)' or 'so as to become obvious (to all)'; *pasak* = Skt. *pratyakṣa*. See above, p. 102, note 4.

[12] *Kam-tān sāmāgin*. See also lines 24 and 50.

[13] *Liyāviyā yutu*, 'it should be caused to be written'; *liyāviyā* = P. *likhāpila*.

[14] *Pas-pol-hi*, Skt. *pañjikā-pustakē* (loc.). See Jētavanārāma inscription, line 28 (above, p. 5). The word *pas* is a derivative, not of *pañjikā*, but of *pañcikā*, the form used in Ceylon and South India. Cf. the titles of works:—*Maudgalyāyana-pañcikā-pradīpa*, *Cāndra-pañcikā*, *Nyāyasāra-pada-pañcikā*. Śrī Dharmārāma Nāyaka-sthavira, the learned editor of the first-named work, says that *pañcikā* is a Māgadhism:—'"*Pañcikā*" *yi ca-kāra madhya pāṭhayama Māgadha-śābdikayanṭa abhimataya. Dākṣiṇātya Saṁskṛta paṇḍitayanṭa da esēmaya*' (Preface, p. xiii, f. n.). Compare, however, Skt. √*pañc* or *pac*, 'to make clear,' of which *pañcikā* may be a derivative, as suggested by Prof. Macdonell.

[15] *Viya-vū* = Skt. *vyaya-bhūta*.

[16] *Maha-pā-vaṭa*, P. *mahā-patta-vaṭṭaṁ*. In reference to the *Mahā-pātra*, 'the large bowl,' the Mudaliyar says, 'a well-endowed vihāra is furnished with a bowl of a large size, which is filled with offerings of rice and other eatables on particular occasions.'

[17] *Labanuvanaṭ*, lit. 'to the receivers.'

[18] *Al-vatu*. I am not sure of the etymology of this word. The Mudaliyar makes it equivalent to Skt. *hasta-vastu*, 'a thing (such as a book) which is or may be carried in the hand,' commonly called *al-pola*, 'hand-book,' or *vaṭṭōru-pola*.

shall be made with the concurrence of [those at the respective] places of business, and such entries[1] as are found false[2] shall be expunged[3] from the account. The sheet of accounts shall [then] be placed in a casket under lock [and key]. Every month the sheets of accounts [so deposited] shall be made public, and a [fresh] statement of accounts be prepared from them. From the twelve statements of accounts [so made] during the year, there shall be compiled a balance sheet at the end of [each] year, which shall be read[4] out in the midst of the community of monks and be [thus finally] disposed of. The employés who infringe these rules shall be made to pay *ge-daṇḍ*[5] fines and be dismissed from the service.

Slab B.

[Ll. 1–3] To the monk who looks after the **Nakā**[6], [there shall be assigned] daily one *näḷiya*[7] of raw rice; for [expenses of] the opening ceremony of the *vassa*[8] season, one *kaḷaňda*[9] and four *aka*[10] [weight] of gold; for the closing festival of the *vassa* season, a similar quantity; to an administrator of [monastic] regulations[11], five *kiriya*[12] [of land] for maintenance[13], as well as one *näḷiya* of raw rice daily; for cost of whitewashing and of flowers, fifteen *kaḷaňd* [of gold] yearly.

[Ll. 3–6] The steward[14], the clerk of the vihāra, the registrar of caskets, the keeper of caskets[15], the almoner[16]—to each of these [shall be assigned]

---

[1] *San* = P. *saññā*.

[2] *Ota*, 'falsehood' (Clough).

[3] *Paḷavay*, lit. 'having caused to disappear.' Cf. *paḷavum* and *pāḷavum* in Jayatilaka's *Eḷu Akārādiya*.

[4] *Janvā*, modern *danvā* (caus. of √*jñā*), 'having made known'; P. *jānāpetvā*.

[5] See above, p. 54, note 3, and p. 103, note 12.

[6] See above, p. 101, note 2.

[7] 'A measure of capacity, about three pints; the twenty-fourth part of a *parrah*, or the thirty-second part of a bushel heaped up' (Clough). According to others, it is equivalent to a seer, or quart.

[8] *Vasan-banā* = P. *vassāna-bhāṇē* (loc.), 'at the reciting of the Buddhist scriptures during the season of retreat.' This evidently refers to the opening festival of the *Vassa* season on the full-moon day of the month of *Āsāḷha* (Skt. *āṣāḍha*), about the middle of June, just as *pavaruṇ-baṇa* (P. *pavāraṇā-bhāṇa*) means 'the preaching of the Doctrine at the closing festival of the Vassa season.' For an account of the ceremonies connected with the *Vassa* season by J. F. Dickson, see *J. C. B. R. A. S.* viii. (1884), pp. 207–31.

[9] See above, p. 28, note 3.

[10] See above, p. 29, note 1.

[11] *Niyam-jeṭak*. See above, p. 101, note 4.

[12] *Kiriya* = P. *karīsa*. Cf. above, p. 3, note 4.

[13] *Jivel*. See above, p. 105, note 4.

[14] *Ā-kāmiyā*. See above, part A, l. 20 (p. 101, note 5).

[15] *Karaňḍu at-samu*. See above, p. 101, note 8.

[16] *Pasak-kāmiyā*. See above, p. 101, note 6.

five *kiriya* [of land]; to the lay warden[1] one *kiriya* and two *paya*[2] [of land] together with two *aḍmanā*[3] of raw rice [daily]; to the one who makes his rounds[4] [as a watchman], two *paya* [of land] and one *aḍmanā* of raw rice [daily]; to the master of festivals[5], one *kiriya* [of land] and a *vasag* from **Damiya.**

[Ll. 7-15] For cost of whitewashing and flowers[6] [shall be given] three *kaḷañd* and two *aka* [of gold] a year; to a servant that attends to the rearing of calves[7], one *kiriya* [of land] and a *vasag* from **Damiya**; for cloths [used] for the merry festival of the great Bōdhi-tree, one *kaḷañda* [of gold]; to a [supplier of] earthen alms-bowls[8], one *paya* [of land] and [daily] two *pata* of raw rice; to one who arranges outside affairs[9] and to a servant that attends to matters arising in [connexion with] the royal house[10]—to each of these, one *kiriya* and two *paya* [of land] together with two *aḍmanā* of raw rice [daily]; to an *oḷ-kämiya*[11], two *paya* [of land] and one *aḍmanā* and two *pata* of raw rice [daily]; to a *perevāḷiya*[12] of the **Piyangal** [monastery], two *paya* [of land]

---

[1] *Pirivahanu-vata-kämiyak-haṭ*, lit. 'to one who performs the duties of a warden.' This official is called simply *Veher-pirivahanuvā* in part A, l. 20. Cf. also *vat-himiyan* above, p. 35, note 7.

[2] See above, p. 36, note 7.

[3] I have not been able to find out the exact value of an *aḍmanā*. It is clear from the present record that its capacity is more than two *pata*, that is to say more than half a quart or seer, a *pata* (prob. P. *pasata*) being equivalent to one-fourth of a seer or *nāḷiya*. As suggested by Rhys Davids, it is probably another name for the *nāḷiya* (*Ancient Coins and Measures of Ceylon*, p. 20).

[4] *Särāyin*. See *E. S.* No. 1583 and compare *dāgä raknānaṭ* below, l. 52.

[5] *Mañgul-jeṭa* = P. *maṅgala-jeṭṭha*.

[6] *Setuvamaṭ mal milā*. I am not quite sure of the meaning of this phrase. The above is the rendering adopted by Müller and the Mudaliyar. See also l. 3.

[7] *Vatsikā-kämiya*. Müller's rendering is 'one who prepares medicine'; that of Mudaliyar 'a servant of one year'; but the commonest meaning of Skt. *vatsikā* is 'a female calf,' and *vatsikā-karmika* may, therefore, very well mean 'a cow-herd', as suggested by Dr. Fleet.

[8] *Māṭi-patak-haṭ*. As the dative suffix *haṭ* is used only with personal nouns in the present record, the word *māṭi-pata* (Pkt. *maṭṭiā-patta*) with its indefinite suffix *-k* or *-ek* (*L. S. S.* § 42) must refer to a maker or supplier of earthen alms-bowls. According to Müller, it means 'a plasterer.'

[9] *Piḷassamak*. I am not sure of my rendering. Compare, however, the note on *dummal-assamun* above, p. 104, note 1. Müller takes it to mean 'one who throws away dead flowers,' and the Mudaliyar translates it by 'scavenger.'

[10] *Raj-ge upäni kämiyak*. This means, according to Müller, 'a workman born on the ground of the king'; and according to the Mudaliyar, 'a workman born in the king's house.'

[11] Both Müller and the Mudaliyar take this servant to be 'a masker,' following Upham's designation of the *oli* caste of drummers and dancers, in his *Sacred and Historical Books of Ceylon*, iii. p. 350.

[12] The meaning of this word is not clear. Both Müller and the Mudaliyar translate *piyangal perevāḷiyak* by 'one who spreads cloths on the stone-ceiling'; but Piyangal is the name of a monastery. See above, p. 53, note 1.

Tablets of Mahinda IV at Mihintale.

Slab B.

Scale 1¾ inches to 1 foot.

From an ink-impression supplied by the Archaeological Commissioner, Ceylon

and a *vasag* from **Damiya**; for [cost of] cloths used at the *Ruvanasun* festival of the great Bōdhi-tree, one *kaḷan̆da* [of gold]; to a *perevāḷiya* [1] of the [**Salamevan-]Pavu** [2] [monastery], two *paya* [of land] and a *vasag* from **Damiya**; to the head painter, two *paya* [of land] and one *aḍmanā* and one *pata* of raw rice [daily]; to each of the eleven painters, two *paya* [of land] and a *vasag* from **Damiya**; to each of the four servants [3] of the paymaster, one *aḍmanā* of raw rice [daily] and two *paya* [of land] for life [4].

[Ll. 15–16] The servants who accept [5] the robes received by each one of the community of monks in this vihāra, that accepts [5] robes at the close of the Vassa season [6], shall divide the same among themselves.

[Ll. 16–25] To each of the two *atsam* [7] of the vihāra [there shall be granted] two *paya* [of land] with one *aḍmanā* and one *pata* of raw rice [daily]; to the head caretaker of the granary, two *paya* [of land] with one *aḍmanā* and two *pata* of raw rice [daily]; to a caretaker of the granary, two *paya* [of land] with one *aḍmanā* of raw rice [daily]; to a *jeḷ-mava* [8], one *paya* [of land] with one *aḍmanā* and two *pata* of raw rice [daily]; to the warder of the refectory, one *paya* [of land] with one *aḍmanā* and two *pata* of raw rice [daily]; to one who issues orders to *mīn̆ḍi* [9], two *paya* [of land]; to each of the twenty-four hired *mīn̆ḍi* [9] servants, one *paya* [of land] and yearly one *kaḷan̆da* [of gold] for cloths; to a servant [10] that attends to affairs arising in the *sañg-välla*, one *kiriya* [of land] and one *aḍmanā* of raw rice [daily]; to each of the twelve servants that do the cooking, one *kiriya* and two *paya* [of land] from the village **Taḷola-gama**; to the head of these servants, one *aḍmanā* and one

---

[1] See note 12, p. 108.

[2] See above, p. 52.

[3] *Vaḷ-nā väri satarak.* Müller's translation of this is 'four goldsmiths,' and that of the Mudaliyar 'four energetic paymasters.' I do not think *väri* means here 'energetic.' See above, p. 53, note 7.

[4] *Jivel.* See above, p. 105, note 4.

[5] *Sāhana* (pres. part.), 'enduring'; *sāhā* (ger.), 'having endured.' See above, p. 102, note 9.

[6] *Vasāgin.* See also above, p. 28, note 5.

[7] *Veher-atsam*, 'receivers of Vihāra revenue,' according to both Müller and the Mudaliyar. But compare *karaṇḍu-atsamu* above, p. 101, note 8, and also *dāge atsam* in l. 33.

[8] *Jeḷ-mava* may mean 'old mother' (P. *jeṭṭha-mātā*), probably a polite way of referring to an old woman that attends to cleaning work in the monastery.

[9] I cannot make out the meaning of this word. Müller translates it by 'slave,' and the Mudaliyar by 'female servant.'

[10] *Sañg-väli upāni kāmiyak*, 'a workman born on the ground of the monks,' according to Müller and the Mudaliyar. Compare, however, *raj-ge upāni kāmiyak* in l. 9 (above, p. 108, note 10), and the note on *sañg-välla* above, p. 104, note 4.

pata of rice [daily in addition]; to a servant who procures firewood and cooks food, three *aḍmanā* of rice [daily]; to a servant who brings firewood but does not cook, and to a servant who goes on errands, two *aḍmanā* of rice each [daily]; to a servant who [only] cooks on firewood fetched [by others], one *aḍmanā* of rice.

[Ll. 26–30] To the chief of the thatchers[1] of the monastery [shall be assigned] two *paya* [of land] with one *aḍmanā* and one *pata* of rice [daily]; to each of the eleven thatchers[1] of the monastery, two *paya* [of land] and one *aḍmanā* of rice [daily]; to each of the five potters who supply daily five earthen pots (*yalā*), one *kiriya* [of land]; to an alms-bowl-maker who supplies every month ten alms-bowls and ten water-pots, two *kiriya* [of land] and two *aḍmanā* of rice [daily]; to one who supplies a water-strainer every month, one *kiriya* and two *paya* [of land].

[Ll. 30–35] To a physician [shall be assigned] a *niya-päliyā* from **Detisäsena**[2] and a *vasag* from **Damiya**; to a physician who applies leeches[3], two *paya* [of land] and a *vasag* from **Damiya**; to a *maňḍovuva*[4], one *kiriya* and two *paya* [of land] and a *vasag* from **Damiya**; to an astrologer, two *kiriya* [of land] and a *vasag* from **Damiya**; to a barber, one *kiriya* [of land] and a *vasag* from **Damiya**; to the keeper[5] of the 'relic-house,' the chief of the retinue[6] [of attendants], the registrar of shrines, the three superintendents of service by turns[7]—to these [servants], the village **Karandägama** for their maintenance; to those *dum-mal-assam*[8] who serve by turns[7], four *vasag* from **Damiya**; for wicks and oil [used for lights] in the 'relic-house,' one *payala* [of land] from this village [Karandägama].

---

[1] *Pahā vāsi jeṭak.* The above is the rendering of both Müller and the Mudaliyar. But as *vāsi* may also mean 'a dweller,' this phrase can be translated 'the chief of the attendants living in the monastery.'

[2] *Detisäsenen niya päḷiyāk.* I cannot make out the meaning of this phrase. Müller takes *päḷiyā* as another form of *pāḷa*; but *pāḷa* is only one-eighth of a *kiriya*, i.e. about one and a half bushel, which would be too small a grant of land to a physician. With *niya-päḷiyā* compare, however, *nilapalā* and *nilapāḷu*, a name given to 'lands once held *ex officio* from Government, but which from discontinuance of the office have again lapsed to the Crown.'

[3] *Puhuňḍā-vedak*, lit. 'a leech-doctor.'

[4] Probably one who prepares medical decoctions. Müller takes it to mean 'a flower gardener.'

[5] *Dāge atsamak*, 'a receiver of dues of the dāge,' according to Müller and the Mudaliyar. But see above, p. 101, note 8.

[6] *Gaṇa-jeṭuvak*, 'the overseer of the tenantry,' according to Müller. The Mudaliyar takes it to mean 'a chief of a chapter of monks,' but this is not probable, as the inscription deals here with the paid lay servants of the monastic establishment.

[7] *Var*, see above, p. 105, note 3.

[8] See above, p. 104, note 1.

[Ll. 35–41] To the two florists who place[1] white [lotus] flowers in the 'relic-house' [shall be assigned] two *kiriya* [of land] from this village [Karandâgama] and a *vasag* each from **Damiya**; to a keeper[2] of blue water-lilies[3] who supplies flowers at the rate of 120 a month, two *kiriya* [of land] from **Sapugamiya**; to a painter, two *kiriya*; to the district headman[4] who takes care of the 'relic-house,' one *naḷiya* of rice [daily]; to six *dum-mal-assam*[5] of the temple[6] containing the colossal statue of the Buddha, to the devotee who preaches the Buddhist doctrine, to the devotee who is a teacher, and to six [other] devotees—to [all] these, the village **Gutâgama**; to the florist of the temple[6] containing the colossal statue of the Buddha, two *paya* [of land] from this village and a *vasag* from **Damiya**; to the *dum-mal-assam*[5] of this village, two *vasag* from **Damiya.**

[Ll. 41–45] To a *pūṇā-kämiya*[7] of the temple of the auspicious colossal stone-statue [of the Buddha] and to one who officiates[8] [there]—to each of them [shall be assigned] two *paya* [of land] with one *aḍmanā* and two *pata* of rice [daily]; to an official[9] at the place of business [who provides] a cup[10] in which to take oil for the unction of [the statue of] the Buddha in the 'relic-house,' and an unbleached cloth[11] for filtering water and the same [articles] for the image-house also, [there shall be granted] one *kiriya* and two *paya* [of land] with two *aḍmanā* of rice [daily]; to the chief master-artisan[12], all that

---

[1] *Ond.* See above, p. 102, note 8.

[2] *Govuva* = Skt. *gōpaka* (from √*gup*). Cf. *ät-govuva* (or *-govvā*), 'an elephant-keeper.'

[3] *Mahu-nel* = modern *mänel*, 'nymphea stellata' (Clough).

[4] *Raṭ-laduvak*, lit. 'he who has received the country,' probably an officer of the rank of a *raṭē rāla* in later times.

[5] See above, p. 104, note 1.

[6] *Maha-budum-ge.*

[7] *Pūṇā-kämiya*, 'a person attending to the ceremonies connected with the sacred *pūṇa* pot in the temple.' Müller and the Mudaliyar call him 'a person officiating in the temple.' In Clough's *Sinhalese Dictionary* we find the word *pūnāva* (probably the same as *puṇā*, 'a pot,' according to Jayatilaka's *Eḷu Akārādiya*) explained as 'a vessel with many spouts for pouring out water, and used by the Kapuvas in the dēvālaya in the service of the demons; this vessel is considered so sacred, that in cases of great difficulty or importance people are compelled to swear upon it.'

[8] *Kam-usṭumak*, 'one who takes an account of work,' according to the Mudaliyar. See, however, above, p. 104, note 1.

[9] *Kam-tän-leḍaruvak*. In the absence of a better explanation, I follow the Mudaliyar in treating this tentatively as an equivalent of Skt. *karmasthāna-lēkha-dhāraka*.

[10] *Poṭa* most probably connected with Skt. and Pāli *puṭa*.

[11] *Tuḷula*, spelt also *tuḷuru* and *tuḷuḷa*, according to the Mudaliyar. The etymology is uncertain, but compare Skt. *tantraka*, 'unbleached cloth,' and *tūla-paṭa*, 'cotton cloth.'

[12] *Vaḍu-maha-aduruk* = Skt. *vardhaka* + *maha* + *ācārya*. Cf. *maha-äduru*, 'master-carpenter,' in the *Piyummala*, p. 60. *Vaḍu* is used here as a general term for artisans.

belongs to the guild[1] of artisans at **Boṇḍ-vehera**; to two master-artisans, to eight carvers[2] and to two brick[3]-layers—to [all of] these, the village **Vaḍu-devāgama.**

[Ll. 46–50] To each of the two workers[4] in wood [shall be assigned] one *kiriya* [of land]: to each of the two master-lapidaries[5], three *kiriya* [of land]: to each of the two blacksmiths, one *kiriya* [of land]; to the lime-burners, the village **Sunuboḷ-devāgama**: to the six cartmen, the village **Dunumugama**; to the overseer of 'workers[6] by the piece' in the reparation of works, one *kiriya* [of land] with one *aḍmanā* and one *pata* of rice [daily]; to the twelve 'workers[6] by the piece,' one *aḍmanā* of rice each [daily] with two *paya* [of land] for maintenance[7].

[Ll. 50–54] To each of the three warders of the dāgäbas **Navaguṇa-maha-säya, Näṭeviya-maha-säya,** and **Ambulu-dāgäba,** [respectively shall be assigned] two *paya* [of land]; to each of those who sweep[8], go repeatedly round[9] and take care of the dāgäbas, &c. which belong to **Ät-vehera** [and are] on the upper and on the lower rock of this vihāra shall be granted one *vasag* from **Damiya**; to the men who perform service in the 'relic-house,' in the 'image-house' and in the refectory, as well as to the two laundrymen who wash clothes, yellow robes for covering the body with, and head-vestments—to [all] these [servants], three *kiriya* [of land] in the village **Maṅguläva.**

[Ll. 54–58] The roads, high-roads, the hired labourers, and the *melāṭsī*[10] in all the villages and lands belonging to this vihāra shall be taken over as the sole property of this very vihāra. Neither wayfarers nor tramps shall commit trespass. In all the places irrigated by the water of the **Kaṇā-väva** tank, the distribution of water shall be utilized for this vihāra only, in

---

[1] *Sṛṇḍya* seems to be a derivative of an adjectival form of Skt. *srēṇi* (P. *seṇi*), 'a guild of artisans.'

[2] *Sir-vaḍu.* I follow Müller in connecting this with Skt. *churikā+vardhaka*, and treating it as a synonym of *siriyaru* (Skt. *churikā-kāra*) in *Nāmāvaliya*, v. 224. According to the Mudaliyar, *sir-vaḍu* means 'bucket-makers,' *sir* being equivalent to Skt. *sirā*, but *sir* can also be a derivative of *sira*, 'a plough.'

[3] *Uḷu* = P. *iṭṭhikā*.

[4] Or 'wood-cutters'; *kaṭu* = Skt. *kāṣṭha*.

[5] *Miṇir* = Skt. *maṇi-kāra*, 'a goldsmith,' according to Müller.

[6] *Kabiḷi.* See above, p. 37, note 5.

[7] *Jivil.* See above, p. 105, note 4.

[8] *Hämāndā*, lit. 'having swept,' from Skt. *sammṛj*. Cf. P. *sammajjati*, 'he sweeps,' and *sammajjanī*, *sammuñjanī*, 'a broom'; Sinh. *hämaduma* (in *Nāmāvaliya*, 233), *ämadīma* (in *Piyummala*, p. 64).

[9] *Dägā*, lit. 'having repeatedly gone,' from the Intens. stem *jaṅgam-* (or *jāgam-*) of Skt. √ *gam*. Cf. Sinh. *däṅgum*, 'moving, walking.'

[10] See above, p. 53, note 10.

accordance with ancient customs in vogue formerly during the Tamil period [of rule]. No villages or lands belonging to this vihāra shall in any manner be mortgaged or gifted away. The money[1] of [i.e. paid by] those who have acquired [lands] shall be forfeited and be held by the vihāra itself; while those who transferred [the lands] shall be banished to a foreign country.

By Order, these regulations were thus established and they shall be observed without transgression[2].

No. 8. ANURĀDHAPURA: SLAB-INSCRIPTION OF MAHINDA IV NEAR THE 'STONE-CANOE'

THIS inscription lies near the so-called 'stone-canoe,' a few yards to the east of the Thūpārāma dāgāba[3]. It contains forty-nine lines of boldly engraved writing which covers 6′ 5″ by 2′ 8″ of the smoothed surface of the slab. As a result probably of rubbing or grinding things on it, the central portion of the inscription—from lines 10 to 46—is totally obliterated. The effaced letters number from four to thirteen in each line of twenty-five akṣaras on the average, as may be judged from the accompanying plate, No. 16.

The letters which are not so lost are quite clear and can easily be read from the plate itself, the alphabet being the same as that employed in other records of the tenth and early eleventh centuries. Attention may, however, be drawn to the compound akṣaras *vya* (l. 21) and *tyā* (l. 43) not met with before in inscriptions of Mahinda IV or in earlier ones.

That the present record belongs to Mahinda IV there is no doubt, for it agrees with the foregoing tablets at Mihintale in its language and general style, as well as in naming the king simply by his title **Siri Saṅgbo Abahay**. The use, however, of forms like *sirī* (l. 1) for *siri*, *dīv* (l. 2) for *div*, *tyāga* (l. 43) and *karma* (l. 44) seems to indicate traces of the Sanskrit influence noticed by Goldschmidt. Further, the honorific term *vahanse* (l. 41), so common in later inscriptions and books, occurs here, so far as I know, for the first time. Its

[1] *Ranā* = Skt. *hiranya*, 'coined gold' or 'money.'

[2] Lit. 'without having transgressed.'

[3] See Burrows' *Buried Cities of Ceylon*, p. 33.

etymology is obscure. Müller derives *vahan* from P. *upāhana* [1]. I am, however, inclined to connect it with Skt. *bhavān* (P. *bhavaṁ*), by metathesis of *ha* and *va* in Pkt. *havaṁ* [2]; and *sē* with Skt. *chāyā* [3].

The inscription is **dated** in the sixteenth year of the reign of Siri Saṅgbo Abahay, that is of Mahinda IV, on the tenth day of the dark half of the lunar month *Mädindina* (February–March). It is, therefore, only about five months and a half later than the Mihintale tablets.

Its **contents** consist of rules for the administration of certain lands and villages. These set forth the terms upon which grantees and tenants can hold lands, how the produce should be divided, what portion should be set apart for the upkeep of the temple of the Buddha's 'Tooth-relic' (*Daḷ-dā-ge*), how disputes should be settled and fines be levied. The reference to the *Daḷ-dā-ge* is important, for it enables us to identify the 'Tooth-relic-house' (*dāṭhādhātu-gharaṁ*), rebuilt by Mahinda IV in the centre of the town [4], with the ruined site now known as the Daḷadā Māligāva [5], and situated to the south-east of the

---

[1] See *Journal C. B. R. A. S.* 1879, p. 13, f. n.

[2] Cf. AMg. JM. *havaï* = *bhavati* (Pischel's *Pkt. Gram.* § 475), AMg. *havanti* = *bhavanti* (Leumann's *Aupapātika-Sūtra*, 130).

[3] See *E. S.* 1567.

[4] Jhātaṁ nagara-majjhamhi dāṭhādhātu-gharaṁ akā । dhammasaṅgaṇi-gēhañ ca mahāpāḷiñ ca bhūpati ॥ (*Mv.* liv. 45.)

[5] The following is Mr. H. C. P. Bell's account of this ruin:—

'The connexion of the "Dáṭhádhátu-ghara," now universally called the "Daḷadá Máligáwa," with the Tooth-relic dates from the reign of Kírti Śrí Méghavarṇa, 304–32 A.D.

'"In the ninth year of his reign a certain Brahman princess brought the Dáṭhádhátu, or Tooth-relic of Buddha, hither from Káliṅga. The monarch, receiving charge of it himself, and rendering thereto, in the most reverential manner, the highest honours, deposited it in a casket of great purity, and lodged it in the edifice called the Dhammacakka, built by Dévánampiya Tissa in the royal park. Thenceforward that house received the name of Dáṭhádhátu-ghara." (*Mv.* xxxvii. 42, 43.)

'The structure lies immediately to the south-east of the Thúpáráma Dágaba. It stands upon a low raised rectangular site, once walled in (57 ft. in breadth by some 84 ft. deep), which left an open space 15 ft. broad around the shrine except in front. Steps admitted to this terrace on either side of the building.

'In the northern portion is an ancient well, 5 ft. square—one of the best specimens of the many to be seen in Anurádhapura. Its sides were formed of dressed slabs, excellently laid and still virtually plumb; and it had its own diminutive steps.

'The "Daḷadá Máligáwa" building, as it exists at this day, shows a length from east to west of 62 ft. 6 in., recessed slightly towards the middle for 8 ft., and 27 ft. 6 in. in width. This irregularity of wall-line is due to the addition of a vestibule, 35 ft. in length by 27 ft. 6 in. broad, built on to the portico of the original shrine, so as to give it the appearance from outside of one continuous structure: inside the overlapment is obvious.

Thūpārāma dāgäba within its outer enclosure, and only a few yards from the spot where the present inscription is.

The text given below is based on two ink-estampages furnished by the Archaeological Commissioner. Its mutilated state does not admit of a complete translation of the original inscription. Nevertheless, the following rendering which has been checked with that made by the late Mudaliyar Guṇasēkara, when connected with the Archaeological Survey, will be found useful.

TEXT.

1 සිරිබර් කැත කුල කොත් මහාවස් රජ්පරපුරෙන් බට ල
2 ත් දිව් පොළොයොන පරපුරෙන් ගිමවූ සිරි සඟ්බො අබහ
3 ණ් මහරජ්හු තුමා සත් ලැඟු සොළොස් වන හවුරුදුයෙහි
4 මැඬියින්දින් සඳ් අවප් මස්හි දස පස් දවස් සතර් ප

'The first erection was a quadrangular building measuring 27 ft. each way, but relieved in front by a bay vestibule, 19 ft. by 14 ft., with the simplest of portico entrances from a plain moonstone and a couple of steps. The walls of this original shrine (now the *ardha maṇḍapaya*, or inner vestibule, and *garbha-griha*, or sanctum, of the "Daḷadá Máligáwa") were 2 ft. 6 in. in thickness, rising directly from the torus of a finely-moulded basement in stone. The stone door-frame of its vestibule still stands. The adytum which sheltered the Tooth-relic is 21 ft. square, and its sixteen pillars (8 ft. 10 in. in height) all free standing. They are of three kinds: the corner four plain squared; the intermediate four pairs octagonal, and finished with unique elongated capitals, perhaps representing conventionalised lotus buds (Mr. Burrows favours the popular view that "the cuneiform mouldings" are meant to represent the sacred relic, *Buried Cities*, 1894, p. 37); the centre four square of shaft and smoothly polished (the sole instance of polished pillars yet met with), but sliding gradually at the top into a wider abacus. The relic doubtless rested between these centre pillars.

'Of the later *maṇḍapaya*, now the *antarála* [sic] or outer vestibule to the shrine, the interior space is 20 ft. 6 in. by 18 ft. 6 in., and the roof appears to have been supported on twenty-four pillars, of which ten stood just within the walls.

'The stairs at the present entrance to the "Daḷadá Máligáwa" are of the handsomest description. At the foot is a moonstone with concentric bands of varied ornamentation cut in deep sunk relief, around a central full-blown lotus. The innermost band contains sixteen *hansas* overlapping; the second, floriated scroll work; the third, nine of the animals found on these slabs (elephant, horse, lion, bull), passing, like the ducks, from left to right; and a final outermost band of "cobra-leaf" design. This stone is among the finest found at Anurádhapura. (An attempt by S. Jayatilaka Mudaliyar to remove this beautiful slab from Anurádhapura in 1849 was fortunately prevented.)

'Triple dwarfs and water-leaf ornament adorn the risers of the six steps; the magnificent wing-stones are topped by mythical *makaras*, from whose mouths descend thick ornate scrolls ending in volutes. On each of the vertical faces of the terminal stones are carved *Nága* figures, nine-hooded, in the usual pose, grasping a lotus stalk with one hand, and supporting a lotus-filled vase in the other. At their feet are a couple of posturing dwarfs.' (*A. S. C. Report* for 1895, p. 3.)

5 ස්හි අය්වූ උකස් ගැම්හි ඉසා පමණු ගැම්හි ඉසා ගි
6 ය තුවාක් දවස්හි රද් කොලව් වැලැඳෑම්හි සිටි කැබැල්ලෙ
7 හි කලැළි කුඹුර් පෙරෙ වලඳෑම්හි සිටි සෙ වලඳනු කොට් ඉසා
8 සෙසු වියල් තුබූ තුවාක් තැන් පමණු ලදුවන් වියල් නෙරුත් මුත්
9 කැබැලි ලදුවන් වියල් නො නෙර්නා කොට් ඉසා පමණු ලදුවන්
10 වියල් නෙල් තැන්හි පහත් .. .. (ග)ත් කිරි අමුණ බා දෙ කැ
11 බැලි ලදුවන් බෙදු ගන්[නා කොට් ඉසා] .. .. (මෙ)යට් උපන් දෙ විකය
12 ක් ඇත ගම් වැසියන් .. .. [පිරි] කපා බා ගන්නා කොට්
13 ඉසා පෙරෙ කැබැලි .. .. වල්) පියො වැ තුබූ තුවා
14 ක් තැන් වැව් බැඳැ .. .. කැරුණ් හසෙකැ බෙදු
15 ගන්නා කොට් ඉසා .. .. ක් ඇත ගම් වැසි
16 යන් දුව් නැස්මක් .. .. යන් බෙදු ගන්නා කො
17 ට් ඉසා මෙකුන් විය .. .. (බ)ද් වැව්සර් වියල්
18 නෙලැගෙහි වැවූ ප .. .. [ගම්වැ]සියන් පස් දෙන
19 කු කී බා දෙ කැබැලි .. .. කොට් ඉසා පෙරෙ ම
20 ත් ගස් කොලව් අ .. .. [වහ]න්සෙ හුණස්හි වැ
21 ඩ වෙන කලැ කල ව්‍ය .. .. (ම) තුනින් එකක් නි
22 යාගෙන් බෙදු ග[න්නා කොට් ඉසා] .. .. තුවාක් දවස්හි ප
23 මණු ලදුවනට් කුඩ .. .. වැවෙම්හි සිටි වැ
24 ව්මක් ඇත පෙරෙ .. .. කොට් ඉසා මෙකුන් අ
25 යෙළින් ඔත් නැරුළ් හ .. .. මහ වරක් දෙ කැබැ
26 ලි ලදුවග් බෙදු ග[න්නා කොට් ඉසා] .. .. කිත් පකක් දෙ කැබැලි
27 ලදුවන් බෙදු ගන්නා [කොට් ඉසා] .. .. (මු)ලත් දෙඩම් කෙල් කො
28 ස් සෙසු උපො පල .. .. [හවු]රුදු පතා වත්තකට් ළී
29 ඳෑකින් දෙ අකක් (බැ) .. .. න් බෙදු ගන්නා කො
30 ට් ඉසා ගම් වැසිය[න්] .. .. ඇත කුඩින් නො ප
31 ල්වා ගම් වැසිය[න්] .. .. කැබැලි ලදුවන්
32 බෙදු ගන්නා කොට් [ඉසා] .. .. [කැ] බැලි ලදුවන් අනි
33 යා නො කරනු කොට් [ඉසා] .. .. [ත]න්හි මෙලාව්සි
34 ලද්දකු ගන්නා [කොට් ඉසා ගම් වැසිය]න් පස් දෙනකු කී ද
35 ඩ ගන්නා කොට් ඉ[සා] .. .. දෙ කැබැලි ලදුවන්
36 වැ මෙහෙයට් ෙ(ද) .. .. [උ]පන් වියවුලක් ඇත
37 මහා ලෙයක්(හු) .. .. වරු අරක් මෙහෙකැම්
38 යක් හු ඉසා ස .. .. (කු)සල් කැම් ලෙයක්හු
39 ඉසා දඬ(නා ප) .. .. (පි) කාරයක්හු ඉසා ඇ
40 තුළ්වැ මෙ තුවා[ක්] .. .. සාහා දෙනු කොට් ඉ
41 සා එකොළොස් .. .. ගිම්යන් වහන්සෙ
42 පස්වනු ප .. .. කැබැලි ලද් කෙනෙකු
43 න් විචාර කොට් .. .. තහග කරනු කොට් ලිය
44 වා දළ්ද මෙ .. .. ලී කර්ම නො ඉක්මැ වැ

Anurādhapura :—Slab Inscription of Mahinda IV, near the Stone-Canoe.

Scale 1⅞ inches to 1 foot.

From an ink-impression supplied by the Archæological Commissioner, Ceylon.

45 වෙනු සඳහා .. .. තබනු ලදී සතර් පස්ගි
46 දෙමෙළ් ගම්බිම් .. .. [බත්] ගස් කොළ්ගි පෙරෙ සිරි
47 ත්සෙ ගන්නා කොට් ඉ[සා මෙ]ගි පවා මත්තෙ බත් ගස් කො
48 ළ්ගි දසපැකින් පකස් හා සතර් මනවරක් හා ළිඟෙඳකින් දෙ
49 අකස් බැවින් ගනෑ යුතු

TRANSCRIPT.

1 Sirī-bar [1] Käta-kula-kot Okā-vas raj-parapuren baṭ La-
2 -k-dīv [2] poḷoyona parapuren himivū **Sirī [3] Saṅgbo Abaha-**
3 **-y-maharaj-hu** tumā sat-läṅgū soḷos-vana havuruduyehi
4 Mändindin sand avap-mashi [4] dasa-pak davas satar-pa-
5 -shi ayvū ukas-gämhi isā pamaṇu-gämhi isā gi-
6 -ya tuvāk davashi rad-kolaṭ väḷändemin siṭi käbälle-
7 -hi kaḷäḷi-kumbur pere vaḷandamin siṭi-se vaḷandanu koṭ isā
8 sesu viyaḷ tubū tuvāk tän pamaṇu laduvan viyaḷ nerut-mut
9 käbäli laduvan viyaḷ no nernā koṭ isā pamaṇu laduvan
10 viyaḷ neḷ tänhi pahan .. .. (ga)t kirī amuṇā bā de-kä-
11 -bäli laduvan bedā-gan[nā koṭ isā] .. .. (me)yaṭ upan de vikaya-
12 -k äta gam-väsiyan .. .. [piri-]kapā bā gannā koṭ
13 isā pere käbäli .. .. va(l)-piyo-vä tubū tuvā-
14 -k tän väv bändā .. .. käruṇ hasekä bedā
15 gannā koṭ isā .. .. -k äta gam-väsi-
16 -yan duṭ näsmak .. .. -yan bedā gannā ko-
17 -ṭ isā mekun viya- .. .. (ba)-d vävsar viyaḷ
18 neḷäyehi vävū pa- .. .. [gamvä]siyan pas dena-
19 -ku kī bā de-käbäli .. .. koṭ isā pere o-
20 -t gas-koḷaṭ a- .. .. [vaha]nse huṇanhi vä-
21 -ḍa-vena kalä kaḷa vya- .. .. [-ma] tunin ekak ni-
22 -yāyen bedā ga[nnā koṭ isā] .. .. -tuvāk davashi pa-
23 -maṇu laduvanaṭ kuḍī .. .. väṭemin siṭi vä-
24 -ṭmak äta pere .. .. koṭ isā mekun a-
25 -yeḷin ot näruḷ ta- .. .. maha-varak de-käbä-
26 -li laduvan bedā ga[nnā koṭ isā] .. .. -kin pakak de-käbäli
27 laduvan bedā gannā [koṭ isā] .. .. (bu)lat doḍam kel ko-
28 -s sesu upo pala .. .. [havu]rudu patā vattakaṭ ḷi-

[1] Read *siri-bar*. [2] Read *div*. [3] Read *Siri*. [4] Probably for *ava-mashi*.

29 -ndekin de akak (bä-) .. .. -n bedā gannā ko-
30 -ṭ isā gam-väsiya[n] .. .. ăta kuḍīn no pa-
31 -lvā gam-väsiya[n] .. .. käbäli laduvan
32 bedā gannā koṭ [isā] .. .. [kä]-bäli laduvan ani-
33 -yā no karanu koṭ [isā] .. .. [ta-]nhi melāṭsī
34 laddaku gannā [koṭ isā gam-väsiya]n pas denaku kī da-
35 -ṇḍ gannā koṭ i[sā] .. .. de-käbäli laduvan
36 vā meheyaṭ (de) .. .. [u]pan viyavulak äta
37 mahā-leyak-(hu) .. .. -varā arak mehekämi-
38 -yak-hu isā sa- .. .. (ku) sal-kämi-leyak-hu
39 isā daṇḍ(nā) pa- .. .. (-pi) kārayak-hu isā ä-
40 -tuḷvä me tuvā[k] .. .. sāhā denu koṭ i-
41 -sā ekoḷos .. .. himiyan-vahanse
42 pasvanu pa .. .. käbäli-lad-keneku-
43 -n vicāra koṭ .. .. tyāga karanu koṭ liya-
44 -vā **daḷdā-ge** .. .. li-karma no ikmä vä-
45 -ṭenu sand-hā .. .. tabanu ladi satar pas-hi
46 demeḷ gam-bim .. .. [ot] gas koḷ-hi pere siri-
47 -t-se gannā koṭ i[sā me]hi pavā matte ot gas-ko-
48 -ḷ-hi dasapäkin pakak hā satar-mahavarak hā ḷindekin de
49 akak bävin gatā yutu

TRANSLATION.

[Lines 1–4] On the tenth day of the dark half of the [lunar] month of Mädindina[1], in the sixteenth year after the elevation of the regal canopy of the great king **Siri Saṅgbo Abahay,** lord by [right of his] lineal descent from the lords[2] of the soil of the Island of Laṅkā, who were descended from the royal line of the Okkāka dynasty, the pinnacle of the illustrious Kṣatriya race, [it was enacted]:—

[Ll. 4–7] That the kaḷāli[3] fields in that portion of [each of] the mortgaged and gifted villages in the four directions, which in bygone days used to be in the possession of the royal family, shall be held as before.

---

[1] From about the middle of February to the middle of March.

[2] *Lak-div-poḷoyonu.* The Mudaliyar translates, 'who in due course became owner of the ground of the Island of Laṅkā.' But see above, p. 26, note 10.

[3] Probably an agricultural term applied to wet lands.

[Ll. 8–12] That recipients of *pamaṇu* grants of land may clear the jungle[1] in any of the remaining forest[1]-clad places[2]; but recipients of allotments shall not clear the jungle[1].

At the places where recipients of *pamaṇu* grants have cleared the jungle . . . . *kiri* and half [?] *amuṇa*, the recipients of two allotments shall divide among themselves . . . . . If there be a sale of things produced . . . . . the village-residents . . . . . shall divide and take half[3].

[Ll. 13–20] Former allotments . . . . . . at places that have fallen into a wild state, tanks having been constructed . . . . shall divide among themselves . . . . if there be . . . . a damage seen by the villagers . . . . shall divide among themselves. The expenditure of these (persons) . . . . the tanks and ponds[4] adjoining . . . . cultivated in places where the jungle has been cleared . . . . . [The recipients of] two allotments [shall take] the half share recommended by five [village]-residents.

[Ll. 20–25] To trees and shrubs planted[5] before . . . . (harm) done at the time of growth . . . . they shall divide justly and take one-third . . . . during . . . . days . . . . . to the recipients of *pamaṇu* grants, the tenants . . . . . if there be an observance[6] which has been kept up, formerly . . . . . coco-nut trees[7] planted at the request [?] of these persons[8].

[Ll. 25–30] . . . . . . a high road [?], the recipients of two allotments shall divide among themselves . . . . . . the recipients of two allotments shall divide among themselves one fruit[9] out of . . . . betel, oranges, plantain, jack and other fruits of the kind . . . . annually to a garden, at the rate of two *aka*[10] from a *ḷinda* [well ?] . . . . . they shall divide among themselves.

[Ll. 30–35] Village-residents . . . . . if there be, the village-residents . . . . . . without ejecting the tenants . . . . recipients of allotments shall divide

---

[1] *Viyaḷ* = Tamil *viyal*, 'forest, jungle.' Here it probably means 'high lands' as distinct from *kaḷāli* fields.

[2] The Mudaliyar's rendering of this passage runs, 'that those who have been put in possession of all remaining dry or high lands may be ejected, but not the shareholders; the temporary occupants being satisfied with the high lands, paddy lands' . . . .

[3] The Mudaliyar translates, 'the villagers . . . . may cut and take down' . . . .

[4] The Mudaliyar translates, 'in tanks, ponds, high lands and paddy lands, the tanks

[5] *Ol*. See *E. S.* No. 221.

[6] *Vāṭmak*, 'observance' or 'means of subsistence.'

[7] *Nāruḷ* probably = *naraḷu*, Skt. *nārikela*, P. *nāḷikera*, Marāṭhi [illegible]

[8] The Mudaliyar translates, 'ejected from the neighbourhood . . . . a high road.'

[9] *Paka* = P. *pakkaṁ*, 'fruit,' or P. *pakkha*, 'side, division.'

[10] See above, p. 29, note 1.

among themselves . . . . . . Recipients of allotments shall do no injustice . . . . whatever the *Melāṭsls*[1] have received shall be appropriated. The fine recommended by five persons [from among village-residents] shall be recovered.

[Ll. 35–40] . . . . . . recipients of two allotments, for tank-work . . . . Should any dispute arise, the chief clerk . . . . . the warden[2], the steward[3], the administrator of law[4], ... doer of . . . . all these [officials] . . . . shall render assistance[5].

[Ll. 41–45] The eleven . . . . lord . . . fifth . . . . having made inquiries from a recipient of allotments and having caused to be written to the effect that the gift is made . . . . for the purpose of observing without transgression the duties of . . . . the **Tooth-relic-house**[6] . . . . [this] is established.

[Ll. 45–49] [The produce] of trees and shrubs which exist . . . . . . in the Tamil villages and lands [situated] in the four directions shall be appropriated in accordance with former custom. Furthermore, one fruit out of ten fruits[7] of trees and shrubs that may exist in the future [on these lands], as well as four *mahavarak* [high roads?] and two *aka* from [each] *ḷinda* [well?], shall be appropriated.

---

[1] See above, p. 53, note 10.

[2] *Arak-mehe-kāmi*, 'a cook,' according to the Mudaliyar.

[3] The Mudaliyar reads *kusal-kāmi-leyak*, and renders it by 'sweeper.' The above is the English for *kusal-kāmi-leyak*, lit. 'the registrar of skilful workmen.'

[4] *Daṇḍ-nā* = Skt. *daṇḍa-nāyaka*.

[5] *Sāhā* = Skt. *sāhya* or *sāhāyya*. See above, p. 101, note 9.

[6] *Daḷ-dā-ge* = P. *dāṭhādhātu-gēham*.

[7] *Dasa-pakinpakak* may also be rendered 'one division out of ten divisions,' i.e. one-tenth share.

No. 9. DAṀBULLA ROCK-INSCRIPTION[1] OF KĪRTI NIŚŚAṄKA MALLA (1189–1198 A.D.).

THE Rock Temple of Daṁbulla, called in the *Mahāvaṁsa* (lxxx. 22) Jambukōla Vihāra, and built underneath an enormous boulder of gneiss, upwards of 500 feet in height and about 2,000 feet in length, is, from its antiquity, its grandeur, and the richness of its decorations, one of the most celebrated Vihāras of Ceylon.

It is situated about forty-seven miles north-west of Kandy, on the main road to Anurādhapura, which is some forty-two miles further north. The other rock temple of equal fame, Alu Vihāra—where, according to the Sinhalese chronicles, the Buddhist scriptures were first committed to writing, under the patronage of Vaṭṭa-Gāmaṇī Abhaya, in the first century B.C.—lies about twenty-nine miles to the south; while the famous fortress of Sīgiri rises aloft like a gigantic cylinder at a distance of about twelve miles to the north-east.

In their vivid descriptions of the Daṁbulla Vihāra, Messrs. Davy, Forbes, Tennent, and Burrows mention the existence of several inscriptions in the Cave character, and of one, by Kīrti Niśśaṅka Malla, in the Sinhalese script of the twelfth century[2]. As far as I know, only one of the former class has up to now been published[3]. The latter inscription is the record under discussion. It is neatly engraved 'on the rock to the right, immediately after passing the Muragē,' in the courtyard of the temple, and consists of twenty-five lines, covering an area of about 5 ft. 9 in. by 3 ft. 6 in.[4].

As already stated, the **letters** represent the type of the Sinhalese alphabet in use in the twelfth and thirteenth centuries. Their average size is

[1] In the Archaeological Commissioner's list, and on the back of the single estampage sent to me to work at, the locality of the inscription is given as 'Veragala Rock in Kuñchuṭṭu Kōrale.' This is evidently a mistake, which I am sorry I did not detect until after I had deciphered the text, independently of that published by Müller (*A. I. C.* No. 143). It is hardly possible to admit the existence of two independent inscriptions having exactly the same defects both in the text and in the stone.

[2] Davy, *Interior of Ceylon*, pp. 467–73; Forbes, *Eleven years in Ceylon*, vol. i. p. 375; Tennent, *Ceylon*, vol. ii. p. 578; Burrows, *Buried Cities of Ceylon*, p. 20; Cave, *Ruined Cities of Ceylon*, pp. 122–3. For a complete topographical and historical account of the Daṁbulla Vihāra, see Lawrie's *Gazetteer of the Central Province of Ceylon*, pp. 121–30.

[3] By Prof. Rhys Davids in *Ind. Ant.*, vol. i. 1872, p. 139 and by Dr. Müller in *A. I. C.* No. 3. See below, pp. 141–2, for the identification of the king mentioned in it.

[4] With the next number of the *Epigraphia Zeylanica* I hope to issue a collotype facsimile of the inscription, the estampage now available not being good enough for the purpose.

about one inch. A comparison of them with the letters in the inscriptions of Mahinda IV[1] will show clearly the nature and degree of the development of the script in the course of nearly two centuries. The change is not very great, and is mostly noticeable in the akṣaras *a*, *i*, *ta*, *ma* and *ra*.

The **orthography** is quite accurate, and the **language** is, as far as I can judge, in keeping with the style of Kīrti Niśśaṅka Malla's other records; the first three lines, however, which are evidently adopted from some of the inscriptions of Parākrama Bāhu I, form an exception[2]. The phraseology of the records, from the eleventh century onwards, affords unmistakable proof of the strong influence of Sanskrit, due to the general revival of learning[3]. Some of the best and most esteemed Sinhalese authors flourished during this period, namely between the twelfth and the fifteenth centuries, in spite of the fact that Ceylon was then continually harassed by Malabar invasions and internal disturbances[4].

No **date** is given in this inscription of Kīrti Niśśaṅka Malla, or in any other record of his yet known to us, but from other sources the period of his reign can be fixed with tolerable accuracy.

According to all authorities he came to the throne in the second year after the death of Parākrama Bāhu I, the two intermediate kings, Vijaya Bāhu II and Mahinda VI, having held the sceptre only for one year and five days.

Now Parākrama Bāhu's inscription at Galvihāra in Poḷonnaruva states that he held a Buddhist synod at the expiration of 1708 A.B.[5] The *Nikāya-saṅgraha*[6], whilst confirming this date, adds that it was the fourth year of Parākrama Bāhu's reign, in which case his reign began in 1705 A.B. (1161 A.D.)[7].

---

[1] See plates 9, 14 and 15. Regarding the date of the accession of this king, which must fall between 1019 and 1029 A.D., see above, p. 80.

[2] Compare for example the Devanagala inscription, which begins:—*Sirivat apirivat* [for *apiriyat*] *levu ikut guṇa muḷin uturat muḷu Dam̃badivahi an Kät-kula pämili-kaḷa Okāvas rada parapuren baḷa*, &c. (*A. S. C. Report on the Kegalla District*, p. 75).

[3] Compare also the facts adduced, in connexion with the influence of Sanskrit on the dialects of India, in Dr. Franke's *Pali und Sanskrit*, pp. 55 ff., and Prof. Rapson's and Mr. Thomas' able papers on the subject of 'Sanskrit as a spoken language' in *J. R. A. S.*, 1904, pp. 445–52 and 467–70.

[4] See *Brit. Mus. Cat. of Sinhalese MSS.*, Introd. pp. xiv ff.

[5] That is 454 + 1254 A. B. expired. See *A. I. C.* No. 137.

[6] My edition of 1890, pp. 11, 20 and 22.

[7] Following the Ceylon tradition, which places the death of the Buddha not in 543 B.C. but in the middle of 544 B.C. I am indebted to Dr. Fleet for drawing my attention to this fact, which I have since verified as follows:—According to the Sinhalese *pañcāṅga*, the 13th of May, 1900 = the commencement of 2444 A.B. Therefore, the middle of 1 A.D. = the beginning of 545 A.B.; the middle of 1 B.C. = the commencement of 544 A.B.; and the middle of 544 B.C. = the commencement of 1 A.B.

At p. 20, however, we are told that he assumed sovereignty when 1696 years had elapsed since the demise of the Buddha, that is to say, about the middle of 1153 A.D. Both these dates can be accounted for by the fact that he was crowned twice, first as governor of a province[1], in succession to his father Kitti Sirimēgha, and the second time as paramount lord of the island, after he had brought all the other provinces under his rule, in the course of a campaign of about eight years duration[2].

Further evidence as to the period of Parākrama Bāhu's reign is afforded by a stone-inscription on the south wall of the Tiruvālīśvara temple at Ārpākkama, eight miles south-south-east of Conjeveram, dated the fifth year of the Cōḷa king Parakēśarivarman, *alias* Srī Rājādhirājadēva, who reigned approximately between 1146 and 1178 A.D.[3] This record makes mention of Laṅkāpura's campaign in the Pāṇḍya country, which, judging from the sequence of events in the *Mahāvaṁsa*, must have taken place in or after the sixteenth year of Parākrama Bāhu's reign. Counting the regnal years of this king from his first coronation in 1153 A.D., the Pāṇḍyan expedition falls in or soon after 1169 A.D., and this is well within the period of the Cōḷa king's reign, as deduced from quite independent sources.

We thus see that the dates derived from the contemporary record at Galvihāra in Poḷonnaruva and from the *Nikāyasaṅgraha* are fairly accurate, and that we are enabled from them to fix the date of the first coronation of Parākrama Bāhu I in 1153 A.D., the second coronation in 1161 A.D.[2], and his death after a reign of thirty-three years in 1186 A.D.[4]

Accordingly the date of the accession of king Kīrti Niśśaṅka Malla may be definitely placed in the first half of the year 1188 A.D., and the date of the present inscription between 1192 and 1197. This is clear from the fact that, as stated above, he ascended the throne in the second year after the death

---

[1] *Mv.* lxvii. 91–93.

[2] The *Mahāvaṁsa* (lxxii. 362) places the second coronation in the second year of the first. There is, therefore, a discrepancy of about six years between the two accounts.

[3] *Annual Report on Epigraphy* for 1898–9 (Government of Madras, Nos. 922–3, Public), §§ 34–7 and 54. This king is probably identical with Rājakēśarivarman, *alias* Rājādhirājadēva. See Kielhorn's *Supplement to the list of South Indian Inscriptions*, p. 24, No. 21.

[4] The accuracy of this last date is, moreover, proved by the fact that Sāhasa Malla's inscription (*A. I. C.* No. 156) gives 1743 A.B. expired (i.e. 1200 A.D.) as the year of his accession. Now, he came to the throne in the fourteenth year after the death of Parākrama Bāhu I. Therefore, the latter event must have taken place in 1186 A.D. Dr. Fleet states that the actual details of the date of Sāhasa Malla's anointment, given in the Poḷonnaruva inscription, are correct for Wednesday, August 23, 1200 A.D.

of Parākrama Bāhu I, his reign lasted only nine years, and, in the inscription at Ruvanväli Dāgaba (*A. I. C.* No. 145), of the fourth year of his rule, he makes no allusion whatever to his work at the Daṁbulla Vihāra, whilst in most of his other records the contrary is the case.

As regards the king himself, whose full name was **Śrī Saṅghabōdhi Kāliṅga Parākrama-Bāhu Vīrarāja Kīrti-Niśśaṅka-Malla Apratimalla Cakravartin**, we see from his inscriptions that he was the son of Śrī Jaya Gōpa, of the dynasty of the Cakravartins of Kaliṅga, then reigning at Siṁhapura. His mother was queen Pārvatī Mahādēvī [1]; he had two younger brothers, one of whom was king Vikrama Bāhu [2], successor of his son Vīra Bāhu; his two queens were Kāliṅga Subhadrā Mahādēvī and Gaṅgavaṁśa Kalyāṇa, who, as Kalyāṇavatī, held the sceptre of Ceylon for six years after Sāhasa Malla; his daughter was Sarvāṅgasundarī [3]; his son was Vīra Bāhu, who died on the day he succeeded his father to the throne [4], and his nephew (*bhāgineyyako*) was Cōḍa Gaṅga, who slew Vikrama Bāhu, and reigned for nine months, until in turn deposed by the powerful commander Kitti.

It will be seen from the above pedigree of Kīrti Niśśaṅka Malla that he most probably belonged to the dynasty of the Eastern Gaṅgas of the Kaliṅga country, reigning at Siṁhapura. I have not found, as yet, any reference in the Indian epigraphical records to his father, Śrī Jaya Gōpa; the latter may have been a petty Rājā, or he would hardly have allowed so many of his kith and kin to go and settle in Ceylon. But that the city of Siṁhapura was at one time a seat of the rulers of Kaliṅga may be judged from the Kōmarti plates of 'the Mahārāja Caṇḍavarman, the ruler of Kaliṅga,' recording a grant made at Siṁhapura in the sixth year of his reign. Dr. Hultzsch, in his article [5] on these plates, says that 'the city of Siṁhapura is perhaps identical with the modern Singupuram between Chicacole and Narasannapēṭa.'

From the earliest times there were frequent intermarriages between the royal houses of Ceylon and those of Kaliṅga and Pāṇḍya. In consequence, numbers of Indian princes and princesses, with their retinues, immigrated, from time to time, and settled in the island. They became merged in the Sinhalese people, and many held offices under successive kings. They regarded the country

---

[1] See Galpota record (*A. I. C.* No. 148). According to Sāhasa Malla's inscription at Poḷonnaruva (*A. I. C.* No. 156) Śrī Gōparāja of Kaliṅga, probably identical with Śrī Jaya Gōpa, had a second queen named Bahidālōka Mahādēvī whose son, Śrī Saṅghabōdhi Kāliṅga Vijaya Bāhu, came to the throne of Laṅkā as Sāhasa Malla, about four years after the death of Vīra Bāhu son of Kīrti Niśśaṅka Malla.

[2] *Mv.* lxxx. 28. [3] *A. I. C.* No. 148. [4] *Mv.* lxxx. 27. [5] *Ep. Ind.*, vol. iv. p. 143.

as theirs, and the nobles as members of their own race. But the attitude of those who came to the island about the time of Parākrama Bāhu I was evidently different. They seem to have been imbued with a strong national spirit. Their great desire was to keep the sceptre of the island in the hands of their leaders, and to make Ceylon a happy hunting-ground for their kith and kin from the Indian continent. They found the nobles of the Govi-kula, however—practically descendants of their own kinsmen—very powerful, and aspiring to the throne. To counteract this the sovereigns resorted to the well-known tradition of the Vijayan colonization of the island, and proclaimed to the Sinhalese people that they alone were the pure descendants of the race of Vijaya, and that for this reason, as also because they were defenders of the Buddhist religion, the throne of Laṅkā belonged to them and to no other clan. We see this expressly stated in the Galpota and the Daḷadā-Mandira records[1] of Kīrti Niśśaṅka Malla, the king mentioned in the inscription under discussion.

This king was a new arrival. He himself says in his Galpota inscription[2]

---

[1] *A. I. C.* No. 148, Galpota C, lines 21–23: 'Enemies to the doctrines of Buddha ought not to be installed in the island of Laṃkā which is appropriate to the Kāliṅga dynasty, for that would be like substituting a poison-tree for a wishing-tree; but if princes of the Kāliṅga race to whom the island of Laṃkā has been peculiarly appropriate since the reign of Wijaya be sought for and brought hither, they will prove worthy rulers and preserve the religion and the country. Aspire to attain the felicities of both worlds, reflecting that virtue doth conquer the universe. Future sovereigns are thus affectionately exhorted by Kāliṅga Niççaṃka, king of Ceylon.'

No. 149, Daḷadā-Mandira B, lines 8–36: 'Over our island of Ceylon which belongs to the religion of Buddha, non-buddhistical princes from Cola or Kerali or other countries must not be chosen; those who join them and make disturbances shall be called traitors.

'As the crow should not be compared to the swan, nor the donkey to the Arab, nor the worm to the cobra, nor the firefly to the sunshine, nor the snipe to the elephant, nor the jackal to the lion, so should no man of the Gowī tribe be greedy after the sovereignty; however powerful they may be the men of the Gowī tribe should not obtain the kingdom.

'Those who honour as a king servants like themselves with salutations and presents, or receive offices and titles from them, shall be called traitors; whenever a prince of wealth and family joins with such people he destroys himself. Therefore, if you look for and find a prince who has a right to Ceylon and is descended from the race of King Wijaya who first peopled Ceylon, take sides with such a ruler who will take care of religion and the prosperity of the world as if they were his two eyes; and so protect your own families and fortunes.

'As the crow may imitate the gait of the swan and the donkey the Arab steed, as the worm may imitate the cobra and the firefly the sunshine, as the jackal may imitate the lion and the snipe the elephant, so some other caste may emulate the conduct of kings; yet it will certainly not meet with respect but only with ridicule: thus speaks the wise and good king Niççaṃka Malla.'

[2] *A. I. C* No. 148, line 5. It is more probable that he was invited by the Kaliṅga princes

that he was 'invited by the king, who was his senior kinsman, to come and reign over his hereditary kingdom of Lak-diva,' and that he landed with a great retinue, and was duly installed in the office of āpā. The *Mahāvaṁsa* states further that he was the sub-king of Vijaya Bāhu, who was murdered, after a year's rule, at the instigation of a certain Mahinda of Kaliṅga. Kīrti Niśśaṅka Malla rose against the regicide, and, within five days, put him to death and ascended the throne.

He reigned at Poḷonnaruva for nine years. His inscriptions give exaggerated accounts of his prowess, his expedition to the Cōḷa and the Pāṇḍya kingdoms, not mentioned in the Sinhalese chronicles, and his philanthropic and religious acts. There is no doubt that he did everything he could to pacify the unrest prevailing at the time, and to win the people over to his side. He relinquished the revenue for five years, remitted taxes, repaired tanks and other irrigation works, restored inheritances to their rightful heirs, and made various grants of land, serfs, cattle, and money. He familiarized himself with the country and its administration by undertaking tours of inspection and holding durbars of ministers and other civil and military officials, including even municipal councillors [1]. By this means he was able to redress many grievances and do much to safeguard the lives and property of the people.

To commemorate his victorious campaign in Southern India, conducted by his general Lag Vijaya Siṁha, he caused pillars of victory and a Hindu temple (dēvālaya), named Niśśaṅkēśvara after himself, to be erected at Rāmēśvara [2].

His religious acts were many. He reconciled the monks of the three Nikāyas [3], established almshouses in the country and built in his capital city of Poḷonnaruva a beautiful temple for the 'Tooth-relic' and the Ruvanväli-dāgaba, eighty cubits high, which he surrounded with cells for priests and with walls having gateways. In the fourth year of his reign he proceeded to Anurādhapura, worshipped the Ruvanväli-dāgaba there, and effected many repairs to it, as well as to the Maricavaṭṭi and other Vihāras of the town, besides building very many new ones [4]. Subsequently King Kīrti Niśśaṅka Malla undertook similar pilgrimages to Devi-nuvara, Kälaṇi, Miyuguṇa, Daṁbulla and Adam's Peak, and did much to restore the sacred edifices of

---

at the Sinhalese Court, who were plotting to capture the throne for one of themselves. This is clear from the events which led to the accession of Kīrti Niśśaṅka Malla.

[1] See *A. I. C.* No. 146.

[2] See below, p. 134, lines 19–23.

[3] *Ibid.* Nos. 148, 152 and the present inscription.

[4] *A. I. C.* No. 145.

these places. To place on record these deeds, which were crowned by his magnificent work at Daṁbulla, he had the present inscription engraved on a rock close by the Vihāra, giving an account of himself and his pious acts. In the last two lines of the record we find the statement that he 'caused the reclining, sitting, and standing statues [of the Buddha] in the cave of Daṁbulla to be gilt, celebrated a great pūjā at a cost of seven lacs of money, and gave (to this cave) the name of Suvarṇa-giri-guhā 'golden rock-cave'[1].'

[1] The account in the *Mahāvaṁsa* (lxxx. 22–23) runs: 'He built the Jambukola Vihāra also with polished walls and pillars dazzling with gold and silver, the floor whereof was painted with vermilion and the roof covered with gilded tiles. And three and seventy gilded images of the Teacher did the wise king cause to be set up therein.' According to the *Pūjāvaliya* 'he covered the Daṁbulle Vehera with plates of gold; overlaid seventy-three large images with gold; and called it Rangiri-Daṁbulla.' About a century before this event, Vijaya Bāhu I effected repairs in the Vihāra (*Mv.* lx. 60–61).

To enable the reader to form a correct estimate of the above statements, I give here an excerpt from Dr. Davy's accurate description of the Temple as it was in 1819. Sir Archibald Lawrie says in his *Gazetteer of the Central Provinces of Ceylon*, Colombo, 1896, that this description is practically true to the present day, as very little of the Vihāra is changed.

'The Vihāra we first explored is the last in order from the entrance. It is about 54 ft. long and 27 wide; and its shelving roof, which dips rapidly inwards, where most lofty is about 27 ft. high. It contains ten figures of Buddha, and a neat dāgaba about 12 ft. high. The figures are well executed and brilliantly painted, and most of them are as large or larger than the ordinary size of man. The roof and sides of the rock and the front wall are painted of the brightest colours, and illuminated with a number of figures, chiefly of Buddha. The general effect of the whole is exceedingly striking and pretty.

'The next Vihāra, called the Alut Vihāra, is separated from the preceding partly by abutting rock and partly by a wall of masonry, in which there is a door of communication. Its principal entrance is by a door in front. We were taken by surprise on entering this Temple. We were astonished by its great size, the brilliant effect of an immense surface of rock painted of the richest colours, and by the numerous figures of Buddha which it contains, in different attitudes and groups, all coloured in the most lively manner. It is about 90 ft. long, 81 ft. wide, and its shelving roof, where highest, is about 36 ft. high. The figures which it contains are fifty in number. One statue of Buddha, in the recumbent posture, its head on a pillar resting on its right hand, is of gigantic size, about 30 ft. long and well proportioned; its face is handsome, and its expression of countenance remarkably placid and benignant. Seven other statues of Buddha, in the standing attitude, are about 10 ft. high, and all the rest are as large as life, or very little less. Most of them are coloured bright yellow; two or three have red robes, and reminded me of the two classes of Lamas in Tibet, described by Captain Turner, who are distinguished from each other by one wearing red and the other yellow garments. Towards the western end of the Temple there is a well-executed figure of King Kīrti Śrī, the last great benefactor of Daṁbulla, in his robes of state, which very much resemble those worn by the late king.

'Between this temple and the next there is no direct communication; I believe they are separated from each other by a stone wall. The portal by which you enter is in front; it is a lofty archway, guarded on each side by figures in stone, intended to represent Janitors. This temple, called the Mahārāja Vihāra, almost as much surpasses in size and effect the last, as that does the first described. It is about 190 ft. long, about 90 ft. wide, and 45 ft. high where highest; nor does obscurity add

In deciphering the inscription I had no other guide save the single estampage supplied to me by the Archaeological Commissioner of Ceylon. But after I had made out the text, I discovered that it was the one published

---

to its grandeur; for it is perfectly well lighted through numerous windows and several doors in front. It contains altogether fifty-three images, a handsome dāgaba, about 14 or 18 ft. high, the broad circular pedestal of which is ornamented with four figures of Buddha, each facing a different quarter, each seated on the coil of a cobra de capello, and shaded by its expanded hood. As in the two preceding temples, so in this, the images are arranged in a row at a little distance from the sides and inner walls of the room, but not grouped; and as in the last, none are placed near the outer wall, with the exception of the statues of two kings. At the western end of the temple the figures are arranged in a double row. The majority of the statues are Buddhas of different dimensions and in different attitudes; many of them larger, but none of them much, if at all, smaller than life. Besides forty-six figures of Buddha, there is, in company with them, one of Maitri Deiyo Rajjuruwo, who, it is imagined, will be the next Buddha, the successor of Gautama; and of each of the three gods Vishṇu, Saman and Nāta; the first in blue robes, the second in yellow, and the third in robes of white. The statues of the two kings alluded to above, as standing apart against the outer wall, are those of Waḷagam Bāhu and Nissaṅga, at opposite ends of the temple: the first, representing the earliest benefactor of Daṁbulla, is the rudest figure in every respect, and its dress is the simplest and least ornamented; the ears are long, and drawn down in the Malabar fashion; there is a double-headed snake about the neck, the body of which serves as a necklace and the heads as ear-pendants. At the eastern extremity of the temple there is a little recess formed by a high projecting rock, the walls of which are covered with paintings illustrating the history of Ceylon, beginning with the earliest and most fabulous period, and continued down to the introduction of the Bō-tree and the sacred relic. The exploits of Wijaya, the first king, make a conspicuous figure, and cover a great deal of space; more especially the voyage of this hero, which is represented by a boat surrounded by sea-monsters. The dedication of the Island to Buddha after the arrival of the relic is figured by a king guiding a plough drawn by a pair of elephants, attended by priests, &c.

. . . .

'The next and last temple, called the Devarāja Vihāra (because the god Vishṇu is supposed to have aided in the construction of its principal image), is very inferior in every respect to either of the preceding, especially the two last. It is about 75 ft. long, 21 ft. wide, and 27 ft. high, and so dark that I had only a very imperfect view of it, even with the aid of a lamp. It contains six images of Buddha and one of Vishṇu, all of them of ordinary size, with the exception of that just alluded to as the principal figure, which is a gigantic recumbent Buddha about 30 ft. long.

'Whether the cavern in which these temples have been formed is altogether natural, or partly natural and partly artificial, it is not now easy to determine. The probability is that it is principally natural, and that man has had very little to do in excavating it. I am not aware that history throws any light upon this point; and, indeed, it can hardly be expected that it should. All I have been able to collect amounts to this: that the Mahārāja Vihāra was commenced 1,924 years ago by Waḷagam Bāhu, during his retirement in this part of Matale, between the period of his defeat by the Malabars and the recovery of his capital; that it was repaired and embellished 627 years ago by King Nissaṅga, who is said to have laid out in ornamenting it 600,000 pieces of gold, but of what value is not known; and lastly, that the Alut Vihāra was formed sixty-four years ago by King Kīrti Śrī, by whom also the great Vihāra was again repaired. These temples are attached to the Asgiri Vihāra, and are under the care of seven resident priests.'

by Dr. Müller as No. 143 of his *Ancient Inscriptions in Ceylon.* Consequently I have made use of his text, plate, and translation as noted below. I have also consulted Armour's English version of the record, published both in Turnour's *Epitome* (Appendix) and in Forbes' *Eleven Years in Ceylon*, vol. ii. p. 578.

TEXT[1].

1 ශ්‍රී සිරිවත් අපිරියත් ලො ඉකුත් ගුණ මුළිනුතුරන් දඹදිව්හි අත් කැත් කුල
පාම්ලි කළ යසස පුලග කොටැ ලංකාව

2 මනුෂ්‍යාවාස කළ විජය රාජ පරම්පරායෙන් ආ ලක්දිව් පොළොයොන්
පරපුරෙන් හිමි නොමින් ගුණ ගැඹර තෙද නිසල

3 සොම් ගුණවත් දළදප් සත් සෙත් කුළුණුවත් යස සිරින් පුත් **වීර රාජ නිශ්ශංක**
මල්ල ලංකෙශ්වර කාලිඟ පරාක්‍රම

4 **බාහු චක්‍රවර්ත්තීන්** වහන්සේ උදා ගල් මුඳුන් පත් රිවි මඬුලුමෙන් සතුරඳුරු
දුරුලා සිරිලක එක් සැත් කොටැ පෙරැ නො

5 බ(ද) කරවූ වර දී මුළුවූ ලංකාවාසීන්ට පස් හවුරුද්දකට අය හැරැ දිවෙල්
වහල් සරක් පමුණු පරපුරු හා හවුරුදු

6 පතා පස් තුලාභාරයක් බැගින් රන් රුවන් මුතු රිදී ඈ නො එක් වස්තු හා දී දුසථ
ලංකාවාසීන් ස්වස්ථ කරවා තවද මතු

7 වන රජදරුවන් කරවූ වර ව(ඩා) ගෙනැ ලංකාවාසීන් දුසථ නොකළ මැනැවැයි
සිතා උතෙත්ත අමුණට අය එකමුණු තු

8 න් පැළ හා මඬරන් සක හා (මැදෙ) එකමුණු දෙ පැළ හා මඬරන් සතරක්
හා (පැසෙස) පස් පැළ හා මඬරන් තුනක් බැවින් අ

9 ය ගන්නා නියායෙන් හා කැ(තැ අය කොටු කණ්බ අය මඤ වජ්‍ර) ජීවිකා ගෙසින්
හැමැ කලට මැ නො ගන්නා නියා

10 යෙන් (හා) ව්‍යවස්ථා කොටැ දස්කම් කළවුනට (දෙන) ගිර සඳ පමුණු (වෙ)යන්
මියණිසින් සොපද්‍රව (වූ තල්) පතැ ලියා දිගෙ (ගැ)

11 ඤී ගිරි සෙ නො කොටැ උන් උන්ගෙ වංශානුගත වැ බොහො කල් පවත්නා
නියායෙන් තම්බ පතැ පමුණු හසුන් ලියවා දී තාම්බ්‍ර

12' ශාසන පවත් කරවා ලංකාව තුන් යාලක් පැදකුණු කොටැ ගම් නියම්ගම්
රාජධානි ද ගිරිදුර්ග්ග වනදුර්ග්ග ජල

13 දුර්ග්ග පංකදුර්ග්ග ද අත(ම්බු)ල් ප(ක)ක් සෙ බලා ගැනියකුදු අනැඟි රුවනක්
ගෙනැ යන කලැ කුමක්දපි නො කිය

14 න නියායෙන් ගම්වල් නිෂ්කණ්ටක කොටැ මෙ ලක්දිව සෙමෙහි තබා (ච)ඤ
පුබාශායෙන් **සාහිරම** දෙවරක් වැඩැ හය

---

[1] For various readings, see the transcript.

15 පත්වූ පාණ්ඩ්‍යරාජයන් එවූ රාජ කන්‍යාවන් හා හස්ත්‍යශ්වාදි පඬු(රු හා) ගෙනැ
චොඩ ගෞඩා දී නො එක් දෙශයෙහි ගුණ්ණ කැ

16 මැඩ රජදරුවන් හා ගුණෙණින් ශ්‍රී සන්ථාන කොටැ ගුණ්ණ නො කැමැත්තවුනට
තමන්වහන්සෙගෙ ශෞර්ය්‍යාතිශයෙන් මැ භය (එළ)

17 (වා) එ එ රටින් කිසොවරුන් හා පඬුරු ගෙණා මුළු දඹදිවැ ද ප්‍රතිමල්ල
රාජයන් නැති හෙයින් රාමෙශ්වරයෙහි වැඩැ ගිඅැ

18 තුලාභාර වස්තු දානයෙන් (.. .. නොසල) මුළු දළිඳුන් පින් පුරා එතන්හි
බොහො කලක් පවත්නා නියායෙන් ජය සතම්

19 (හ කොටැ නිශ්ශංකෙශ්වරයැ)යන දෙවාලයක් නාවා සිඬුරන් සෙනග පිරිවරා
නැවැත ලක්දිවූ වැඩැ පිවතැ සතුරන් නැති බැ

20 චිත් (දිනුවමනාකෙළෙස්) සතුරන් (වෙදපි) සිතා දඹදිවැ ලක්දිවැ නො එක්
තන්හි සත්‍ර නංවා තිර තුරුවූ දන්වතු

21 (දි) .. .. (පින්පුරා) බොහො කල් ගිනහව තුබූ තුන් නිකාහි
සඟුරුවන් සමඟ කරවා තෙවළා බුදු වදළ බජන

22 [කරවා] .. .. (ඇතුලත් බාහිර) ශාස්ත්‍ර ද පවත් කරවා පෙර රජ්(ජුවසැ)
දුශ්පරිගා(ණ්)යෙනැයි ගිය වෙහෙර මහ සෑ

23 .. .. (අනු)රාධපුරනුවර දෙවි(නු)වර (කැ)ලණි මියුගුණ (ඇ නො එක්)
වෙහෙර කරවා අනන්ත වස්තු (ත්‍යාගකොට) .. ..

24 (ක)රවා (.. .. .. දඹුලුලෙණැ හොත් හුන්) සිටි පිළිම වෙහෙරව (ප)
.. .. (ඝන) රන්මය කරවා (ස)

25 ත් ලක්ෂයක් ධන වියදම් කොටැ මහ පූද කරවා සුවර්ණගිරිගුහායැයි නම් තබා
කරවා වදාළ ශිලාලෙඛයයි

TRANSCRIPT.

1 Śrī sirivat apiriyat lo ikut guṇa muḷin-uturat Dambadivuhi an Kät-kula pāmili kaḷa yakṣa praḷaya koṭā Laṁkāva

2 manuṣyāvāsa kaḷa Vijaya-rāja-paramparāyen ā Lak-div-poḷoyon-parapuren himi nomin guṇa gämbara teda nisala

3 somi-guṇavat[1] daḷadap sat set kuḷuṇu-vat[2] yasa sirin yut **Vīra-rāja Niśśaṁka-Malla Laṁkeśvara Kāliṅga Parākrama-**

4 **Bāhu Cakravarttin**-vahansē udā-gal mundun pat rivi-maṇḍulu-men satur-anduru durulā siri Laka ek-sät koṭā perā no

5 ba(da) karavu-vara dī muḷa-vū Laṁkāvāsīnṭa pas havuruddakaṭa aya hārā divel vahal sarak pamuṇu[3] parapuru hā havurudu

---

[1] Mt. *nisal somiguṇa panad .. udapa.* [2] Mt. *kulaṇu dan.* [3] Mt. *pamuṇa* ; Mp. *samuṇu.*

6 patā pas tulā-bhārayak bägin ran ruvan mutu ridī ā no ek vastu hā dī dustha Laṁkāvāsīn svastha karavā tavada matu-

7 -vana raja-daruvan karavu-vara va(ḍā) genä Laṁkāvāsīn dustha no kaḷa mänäväyi sitā utte amuṇaṭa aya ek-amuṇu tu-

8 -n pāḷa hā maṇḍaran saka[1] hā (mände) ek-amuṇu de-päḷa hā maṇḍaran satarak hā (pässe) pas-pāḷa hā maṇḍaran tunak bävin a-

9 -ya gannā niyāyen hā kä(tä aya keṭu kaṇaba aya manda vajra)[2] jīvikā-heyin hämä kalaṭa-mä no gannā niyā-

10 -yen (hā) vyavasthā koṭä das[3]-kam kaḷavunṭa (dena) hira sanda pamuṇu (ve)yan-mīyan-visin sopadrava(-vū tal-)patā liyā diye (hä-)

11 -ndi hiri-se no koṭä un-unge vaṁśānugata[4]-vä boho kal pavatnā niyāyen tamba-patā pamuṇu hasun liyavā dī tāmbra

12 śāsana pavat-karavā Laṁkāva tun yālak pädakuṇu koṭä gam niyam-gam rājadhāni da giri-durgga vana-durgga jala-

13 durgga paṁka-durgga da at-aṁbul pa(ka)k-se balā gāniyakudu anäṅgi ruvanak genä yana kalä kumak-dayi no kiya-

14 -na niyāyen gam val niṣkaṇṭaka koṭä me Lak-diva semehi tabā (dva)nda-[5] yuddhāśāyen **Pāṇḍī-raṭa** de-varak väḍä bhaya-

15 -patvū Pāṇḍya-rājayan evū rāja-kanyāvan hā hasty-aśv-ādi paṇḍu(ru[6] hā) genä **Coḍa Gauḍ**-ādi no ek deśayehi guṇa kä-

16 -mäti rajadaruvan hā guṇen mitra santhāna koṭä guṇa no kämättavunṭa taman-vahansege śauryyātiśayen-mä bhaya (eḷa)-

17 (-vā) e e raṭin bisovarun hā paṇḍuru genvā muḷu Dambadivä da pratimalla-rājayan näti heyin **Rāmeśvarayehi** väḍä hindä

18 tulābhāra vastu dānayen (..[7] .. no saḷa) muḷu diḷindun sit purā etanhi boho kalak pavatnā niyāyen jaya-stam-

19 (-bha koṭä Niśśaṁkeśvarayä)-yana devālayak naṁvā sivuraṅg senaṅga pirivarā näväta[8] Lakdivu[9] väḍä piṭatä saturan näti bä-

20 -vin (dinuvamanā[10] keḷes) saturan (ve-dayi) sitā Dambadivä Lakdivä no ek tanhi satra naṁvā niraturu-vū dan-vatu

21 (dī) .. .. (pin purā) boho kal bhinnava[11] tubū tun nakāhi saṅgu-[12] -ruvan samaṅga karavā Tevaḷā Budu[13]-vadan da bajana

---

[1] Mt. and Mp. *sāka*. [2] Mt. *kāti aya da kaṭu kaṇabā aya daku vajra*. [3] Mt. *dasa*.

[4] Mt. *vaṁśānuyāta*. [5] Read *dvandva*-. [6] Mt. °*rā*. [7] Mt. *ese no saḷa*.

[8] Mt. *nävätā*. [9] Mt. °*diva*. [10] Mt. *ramaṇī* . . . . . . *sasaturan äva da yi*.

[11] Mt. *hinnava*. [12] Mt. *saturuvan*. [13] Mt. *Buduva danda vedā na*.

22 [karavā] .. .. (ätulat bāhira) śāstra da pavat karavā perä raju(n davasä) duṣpariha(ṇi-)-yen näsī giya vehera maha-sā

23 .. .. (Anu)rādhapura-nuvara Devi-(nu)vara (Kā)laṇi Miyuguṇa (ā no ek) vehera karavā ananta vastu (tyāga koṭa) .. ..

24 (ka)ravā (. .. .. Dambulu[1]-leṇä hot hun) siṭi piḷima veheraṭ (pa)[2] . .. . (ghana) ranmaya karavā (sa-)

25 -t lakṣayak dhana viyadam koṭā maha puda karavā **Suvarṇṇa-giri-guhā-**-yäyi nam tabā karavā vadāḷa śilā-lekhayayi[3]

TRANSLATION.

[Lines 1–4] Hail! The illustrious monarch **Vīrarāja Niśśaṅka-Malla Laṅkēśvara Kāliṅga Parākrama-Bāhu Cakravartin**[4], abounding in a multitude of virtuous qualities, which are pre-eminent in the boundless world; lord by (right of his) lineal descent from the lords[5] of the soil of the island of Laṅkā, who were descended from the race of King Vijaya, that threw into shade the other Kṣatriya races of Daṁbadiva[6], and that made Laṅkā a habitation for man by extirpating the Yakṣas; [His Majesty] who is gloriously endowed with qualities which are manifold, deep, majestic, unchangeable, and gentle, haughty, (yet) full of sympathy for the happiness of living beings, dispersed his enemies, just as the (brilliant) orb of the sun, which has risen above the summit of the mountain[7] of the morn, dispelleth darkness, and brought the prosperous Laṅkā under one canopy (of dominion).

[Lines 5–6] He [thereafter] relinquished the revenue for five years in

---

[1] Mt. . . . *härajthi da gal . . no hot hun siṭi.*

[2] Mt. *paḍeka . . sana ranmaya.*

[3] The whole of this line is transcribed from Müller's text, the estampage supplied by the Archaeological Survey being imperfect.

[4] For this king's full name, as given in the Galpota inscription (*A. I. C.* No. 148), the two titles Śrīsaṅghabōdhi and Apratimalla should be added to the above list. In Ceylon historical works he is commonly referred to by his shorter title Kīrti Niśśaṅka Malla. The above high-sounding epithets may be translated:—'the heroic and fearless royal warrior, lord of Laṅkā and the mighty-armed emperor of the Kaliṅga (dynasty).'

[5] *Lak-div-polоyоn.* See above, p. 26, note 10.

[6] Skt. *Jambudvīpa*, India.

[7] *Udà-gal* = Skt. *udaya-giri.*

favour of those inhabitants of Laṅkā who had become impoverished by the payment aforetime of inordinate taxes. By gifts of *divel*-lands, serfs, and cattle, by restoring permanent grants and inheritances [1], and by annual donations of wealth, five times (his) weight in the balance, consisting of gold, precious stones, pearls, silver, &c., he enriched those inhabitants of Laṅkā who were in straitened circumstances.

[Lines 7-9] Moreover, from a desire that succeeding kings should not (again) impoverish the inhabitants of Laṅkā, by levying excessive imposts, he ordained that the revenue should be collected (only) at the rate of one *amuṇa* and three *pāḷas* and six *maṅḍarans* [2] for an *amuṇa* (extent of land) of the best (soil) [3], one *amuṇa* and two *pāḷas* and four *maṅḍarans* for (an *amuṇa* extent of land) of medium (quality), and five *pāḷas* and three *maṅḍarans* for that of the last (quality). Since 'those who laboured with the bill-hook in clearing thorny jungles (for cultivation) earned their livelihood distressfully' [4] they should be always exempt from taxation.

[Lines 10-11] He also made it a rule that when perpetual grants [5] of land were made to those who had done loyal services, such benefactions should not be made evanescent, like lines drawn upon water, by being written on palm leaves liable to be destroyed by mice and white ants; but that they should be engraved on plates of copper, so as to endure long unto their respective posterity.

[Lines 12-16] Thrice he made the circuit of Laṅkā. He examined the villages, the towns and cities (thereof, and explored) the mountain and the forest fastnesses [6], as well as those surrounded by water and by marshes. So much so, that he had as precise a view (of the whole of Laṅkā) as if it were a ripe

---

[1] Cf. also the charitable acts of Vijaya Bāhu on his accession to the throne the year before Niśśaṅka (*Mv.* lxxx. 4).

[2] '*Maḍaran*,' according to Forbes, signifies 'a fine paid by a cultivator to a proprietor of land on receiving it for cultivation' (vol. ii. p. 351).

[3] Müller translates *uite amuṇa*, *mānde amuṇa* and *pässe amuṇa*, by 'the first *amuṇa*, the middle *amuṇa* and the last *amuṇa*.' This hardly gives sense. I think, therefore, Forbes is correct in taking these terms to be the classification of fields according to their fertility (l.c.).

[4] The letters on my estampage not being clear, I am not able to decipher this passage satisfactorily. This is the rendering given both by Forbes (l.c.) and Müller (*A. I. C.* p. 125). The idea seems to be that all *ċhena* cultivation should be free from taxation. See this king's Galpota inscription (*A. I. C.* No. 148 A, line 18).

[5] *Hira-sanda-pamuṇu* = grants which are in force so long as the sun and moon exist.

[6] *Durga* = lit. a place difficult of approach.

nelli-fruit[1] in his hand. And he freed the villages and wildernesses of lawlessness so thoroughly that even a woman might carry a precious jewel, and not be asked 'What is it?' (Thus) did he keep this Island of Laṅkā in a peaceful state. Then, with a desire for war[2], he twice invaded the **Pāṇḍya** country and accepted, as tributes (of homage), the royal maidens and also the elephants, horses, &c., sent by the terrified kings of the Pāṇḍyas. He, moreover, established[3] friendly alliances with such of the princes of **Cōḍa, Gauḍa** and of many other countries as were desirous of (his) goodwill; but unto those who did not wish such friendship he struck terror by the very superiority of his own valour.

[Lines 17–19] He exacted from such kingdoms princesses, together with (other) tributes (of homage) and, as then there remained no hostile kings in the whole of Daṁbadiva, he tarried at **Rāmēśvara.** Here he made donations of wealth equal to his weight in the balance and filled (with satisfaction) the hearts of all the poor. He had pillars of victory set up there as lasting monuments[4] and he caused a temple (*dēvālaya*) named **Niśśaṅkēśvara** to be built.

[Lines 19–23] Thereafter, escorted by (his) fourfold army, he returned to the Island of Laṅkā. Then, reflecting that since he had (now) no external enemies, he (should conquer) the [internal] enemies[5] of evil passions, he caused almshouses to be erected at many places in Daṁbadiva and in the Island of Laṅkā, and also had alms distributed constantly. . . . He reconciled the clergy of the three Nikāyas[6], that had been separated for a long time, honoured the word of the Buddha (as contained) in the Tripiṭaka, and promoted science. . . . (He restored also) the Vihāras and Dāgabas which had fallen into ruin in consequence of the calamities that had befallen (the land) during the days

[1] *At-ambul* = Skt. *hastāmalaka*, 'the fruit of the Myrobalan in the hand,' a simile used by Sanskrit writers for something quite clear or palpable.

[2] *Dvanda-yuddha* for *dvandva-yuddha* = lit. 'duel' or 'single combat.'

[3] *Santhāna* for *saṁsthāna*.

[4] Lit. 'so as to last a long time.'

[5] Cf. *yuddhaṁ kilēsacōrēhi karissāmi sudujjayaṁ*. 'I will wage a war very difficult to win, with the robber bands of evil passions' (*Mv.* xxvi. 3). This is undoubtedly the sentiment expressed here. It is repeated in this king's other inscriptions as follows:—(a) *pitatā saturan [illegible] me [illegible] dinurāmana kelesa saturan vedayi sitā* (*A. I. C.* No. 147, Thūpārāma, viii, lines 2–3); (b) *[illegible] saturan [illegible] paralovā saturan danumhayi sitā* (*A. I. C.* No. 148, Galpota B, line 21). The letters in my estampage are too faint to make out every word in the passage with absolute certainty.

[6] Namely, the Mahāvihāra, the Abhayagiri and the Jētavana fraternities. See *Mv.* lxxviii. 20 27.

of former kings. . . . (Moreover) he built many Vihāras in **Anurādhapura, Devi-nuvara, Kälani, Miyuguṇa,** &c., and made donations of vast riches.

[Lines 24–25] He caused (the reclining, sitting and) standing statues [of the Buddha] in the cave of **Daṁbulla** to be gilt, ... celebrated a great *pūjā* at a cost of seven lacs of money, and gave (to this cave) the name of **Suvarṇa-giri-guhā** 'golden rock-cave.' (To this effect) the rock-inscription was executed and proclaimed.

No. 10. RIṬIGALA INSCRIPTIONS

THE 'hill-range' of Riṭigala, towering as it does above the surrounding flat country, with forest-clad slopes and lofty peaks, is conspicuous from whatever side you enter Māṭambuvā Kōraḷe. Its commanding position about twenty-five miles south-east of Anurādhapura, the ancient capital, and eighteen miles north-east of Daṁbulla, as well as the shelter which its numerous rocks and caves afford, may account for its importance in ancient times, both as a stronghold of contending clans and as a place of refuge for fugitive princes and religious devotees. The very name of the mountain seems to emphasize this idea, for *riṭi-gala* means 'a safety-rock', *riṭi* being a derivative of the Sanskrit *ariṣṭi*. In the *Mahāvaṁsa* it is called *ariṭṭha-pabbata*, and this identification is confirmed by Mr. Bell's discovery of the name *ariṭa-gama* in two of the inscriptions found in the place, one at Kuḍā-arambädda-hīnna and the other at Vēväl-tänna. *Ariṭṭha-pabbata* may, of course, mean 'the mountain of Ariṭṭha', considering that a prince named Mahā-Ariṭṭha, a nephew of king Dēvānampiya Tissa, played an important part in the latter's reign (*circa* 247–207 B.C.).[1]

Owing to the belief prevalent amongst the ignorant villagers in the neighbourhood, that Riṭigala is even now infested by Yakṣas, few dare approach the place in search of honey or game, for fear of incurring the wrath of the demons.

[1] Cf. *Mv.* xvi. 10–11; xviii. 3; xix. 12, 65. See also Windisch's interesting note on the meaning of the expression *mahā-ariṭṭhako maṇi*, occurring in the Mārasaṁyutta (par. 2) of the Saṁyutta-nikāya (*Z. D. M. G.* xlix. pp. 285–6). For the date of Dēvānampiya Tissa's reign, see below, p. 143.

As a consequence the whole mountain-range remained more or less untrodden, except by a few officials and one or two botanists, until the Archaeological Commissioner (Mr. H. C. P. Bell) explored it 'from end to end' in 1893 and discovered numerous rock-caves and ruins, as well as many inscriptions. A full account of his exploration is given in his annual report for 1893[1].

As mentioned above, Mr. Bell's discovery of the occurrence of the name of *arița-gama* in two of the inscriptions settles the identity of Rițigala with Arițțha-pabbata (or -sēla) in Pāli writings, especially as no other mountain is known to have had this appellation. All notices of Rițigala or Arițțha-pabbata in Sinhalese works must, therefore, refer to this mountain.

A manuscript *kaḍa-im-pota*, 'boundary-book', in the Colombo Museum Library gives the following curious account :—

Rițigal nam parvatayeka. Kalukohovila pokunak äta. Ehi purā-tana pūḍāvek ratran vamāraunēya. Ema Rițigala sat-ruvan uṇa-paňdurak äta. Tudas maha raṭa kiḍa-imaḷa lakṣayak akṣara keṭū śilā-stambhayan siv-diga pihiṭuvana laddēya.

'There is a mountain by the name of Rițigal wherein is a pond containing *kalu-kohovila* plants. A leech in it formerly disgorged gold. In the same Rițigala there is a seven-gemmed bamboo bush[2]. At the four quarters are planted monoliths, which are inscribed with a lac of characters, for the purpose of marking the boundaries of the fourteen great territories.'

In the *Samantakūṭa-vaṇṇanā*[3], a thirteenth-century Pāli poem on Adam's Peak by Vēdēha Thēra, Rițigala is mentioned, amongst other historic moun-

[1] *Ceylon Sessional Papers*. xxxviii, 1904, pp. 8–10.

[2] Cf. *Dv*. xi. 15.

[3] vv. 516–17 of the Colombo edition of 1890:

Rammē tadā Ratanadīpa-varamhi Laṅkā-
Lōkābhidhāna-Harikaṇḍaka-Yakkhadāsē
Ōdumbarē Sumanakūṭaka-Taṇḍuleyyē
Sēlēsu Māragiri-Missaka-'Riṭṭha-nāmē

Ye 'ññē pi santi girayō vana-rāmaṇeyyā
Gaṅgā nadī giri-guhā sikatā talā ca
Tatthārasanti rabhasā pharusātiruddā
Pāṇātipāta-niratā saṭha-kūṭa-yakkhā.

'At that time the Yakṣas, who were wicked, abusive, very cruel, and cunning, and who were continually engaged in taking away animal life, haunted the mountains Laṅkā [Lag-gala], Lōka [Log-gala], Harikaṇḍaka [Hirikaḍa], Yakkhadāsa [Yakdessā-gala], Ōdumbara [Dimbulā-gala], Sumana-kūṭa [Adam's Peak], Taṇḍuleyya, Māra-giri [Māragala], Missaka [Mihintale], Ariṭṭha [Riṭigala], and such other rocks which grace the woods and [they haunted also] rivers and streams, rock-caves and sandy plains of the delightful Island of Gems (Ceylon).'

tains, as one of the haunts of the aborigines of Ceylon, named Yakṣas, at the time of the supposed first visit of Gōtama Buddha to Ceylon, in the ninth year after his attainment of Buddhahood (*circa* 519 B.C.).

The *Mahāvaṁsa* (x. 63–72) gives a quaint description of a battle which took place on the mountain between Paṇḍukābhaya and his uncles (*circa* 377 B.C.), in which the former received the help of the Yakṣas. The following is Turnour's translation of the passage in question :—

'Conducting her [i.e. Cētiyā, a female Yakṣa] to the Dhūmarakkha mountain, he obtained a great accession of warlike power by making her his battle-steed. There, at the Dhūmarakkha mountain, he maintained his position for four years.

'Departing from thence with his forces, he repaired to the mountain Ariṭṭha. There, preparing for the impending war, he remained seven years.

'Leaving two uncles (Abhaya and Girikaṇḍaka), the other eight uncles, uniting in hostility against him, approached that mountain Ariṭṭha. Throwing up a fortification at Nagaraka, and conferring the command (on the person selected), they surrounded the Ariṭṭha mountain on all sides.

'The prince having consulted with the *yakkhiṇī*, in conformity with her advice he sent forward a strong party (in the character of a deputation), placing in their charge his insignia of royalty, as well as the usual offerings made as tribute and his martial accoutrements: and enjoined them to deliver this message (from him): "Take all these things: I will come to ask your forgiveness." And they (the enemy) were lulled to security, thinking "We will seize him when he enters our camp": then the prince, mounting his *yakkha* mare, and surrounded by his whole army threw himself into the midst of the fight. The *yakkhiṇī* set up a loud shout. His (the prince's) army without, as well as (the deputation) within (the enemy's camp) answered with a tremendous roar. The whole of the prince's army having slaughtered many of the enemy's men, as well as the eight uncles, they made a heap of their (decapitated) heads. The commander (of the enemy's army) having fled, and concealed himself in a forest, from that circumstance that forest is called the *Senāpati* (commander's) forest.

'Observing the skulls of his eight uncles surmounting the heap of heads, he remarked: "It is like a heap of *labu* fruit." From this circumstance (that place) was (from Nagaraka) called Lābugāma.

'Thus this Paṇḍukābhaya, the victorious warrior, from thence proceeded to the capital of his maternal great uncle Anurādha.'

The Yakṣas of Riṭigala were afterwards much favoured by this king. He conferred high offices on them and treated them respectfully. But with the increase of the Sinhalese population and the establishment of Buddhism, Yakṣas seem to have lost their influence, and Riṭigala, their stronghold, became a suitable spot to build Vihāras on. Thus king Sūra Tissa, who reigned *circa* 187–177 B.C.[1], built the Laṅkā Vihāra at the foot of the Ariṭṭha mountain[2]. In the following century king Lajji (or Lañja) Tissa (*circa* 59–49 B.C.)[1] erected 'the Ariṭṭha and the Kandarahīnaka Vihāras[3].'

Nearly a thousand years later, Sēna I (*circa* 897–917 A.D.)[4] 'built, as it were by a miracle, a great Vihāra at Ariṭṭha-pabbata, and endowed it with great possessions, and dedicated it to the Paṃsukūlika brethren. And he gave to it also royal privileges and honours, and a great number of keepers for the garden, and servants, and artificers[5].'

These statements in Sinhalese and Pāli works, as to the ancient importance of Riṭigal-danavva, receive ample support from the ruins and inscriptions found in the place. According to Mr. Bell's account, the latter consist of more than thirty-two cave and rock records. Of these I am able to deal here with the following only:—

I. Āṇḍiyā-kanda[6].

Ten cave-inscriptions on caves Nos. 314–323.

[1] Cf. the dates in the accompanying genealogical table. [2] *Mv*. xxi. 6.
[3] *Ibid*. xxxiii. 27. [4] See below, p. 158. [5] *Mv*. l. 63–64.
[6] Mr. Bell's account of this 'east spur of Riṭigala' runs:—

'There are a score or more [caves], and all lie beneath boulders within a quarter of a mile radius, but at different levels—the fall in some cases being steep. The caves, as a whole, are far the finest yet explored in the North-Central Province.

'Cave 19. A magnificent natural cavern formed by a long boulder rock, 56 ft. in height, which on the south rests on lower flattish rock, leaving an open space beneath, 96 ft. in length by 27 ft. wide, widening to about 50 ft. The cave fronts N.E. and also S.E., where the roof ends in a high point. Under part of the cave are remains of a small brick and mud-built room.

'Cave No. 10. A detached boulder rock (nearly 80 yards in circuit), which overhangs on three sides. The shelter below was divided into at least four or five rooms for the *Wanawása* priests, who once occupied these caves.

'Of the twenty-one caves noted more than half have inscriptions, some of great palaeographical interest.

'That of Cave No. 9 is historically valuable: it is among the few (like that at Dambulla) distinctly connected with a royal donor, one of the earliest kings. It runs:—*Devanapiya Maha Rajha Gamaṇi Tisaha puta Devanapiya Tisa A* [*baha*] *leṇe agata anagata chadu* [sic] *disa sagasa leṇe*, "Cave of Tisa A [baya], beloved of the gods, nephew (lit. son) of the great King, beloved of the gods, Gamini Tisa [is granted to] the monks from the four quarters, present and absent." This record may well belong to Waṭṭagámiṇi Abaya (104 B.C.), and his uncle, the great ruler Duṭṭhagámiṇi (161 B.C.).' See *A. S. C. Report for* 1893, p. 9.

II. Karaṁbā-hīnna [1].

One out of two cave-inscriptions.

III. Nā-ulpata [2], called also Nā-arambädda-hīnna.

One cave-inscription and three rock-inscriptions.

IV. Vēväl-tänna [3].

One cave-inscription and one rock-inscription.

I. Āṇḍiyā-kanda Cave-inscriptions (pl. 18).

These consist of ten records, each inscribed on the brow of a cave below the 'drip-line,' in Brāhmī script of the first and second centuries B.C.

It will be seen from the accompanying plate, No. 18, that the **letters**, though on the whole they resemble those of the Vessagiri cave records [4], yet exhibit forms which, on palaeographic grounds, seem to belong to different periods. According to the antiquity of these types and their occurrence in each record, I have arranged and numbered the inscriptions on the plate.

The **letters** in No. 1 are mostly of Aśōka type. There is no general shortening [5] of vertical strokes, or the thickening of their upper ends or undue elongations of their lower ends, such as is noticeable in later records. Many

[1] This is the north-west spur of Riṭigala. The two caves are 'under one boulder, each with an inscription below its "drip-line"' (*Ibid.* p. 8).

[2] The following is Mr. Bell's account of this site, on the west and south-west spur of the mountain:—

'Kuḍā-arambędda-hīnna. There are more than a dozen caves scattered among the boulders, mostly to the west of the [Nā-ulpata] ęla. Six at least have inscriptions.

'On the top of the boulder, beneath which is cave No. 14, are cut four important inscriptions, confirming the "Mahāwaṇsa" record. One reads:—[*La*]*jaka Tisa maharaḥ vihara kararaya Abadaḷuka vari saga dini*, "The Maharaja Lajaka Tisa caused [this] viháré to be built [and] bestowed on the monks the Abadaluka tank." A second runs:—*Gamaṇi Abayi kubara saga dini*, "[King] Gamaṇi Abaya bestowed the [tract of] fields on the monks." In a third occurs the ancient name of Riṭigala ("*Ariṭa*").

'These records of the first and second century B.C. belong to Lajji Tisa (119–109 B.C.) and his younger and more famous brother Waṭṭagámaṇi Abhaya (104–76 B.C.)' (*Ibid.* p. 9). Compare, however, my article on them at pp. 147–9, which places their date in the second or third century A.D.

[3] 'The high valley, lying between Riṭigala and the somewhat lower eastern spur, parallel and connected, known as Áṇḍiyá-kanda.

'The *tęnna* is the small hill-girt flat valley two miles up from "Banḍá Pokuṇa." Not more than a quarter of a mile in breadth at its centre, it narrows down at the south end; and here, and at the north, the descent is steep. In length it may be three-quarters of a mile. It is strewn with countless boulders, except about the centre, where the ground may have been anciently utilized for a Buddhist temple' (*Ibid.* p. 10).

[4] See above, plates 5 and 6.

[5] Except in the case of the cerebral *ṇ*.

of the characters closely resemble those in the Girnār and Siddāpura edicts of Aśōka. Some, such as *ga*, *ma*, *śa*, *sa*, are more or less like those of Jaugaḍa and Kālsi, whilst *ṇi*, *ṇa*, and *pa* seem to agree with the types in Ghasundi and Bhaṭṭiprolu records. In *ra* a slight thickening of the top is noticeable. The examples of *ya* definitely confirm Bühler's theory[1] that the vertical line and the curve of this particular type were written separately. The angular form of medial *i*, and the manner in which this vowel and *e* are attached to vertical strokes, point to their antique character.

All these facts, coupled with the absence of younger forms of *ta*, *la*, *ha*, and especially of the secondary form of *ma* peculiar to Ceylon, namely ʊ[2], all of which occur both in the Tōnigala and in the Vessagiri inscriptions, would compel us to give this record a date anterior to 200 B.C., but for the mention of two kings, **Devanapiya Maharaja Gamiṇi Tisa** and his son **Devanapiya Tisa A(baya)**, who, as I shall show further on, must have reigned in the first century B.C. This confirms the fact, already noticed by palaeographists, both Indian and European, that in epigraphical records the alphabet employed is often more archaic in type than that of other writings of the same period[3].

The inscriptions Nos. 2-7 still retain nearly all the archaic forms discussed above, though the akṣara *ma* in Nos. 2 and 6 has a more open top, and *da* in No. 5 a more angular form. The akṣaras *a*, *ca* and *sa*, too, vary a little from those in No. 1.

The inscriptions Nos. 8–10, on the other hand, contain several advanced types of letters. These are the secondary forms of *ma*, the slightly angular *da* and *ṭha*, and, in No. 10, *le* with a short vertical stroke. Note also that the akṣara *bha* in No. 10 has its top vertical line on the left instead of on the right, nearly resembling the one in the Bhaṭṭiprolu record.

Differences such as these exist even in the Aśōka inscriptions, but their repeated occurrence in Nos. 8–10 is a sufficient proof of the later date of these records, as compared with Nos. 1–7. In any case they cannot, I think, be later than the **second half of the first century**, B.C.

As regards peculiarities in **orthography, phonology** and **grammar**, the present records fully agree with those of the Vessagiri caves, as noticed above on pp. 14-16. Their **phraseology**, too, is alike, and shows a marked resemblance to that of the early cave-inscriptions of India, one of their favourite expressions being *catu-disa sagasa dine*, which M. Senart has rightly translated

---

[1] *Indische Palaeographie*, p. 36. See also above, p. 14.
[2] Cf. also the old Burmese *ma*. See Bühler's *Indische Palaeographie*, p. 30, par. 14.

'given to the universal saṅgha[1],' without distinction of sect. Most of the proper names, also, are to be met with in Indian lithic records. The word *bata* in Nos. 5 and 7 calls for a few remarks: it occurs as *bhata* in the Bedsa cave-inscription (No. 2) of W. India, and as *bhatu* in No. 10 here. Bhagwānlāl Indrajī connected it with Skt. *bhaṭṭa* [*sic*], 'a warrior[2],' and Bühler with Skt. *bhakta*, 'devoted[3].' Both these scholars seem to have overlooked the possibility of its being a derivative of *bhrātṛ*, 'brother,' used as a term of endearment or honour, in speaking of a kinsman or of a member of the same religious order[4]. The first two forms represent the Pāli Nom. *bhātā*, and the third the base *bhātu*[5]. In the modern Indian vernaculars this word exists under the forms *bhāū* (Marāṭhi), *bhāu* (Sindhi), *bhrāū* (Panjābi) and *bhāī* (Hindi), and these, I am told[6], are attached to proper names either honorifically or as a term of endearment, e.g. Bhāū Dīkṣita, Bhāū Gōvinda.

Bhata and *bata* may also be derived from Skt. *bhartṛ*, Pkt. *bhattu*[7], 'lord,' but I prefer the former etymology, at least for the present[8].

Another point to be noticed is the use of the title *parumaka*. It will be seen from the examples in Nos. 2, 3 and 8[a] that it is a term applicable to both men and women.

The **contents** of these records deal with gifts of caves to the Buddhist clergy and would be of no real historical value, but for the fact that inscription No. 1 makes mention of the names of two Ceylon kings, **Devanapiya Maharaja Gamiṇi Tisa** and his son **Devanapiya Tisa Abaya.** Now in going through the known inscriptions written in Brāhmī characters of the most ancient type, we come across the following names of kings:—

(1) Devanapiya Maharaja Gamiṇi Tisa (Daṁbulla rock, *A.I.C.* No. 3 and below, No. 1).

(2) Devanapiya Tisa Abaya (below, No 1).

(3) Devanapiya Maharaja Gamiṇi Abaya (Tōnigala and Galleṇa Vihāra, *A.I.C.* Nos. 1–2).

(4) Tisa, son of No. 3 (Galleṇa Vihāra, *A.I.C.* No. 2).

(5) Devanapiya Tisa-maharaja } Maharatmale rock,
(6) Devanapiya Puṭikana Gamiṇi Abhaya-maharaja } above, p. 59.

[1] See p. 144, note 5. [2] Burgess, *Cave-inscriptions*, p. 26.
[3] *A.S.W.I.* vol. iv. p. 89. [4] For this use, compare the Roman *fratres Arvales* (Mr. A. B. Keith).
[5] For other examples of the shortening of the original long *ā*, see above, p. 15.
[6] By Dr. Hoey and Prof. Blumhardt. [7] Cf. Pischel's *Prākrit Grammar*, §§ 389–90.
[8] I think, however, that it is *bhaṭṭa* as a term of honour (as in Bhaṭṭa Nārāyaṇa). Cf. *parumaka*, with which it alternates in the case of Sōṇa on p. 145 (Mr. A. B. Keith).

Of these, No. 3 has been correctly identified with Vaṭṭa-Gāmaṇī Abhaya[1], No. 4 with Mahācūla Mahā-Tissa, the adopted son of Vaṭṭa-Gāmaṇī[2], and Nos. 5 and 6 with Vaṅkanāsika Tissa and Gajabāhuka Gāmaṇī[3] respectively. There remain, therefore, only Nos. 1 and 2 to be identified. Dr. Müller's supposition[4], that No. 1 refers to the same Tisa as No. 4, is not convincing on palaeographic grounds. Judging from Prof. Rhys Davids' eye-copy of the Daṁbulla record, published in *The Indian Antiquary*, vol. i. p. 140, its characters are of the same type as those in the Āṇḍiyā-kanda cave-inscription, No. 1, now under discussion, where this very name Devanapiya Maharaja Gamiṇi Tisa occurs. And for reasons explained above, this type is slightly more archaic than that of the alphabet of the Tōnigala inscription ascribed to Vaṭṭa-Gāmaṇī. It would, therefore, be more reasonable to identify **Devanapiya Maharaja Gamiṇi Tisa** with Vaṭṭa-Gāmaṇī's father, King **Saddhā Tissa**, than with his adopted son, Mahācūla Mahā-Tissa. As for the title Gamiṇi (P. Gāmaṇī), the *Mahāvaṁsa* explicitly states that it was first given to Saddhā Tissa's elder brother Duṭṭha-Gāmaṇī because of his sovereignty over Mahāgāma[5]. But the former also ruled in Mahāgāma and may, therefore, equally have used the title.

Another argument in favour of this identification is that it enables us to recognize No. 2, Devanapiya Tisa Abaya, the son and donor of the cave, as no other than king Lajji (or Lañja) Tissa, the eldest son of Saddhā Tissa[6], whose connexion with Riṭigala is shown by his building the Ariṭṭha Vihāra, as noticed above. This king, moreover, supplied 'medicinal drugs for the itinerant priests, and, inquiring always of the priestesses, "What do ye need?" he provided what they wanted and the rice requisite for their maintenance.'

The accompanying genealogical tree will show more clearly how the kings named above were related to one another. In fixing the dates of their rule, I have taken as my starting-point the date of the coronation of Aśōka, which, according to the calculation below[7], took place in or about the year 265 B.C.

[1] See *A. I. C.* p. 25 and M. Boyer's article in the *Journal Asiatique* for Nov.–Dec. 1898.

[2] *A. I. C.* p. 26, footnote. [3] *Ibid.* p. 27 and above, p. 59. [4] *A. I. C.* p. 26.

[5] *Mahāgāmē nāyakattaṁ* (*Mv.* xxii. 71), which the Ṭīkā explains by '*Mahāgāmē Vaḍḍhamāna-nāmakamhi nagarē attanō nāyakabhāvaṁ.*' [6] Cf. *Mv.* xxxiii. 14.

[7] The accession of Candragupta has been fixed with tolerable certainty in the year 321 B.C. This king reigned 24 years, and his successor Bindusāra 28 years. Then Aśōka in 269 (i.e. 321–52) B.C. came to the throne; but it was only four years later (265 B.C.) that his coronation, said by all the Ceylon chronicles to have taken place 218 years after the death of the Buddha, followed. If this is accepted, the Buddha's death must be placed in 483 B.C. (i.e. 265 + 218). The difference then between this and 544 B.C., the date of his death according to the Sinhalese tradition (above, p. 122, note 7), is just 61 years. For a striking confirmation of this computation, see below, pp. 156–7, and for a full

N.B. The dates given here are reckoned on the supposition that the Buddha died in 483 B.C. See p. 142, note 7, and pp. 156–7. If, however, the tradition now current in Ceylon, which places the date of his death in 544 B.C. (p. 122, note 7) is to be followed, it will be necessary to make the dates earlier by 61 years. Paṇḍukābhaya's reign would accordingly be *circa* 438–368 B.C. and that of Gajabāhuka-Gāmaṇi 116–138 A.D.

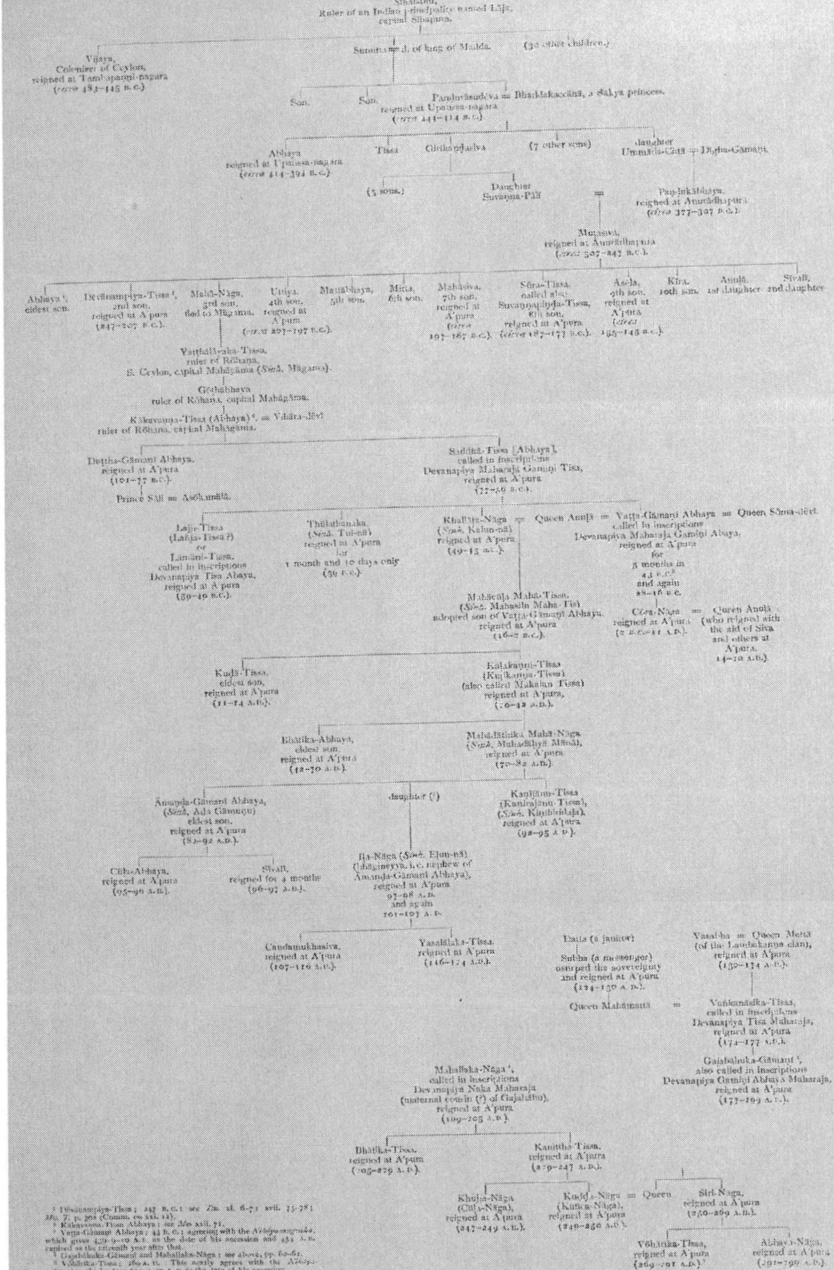

[1] Dēvānampiya-Tissa; 247 B.C.: see *Dīp.* xi. 6–7; xvii. 75–78; *Mv. T.* p. 303 (Comm. on xxi. 12).
[2] Kākavaṇṇa-Tissa Abhaya: see *Mv.* xxii. 71.
[3] Vaṭṭa-Gāmaṇi Abhaya; 43 B.C.; agreeing with the *Nikāya-saṅgraha*, which gives 439–9–10 A.B. as the date of his accession and 454 A.B. expired as the fifteenth year after that.
[4] Gajabāhuka-Gāmaṇi and Mahallaka-Nāga: see above, pp. 60–61.
[5] Vōhārika-Tissa; 260 A.D. This nearly agrees with the *Nikāya-saṅgraha*, which gives 752–4–10 A.B. as the date of his accession.

[*To face p.* 142.]

The *Dīpavaṁsa* (xi. 13–14) tells us that when seventeen years had elapsed after the coronation of Aśōka Muṭasiva died, and six months after, Dēvānampiya Tissa was crowned king of Ceylon. Therefore the latter event happened in 247 B.C.[1]

I have verified this date by means of other dates given in Pāli and Sinhalese chronicles. For example, Mahāsēna died when 844 years nine months and twenty-five days had elapsed since the demise of the Buddha[2], i.e. in 845 A.B. According to all authorities, the number of years that expired from the accession of Dēvānampiya Tissa down to the death of Mahāsēna approximately amounts to 609 years. Therefore, the former came to the throne in 236 (i.e. 845 – 609) A.B., and this is equivalent to 247 B.C., taking 483 B.C. as the date of the death of the Buddha[3]. This shows that the Sinhalese chronicles are after all not far wrong in their dates fixing the relative sequence of events.

As regards the names of the other personages mentioned in the present inscriptions, it will be seen from Nos. 3 and 8ᵃ that Her Eminence Anuḍi had two sons, namely Parumaka Utiya (P. Uttiya) and Parumaka Tiśa (P. Tissa). I am inclined to identify this lady with Anuḷā, queen successively of Khallāṭanāga and of his younger brother Vaṭṭa-Gāmaṇī, the change of cerebral *ḍ* to cerebral *ḷ* not being uncommon in Pāli and Sinhalese phonology[4]. Parumaka Tiśa would then be no other than her son Mahācūla Mahā-Tissa, as shown in the genealogical tree. This king was also the donor of the cave-temple, Galleṇa Vihāra[5]. The names of the remaining donors are Tiśa Tera (P. Tissa-Thēra), Bata Nada[6] (P. Bhātu-Nanda), Bamaṇa Utara Puśaguta[7] (Skt. Brāhmaṇōttara Puṣya-Gupta), Bata Śivaguta[8] (P. Bhātu-Sivagutta), Baḍakarika[9] Majhima (P. Bhaṇḍākārika Majjhima), Parumaka Śona and Bhatu Śoṇa.

---

discussion of the above dates, see Fleet, *J.R.A.S.*, 1906, p. 984 and 1909, pp. 1–34. The author has kindly permitted me to peruse the latter in proof after he had seen the above note in print.

[1] Cf. *Dv.* xvii. 78, where it is definitely stated that Dēvānampiya Tissa was crowned when 236 years had elapsed from the death of the Buddha. This is equivalent to 483 – 236 = 247 B.C.

[2] So stated in the Sinhalese historical works. The *Nikāyasaṅgraha* places the accession of Mahāsēna in 818 A.B. expired. His death would accordingly fall in 846 A.B.

[3] Again the Galvihāre inscription of Parākrama Bāhu I (*A.I.C.* No. 137) and the *Nikāyasaṅgraha* (p. 22) together give us the date 454 A.B. as the fifteenth year of Vaṭṭa-Gāmaṇī. If we deduct from this 218, the number of years that elapsed since the accession of Dēvānampiya Tissa, we get 236 A.B. i.e. 247 B.C. (483 – 236) as the date of his accession.

[4] Cf. *L.S.S.* § 22.

[5] See *A.I.C.* No. 2.

[6] Cf. Bata Pala in Vessagiri cave-inscription, No. 8, above, p. 21.

[7] Cf. Utaradāsaka in Mathura inscription No. 1 (*Ep. Ind.* vol. ii. p. 198); Utaradatā, Utaramitā, Naṁdutarā, as well as Pusadata in Sāñchi records (*op. cit.* vol. ii. pp. 386–7); Puṣya-Gupta in Junāgaḍh inscription of Rudradāman, l. 8 (*op. cit.* vol. viii. p. 43).

[8] Cf. Sivaguta in Nāsik No. 4 (*Ibid.* p. 71).

[9] See above, p. 73, also Nāsik cave-inscription No. 19, l. 2 (*op. cit.* vol. viii. pp. 91, 92).

No. 1.

Devanapiya maharajha[1] **Gamiṇi-Tisaha** puta Devanapiya **Tisa-A[baya]ha** leṇe agata anagata catu-di-disa[2] śagaśa[3] (di)[ne]:

The cave of Devanapiya[4] Tisa Abaya, son of the great king Devanapiya Gamiṇi Tisa, is given to the Buddhist priesthood from the four quarters[5], present and not present.

No. 2.

Parumaka **Anuḍiya** da(na) agata anagata catu-diśa śagaśa[3]:

The gift of Her Eminence Anuḍi to the Buddhist priesthood from the four quarters, present and not present.

No. 3.

Parumaka **Anuḍi**-puta parumaka **Utiya**[6] leṇe sagasa:

The cave of his Eminence Utiya, son of Her Eminence Anuḍi [is given] to the Buddhist priesthood.

No. 4.

a.

Tiśa-teraśa[7] dane śagaśa[3]:

Tissa Thēra's gift to the Buddhist priesthood.

b.[8]

Tiśa[9]-teraha dane agata anagata catu-diśa śagaśa[3]:

Tissa Thēra's gift to the Buddhist priesthood from the four quarters, present and not present.

---

[1] Read *-raja.*

[2] Read *catu-disa*: the syllable *di* is engraved twice erroneously.

[3] Read *sagasa.*

[4] Regarding this royal title, see above, pp. 62, 63.

[5] Cf. M. Senart's remarks on the expression *catu-disa-sagasa dine* in *Ep. Ind.* vol. vii. p. 59; also above, p. 18.

[6] *Utiya* (P. *Uttiya*) is a masculine proper name often met with in Pāli literature, for example the brother of king Dēvānampiya Tissa was 'known by the name of prince Uttiya' (*Mv.* xx. 29). According to inscription No. 10 (*b*), however, the name here may be *Uti.* If so, the feminine genitive termination, *ya*, which we see in No. 2, is used here with a masculine noun in *i*.

[7] Read *Tisa-terasa.*

[8] From an eye-copy.

[9] Read *Tisa.*

No. 5.

Bata **Nadaha** leṇe:

The cave of Brother Nanda.

No. 6.

Bamaṇa **Uta(ra) Puśagutaha** leṇe:

The cave of Brahman Utara Puśaguta (Uttara Pussa-gutta).

No. 7.

Bata **Śivagutaha** leṇe catu-diśa śagaśa[1] dine

The cave of Brother Śivaguta is dedicated to the Buddhist priesthood from the four quarters.

No. 8.

a.[2]

Parumaka **Anuḍi**-puta parumaka **Tiśaha** dane śagaśa[1]

The gift of His Eminence Tissa, son of Her Eminence Anuḍi, to the Buddhist priesthood.

b.

Baḍakarika **Majhimaha** leṇe śagaśa[1]

The cave of Majjhima the Treasurer [is dedicated] to the Buddhist priesthood.

No. 9.

Parumaka **(Śo)naha**[3] leṇe śagaśa[1]

The cave of His Eminence Sōṇa [is given] to the Buddhist priesthood.

No. 10.

a.

Bhatu-**Śoṇaśa**[4] leṇe Mahaśudaśane[5] catu-diśa saghaśa[6] patiṭh(i)te[7]

The cave [called] Mahāsudassana of Brother Sōṇa is established for the Buddhist priesthood from the four quarters.

---

[1] Read *sagasa.*

[2] From an eye-copy furnished by the Archaeological Commissioner. This inscription ought really to follow No. 3. In the absence of an ink-impression or a photograph no facsimile of it can be given.

[3] Read *Soṇaha.*

[4] Read *Soṇasa.*

[5] Skt. *mahāsudarśana.*

[6] Read *saghasa.*

[7] P. *patiṭṭhita.*

b.[1]

Parumaka **Uti**[2] -puta parumaka (Ba) .. (da) .. .. (ha) .. ga .. le[ṇe] catudiśa [śa]gaśa[3]

The cave of His Eminence Ba .. da .. .. son of His Eminence Uti [is given] to the Buddhist priesthood from the four quarters.

II. Karaṁbā-hinna Cave-inscription (pl. 19).

This record belongs to the same period as Nos. 8–10 of the foregoing ones, that is to say about the second half of the first century B.C. The akṣara *ta* in *bata* has a more or less semicircular basis, which is distinctly a more advanced type of the angular *ta*[4]. The letters *a*, *ma* and *ṇa* have also the usual characteristics of younger types. *Ga* in the word *anagata* is engraved upside down.

It will be seen that the owner of the cave was **Bata Maha-Tisa**; and he may be identified with king Mahācūla Mahā-Tissa, the adopted son of Vaṭṭa-Gāmaṇī, both owing to the similarity of the name and to the fact that he lived about this period and took part in the dedication of caves to the Buddhist clergy[5].

Bata Maha-Tiśaha leṇe agata anagata

The cave of Brother Mahā-Tissa [is given to the Buddhist priesthood from the four quarters], present and not present.

III. Nā-ulpata *alias* Nā-arambädda-hinna (pl. 19).

(*a*) The Cave-inscription.

The **characters** of this record are more or less of the same type as those of Nos. 2–7 above. I would, therefore, place it amongst the inscriptions of the first century B.C. A point of interest in its contents is the fact that the donor of the cave was a Thēra named Budarakita (P. Buddharakkhita). Buddhist monks appear as donors also in Indian inscriptions, as for example in those of the Sāñchi Stūpa[6] of about the second century B.C., as well as in Kanheri Cave-inscriptions[7] of the fourth century A.D. They must, therefore, have been

---

[1] From an eye-copy.
[2] Read *sagasa*.
[3] See *A.I.C.* No. 2.
[4] Probably Utiya, the son of Anuḍi in No. 3.
[5] Cf. Bühler's *Indische Palaeographie*, p. 36.
[6] *Ep. Ind.* vol. ii. pp. 97–112.
[7] *A.S.W.I.* vol. v. p. 77.

Ritigala.—Aṇḍiyākanda Cave-Inscriptions.

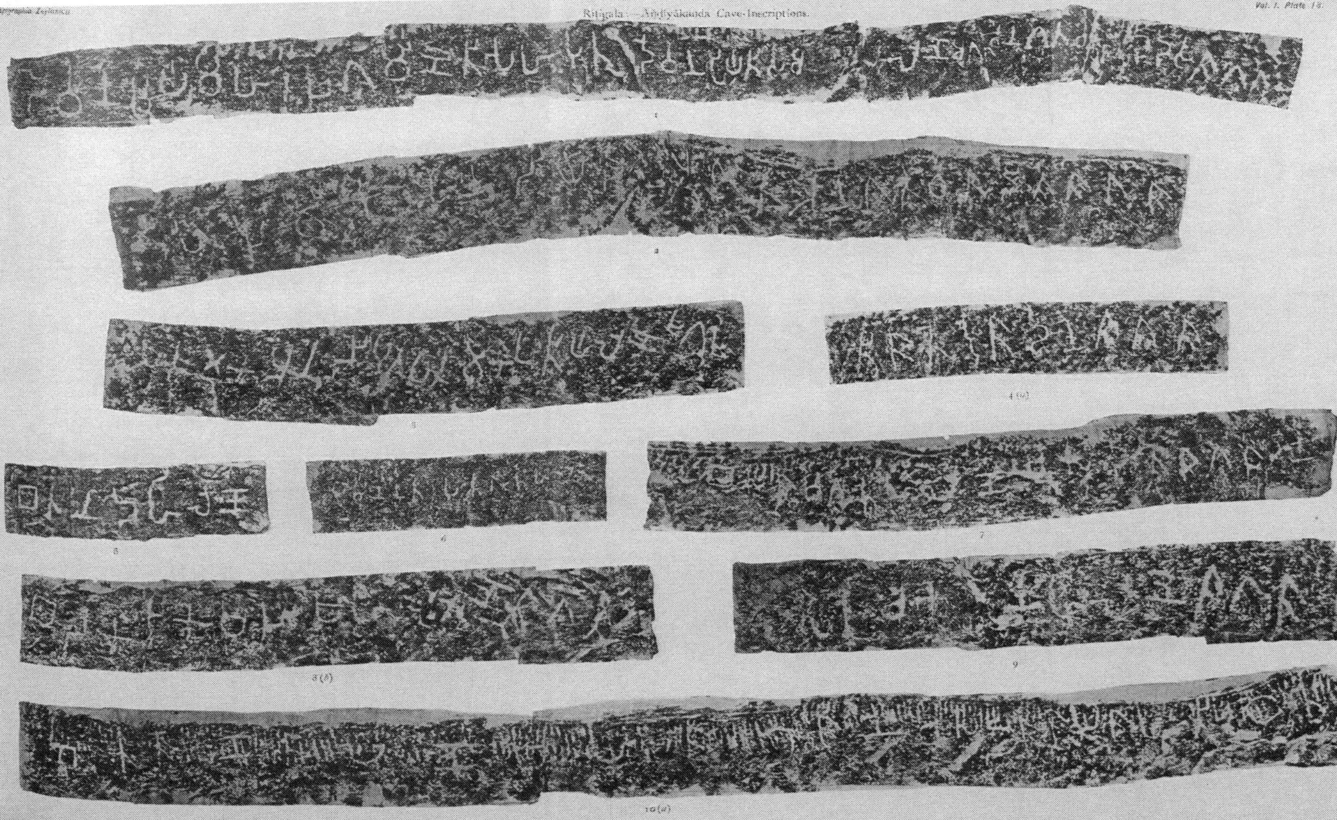

1, 2, 3, 4 (a), 5, 6, 7, 8 (b), 9, 10 (a)

From ink-impressions supplied by the Archaeological Commissioner, Ceylon.

allowed in early times to possess personal property[1] (P. *puggalika vatthu*) which they could bestow on the Order to be used as their common property (P. *saṅghika vatthu*) as in the case of the present cave, or spend on religious undertakings, as at Sāñchi.

Budarakita-teraha śagha[2] -da(ne)

Buddharakkhita Thēra's gift to the Buddhist priesthood.

(*b*) The Rock-inscriptions.

According to the Archaeological Commissioner's description of this site, quoted above, there are four inscriptions on this boulder. The photograph before me shows three of them, of which the third is reproduced here (pl. 19) from an ink-estampage supplied by the Archaeological Survey.

The photograph is not worth reproducing, as it seems to have been taken after the letters on the stone had been chalked over.

The first inscription has three lines, the second, one, while the third has two lines, about 15 feet long, each letter being 5 to 8 inches in height and breadth. Judging from the photograph, the size of the letters of the first two inscriptions must be about 2 to 4 inches.

They are all written in the same type of character, and it will be seen from the facsimile of the third inscription that this type agrees with that of the Maharatmale Rock-inscription (pl. 13 above), and that it must belong to a period between 150 and 300 A.D. The phraseology of the inscriptions, too, shows that they must have been written in the second or third century A.D. For example, in the pre-Christian inscriptions of Tōnigala, Galleṇa and Daṁbulla[3], as well as in the cave record of Āṇḍiyā-kanda, No. 1 of the present Riṭigala mountain, we find the title *maharaja* inserted always between the epithet *Devanapiya* and the name of the king; whilst in the inscriptions of the second or third century A.D., such as those of Maharatmale[4] and Mihintale[5], it comes after the name of the king.

Owing to the insufficiency of material I am unable to edit the three inscriptions in question; but I give below what I have succeeded in deciphering from the photograph mentioned above, and from an eye-tracing sent me by the Archaeological Commissioner.

---

[1] Cf. Bühler's remarks in *Ep. Ind.* vol. ii. p. 93.
[2] Read *sagha*.
[3] *A. I. C.* Nos. 1–3.
[4] Above, p. 61.
[5] *A. I. C.* No. 20.

TRANSCRIPT.

a.

1 .. .. .. [La]jaka Tisa maharaji vihara karavaya Abadaḷaka-vavi saga dini
2 .. .. .. me te hu ṇa .. ta ṇa ka ya ka ti ra ga ṇa ka ca .. keta ka ba na ka ca ....
3 .. .. vavi biku-saga-haṭaye dini

b.

1 Gamiṇi Abaye kubura saga dine

c.

1 .. .. ha .. .. (ma)harajaha putaha Devanapiya Laja
2 .. .. sa ma .. .. [ma]haraja Ariṭe hamaṇa saha .. .. haṭaye batavaṭita raja .. ..

TRANSLATION.

a.

The great king Lajaka Tisa having caused the construction of the Vihāra dedicated the Abadaḷaka Tank to the Buddhist priesthood.

. . . . field . . . . . .

. . . . tank [he] dedicated to the community of monks

b.

Gamiṇi Abaya bestowed the tract of fields on the Buddhist priesthood

c.

The great king . . . . . . (grandson (?) of the great king) Devanapiya Laja[ka Tisa], son of the great king . . . . . . the ever-devoted king [dedicated] . . . . . . for the maintenance of the fraternity at Ariṭa.

REMARKS.

It is apparent from the above version that the three records belong to three different kings, namely, **Lajaka Tisa, Gamiṇi Abaya,** and another—a son or grandson—whose name is unfortunately missing from the fragment of the third inscription before us. Mr. Bell (see p. 139, note 2) has identified Lajaka Tisa with Lajji Tissa, and Gamiṇi Abaya with Vaṭṭa-Gāmaṇī Abhaya, who reigned in the first century B.C. This identification is, however, not tenable, for the inscriptions belong, on palaeographic grounds, to the second or third century A.D., and they refer to contemporaneous events. Among the kings of the latter period who were great patrons of the Buddhist Order, the names of three are familiar to us from the rock-inscriptions at Maharatmale (above, pp. 59–61) and on the Mihintale mountain (*A. I. C.* No. 20). They are: (1) Vaṅkanāsika, *alias* Devanapiya Tisa-maharaja, (2) his son, Gajabāhu I, called also Gayabāhu Gāmiṇi Abhaya, and (3) their relative, Mahallaka Nāga, called in inscriptions Devanapiya Naka-maharaja. I am positive that these are the kings referred to in the present records. Lajaka Tisa can be no other than Vaṅkanāsika Tisa, the son of Vasabha, because Laja (P. Lajja or Lañja), called also Lämiṇi or Lämāṇi (P. Lambakaṇṇa), was the name of his clan or family[1].

The third king in question must be Naka-maharaja, called in the *Mahāvaṁsa* Mahallaka Nāga, judging from the reference, in the Mihintale inscription (*A. I. C.* No. 20), to the tank at Ariṭa-gama mentioned above, and to the gifts bestowed on the monks at Vihirabijaka and Muṭigutika as confirmed by the Maharatmale inscription of this king[2].

IV. Vēväl-tänna (pl. 19).

(*a*) The Cave-inscription.

This consists of a single line above five rudely engraved *maṅgala* symbols, namely:—

(1) A *svastika*, (2) a *caitya*, (3) a *cakra*, (4) what some call a Buddhist trident, others an ornamental footprint[3], but what seems to me to be a glorified *ma* representing the initial akṣara of the word *maṅgala*[4], (5) a smaller figure of No. 4.

It is written in the pre-Christian Brāhmī script, the type of the characters closely resembling that of the Vessagiri records[5]. Hence the date of this inscription may be placed in the first century B. C.

As to the grammar, attention may be drawn to the instrumental in *ena* and to the past participle passive in *ta*, in the expression *Puśagutena karita* for P. *Pussaguttēna kārita*.

The facsimile of the inscription in pl. 19, though prepared from a photograph

[1] See *Mv.* xxxv. In all the Sinhalese historical works, Lajji Tissa, the son of Saddhā Tissa, is called Lämāṇi Tissa, and Vasabha (Sinh. Vähäp), the father of Vaṅkanāsika Tissa, is put down as a descendant of the Lämāṇi race. Hence Vaṅkanāsika Tissa could very well have been called Lämāṇi or Lajji Tissa.

[2] See above, pp. 58–65.

[3] See Dr. Vogel's article on two rock-inscriptions in the Kāṅgra Valley (*Ep. Ind.* vol. vii. p. 119).

[4] For other examples of these devices and discussions thereon, see Bühler's *Indische Palæographie*, p. 85.

[5] See above, plate 5.

which seems to have been taken after the letters had been chalked over, may be relied upon, with the exception of the seven akṣaras enclosed in parentheses in the following transcript.

TRANSCRIPT.

Mahamata-Bamadata-puta purumaka (Pu[1])śagutena (ka[2])ri(ta[3]) (bada-tuba[4])

TRANSLATION.

(The auspicious stūpa)[5], which was caused to be constructed by His Eminence Puśaguta (Puṣya-gupta), son of the Mahamata[6] Bama-data (Brahma-datta).

(*b*) The Rock-inscription.

The three symbols or letters on the top left corner and the two lines of Brāhmī script, about six feet long, make up this record, as may be seen from the facsimile in pl. 19. The **characters** are about 2 to 4 inches each in size. Their type is the same as that of the foregoing cave-inscription. Note, for example, the close similarity of the akṣaras, *ka*, *da*, *pa*, *ma*, *śa* and *ha* to those in the Aśōka inscriptions. The remaining letters, with the exception perhaps of *ga*, are also of antique type. I would, therefore, place the execution of this record in the same century as the Āṇḍiyā-kanda Cave-inscription No. 1 (above, p. 144), or in the century previous to it, that is to say in the first or second century B. C.

The **language** of the inscription likewise lends support to this assumption of its antiquity, for, like the foregoing record, it is really composed in Prākrit and contains most of the phonological peculiarities occurring in the Bharhut and other Indian inscriptions of the kind, as noticed in my article on the Vessagiri records, above, pp. 15–17. The retention of palatal *ś* in *Puśa* (Skt. *Puṣya*, Mg.

---

[1] The letter is clear on the photograph, though chalking has made it look like *ra*.

[2] Possibly *kā*.

[3] This may be *te*.

[4] The photograph cannot be relied upon as regards these four akṣaras. I am inclined to read them as *bada-guha* (Skt. *bhadra-guhā*), 'auspicious cave' or *buda-guha* (Skt. *bauddha-guhā*), 'Buddhist cave.' This is, of course, purely conjectural.

[5] *Bada-tuba* = P. *bhadda-thūpa*. Cf. *thuba* (for *thūpa*) in Kanheri Cave-inscription, No. 10 (*A. S. W. I.* vol. v. p. 78). Our inscription being engraved on the brow of the cave, it obviously refers to the formation of the cave itself. Hence *guhā* is more probably the word on the stone than *tuba*.

[6] See below, p. 153.

Puśśa, P. *Pussa*) and *Tiśa* (Skt. *Tiṣya*, Mg. *Tiśśa*, P. *Tissa*), as well as the occurrence of nom. sing. in *e*, as in *Bahike*, *Puśagute*, show a tendency to Māgadhīsm, while the instrumental terminations *ena* and *ehi*, and the passive construction found in both these records, make clear the Pāli or Prākrit character of the language.

Regarding the three symbols or letters ȣ ⱶ ɣ on the left top corner of the inscription, my friend Dr. Hoey thinks that they belong to the first line, which the engraver abandoned when he found he had made a mistake in the second and third akṣaras, and that he evidently forgot to score them out before beginning the line afresh.

While admitting this possibility, I am still inclined to believe they represent a date[1]. M. Boyer, in his able article on the Tōnigala and other Indian inscriptions, in the *Journal Asiatique*, Nov.-Dec. 1898, has with good reason pointed out that the symbol ȣ in the Tōnigala record stands for ∝, the Brāhmī symbol for the number 10. This may also be the case in the present instance, for there is very little difference between the Tōnigala ȣ and the ȣ of this record, both accidentally resembling the akṣara *ma* of the pre-Christian Brāhmī script[2]. The sign ⱶ, which comes next, is undoubtedly the number 5. Its type is older than that found in Nāsik, No. 16[3], judging from the fact that the vertical line of the former is longer and is void of any thickening of its upper portion, such as is noticeable in the latter.

The third symbol is difficult to be deciphered. It looks like a cursive *sa* or *su*. If the former, it may be an abbreviation of *savachare* or *savacharahi* and the date 15 *sa*. will then mean 'in the fifteenth year,' although in Indian inscriptions *savachare* or *sa*. is as a rule written before the figure[4].

If, on the other hand, it is a modified form of *su*, it may stand for the numerical figure 100 or 200. This is, however, not probable, for two reasons. First, if the three signs are meant either for 215 or 115, the figure *su*, which is third here, ought to come first, as in the case of the number 256 in the Aśōka inscriptions of Sahasrām, Rūpnāth and Siddāpura. Secondly, neither 215 nor 115 can very well stand for the number of years since the Buddha's death. If it must be a date, it can only be one reckoning from the introduction of Buddhism into Ceylon 'in the 236th year of the Buddha, which was the eighteenth

---

[1] They may not have been a date at all, but mere mason's marks (Mr. A. B. Keith).

[2] Cf. the numerical system in Malayālam, according to which the akṣara ൧ *ma* = 10. This proves that the above sign was at one time identified with the Brāhmī akṣara *ma*, and that its numerical value is ten.

[3] See *A. S. W. I.* vol. iv. Pl. liv.

[4] See for examples the dated inscriptions of Mathurā and Nāsik in *Ep. Ind.* vol. ii. pp. 201–12, and vol. viii. pp. 59–96.

year of the reign of Aśōka.' The date of the inscription would accordingly be 451 (i.e. 236 + 215) A. B., which is equivalent to either 32 or 93 B. C.[1] On palaeographic grounds there cannot be any objection to this date, but in consideration of the irregularity of the order of the numerals and the total absence of any indication of the era, I prefer the reading 15 *sa*.

The name of the king, in the fifteenth year of whose reign the event recorded in the inscription took place, is omitted here, as it is in the dated inscriptions from Mathurā[2]. But it seems probable from the Āṇḍiyā-kanda cave-inscription No. 1, in the neighbourhood, described above, and from Lajji Tissa's connexion with Riṭigala, that the number refers to the regnal years of his father, Saddhā-Tissa, who reigned, according to the genealogical table, from 77–59 B. C., and, according to Wijēsiṇha's list, 137–119. The date of this record would, therefore, fall either in 62 or in 122 B. C.

The only other king that can be suggested in this connexion is Vaṭṭa-Gāmaṇī. If, as M. Boyer says, the Tōnigala inscription is dated the fourteenth year of this king, then the present record must have been inscribed in the following year, which would be the year in which he resumed the sovereignty (28 or 89 B. C.)[1].

As to the personages mentioned, we see from the foregoing cave-inscription in this locality that Purumaka Puśaguta was the son of Mahamata Bamadata. From this it is obvious that the word *puta* here refers not only to the first name, Purumaka Bahika, but also to the three names following it, namely Purumaka Puśaguta, Purumaka Mita and Purumaka Tiśa, and that all these four chieftains were the sons of the minister Bamadata.

TRANSCRIPT.

(1) 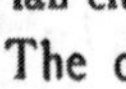
(2) Mahamata Bamadata puta[3] purumaka Bahike purumaka Puśa-gute
(3) Purumaka Mite purumaka Tiśe etehi karite Ariṭa-maha-gama

TRANSLATION.

In the fifteenth year (?), the sons of the Mahamata Bamadata [namely] His Eminence Bahika, His Eminence Puśaguta, His Eminence Mita and His Eminence Tiśa—by these [chieftains] was formed the great village Ariṭa.

---

[1] Taking 544 B. C. as the date of the death of the Buddha, this being the tradition now current in Ceylon. See, however, above, p. 142, note 7, and below, pp. 156–7.

[2] See *Ep. Ind.* vol. ii. p. 201.

[3] Or *pute*.

Kitigala Inscriptions.

Karambä-hinna cave.

Nä-ulpata cave.

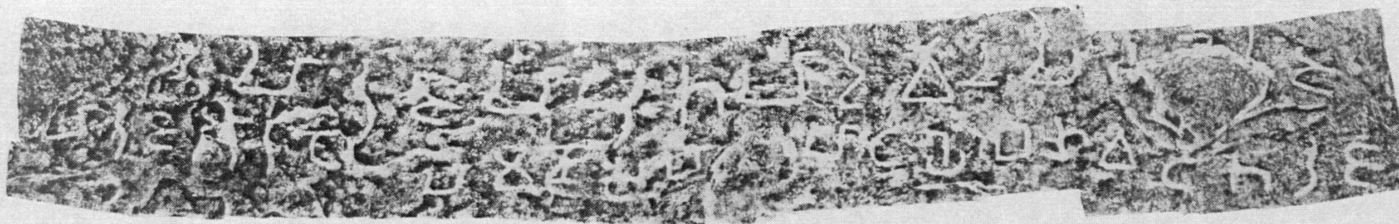

Nä-ulpata rock.

Veväl-tänna rock.

Veväl-tänna cave.

From mix-impressions supplied by the Archaeological Commissioner, Ceylon.

REMARKS.

Mahamata = Skt. *mahāmātra*, Pāli *mahāmatto*, a title which occurs repeatedly in Buddhaghōsa's commentaries [1] and in the edicts of Aśōka. It is analogous to *mahāmātya* (P. *mahāmacco*) and was used by Aśōka as a general term for all officers of high rank entrusted with administrative powers in civil, judicial, political, and even religious matters, e. g. *dhamma-mahāmāta*.

Bama-data = *Brahma-datta*. In Sāñchi-stūpa votive inscriptions, No. 30, *Bahadata* [2]; Pkt. *Bambhadatta* and *Bamha-*; Sinh. *Bamba-dat*.

Purumaka same as *parumaka*. See above, pp. 17, 26 n. 1.

Bahike. Cf. *Bāhiya* in *Mv*. xxxiii. 59.

Karite = *kārite*.

Arita-maha-gama = P. *Ariṭṭha-mahā-gāma*, the crude form *gama* being used for the nominative [3].

No. 11. KIRIBAT-VEHERA [4] PILLAR-INSCRIPTION.

THIS inscription was discovered by the Archaeological Commissioner (Mr. H. C. P. Bell), in 1891, in the jungle close by the ruined dāgaba known as Kiribat-Vehera [5], about 3½ miles to the north of the town of Anurādhapura. The site has since been thoroughly excavated [6].

---

[1] See passage from *Sumaṅgala-vilāsinī* quoted in Alwis' *Pāli Grammar*, p. 99, and the story of Abhaya-rājakumāra in the *Dhammapadaṭṭhakathā*, p. 426 of the Colombo edition of 1886.

[2] *Ep. Ind.* vol. ii. p. 100.

[3] Cf. Bühler's remarks in *Ep. Ind.* vol. i. p. 375.

[4] The location of this inscription is given according to the information supplied by the Archaeological Survey of Ceylon.

[5] 'This ancient dāgaba is in present appearance a small hill covered with grass (through which brick débris shows up freely), shaded heavily by trees. In height it rises to about 30 ft., and the tape run round the bottom of the slope gave a circumference of over 200 yards.

'The jungle round was explored, but beyond a solitary pillar bearing an inscription of the tenth century, the only other relic of the past discovered was a piḷima-gē (image-house) on four tall squared pillars, which once supported a roof over a large standing figure of the Buddha, now fallen on its face.

'The trunk of the image is cracked, and the lower limbs and one arm are gone, but the head is apparently intact. What remains of the figure measures from crown of head to waist 9 ft. 1 in.' (*A. S. C.* Report for 1891, p. 2).

[6] For a detailed report of the excavations conducted by the Archaeological Commissioner and myself, and of the ruins unearthed, see *A. S. C.* Reports for 1892, p. 5, and 1893, p. 4.

The inscription is in a fairly good state of preservation, as may be judged from the accompanying facsimile (pl. 20). It is engraved from top to bottom on the four sides of a quadrangular pillar of stone, about 5 ft. long by 10 in. square.

The letters are from one to two inches in size. They exhibit the type of the Sinhalese alphabet of the tenth century A. D., and vary but little from the form of script in the slab-inscriptions of Dappula V and Kassapa V, described above at pp. 23 and 41. The akṣaras that look more antique are *a*, *i*, *ba*, *ma*, and *ra*. As they resemble those in Kassapa's record more than those in the later inscription of Dappula V, I would place this record in a period immediately preceding Kassapa's reign.

The inscription itself is dated in the fourteenth year of a king called **Siri Saṅgbo** (Skt. *Śrī Saṅghabōdhi*). It was set up by royal order in the presence of three officials named (1) Sabā-vaḍunnā Salayem [1], the body-guard [2] of the Pāṇḍyan king Dāpuḷa, (2) (Ro)ṭu Pullayem [1], and (3) Kiling Agbo [3] (P. Kaliṅga Aggabōdhi). It proclaims certain privileges or immunities attached to the dispensary (*behed-ge*) at Bamuṇ-kumbara.

The name of Siri Saṅgbo is an epithet adopted by many kings. In the present instance it refers most probably to Kassapa IV, the younger brother and successor of Udaya I [4], and the predecessor of Kassapa V. The only other king who reigned more than fourteen years in the tenth century, and who was also called Siri Saṅgbo [5], was Sēna II, the father of Kassapa V; but the following facts show that Kassapa IV was the king in question :—

1. The advanced form of the alphabet, as discussed above.

2. The striking similarity of the phraseology of this record with that of the Mahākalattäwa inscription [6] of the fifteenth year of Siri Saṅgbo, which treats of an endowment to a nunnery built by the chief scribe Sēna in honour of his mother Nālā [7]. This scribe was evidently the one who, according to the

[1] These seem to be corrupt forms of South Indian names. For another official of the name of Sabā-vaḍunnā, see Vessagiri slab-inscription of Mahinda IV, l. 33 (p. 32, above).

[2] *Mekāppara*=Tamil *mey-kāppar*. See above, p. 38, note 2.

[3] Possibly these two were also body-guards of Dāpuḷa, and the word *mekāppara* refers to all three.

[4] See Moragoḍa pillar in *A. S. C.* Seventh Progress Report, 1891, p. 61.

[5] See above, pp. 23 and 42.

[6] *A. I. C.* No. 110.

[7] Nālā was the daughter of Mahinda, lord of Ruhuṇa, by Dēvā the daughter of Dappula II (*Mv.* xlix. 10–13). She eloped with Udaya, the brother of Sēna I, and governor of the southern country (*Mv.* l. 8–9). Their issue was the chief scribe Mahālēkhaka Sēna (Sinh. Mahalā Sen), who must, therefore, have lived in the reign of Kassapa IV.

Mahāvaṁsa[1], also 'built a noble house, called Mahālēkhaka-pabbata, for the use of the monks of the Mahāvihāra' in the reign of Kassapa IV.

3. The subject-matter of the record, which is a benefaction to a dispensary. It is distinctly stated in the *Mahāvaṁsa*[2] that Kassapa IV built hospitals at Anurādhapura and in the city of Pulatthi 'for the prevention of pestilential diseases. And to these buildings he granted fruitful lands and gardens with keepers, and furnished them also with means for the support of images. In divers places in the city he built dispensaries[3] for medicine, and caused rice and cloth to be given to the Paṁsukūlika monks.'

Touching the **date** of Kassapa IV, I have, at p. 123 above, proved that the first coronation of Parākrama-Bāhu I took place about the middle of 1153 A.D., or 1696 A.B. expired. Calculating from this date backwards, and subtracting from it 107, the total of the regnal years of the six kings that preceded him, we get 1046 A.D., or 1589 A.B. expired, as the date of the accession of Parākrama Pāṇḍya (No. 121 of Wijēsiṇha's table). Now with the aid of the dates of the Tanjore and the Manimaṅgalam inscriptions of South India, as computed by Professors Hultzsch and Kielhorn, I have shown, at p. 80 above, that the eleven kings, from Udaya III down to Parākrama Pāṇḍya (Nos. 111 to 121 of Wijēsiṇha's table), must have reigned between 1015 and 1046 A.D. Here is, therefore, a striking agreement of dates derived from two absolutely independent sources. It is true that the former reckoning makes 1046 A.D. the year of the accession of Parākrama Pāṇḍya, whilst, according to the latter calculation, he was defeated by the Cōḷa king, Rājādhirāja I, in or before 1046 A.D. But this slight difference is of no real consequence, considering that at this period Ceylon was in a state of complete anarchy, and the compiler of this portion of the *Mahāvaṁsa* must very naturally have found it difficult, at a later period, to fix the precise length of the nominal reigns of the successive rulers who held sway in the south of the island. Of Parākrama Pāṇḍya, the *Mahāvaṁsa* says that he reigned for two years, and was slain in battle by the Cōḷians. The *Pūjāvaliya*, on the other hand, credits him with only one year's reign, the *Rājāvaliya* with six, and the *Rājaratnākara* merely states that during his reign the Tamils made a disastrous invasion of Ceylon.

---

[1] Chap. lii. 33. [2] Chap. lii. 25–28.

[3] P. *bhēsajja-gēhaṁ* = Sinh. *behed-ge*, 'medicine-house.' This is the actual word used in the present inscription.

In view of these discrepant statements it may be safer to rely on the dates deduced from contemporary epigraphical records, and to place the accession of Parākrama Pāṇḍya, and probably his death too, in 1046 A. D. And we are accordingly enabled to fix the dates of accession of the following kings :—

No. 111	Udaya III	1015 A. D.	= 1496 A. B. expired
" 112	Sēna IV	1023 "	
" 113	Mahinda IV	1026 "	
" 121	Parākrama Pāṇḍya	1046 "	= 1589 A. B. expired
" 127	Parākrama Bāhu I	1153 "	= 1696 A. B.[1] expired
" 130	Kīrti Niśśaṅka Malla	1189 "	
" 135	Sāhasa Malla	1200 "	= 1743 A. B.[2] expired

Counting further backwards from Udaya III, it will be seen from the *Mahāvaṁsa* that Kassapa IV (the Siri Saṅgbo of the present inscription) came to the throne fifty-one years and seven months before that monarch, i.e. in 963 A. D.; and, according to the *Pūjāvaliya* forty-seven years and seven months before him, i. e. in 967 A. D. As the present record was set up in the fourteenth year of Kassapa's reign, its date must be either 977 or 981 A. D.

It will perhaps not be out of place to record here an important discovery which I believe I have made in connexion with the much discussed date of the death of the Buddha.

From the above computation it is apparent that, as far back as the time of Parākrama Pāṇḍya (1589 A. B. expired = 1046 A. D.) the traditional date in Ceylon of the death of the Buddha was, as it is now, 544 B. C. But, previous to this period, the Buddhist era seems to have been different. And this can be proved from the *Mahāvaṁsa* itself. According to this chronicle, a period of ninety-three years and eight days intervened between the accession of Udaya III and that of Parākrama Pandya in 1590 A. B. current. The former, therefore, came to the throne in the year 1497 A. B. (i.e. 1590 minus 93). The date of his accession, according to my calculation, shown above, is in 1015 A. D. It is thus clear that 1497 A. B. is nearly equivalent to 1015 A. D., and that the difference between these two dates, namely 482, is the number of years that must have elapsed between the death of the Buddha and the beginning of the Christian era. In other

[1] Galvihāra Inscription (*A. I. C.* No. 137) and *Nikāyasaṅgraha*, pp. 20 and 22. See also above, pp. 122–3.

[2] Sāhasa Malla Inscription (*A. I. C.* 156). See also above, p. 123, note 5.

words, the Buddha died in 483 B.C. And this, as it happens, agrees with the date of his death determined, from other sources, by Dr. Fleet[1], and by myself above, at p. 142, note 7.

If the foregoing calculation is correct, it follows that the compiler of that portion of the *Mahāvaṁsa* which treats of the kings mentioned above, lived at a period when 544 B.C. was the accepted Buddhist era in Ceylon. And he must have found dated records which place the accession of Udaya III in 1497 A.B. current, and that of Parākrama Bāhu I in 1697 A.B. He must, moreover, have been in a position to fix accurately the date of the accession of Parākrama Pāṇḍya in 1590 A.B., either by means of dated historical events, or by calculating backwards, from the reign of Parākrama Bāhu I, the regnal years of the five kings who reigned between these two monarchs.

There remain then the years between the accession of Udaya III, in 1497 A.B., and that of Parākrama Pāṇḍya in 1590 A.B. to be accounted for. This was, as stated above, a time of internal wars and foreign invasions, and complete anarchy seems to have prevailed in Ceylon. It is, therefore, most probable that the chronicler could not obtain accurate information regarding the length of the reigns during that period. He found that Udaya III began his reign in 1497 A.B., and Parākrama Pāṇḍya in 1590 A.B., and, at the same time, he was ignorant of the important fact that these two dates represented two different Buddhist eras, the former placing the death of the Buddha in 483 B.C., and the latter in 544 B.C. He must, therefore, have taken it for granted that the intervening period was ninety-three years (i.e. 1590 – 1497 A.B.) instead of thirty-one (i.e. 1046 – 1015 A.D.), and he accordingly adjusted the duration of the reigns, giving longer periods to those kings as to whose reigns he had no definite information.

Reverting to the present record, it will be seen that one of the officials, Sabāvaḍunnā, if not all the three who proclaimed the king's order, was a member of the body-guard of a Pāṇḍyan Rājā named Dāpuḷa. Another of the body-guard of this Rājā was instrumental in promulgating the Mahakalattäwa inscription (*A.I.C.* No. 110), which is dated in the fifteenth year of Siri Saṅgbo, that is to say, a year after the present one. There is nothing in the two records to show who this Pāṇḍyan Rājā was, but it is possible, considering the nearness of date, that he was the one who came to Ceylon

[1] See his article in *J.R.A.S.*, 1909, pp. 1–34, a printed proof of which he has kindly sent me for my use.

and sought the help of Sēna II to obtain the Pāṇḍyan sovereignty. According to the *Mahāvaṁsa*, Sēna II (917–952 A.D.[1]) himself was at the time making preparations to invade that country in retaliation for the Pāṇḍyan invasion of Ceylon during the reign of his predecessor Sēna I (897–917 A.D.[1]). He, therefore, welcomed the Pāṇḍyan prince, and sent him back with a large army commanded by Sēna's chief captain. The Sinhalese defeated the Pāṇḍyan king, took Madura and placed their nominee on the throne. Rai Bahadur Venkayya Avargaḷ, in discussing this event[2], mentions four princes, namely, (1) Māyā-Pāṇḍya, (2) a relation of his, (3) Varaguṇa, and (4) Ugra-Pāṇḍya, with one of whom the Pāṇḍyan ally of the Sinhalese may be identified. As, however, none of these is known to have borne the name Dappula or Dāpuḷa-Pāṇḍya, we are still in doubt as to the identity of the Dāpuḷa-Rājā referred to in our inscription.

TEXT.[3]

	A.		B.
1	සිරිස	1	.. ..
2	ග්ගබො	2	(වැගු)ණ ම
3	මපුර්මු	3	ගා (රා)දය
4	කා තුඩුස්	4	න් බමුණ් ගු
5	වය්(ෆ)ය වැප	5	ඛරඬ බෙ
6	පුර පොහො	6	ගෙද් ගෙව
7	දවස් වදා	7	දුන් උතුර්මෙ
8	ලසින් පාඩි	8	ගිරිවතත
9	රද් දපුල ව	9	ව පැදුම් දෙ
10	ඨ වෙකාප්ප	10	සෙන් වෙගෙ
11	ර සබාවමු	11	ර් වතත ගි
12	ස්නා සල	12	මි කොව ඉ
13	සෙම් ඉසා	13	සා දකුණ්
14	(සෙමු) පුල්ල	14	දෙසෙන් මි
15	සෙම් ඉසා	15	ගස ගි

[1] This date is based on my calculation shown above. According to Wijēsiṇha's list, Sēna II reigned from 866 to 901 A.D., and Sēna I from 846 to 866 A.D. The *Nikāyasaṅgraha* places the accession of Sēna I in 1362 A.B. expired.

[2] See *Progress Report of the Asst. Archaeological Superintendent or Epigraphy, Southern Circle*, 1907–1908, p. 68.

[3] For alternative readings, see the transcript.

Kiribat-Vehera Pillar-Inscription.

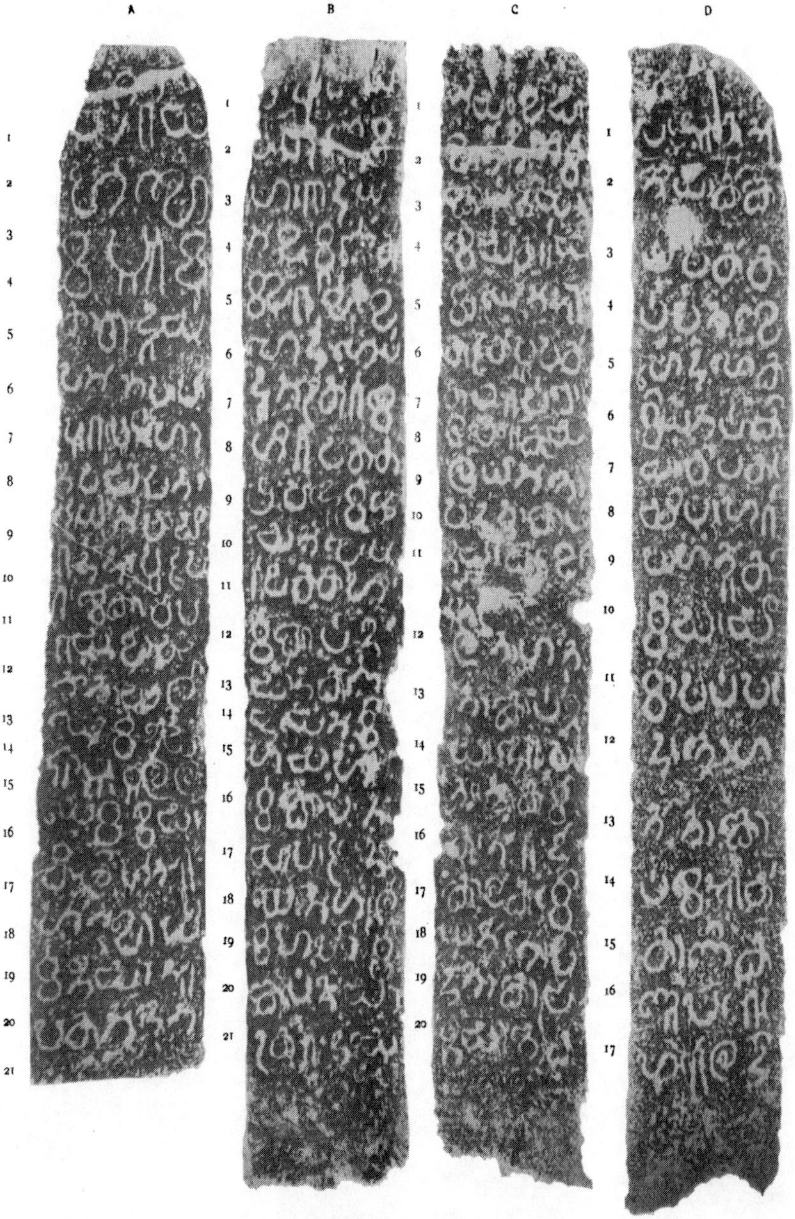

From an ink-impression supplied by the Archaeological Commissioner, Ceylon.

16 කිලින් අ
17 ණ් බොසි
18 මි ඉසා අ
19 ප තුන් ඟෙදන

16 මි කොට් ඉ
17 සා පැලෑ දෙ
18 සෙත් ගැල්
19 මග ගිම්
20 කොංට් ඉසා
21 උතුරු දෙසෙ

C.

1 න් සංබඩෑ
2 බැද්ද ගිම්
3 කොට් ඉසා
4 මෙ සතර් සී
5 මායෙන් ඈ
6 තුළන් වූ වත්
7 තට රද් (කො)
8 ල්(වැර්) කුස
9 ලයන් නො
10 වද්නා කොට්
11 ඉසා කැබෑ
12 ලි නො ගත්
13 නා කොට් ඉ
14 සා දෙරුව
15 නෑ දෙකම්
16 තැන් රද්
17 කොල් කැඹී
18 යන් නො ව
19 ද්නාං කොට්
20 ඉසා නො ක

D.

1 වෑ සුතු අ
2 නියාක් කො
3 ට් වත්ත
4 ට් වන බෙ
5 ෂෙහද් නෙ කෑ
6 මියනට් කි
7 යා පිවතෑ
8 සිවෑ හර්
9 වා ගතුත්
10 මිසෑ සී
11 මාවට් වෑ
12 දූ නො ග
13 න්නා කො
14 ට් මෙ අත්
15 තාණී ක
16 ණු පැරැ
17 හැර් ලදී

TRANSCRIPT.

A.

1 **Siri Sa-**
2 **ňg-bo**
3 mapurmu-
4 -kā tudus
5 vann(e) Väp
6 pura poho
7 davas vadā-
8 -ḷayin Pāňḍi

B.

1 .. ..
2 (vä gu)ṇa ma-
3 -hā (rā)daya-
4 -n Bamuṇ ku-
5 -mbarab[1] be-
6 -hed-geṭ
7 dun Utur-me-
8 giri-vatta-

---

[1] Read *kumbara.*

9 rad **Dāpuḷa**-va-
10 -rā me-kāppa-
11 -ra **Sabāvaḍu**-
12 -**nnā Sala**-
13 -**yem** isā
14 **(Roṭu)**[1] **Pulla**-
15 -**yem** isā
16 **Kiliṅg A**-
17 -**g-boyi**-
18 -**m** isā a-
19 -pa tun dena

9 -ṭ pädum de-
10 sen vehe-
11 -r vatta hi-
12 -m koṭ i-
13 -sā dakuṇ
14 desen mı
15 gasa hi-
16 -m koṭ i-
17 -sā päḷā de-
18 -sen gäl
19 maṅga[2] him-
20 koṭ isā
21 uturu dese-

C.

1 -n Saṁbaḍā
2 ḥädda him-
3 koṭ isā
4 me satar si-
5 -māyen ä-
6 -tuḷat vū vat-
7 -taṭa rad-(ko-)
8 -l (väri)[3] kusa-
9 -layan no-
10 -vadnā koṭ
11 isā käbä-
12 -li no gan-
13 -nā koṭ i-
14 -sā deruva-
15 -nā dekam-
16 -tān rad-
17 -kol kämi-
18 -yan no va-
19 dná koṭ
20 isā no ka

D.

1 -ṭā yutu a-
2 -niyák ko-
3 -ṭ vatta-
4 -ṭ vana be-
5 -hed ge kä-
6 -miyanaṭ ki-
7 -ya piṭata
8 siṭā har-
9 -vā ganut
10 misā si-
11 -māvaṭ vä-
12 -dā no ga-
13 -nnā ko-
14 -ṭ me at-
15 -taṇi ka-
16 -ṇu pära-
17 -här ladi

[1] Or *Koṭu*.
[2] Read *maga*.
[3] *Pora* may be suggested as an alternative reading.

TRANSLATION.

Whereas on the *upōsatha* day of the full moon of [the lunar month of] *Väp* [Sept.–Oct.], in the fourteenth year [of his reign], His Majesty **Siri Saṅgbo** declared [the following immunity], we, the three persons, **Sabāvaḍunnā Salayem**, body-guard of the Pāṇḍyan king **Dāpuḷa, (Roṭu-)Pullayem** and **Kiliṅg Agbo**[1] [do hereby notify] that [the garden called] Upper Megiri-vatta[2] which . . . the virtuous great king has granted to the dispensary at Bamuṇ-kumbara shall be bounded on the east by Veher-vatta[3], on the south by the Mī tree[4], on the west by the cart-road, and on the north by the Saṁbaḍä jungle; that the garden within these four boundaries shall not be entered by skilled servants[5] of the royal family; that no allotments[6] shall be taken; that no officials of the royal house holding two appointments[7] shall enter [the garden]. Should any person enter after committing an offence, he shall be arrested only outside the precincts after the officials of the dispensary have been informed and [the offender] has been made to turn back, but no arrest shall be made by trespassing within the precincts.

[To this effect] this edictal pillar[8] of immunity was proclaimed.

---

[1] Skt. *Kaliṅga Agrabōdhi.*

[2] *Utur-me-giri-vatta* may also be rendered 'this Giri-vatta (hill-garden) on the north side.'

[3] *Veher-vatta* = literally 'temple-garden.'

[4] *Mī-gasa*, 'wild sapota tree, *Bassia longifolia* (Sapotaceae).' See Clough's *Sinhalese Dictionary.*

[5] *Rad-kol väri kusalayan.* I am not sure of the meaning of this phrase. The above is offered tentatively. Regarding *väri*, see above, p. 53, note 7. The reading *rad-kol pora kusalayan* = 'champion fighters of the royal family.'

[6] *Käbäli*, see above, p. 37, note 5.

[7] *Deruvanā dekamlān.* The meaning of this expression is not clear to me. It occurs in the Padaviya pillar-inscription (*A. S. C.* A'pura, Seventh Progress Report, p. 61). Compare also *deruvānā dekamlān vässan* in the Vessagiri slab, above, p. 37, note 7.

[8] *Attāṇi-kaṇu pärähär.* Cf. *vävasthā-pahaṇa*, above, p. 36, note 1. *Attāṇi* = Skt. *āsthāni*, Tamil *attāṇi*, in the sense of 'the Presence,' i. e. the king in council. *Pärähär* = P. *parihāra.* Cf. Nāsik, No. 14 (*A. S. W.*, vol. iv, p. 106).

No. 12. ĪRIPINNIYĀVA PILLAR-INSCRIPTION

ĪRIPINNIYĀVA is a deserted village with a fairly large *pokuṇa* (pond) situated about one and a half miles east of Tittagōnāva in Kuñcuṭṭu Kōrale, North-Central Province.

The inscribed pillar was discovered by me on August 17, 1892. It was then lying prone in the dense thicket to the north-east of the *pokuṇa*. Some 300 feet west, a mound, 42 ft. × 36 ft., marks the site of a ruined Vihāra built facing east. Eight of its pillars, measuring 7 ft. × 1 ft. × 1 ft. 4 in. each, appear above ground. About 110 feet north of these stands the dāgaba of the monastery, which is also in ruins. It has for its eastern *mal-āsana* or altar a quadrangular slab of stone, 11½ ft. × 4 ft. 3 in., smoothed and edged with the usual moulding, while another flag with the conventional Buddha's footprint carved on it serves as its southern altar.

The inscribed pillar is 9 ft. 10 in. long, the pot or *kalaśa* shaped capital being 1 ft. in length, the quadrangular shaft 6 ft. 10 in. × 9 in. sq., and the part let into the ground 2 ft. The first side of the shaft contains twenty-six lines of writing, the second twenty-nine, the third twenty-seven, and the fourth thirty-four.

The **letters**, one to two inches in size, are fairly well preserved[1]. They represent the alphabet of the **tenth century A.D.** Their type, however, is older than that of the Kiribat-vehera pillar-inscription of about 977 A.D.[2] A comparison of the akṣaras *i*, *ka*, *ya*, and *ra*, as well as the medial vowel-sign in *ku* in our inscription, with their later forms *i*, *ka*, *ya*, *ra*, and *ku* in the other, will suffice to make this fact apparent.

As regards peculiarities of writing and spelling, attention may be drawn to the use of the cerebral *ṇ* in *radāṇan* (side A, l. 14), and to the method of writing conjoint consonants one above the other, in some cases with the *virāma* sign on the first, and the vowel sign on the second, e. g. *ṭṭhā*, *nva*, *sva*, *sti*. In the words *samaṇan-vara* (D, ll. 20–21) and *dunnu*

[1] See accompanying Plate 21.

[2] See above, p. 156, and compare Plate 20.

(l. 33), the akṣaras *ma* and *va* of the former, and *nu* of the latter, are engraved below the line, evidently either for want of space, or as corrections.

The **language** of the inscription, with the exception of one or two clauses and the names of the lands dealt with, is identical, word for word, with that of the Raṁbäva pillar[1] of the same year, and of the same king **Abhaya Salamevan Mapurumukā**, agreeing as it does generally with the style and phraseology of other records[2] of the tenth century A.D.

The **contents** tell us that the Generalissimo[3] named **Kuṭṭhā** built the **Sen-Senevirad-pirivena**[4], and that subsequently Mekāppar[5] **Guligamu Araḷeyim** and Mekāppar **Keḷālāsendeyim**, [both] belonging to this general's family, and **Kuṇḍasalā Saṅgdeṭim**[6] of the family of the Chief Secretary[7] **Varāg-Senā-Rak-samaṇa**, came together by Order of His Majesty **Abhaya Salamevan**, in the month of *Undvāp* (Nov.–Dec.) of the first year of his reign, and granted certain immunities (*pärähära*) to **Posonavulla**, in **Sulinnarugama**, already dedicated to the *pirivena*.

Now, on palaeographic and linguistic grounds we have placed the date of this inscription in the tenth century A.D. And on looking through the narrative of events of this period in the *Mahāvaṁsa*, we happily find a full corroboration of the grant, for it is related at ch. li. 88 that **Kuṭṭhaka**[8], the valiant chief captain (*sēnāpati*) of king **Sēna II**, 'built the parivēṇa **Sēna-Sēnāpati**, and endowed it with great possessions.' This Generalissimo is also mentioned in the Raṁbäva[9] and the Poḷonnaruva[10] inscriptions, and is most

---

[1] See below, p. 172.

[2] Cf. *A.I.C.* Nos. 110 to 115 and 119. See also Mr. Bell's remarks on No. 119 in *A.S.C. Seventh Progress Report*, p. 59, note 2. This inscription is undoubtedly another proclamation of the king *Abhaya Salamevan* of the Iripinniyāva and the Raṁbäva pillars.

[3] *Senevirad*=P. *Sēnāpati-rāja*; *Kuṭṭhā*=P. *Kuṭṭhaka*.

[4] P. *Sēna-Sēnāpati-rāja-parivēṇa*.

[5] *Mekāppar* for *mey-kāppar*, 'body-guard,' a Tamil title. See above, p. 38, note 2.

[6] Skt. *saṅgha-jyēṣṭha-svāmī*.

[7] *Maha-le*=Skt. *mahā-lēkhaka*, and *Varag-Sena*=prob. P. *Vajiragga-Sēna*.

[8] Wrongly *Tuṭṭhaka* in the printed Pāli and Sinhalese recensions, and also in many manuscripts. As Mr. Bell points out (*A. S. C. Seventh Progress Report*, p. 59, note 2), 'the resemblance between the Sinhalese *k* and *t* in MSS. is doubtless responsible for the error.' The correct reading *Kuṭṭhaka* is, however, to be found in the MS. copy of the *Mahāvaṁsa* in the Indian Institute, Oxford, bearing the press-mark 'Cupb. B, No. 24 (ii).' See fol. 76, l. 7. *Kuṭṭhā* is obviously the Sinhalese form of P. *Kuṭṭhaka*.

[9] See below, p. 172.

[10] *A.I.C.* No. 119.

Îripinniyâva Pillar-Inscription.

A B C D

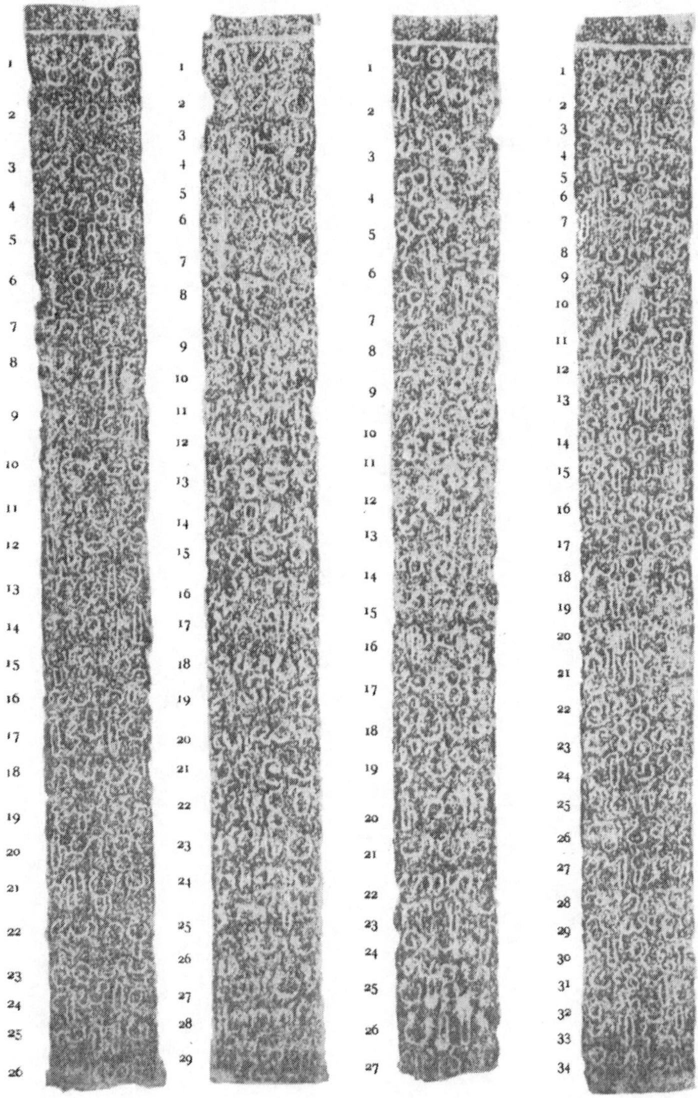

From an ink-impression supplied by the Archaeological Commissioner, Ceylon.
Scale about 1¼ inches to 1 foot.

probably identical with the very *sēnāpati* who successfully conducted a campaign in the Pāṇḍiyan country in the ninth year of the reign of king Sēna II, as related in verses 27–47 of the same chapter of the *Mahāvaṁsa*, and in the Elleväva and the Äṭavīragolläva inscriptions [1].

These facts, important as they are, do not, however, justify us in inferring that the present edict was issued by Sēna II (917–952 A. D.). It deals, not with the building of the *pariveṇa*, but with the granting of immunities to a land already dedicated to it. The latter event may, therefore, have taken place long after the former, especially in view of the fact that two of the officials who proclaimed the royal order take their family name [2] from Kuṭṭhā. Moreover, the close similarity which exists between the form of script in the Moragoḍa pillar [3] of Kassapa IV (963–980 A. D.) and that of the present inscription also leads us to assign the latter to a date later than that of Sēna II.

It may further be pointed out that the names Abhaya Salamevan and Siri Saṅgbo are *birudas* adopted by several kings, the former even by queen Līlāvatī [4] as late as the thirteenth century A. D In inscriptions, so far as we know them, Sēna II is referred to only by the title Siri Sangbo. He may, of course, have also used the title Salamevan (P. Silāmēghavaṇṇa), adopted by his predecessor Sēna I [5]; but a mere supposition of this kind cannot counteract the foregoing reasons against the identification of king Abhaya Salamevan of the Poḷonnaruva, the Raṁbäva, and the present records with Sēna II. We know that the name Abhaya Salamevan occurs as a *biruda* of both Kassapa V (980–990 A. D.) and Dappula V (990–1002 A. D.), but their inscriptions palaeographically belong to a much later date. We have, therefore, no alternative but to assume, at least tentatively, that king **Abhaya Salamevan** of our inscription was one of the two kings who reigned between Sēna II and Kassapa V, namely Udaya I (952–963 A. D.) and Kassapa IV (963–980 A. D.) [6].

Touching the officials mentioned in the grant, nothing definite is as yet known. *Varäg* can be a Sinhalese derivative of P. *Vajiragga*, but this alone does not warrant us in identifying the Chief Secretary **Varäg** of our inscription with the Chief Captain **Vajiragga** who led a punitive expedition to Ruhuṇa

[1] See *A. I. C.* Nos. 116–117, and *A. S. C. Seventh Progress Report*, p. 45.

[2] For a discussion on this point, see below, p. 193.

[3] See below, p. 201.

[4] See below, p. 177.

[5] *Mv.* l. 43.

[6] These dates are based on the calculations on p. 156 above.

in the reign of Udaya I[1]. The names **Rak-** or **Arak-samaṇa** and **Kuṇḍasalā** occur in other lithic records. The first seems to be a *biruda* or an official title of the head of a family, and the second a personal name with some special signification, as may be surmised from its constant recurrence after the former, e. g.:—

Mahale Dāpuḷā-Araksamaṇan varā Kuḍasalā Daḷsivim (*A. I. C.* 110).

Mahalekā-Araksamaṇan varā (van) Kuḍasalā (*Ibid.* 113).

Mahale Ramuk-kaňdu Vadurā-Raksamaṇan varā vana Kuḍasalā Vata-käminilā (*Ibid.* 116, *A. S. C. Seventh Progress Report*, p. 45).

Vaṭarak Saňgā-Raksamaṇan varā Kuḍasalā Vatkäm-deṭim (above, p. 34).

Mahale Varāg-Senā-Raksamaṇan varā Kuṇḍasalā Saňg-deṭim (present record).

The rivulet (*hoya* or *oya*), and the dam across it, referred to on side A (l. 26) and on B (ll. 1–11), may be identified, the former with Mora-oya, which flows by the village, and the latter with the ruined anicut, about three-quarters of a mile to the south[2]. The statement in our inscription that twelve *kiriyas* 'sowing-extent' of land was set apart, with certain immunities, for the special purpose of building this anicut goes to show that both the anicut, and the canal (*yōda-äla*) connected with it, are works of the tenth century A. D.

---

[1] *Mv.* li. 105, 126.

[2] Mr. Bell in his *Seventh Progress Report*, 1891 (p. 33), gives the following account of the irrigation works here:—

'The *Tavalam-halmillęwa-oya* being found insufficient to supply *Wahal-kaḍa-vęwa*, resort was had to the *Mora-oya.* From the river a channel, now called "Yóda-ęla," was cut for a distance of seven or eight miles to unite with the *Tavalam-halmillęwa-oya* within *Wahal-kaḍa* tank.

'I examined the water-course from its confluence with the *Tavalam-halmillęwa-oya* up to the anicut on the *Mora-oya* which divided the stream. The general course of the *ęla* is east-north-east.

'The anicut, constructed on the *Mora-oya* to enable the water to flow down the Yóda-ęla, is in the forest, half to three-quarters of a mile from Namaḍa-vęwa village. It is completely washed away, except a few blocks (average 3 ft. 3 in. by 1 ft. 9 in. by 1 ft. 2 in.) here and there in the bed. The breadth of the dam was nearly 70 ft., and the *ęla* starts from the right bank of the *Mora-oya* immediately above it. The anicut was well placed, for, fifty to sixty yards below, the river narrows to 50 ft., and passes through a gorge only 13 ft. wide with large boulders on either side, probably natural, but confidently believed by the natives to be the work of the giants of old. This would further aid in keeping the water back to pass down the Yóda-ęla.'

TEXT.

A.

1 ස්වස්ති ශ්‍රී
2 අභය
3 සලමෙ
4 වන් මපු
5 රුමුකා ප
6 ලඹු වන්
7 නෙ උඅ්වැ
8 පැ අව
9 දසවක්
10 දවස් ම
11 හවෙගෙ
12 ර කුමබා සෙ
13 නෙවිරදු
14 ණන් කැර
15 වූ සෙන්
16 සෙනෙව්
17 රද් පිරිබෙ
18 නව වදු
19 ල සුළින්ග
20 රුගැමැ
21 ආවූ සො
22 සොනවු
23 ල්ලව් පෙ
24 රෙ සිරිත්
25 සකුර් ව
26 ඩා හොය

B.

1 කොඩැබ
2 ද් බඅ්ව
3 න්නව් සො
4 සොනවු
5 ල්ලව්
6 මහමඩල
7 .(යෙ)න්වන්
8 දෙලොස්
9 කිරියැ දිය
10 බෙදුම් නො
11 ගන්නා කො
12 ව් ඉසා ම
13 හ මඩලෙ
14 ත් මෙ වන්
15 මෙලාත් [1]
16 සි නො ව
17 ද්නා කොව්
18 ඉසා වදු
19 ලෙසින් මෙ
20 සොසොන
21 මුල්ලව්
22 දෙකම් තැ
23 ත් දෙරුව
24 (නැ) නො ව
25 ද්නා කොව්
26 ඉසා පි
27 යො වදු
28 රන්නන් නො
29 වද්නා කො

C.

1 ව් ඉසා
2 රව් ලදු ප
3 ස් ලදු
4 මෙලාව්
5 සින් හෙ
6 ළ් කුලී දෙ
7 මෙළ් කුලී
8 ගැල් මීවූ
9 ත් ගම් (ගො)
10 න් බිලි බ
11 ත් බිලි
12 සාල් දි
13 හි කිර්
14 තෙල් නො
15 ගන්නා
16 කොව් ඉ
17 සා මත්
18 දිව් පිය
19 දිව් සො
20 රුන් කො
21 වා වන්
22 නො ගන්
23 නා කොව්
24 ඉසා හු
25 වර් මහ
26 වර් රද්
27 කොල් (කැ)

D.

1 මියන් නො ව
2 ද්නා කොව් ඉ
3 සා වැරියන්
4 නො ගන්නා
5 කොව් ඉසා
6 අත්තාණී පැ
7 රැහැර දෙන්න

[1] මෙලාවසි—ඇතැම්

8 ව වදෘලෙසි
9 ත් අ සෙනෙ
10 මිරද් කුඹිකා
11 වරුවත් මෙ
12 කාප්පර් ගුලී
13 කමු අරලෙ
14 සිම ඉසා
15 මෙකාප්පර්
16 කෙළාලාසෙ

17 සෙදසිම ඉ
18 සා මගලේ
19 වරුශ්සෙ
20 සා රණ්සමිණ්
21 ස්වරු කුඩස
22 ලා සග්දෙ
23 සිම ඉසා
24 අප් මෙ
25 තුවාක්දන

26 මො වදෘලෙ
27 ත් අඩුද් සො
28 සොනබුල්
29 ලෙ සිමා
30 ඇතුළු කො
31 ව මෙ අත්
32 තාණ් පැරු
33 හැර දුන්නු
34 මග

TRANSCRIPT.

A.

1 Svasti śri
2 **Abhaya**
3 **Salame-**
4 **-van** Mapu-
5 -rumukā pa-
6 -ḷamu van-
7 -ne Undvä-
8 -pä ava
9 dasa-vak
10 davas Ma-
11 -ha-vehe-
12 -rä **Kuṭṭhā** Se-
13 -nevi-radā-
14 -ṇan kärä-
15 -vū **Sen-**
16 **Senevi-**
17 **rad Pirive-**
18 **-naṭ** vadā-
19 -ḷa **Suḷinna-**
20 **-ru-gämä**
21 **ävū Po-**
22 **-sonavu-**
23 **-llaṭ** pe-
24 -re sirit
25 śakur va-
26 (-ḍā) hoya

B.

1 (hoḍä ba-)
2 (-d band-va-)
3 -nnaṭ **Po-**
4 **-sonavu-**
5 **-llaṭ**
6 (Maha-maṇḍala-)
7 (-ye)n van
8 doḷos
9 kiriyä diya-
10 bedum no
11 gannā ko-
12 -ṭ isā Ma
13 -ha-maṇḍa(le-)
14 (-n) me van
15 meläṭ-[1]
16 -si no va-
17 -dnä koṭ
18 isā vadā-
19 -ḷeyin me
20 **Posona-**
21 **-vullaṭ**
22 de-kam-tä-
23 -n deruva-
24 -nā no va-
25 -dnā koṭ
26 isā pi-
27 -yo vadā-
28 -rannaṅ no
29 vadnā ko-

C.

1 -ṭ isā
2 raṭ-ladu pa
3 -s-ladu
4 meläṭ-
5 -sin He-
6 -ḷ-kulī De-
7 -meḷ-kulī
8 gäl mīvu-

---

[1] *meläṭsi* in other places.

9 -n gam-go-
10 -n bili-ba-
11 -t bili-
12 sāl di-
13 -hi-kir
14 tel no
15 gannā
16 koṭ i-
17 -sā maṅg-
18 dīv piya-
19 dīv so-
20 -ruṇ ko-
21 -ṭā van
22 no gan-
23 -nā koṭ
24 isā su-
25 -var maha-
26 -var rad-
27 kol (kä-)

D.

1 -miyan no va-
2 -dnā koṭ i-
3 -sā väriyan
4 no gannā
5 koṭ isā
6 attāṇi pä-
7 -rähāra denna-
8 -ṭ vadāḷeyi-
9 -n ā Sene-
10 -virad **Kuṭṭhā-**
11 varā van Me-
12 -kāppar **Guli-**
13 **-gamu Araḷe-**
14 **-yim** isā
15 Mekāppar
16 **Keḷāläse-**
17 **-ndeyim** i-
18 -sā Mahale
19 **Varāg-Se-**
20 **-nā-Rakṣamaṇa-**
21 **-n-varä Kuṇḍa-sa-**
22 **-lā Saṅg-de-**
23 **-ṭim** isā
24 āp me-
25 -tuvāk dana-
26 -mo vadāḷe-
27 -n avud **Po-**
28 **-sonavul-**
29 **-le** sīmā
30 ätuḷu ko-
31 -ṭ me at-
32 -tāṇi pärä-
33 -hära dunnu-
34 -maha

TRANSLATION.

Hail! Prosperity! On the tenth day of the waning moon of the [lunar month] *Und-väp* (Nov.–Dec.) in the first year [of the reign] of His Majesty **Abhaya Salamevan.**

Whereas it was declared[1] [by His Majesty] in respect of **Posonavulla** in **Sulinnaru-gama,** dedicated to [the monastery] **Sen-Senevirad-pirivena,** which was caused to be built at the **Mahāvihāra** by the Commander-in-Chief **Kuṭṭhā,** that the privileges[2] formerly extended to it should [now] be augmented; that

[1] *Vadāḷeyin* (side B, ll. 18–19).

[2] *Pere-siril-sakur* (A, ll. 23–25)=Skt. *pūrva-caritra-satkāra* (P. *sakkāra*), 'honours paid according to former custom.'

the distribution of water[1] in the twelve *kiriyas*[2] ['sowing-extent' of land] assigned to it from the **Maha-maṇḍala**[3] for the purpose of having a dam constructed across the water-course of the *hoya* (stream), should not be appropriated; and that the *melāṭsin*[4] that came from the same Maha-maṇḍala should not enter [Posonavulla].

And whereas it was declared that a Warrant of Council[5] be granted to the effect that persons holding [the management of] two offices[6], or enforcers of customary practices[7], should not enter this **Posonavulla**; that district headmen[8], or keepers of (district) record books[9], should not appropriate the *melāṭsin*, the Sinhalese[10] coolies[11] or the Tamil coolies, the carts, the buffaloes or the village oxen, gifts[12] of boiled or raw rice, curdled milk or oil[13] [belonging to Posona-

---

[1] *Diya-bedum* (B, ll. 9–10). The above is the literal translation, but the context seems to suggest an irrigation tax levied in proportion to the water distributed. The freedom from this tax is the immunity granted to the twelve *kiriyas*, the extent of land assigned to Posonavulla. The expression *diya-bedum no gannā koṭ* occurs frequently in lithic records, but its technical meaning is not quite clear. We see, however, from the Perumäiyan-kuḷam rock-inscription (above, pp. 66–74) and from the *Mahāvaṁsa* (xxxv. 48), that a tax on water, called *dakapati* (P. *dakapatti*), used to be regularly levied. *Diya-bedum* of the tenth-century inscriptions is probably a later term for the same tax. See also below, p. 199, note 8.

[2] See above, p. 3, note 4.

[3] *Maha-maṇḍala*=Skt. *mahā-maṇḍala*. This may be the name of a district. Cf. *Go-maṇḍla* in the Raṁbāva pillar (l. 13) below, p. 172, *Īṛa-maṇḍalam*, the Tamil name for Ceylon, and *Mahā-maṇḍalē-śvara*, the title of certain South Indian kings. *Mahā-maṇḍala*, like the *amālya-maṇḍala* in the Puliyan-kuḷam Slab of Queen Līlāvatī (p. 180, below), may also mean 'the great Council,' referring probably to the king's Advisory Council, in which case the preposition 'by' should be substituted for 'from' in the translation.

[4] See above, p. 53, note 10.

[5] *Attāṇi-pārāhāra* (D, ll. 6–7) = Skt. *āsthāni-parihāra*, lit. 'Council immunity.' See above, p. 161, note 8.

[6] *Dekamtän deruvanā*. The meaning of this phrase is still not clear to me. See above, p. 37, note 7, and p. 161, note 7, and below, p. 207, note 3.

[7] See below, p. 207, note 1.

[8] *Raṭ-ladu*=Skt. *rāṣṭra-labdha*, lit. 'recipients of districts.' See below, p. 206, note 7.

[9] *Pas-ladu*=Skt. *pañjikā-labdha*, see below, p. 206, note 8. Guṇasēkara Mudaliyar's rendering of *raṭ-ladu pas-ladu* is 'those who have obtained the (whole) kingdom or a part thereof.'

[10] *Heḷ*=Skt. *Siṁhala*. Cf. *Heḷa-diva*=Skt. *Siṁhala-dvīpa*, 'the Island of Ceylon.'

[11] *Kulī*. See Mihintale tablet B, l. 55, above, pp. 97 and 112. Hindī, Panjābī, &c., *kulī*, 'a hired labourer.' Modern Sinh. *kulī*, Tamil, Telugu, &c., *kūli*, mean 'wages.'

[12] *Bili-bat* and *bili-sāl* evidently refer to what in modern times are called *aḍukku*—presents of rice (and other provisions) usually made to officials on circuit. I do not think *bili* here means an offering to a god.

[13] *Dihi-kir* (Skt. *dadhi*+*kṣīra*) taken separately mean 'curds and milk.' *Tel*=P. *tēla*, 'sesamum oil.' Here probably *gi-tel*, 'clarified butter.'

vulla]; that those who live by highway robbery [1] or by vagrant habits [2], thieves, or those who come [for shelter] after committing assaults [3], should not be admitted; that goldsmiths [4] or chief artisans (?) [4], or servants [5] of the royal family, should not enter; and that farm labourers [6] should not be appropriated.

We, all of us, [namely:—] Mekāppar [7] **Guligamu Araḷeyim** and Mekāppar **Keḷālāsendeyim** [both] of the family [8] of the Commander-in-Chief **Kuṭṭhā**, and **Kuṇḍasalā Saṅgdeṭim** [9] of the family [8] of the Chief Secretary **Varāg-Senā-Raksamaṇa**, having come together by Order, have [now] defined the boundaries of **Posonavulla**, and have given this Warrant of Council (*attāṇi pārūhāra*).

---

[1] *Maṅg-dīv*=Skt. *mārga-jīva*. Cf. *maṅg-giva*, above, p. 97, l. 55.

[2] *Piya-dīv*=Skt. *pāda-jīva*. Cf. *piya-giva* (l. c.).

[3] Probably 'murder.' Cf. *minī-keṭū*, above, p. 47 (l. 18). See also below, p. 207, note 6.

[4] *Suvar*=Skt. *suvarṇa-kāra*, Sinh. *suvankaru*, *suvaru* (*Nām.* and *Ruvan.*); *mahavar*=Skt. *mahā-kāra* (?). Cf. Sinh. *maha-āduru*=Skt. *mahā-ācārya*, a title applied to a master-carpenter. Both these words may also be rendered:—*suvar* or *suvaru*=Skt. *sūpakāra*, 'a cook' (*E. S.*, p. 92, and *Piyum*, p. 56), or Skt. *sūtra-kāra*, 'a weaver,' and *mahavar*=Skt. *matsya-kāra*, P. *maccha-kāra*, 'fisher' or 'fish-monger' (P. *maccha* being equivalent to Sinh. *maha*) or Skt. *māṁsa-kāra*, 'butcher.' The statement in the *Mahāvaṁsa* (xlix. 48) that Aggabōdhi VIII 'forbade the bringing in into the inner city of flesh, fish, and strong drinks, on the Upōsatha days,' lends support to this derivation.

[5] *Kāmiyan*. In the *Ruvanmal* and *Piyummal* vocabularies (pp. 49–50 of the printed edition) *kāmi* is given as a synonym for *lēkama*, 'clerk' or 'secretary.'

[6] *Vāriyan*, see above, p. 53, note 7.

[7] See above, p. 164, note 5.

[8] *Varā van*. See below, pp. 193–194, for an explanation of these two words.

[9] Skt. *saṅgha-jyēṣṭha-svāmī*.

No. 13. RAMBĀVA PILLAR-INSCRIPTION

THE village of Rambāva lies on the right bank of the *Yōda-äla*, mentioned above, at a distance of about three miles north-east of Īripinniyāva. It was visited by the Archaeological Commissioner (Mr. H. C. P. Bell) in September, 1891, and by me as his assistant in August of the following year. Mr. Bell discovered 'the square inscribed pillar, leaning over at an angle of thirty or so degrees' on the bund of the tank, and made a tolerably accurate copy[1] under difficulties, and in spite of the much worn state of the stone.

The pillar measures 5 ft. 10 in. by 1 ft. square. All its four sides are inscribed, side A containing seventeen lines of writing, B nineteen, C nineteen, and D sixteen.

The **akṣaras** are on the whole well preserved, and are each about 1½ in. in height and breadth[2].

The **date** of the inscription is the middle *poho* day of the bright half (i.e. the full moon day) of the lunar month, *Hil* (Oct.–Nov.), in the first year of the reign of king **Abhaya Salamevan.** It is, therefore, only a little over five weeks earlier than that of the **Īripinniyāva** pillar described above. Hence in type of **letters,** and in style of **language,** the two records agree completely, the text on sides B and C of the present pillar being, moreover, the same, word for word, as that on sides B (l. 26) and C of the other. In **orthography,** however, there are a few differences more or less of phonological importance. We find here *mapurmukā*, *manḍla*, *vadāḷein*, *sendeim*, and *dunmaha*, instead of *mapurumukā*, *manḍala*, *vadāḷeyin*, *sendeyim*, and *dunnumaha* in the Īripinniyāva pillar.

The **subject** of the two inscriptions is also the same. Both deal with the granting of immunities in respect of certain lands dedicated to the **Sen-Senevirad-pirivena,** built by the Commander-in-Chief **Kuṭṭhā** at the Mahāvihāra. These privileges refer in the present instance to the four *payaḷas*[3] 'sowing-extent' of land in **Gälinduru Gomanḍla**[4].

The officials, instrumental in conferring the *attāṇi pärähära* (Council Warrant), are likewise identical in both cases. What I have written about them, and about their king, **Abhaya Salamevan,** and his identity in the foregoing article, is applicable here also.

---

[1] Since published with transcript and translation as appendix E to the *Seventh Progress Report*, 1891. See pp. 25, 59, and 60.

[2] See Plate 22.

[3] *Payala*, modern Sinh. *pāla*. See above, p. 55, note 3.

[4] P. *Gō-maṇḍala*, 'cattle-pen.'

TEXT.

A.

1 ස්වස්ති ශ්‍රී
2 අභය්
3 සලමෙව
4 ණ් මපුර්මුකා
5 පලඹුවන්නෙ
6 ගිලෑ පුර මැ
7 ඤී පොහො ද
8 වස් කුඹා සෙනෙ
9 විරදුණන් මග
10 වෙහෙරැ කැර්වූ සෙ
11 ණ් සෙනෙවිරද් පිපි
12 වෙනව වදාළ ගෑ
13 ලිඳුරු ගොමඩ
14 ල සතර් පය
15 ලව දෙකම්තැන්
16 දෙරුවනෑ නො ව
17 ද්නා කොට ඉසා

B.

1 පියොවදාර
2 න්නත් නො වද්
3 නා කොට ඉසා
4 රව ලදූ පස්
5 ලදූ මෙලාව
6 සින් හෙල් කුලී
7 දෙමෙල් කුලී ගැල්
8 මිවුන් ගම් ගො
9 න් කිලි බත් කි
10 ලි සාල් දිගිකි
11 ර් තෙල් නො ගන්
12 නා කොට ඉසා
13 මන්දිව පි
14 යදිව සොරු
15 න් කොඩා[1] වන්
16 නොගන්නා කො
17 ට ඉසා සුව
18 ර් මහවර් රද්
19 කොල් කැමියන්

C.

1 නො වද්නා කො
2 ට ඉසා වැ
3 රියන් නො
4 ගන්නා කො
5 ට ඉසා
6 අත්තා
7 ණී පැරැගෑ
8 ර් දෙන්නට
9 වදාලෙඉන්
10 අ සෙනෙවි
11 රද් කුඹාව
12 රැ වන් මෙකා
13 ජ්පර ගුලි
14 ගබු අරලෙඹු
15 ම ඉසා මෙකා
16 ජ්පර් කෙලලා
17 සෙපෙඳුම් ඉ
18 සා මහලෙ
19 වරණ් සෙනා

D.

1 රක්සම(ණ)
2 ස්වරැවත්
3 කුඩසලා
4 සග්දෙමි
5 ම ඉසා අ
6 ජ මෙතුවා
7 ක් දනමො ව
8 දෑලෙඉන් අ
9 වුද් ගැලිඳුරු
10 ගොමඩල
11 සතර පය
12 ලැ සිමා
13 ඇතුළු කො
14 ට වෙ අත්තා
15 ණී පැරැගෑ
16 ර් දුන්මහයි

---

[1] වා

TRANSCRIPT.

A.

1 Svasti śrī
2 **Abhay**
3 **Salameva-**
4 -**n** mapurmukā
5 paḷamu-vanne
6 Hilä pura mä-
7 -ndi poho da-
8 -vas **Kuṭṭhā** sene-
9 -vi-radāṇan Maha-
10 veherā kärvū **Se-**
11 -**n-Seṇevirad-piri-**
12 -**venaṭ** vadāḷa **Gä-**
13 -**linduru Gomaṇḍ-**
14 -**la** satar paya-
15 -laṭ de-kam-tän-
16 deruvanā no va-
17 -dnā koṭ isā

B.

1 piyo-vadāra-
2 -nnan no vad-
3 -nā koṭ isā
4 raṭ-ladu pas-
5 ladu melāṭ-
6 -sin Heḷ-kulī
7 Demeḷ-kulī gäl
8 mīvun gam-go-
9 -n bili-bat bi-
10 -li-säl dihi-ki-
11 -r tel no gan-
12 -nā koṭ isā
13 maṅg-diva pi-
14 -ya-diva soru-
15 -n koṭhā[1] van
16 no gannā ko-
17 -ṭ isā suva-
18 -r mahavar rad-
19 -kol kämiyan

C.

1 no vadnā ko-
2 -ṭ isā vä-
3 -riyan no
4 gannā ko-
5 -ṭ isā
6 attā-
7 -ṇi pärähä-
8 -r dennaṭ
9 vadāḷein
10 ā Senevi-
11 rad **Kuṭṭhā**-va-
12 -rā van Mekā-
13 -ppar **Guli-**
14 -**gamu Araḷei-**
15 -**m** isā Mekā-
16 -ppar **Keḷalā-**
17 -**sendeim** i-
18 -sā Mahale
19 **Varag-Senā**

D.

1 **Raksama**(ṇa-)
2 -**n**-varā van
3 **Kuṇḍasalā**
4 **Saṅg-deṭi-**
5 -**m** isā ā-
6 -p metuvā-
7 -k danamo va-
8 -dāḷein a-
9 -vud **Gälinduru**
10 **Gomaṇḍla**
11 satara paya-
12 -lä sīmā
13 ātuḷu ko-
14 -ṭ me attā-
15 -ṇi pärähä-
16 -r dunmahayi

[1] Read *koṭā*.

Raṁbâva Pillar-Inscription.

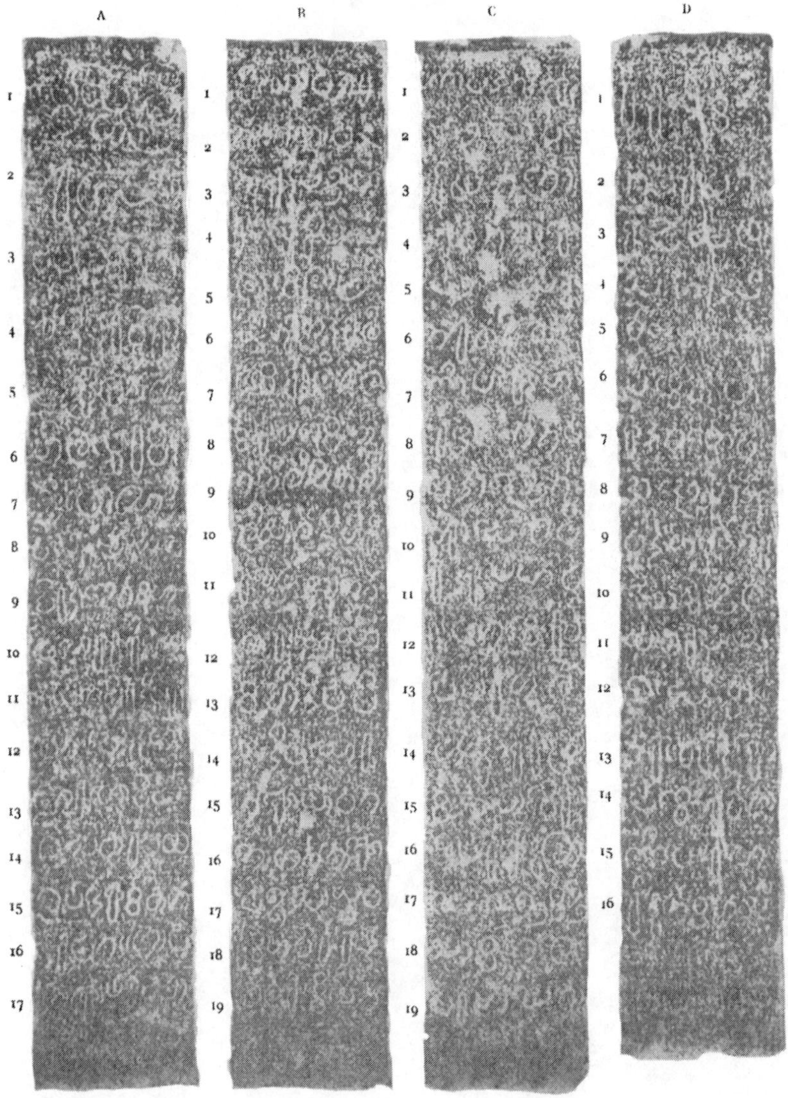

From an ink-impression supplied by the Archæological Commissioner, Ceylon.
Scale about 1½ inches to 1 foot.

TRANSLATION.

Hail! Prosperity! On the middle *poho*[1] day of the waxing moon [of the lunar month] of *Hil*[2] in the first year of [the reign of] His Majesty **Abhay Salamevan.**

Whereas it was declared[3] [by His Majesty] in respect of the four *payalas*[4] ['sowing-extent' of land] in **Gäliňduru Gomaňḍla,** dedicated to the monastery **Sen-Senevirad-pirivena,** which was caused to be built by the Commander-in-Chief **Kuṭṭhâ** at the Mahāvihāra, that a Warrant of Council be granted to the effect that persons holding [the management of] two offices[5] should not enter it; that enforcers[6] of customary practices should not enter; that district headmen[7] or keepers[8] of district record books[8] should not appropriate the *melāṭsin*, the Sinhalese coolies[9], the Tamil coolies, the carts, the buffaloes, the village oxen, gifts of boiled or raw rice[10], curdled milk or oil[11] [belonging to the said four *payalas*]; that those who live by highway robbery[12] or by vagrant habits, or thieves, or those who come [for shelter] after committing assaults[13] should not be admitted; that goldsmiths[14], chief artisans (?), or servants[15] of the royal family should not enter [the said four *payalas*]; and that farm labourers[16] be not appropriated.

We, all of us, [namely:—] Mekāppar **Guligamu Araḷeim,** and Mekāppar **Keḷalâ-Sendeim**[17] [both] of the family of the Commander-in-Chief **Kuṭṭhâ,** and **Kuňḍasalâ Saňgdetim** of the family of the Chief Secretary **Varag-Senâ-Raksamaṇa,** having come together by Order, have [now] defined the boundaries of the four *payalas* [of land] in **Gäliňduru Gomaňḍla,** and have granted this Warrant of Council.

---

[1] Possibly the full moon, this being the middle *upōsatha* day of the month. Sinh. *pohoya*, *pohō*, *boho*, *pōya* or *pō* = P. *upōsatha*.

[2] Modern Sinh. *Il*, October–November.

[3] *Vadāḷein* (side C, l. 9).

Modern Sinh. *pāla*. See above, p. 55, note 3.

[5] See above, p. 170, note 6, and below, p. 207, note 3.

[6] See below, p. 207, note 1.

[7] See above, p. 170, note 8, and below, p. 206, note 7.

[8] See above, p. 170, note 9, and below, p. 206, note 8.

[9] Guṇasēkara Mudaliyar translates *heḷ* by 'hills,' and *kulī* by 'huts.' See above, p. 170, notes 10 and 11.

[10] See above, p. 170, note 12.

[11] See above, p. 170, note 13.

[12] See above, p. 171, notes 1 and 2.

[13] See above, p. 171, note 3, and below, p. 207, note 6.

[14] See above, p. 171, note 4.

[15] See above, p. 171, note 5.

[16] *Vāriyan*, 'unfriendly persons,' according to Guṇasēkara Mudaliyar, but see above, p. 53, note 7.

[17] *Keḷālāsendeyim* in the Īripinniyāva pillar, above, p. 171.

No. 14. THE SLAB-INSCRIPTION MARKED $\frac{D}{8}$ OF QUEEN LĪLĀVATĪ

THIS inscribed slab is one of a number now lying at the premises of the Archaeological Commissioner's Office at Anurādhapura. Nobody seems to know for certain its original home; but as it is placed together with those from Puliyan̲-kuḷam[1], a small village about two and a half miles north-east of the present town of Anurādhapura, it also is supposed to have come from the same locality.

The ruins at Puliyan̲-kuḷam consist of a dāgaba and three Vihāras within a raised site, about 300 ft. square, banked up by a moulded revetment of large stone slabs and surrounded by about forty buildings, mostly monks' residences, within an outer quadrangle, 330 by 360 yards. To these may be added a *pokuṇa* (pond) near the northern outer gate, a *piḷima-gē* (image-house) for a colossal figure of the Buddha, and one or two other buildings[2].

In the course of excavation Mr. Bell discovered several inscribed slabs at the *piḷima-gē* and in the stone revetment of the stylobate of the dāgaba. Three of them are marked respectively $\frac{C}{6}$, $\frac{C}{7}$, and $\frac{C}{8}$. The slab dealt with here is marked $\frac{D}{8}$. It bears an inscription in twenty-nine lines, boldly carved on a surface, 4 ft. by 2 ft., smoothed and ruled for the purpose. The **letters**, of which the average size is about $1\frac{1}{2}$ inches, represent the type of the alphabet of the **twelfth** and **thirteenth** centuries. They agree in every detail with those of the Daṁbulla inscription of king Kīrti Niśśaṅka Malla (1187–1196 A. D.)[3]. Their difference from the earlier alphabet employed in the inscriptions of Mahinda IV[4] is specially noticeable in the akṣaras *a*, *ja*, *ma*, *ra*, *ḷa*, and *ḷu*. The **language** too, bristling as it does with Sanskrit *tatsamas*, is in keeping with the style of other inscriptions of the twelfth and thirteenth centuries.

The **contents** tell us that Her Majesty **Abhā Salamevan Līlāvatī** ruled

---

[1] So called probably from a Śaiva temple or shrine that may have existed in the village, for the Tamil name புலியன்குளம் *Puliyan̲-kuḷam* signifies the tank of *Puliyan*, 'he who [wears the skin of] a tiger,' i.e. either Śiva (புலித்தோலுடையோன் *Pulittōluḍaiyōn̲*) or a Śaiva ascetic.

[2] For a full account of this important group of ruins, see the Archaeological Commissioner's Reports for 1891 (p. 3), 1896 (p. 3), 1897 (pp. 4–6), and 1898 (pp. 3–4), as well as the *Sixth Progress Report*, 1891 (pp. 1–2).

[3] At p. 123, above, I stated that the date of this king's accession might be placed in the first half of 1188 A. D. But on further calculation I find that this event could very well have taken place six months earlier, i. e. in the latter half of 1187 A. D.

[4] Cf. Plates 14–16.

the island with the aid of a Council of Ministers. At Anurādhapura she built a *dāna-śālā* (almshouse), and close to it a *masisaya*[1] (probably a platform), endowing them with land, slaves, and cattle for the perpetual maintenance of charity.

No date of any kind is given in the inscription. Līlāvatī's intermittent rule can, however, be fixed from other sources. We know from the Sinhalese chronicles that Parakkama Bāhu I had two queens, namely Līlāvatī and Rūpavatī, daughters of his uncles, Sirivallabha and Kittisirimēgha respectively. Soon after Parakkama Bāhu's death in 1186 A. D., there were perpetual intrigues, among the Kāliṅga and Sinhalese princes and officers of state, for political ascendancy[2]. In consequence, very few of the succeeding sovereigns were able to rule long. They were either murdered or deposed.

Līlāvatī was the seventh sovereign to hold the sceptre after the death of her husband, Parakkama Bāhu I, eleven years previously. She was placed on the throne by the powerful Chief of the Army, Kitti[3], who may be identified with the Lag Vijayasiṅgu Kit mentioned in the Abhayaväva pillar[4] as her *agrāmātya* or prime minister. Both in this inscription and in that under discussion, she adopts the *biruda* Abhā Salamevan, so common in tenth-century records[5].

From subsequent events it is apparent that Kitti's rule through Līlāvatī was not altogether popular. He himself perhaps was not satisfied with her. His co-ministers preferred a prince of the Kāliṅga dynasty to reign over them. He, therefore, deposed[6] Līlāvatī after she had reigned about three years (1197–1200 A. D.). He then invited Sāhasa Malla, half-brother of king Kīrti Niśśaṅka Malla[7], over from India, and installed him on the throne on Wednesday, August 23, 1200 A. D.[8]

As to the fate of this monarch nothing is known. The chronicles merely

---

[1] See below, p. 181, note 11.

[2] See my remarks on p. 125 above. Though both the parties were related to one another by intermarriage, yet the Kāliṅgas considered themselves as members of a race distinct from and superior to the Sinhalese, and their leaders as rightful heirs to the throne of Ceylon. This is well illustrated by the objections raised by queen Ratanāvali, mother of Parakkama Bāhu I, to the marriage of her daughter Mittā to Mānābharaṇa, son of her brother-in-law, Sirivallabha (*Mv.* lxiii. 6–16).

[3] *Mv.* lxxx. 30–31.

[4] *A. I. C.* No. 157 (pp. 69, 104–105, and 137). Dr. Müller's remarks, as well as his translation of the text, need some modification. The *Mahāvaṁsa* does not say that General Kitti ever married Līlāvatī, nor does the text connote the idea that Abhā Salamevan was Līlāvatī's consort.

[5] See above, p. 165. Dr. Müller wrongly took the title to be the name of a king, and fell into the error of regarding him as her royal consort.

[6] The reasons for taking this step are given in Sāhasa Malla's inscription at Poḷonnaruva (*A. I. C.* No. 156).

[7] See above, p. 124, note 1.

[8] See above, p. 123, note 4.

state that he ruled for two years, and that thereafter a general called Āyasmanta[1] reigned at Poḷonnaruva, the then capital of Ceylon, for seven years, that is to say, six years through Kalyāṇavatī, the dowager-queen of Kīrti Niśśaṅka Malla, and one year by placing on the throne a three-months-old prince named Dhammāsōka. Then a governor named Anikaṅga, with a large army from the Cōḷa country, invaded the island, put both Āyasmanta and his protégé to death, and took up the reins of government. But after seventeen days one of his own generals, called Camūnakka, killed him in turn, and installed the old queen Līlāvatī again on the throne. Through her he ruled the country for one year, when Lōkissara came from the opposite coast with a Tamil army, and took possession of the throne for nine months. Thereafter Parakkama of the Kālanāgara race, the chief of the army, anointed the queen Līlāvatī for the third time, and administered the government through her for seven months until they were deposed by the Pāṇḍiyan king Parakkama.

The dates of these events may be fixed with the aid of the calculations on p. 123, above. According to them Līlāvatī was on the throne first from 1197 to 1200 A.D., secondly in 1209, and lastly in 1211. The present grant was most probably made during the first period, when the government was administered by Kitti Sēnāpati, called also in Sinhalese Lag Vijayasiṅgu Kit Senevi, if we may trust a similar inscription at Abhayavāva[2] dated the third year of his administration as Līlāvatī's prime minister.

In conclusion, it may perhaps be of interest to mention that in spite of the unsettled state of the country a good number of scholars flourished about this period both at Poḷonnaruva and elsewhere in the island. They have left us some of the best productions in Pāli and Sinhalese literature[3]. Under the patronage of Kitti Sēnāpati the Sinhalese poem *Sasadāvata* and probably *Muva-dev-dāvata* also were composed between 1197 and 1200 A.D., while under that of the minister Parakkama, Dhammakitti Thēra[4] composed the Pāli poem *Dāṭhāvaṁsa* in 1211 A.D.

---

[1] So stated in *Mv.* lxxx. 33. But in the *Pūjāvaliya* and in the *Rājāvaliya* this general is called Abō Seneviraja (°rada). In the Sāhasa Malla's inscription (*A.I.C.* No. 156) both the titles Āyuṣmat and Abōnā are applied to Lag Vijayasiṅgu Kit (Pāli, Kitti). Hence the person referred to by Āyasmanta (the Pāli form of the nominative plural of Skt. Āyuṣmat) in the *Mahāvaṁsa* may have been no other than this old general who first installed Līlāvatī on the throne.

[2] *A.I.C.* No. 157.

[3] See *Catalogue of the Sinhalese MSS. in the British Museum*, Introd. pp. xiv–xvii.

[4] See *J.R.A.S.* for 1896, p. 200.

TEXT.

1 සිරිබර ඔකාවස් රජ්පරපුරෙ
2 (නි) මුහුන් මැලි විසල් ගුණගණෙ
3 න් දුළු සියලු කලා තෙර පැමිණි අඟා
4 සලමෙවන් ලීලාවතී ස්වාමින් ව
5 හන්සෙ තමන් වහන්සෙ පරම්පරා
6 යාත ත්‍රිසිංහල රජය ධැමින් සෙමි
7 න් පැමිණෑ එකාතපත්‍ර කොටැ ප්‍රඥුචිත්‍ර
8 ම භක්ති සම්පන්න අමාත්‍ය මඩළ ඇ
9 ති කොටැ ස්වමඩළය පරමඩළයෙහි
10 රුපද්‍රව කොටැ ලොක ශාසන සෙ
11 මෙහි තබා දස රාජ ධර්මයෙන් ර
12 ජ කරනසෙගයෙක් අනුරාධපුරෙ
13 ඟි නාත් දෙසෙහොසළ මුළු දිළිඳු
14 න් සිත් පුරා දන් දෙනු සඳහා ස
15 ලබල් මෙබාම් නම් විරුදුයෙන් දා
16 න ශාලාවක් රක්ෂිත ගොපිත කො
17 ටැ කරවා එව කුළුබවු ඇවූ දෙය
18 පසිඳිනා පරිද්දෙන් ශාලාව සමී
19 පයෙහි නානා දෙශී ව්‍යාපාරයක් ල
20 වා සල බලම් මෙබාම් නම් මසිස
21 ය කරවා ගිර සඳ පමුණු කොටැ හ
22 කරගොඩ වරුපහින් කිපුවට තුන් යා
23 ළක් හා කිලිංනාවියළින් යාළක් හා
24 වහල් තිසක් හා එළ සරක් මී ස
25 රකින් ගෙළසික්[1] ලවා වදාරා නි
26 ති දන් පවත්නා පරිද්දෙන් මෙ කො
27 ටැ වදාළ සුචරිතය මතුවන රජද
28 රුවනුදු දෙ ලො වැඩ සලකා තුබූ ප
29 රිද්දෙන් තබා රක්ෂාකරනු මැනැවි

---

[1] ගෙළසියක්

TRANSCRIPT.

1 Siri-bara Okāvas raj-parapure-
2 (-hi) mundun māli visal guṇa geṇe-
3 (-n) duḷu siyalu kalā tera pāmiṇi **Abhā**
4 **Salamevan Līlāvatī** svāmin-va-
5 -hanse taman-vahanse paramparā-
6 -yāta Tri-Siṁhaḷa[1] rajaya dhāmin semi-
7 -n pāmiṇā ekātapatra koṭā prajñā vikra-
8 -ma bhakti sampanna amātya-maṇḍaḷa ā-
9 -ti koṭā sva-maṇḍaḷaya para-maṇḍaḷayen ni-
10 -r-upadrava koṭā loka śāsana se-
11 -mehi tabā dasa rāja dharmmayen ra-
12 -ja karanaseyek **Anurādhapure-**
13 -hi nan desen osaḷa muḷu diḷindu-
14 -n sit purā dan denu sandahā **Pa-**
15 **-labalavi-medhāvi** nam viruduyen dā-
16 -na-śālāvak rakṣita gopita ko-
17 -ṭā karavā eṭa kuḷubaḍu āvū deya
18 pasindinā paridden śālāva samī-
19 -payehi nānā dēśī vyāpārayan la-
20 -vā **Palabalavi-medhāvi** nam (masisa-)
21 (-ya) karavā hira sanda pamuṇu koṭā (**Ha-**)
22 **-kara-goḍa**-varu-patin bijuvaṭa tun yā-
23 -ḷak hā **Kiliṁnā**-viyaḷin yāḷak hā
24 vahal tisak hā eḷa-sarak mī-sa-
25 -rakin yeḷasik[2] lavā vadārā ni-
26 -ti dan pavatnā paridden me ko-
27 -ṭā vadāḷa sucaritaya matu-vana raja-da-
28 -ruvanu-du de-lo-väḍa salakā tubū pa-
29 -ridden tabā rakṣā-karanu mānävi

---

[1] Read *Siṁhaḷa*. [2] Read *yeḷasiyak*.

Slab-Inscription (11/8) of Queen Lilāvati.

From an ink-impression supplied by the Archaeological Commissioner, Ceylon.

Scale about 2 inches to 1 foot.

TRANSLATION.

[Lines 1–7] Her Majesty **Abhā Salamevan Līlāvatī,** the most pre-eminent[1] in the royal line of the illustrious Okkāka dynasty, who shines with a multitude of all-pervading virtues, and who has reached the [farthest] shore of all arts, has justly and fairly[2] attained to the sovereignty of Tri-Siṁhala[3], which came to her by hereditary succession, and has brought it under one canopy [of dominion].

[Lines 7–12] By creating a Council[4] of wise, brave, and faithful ministers, she has freed her own kingdom from the dangers [arising] from other kingdoms[5], and [thus] placing the people and the Buddhist Church[6] in a peaceful state, Her Majesty reigns in accordance with the ten virtues belonging to royalty[7].

[Lines 12–21] For the purpose of giving alms to the full satisfaction[8] of the poor that throng into Anurādhapura from various quarters, she caused an almshouse with the title[9] of **Pala-balavi-mēdhāvi** to be established, protected, and maintained. And for the supplying of spices,[10] and the like [required] for it, she caused the platform[11] called **Pala-balavi-mēdhāvi** to be built in the neighbourhood of the almshouse by traders of divers countries.

---

[1] *Mudun-māli* = Skt. *mūrdhan* + *mālikā*, 'the head-garland.'

[2] *Dhāmin semin* = P. *dhammēna samēna*. Cf. the expression *dhammēna samēna aṭṭaṁ vinicchineyyātha*, 'You should judge the case with justice and impartiality.' Clough (*Sinh. Dict.* s. v.) renders *semin* by 'slowly, gently, peacefully.' The former is derived from Skt. *sama* and the latter from Skt. *śama*, both through Pāli and Prākrit *sama*.

[3] The three ancient divisions of Ceylon were *Ruhuṇu*, *Māyā*, and *Pihiṭi*, Southern, Central, and Northern respectively.

[4] *Maṇḍala* here in l. 8 means 'assembly,' in the next line 'territory.'

[5] Cf. *sva-maṇḍalaya para-maṇḍalaya* in Niśśanka Malla's inscription at Poḷonnaruva (*A. I. C.* No. 148 B, l. 7).

[6] *Lōka-śāsana* (l. 10) = *lōkayada śāsanayada* in Niśśanka Malla's inscription at Ruvanväli Dāgaba (*A. I. C.* No. 145, l. 19).

[7] *Daśa-rāja-dharma*. See glossary to the Sinhalese version of the *Mahāvaṁsa*, Pt. II, for an enumeration of the ten kingly virtues.

[8] *Sit-purā*, lit. 'having filled (their) hearts,' i. e. to their hearts' content.

[9] *Viruda* or *biruda*.

[10] *Kuḷu-baḍu*, 'pungent substances, such as dry ginger, pepper, &c.' (Clough's *Sinh. Dict.*).

[11] *Masisaya*. I am not sure of the meaning of this word. In Clough (*op. cit.*) *māsise* means 'platform, palm of the hand.' Cf. also *māssa*, Skt. *mañca*, 'platform.'

[Lines 21–29] Her Majesty [thereafter] granted in perpetuity[1] three *yāḷas*[2] 'sowing-extent' [of land] from the tract of fields at **Hakara-goḍa,** one *yāḷa* from **Kilimnā**-viyaḷa, 30 serfs, 150[3] [head of] oxen and buffaloes. And she did [all] this in order that alms might be given constantly.

May future sovereigns also, having regard to the good of the two worlds, keep it up as it has been kept up, and [continue to] give their protection.

No. 15. PULIYAṈ-KUḶAM SLAB-INSCRIPTION (?) OF UDĀ MAHAYĀ

AS stated above, on p. 176, this slab was unearthed in 1898 at the *piḷima-gē* (image-house) of the ruined monastery at Puliyaṉ-kuḷam. It measures nearly 6 ft. × 2 ft. Its shape, pointed at the lower end and rough on three of its sides, indicates that it must have originally stood upright, fixed in the ground two feet deep and built into the wall of the building, leaving the inscribed side alone exposed to view.

The inscription is neatly engraved in forty-four lines on a smoothed surface, 3 ft. 11 in. × 2 ft. 1 in., edged with the usual moulding in relief. The **letters** exhibit the type of the alphabet of the last quarter of the tenth or the first of the eleventh century A. D.[4] A careful comparison of akṣaras such as *a*, *i*, *ṭa*, *ba*, *ma*, *ra*, and *la* with those of the Vessagiri slabs Nos. 1 and 2[5] respectively of the second year of Dappula V (i. e. 992–993 A. D.)[6] and the ninth year of Mahinda IV (1035–1036 A. D.) will show that our inscription must have been engraved sometime between these two dates. The **language** also supports this view, containing as it does phrases[7] occurring in records of both the tenth and the eleventh centuries. As to the **grammar**, it is interesting to see in *mahayā-ge* (l. 35), *mahayā-gehi* (l. 44), and *rad-gehi* (l. 38), the gradual transition of *ge*, *gehi* (P. *gēhamhi*, 'in the house') to the position of a genitive case suffix[8].

---

[1] *Hira-sanda-pamuṇu*, lit. 'sun-moon-gift,' i. e. a grant that should be valid so long as the sun and moon exist.

[2] *Yāḷa* = 20 *ammaṇa* of grain or 20 head of cattle. See above, p. 103, note 11.

[3] *Yeḷa-sik* for *yeḷa-siyak*.

[4] See accompanying Plate 24.

[5] See above, Plates 8 and 9.

[6] These dates are based on the calculations on p. 156, above.

[7] See my notes on the translation, below, pp. 187–190.

[8] See also Geiger's *Litt. u. Spr. d. Singh.* § 40.

The **contents** state that **Udā Mahayā's**[1] father was **Mihind**[2] **Mahayā**, his mother **Kitā Räjna**[3], and his son **Kitagbo Āpā**[4]; that he was *Yuva-rāja* (heir-apparent), and that he established the monastery **Udā-Kitagbo**, naming it after himself and his son. Then, in the twelfth year of the reign of **Abā Salamevan**[5], he instituted rules for its general up-keep, the protection of its property, and the continuance of its monastic duties. In these regulations occur references to (*a*) **Puvaram-vehera** (P. *Pubbārāma-vihāra*) of the **Kapārā** fraternity, most probably the one built by Sēna I (897–917 A. D.) and his queen Saṅghā at Abhayagiri, the head-quarter of this Order[6]; (*b*) **Tusaya** and **Soliya**; (*c*) **Saṅgsana,** perhaps incorrectly for **Saṅgsena** (P. *Saṅghasēna*), being either the Vihāra built by Sēna I[7], or that by Kassapa V[8], or by his mother Saṅghā, queen of Sēna II, and (*d*) **Sak-maha-ämäti** (P. *Sakka-mahā-amacca*), the title by which the steward or the *dāyaka* of the monastery was called. It is evidently the same as *Sakka-sēnāpati*, which appears from the *Mahāvaṁsa*[9] to have been an office connected with the management of Buddhist monasteries and the like. The steward referred to here was probably the grandson of Kassapa V[10].

The king **Abā Salamevan** has been correctly identified by Mr. Bell with **Dappula V,** whom we know from inscriptions as the son of Sēna II by his sub-queen Dēvā[11], his other son, Kassapa V, being by his chief queen Saṅghā. Dappula reigned for twelve years (991–1003 A. D.); his successor, **Udaya II,** for only three years. Of this king's relationship to his predecessors the chronicles give us no information whatever; but if our inscription is to be relied on, he could be no other than **Udā** Mahayā, because we are told in it that he held the office of sub-king, *Yuva-rāja*, in the last year of Dappula's reign. He must, therefore, have ascended the throne in the following year. His parents Mihind and Kitā may be identified with Mahinda, the brother of Sēna II[12], and Kittā, the daughter of Kittaggabōdhi[13]. The following genealogical tree will show the relationship more clearly[14].

---

[1] P. *Udaya Mahāpāda*. [2] P. *Mahinda*. [3] P. *Kittā Rājinī* (cf. *Mv*. l. 60).

[4] P. *Kittaggabōdhi Adipāda*. [5] P. *Abhaya Silāmēghavaṇṇa*.

[6] *Mv*. xlv. 29, l. 69, and the slab-inscription of Kassapa V, l. 13, above, pp. 42, 47, and 52.

[7] *Mv*. l. 70. [8] *Mv*. li. 86, and above, pp. 42 and 51. [9] lii. 52–53.

[10] *Mv*. lii. 79. [11] See above, pp. 23–24. [12] *Mv*. li. 7.

[13] *Mv*. l. 50, 57, 60, and li. 16–17.

[14] This genealogical tree has been compiled independently of that given as appendix No. 4 in Mr. Still's useful *Index to the Mahāvaṁsa* (Colombo, 1907), and in consequence contains differences and additional matter.

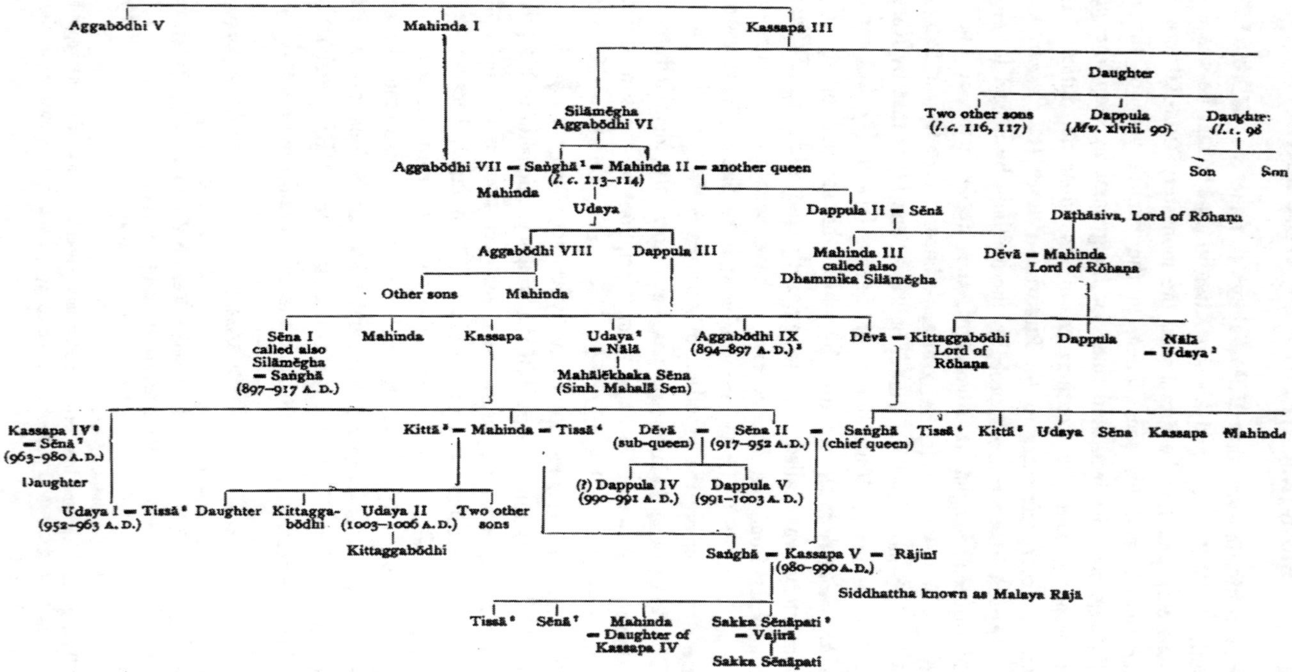

[1] Probably step-sister of Mahinda II.
[2] These dates are deduced tentatively from the calculations on p. 156, above.
[3] Same prince.
[4–7] Same princesses : the relationship of 6 and 7 is obscure.
[8] See Moragoḍa inscription below, p. 200.
[9] This may have been the official title of Mahinda, in which case Vajirā may be taken as the name of his wife, the daughter of Kassapa IV.

TEXT.

1 සිරිබර කැතකුල කොත් ඔකාවස් පරපුරෙන් බ

2 ට සව්ගුණමුළින් උතුරත් මිහිඳු මහයා සිරි

3 සරඟු පිණිසැ විමල්ගුවන්හි පාළ නව බ(ග්ල)

4 සඳ්ලෙයස්බඳු කුලෙන් සමදැ කිසා රජ්න කුසි

5 න් දැනැ දුනු සැණැගිමෙ ඇපා යුවරද් කිසෙව් තනැ

6 පැමැණැ සිපැරැක්මෙන් වැජැඹැ සියල් රුපු දප් කි

7 ඳැ රිවිතික් තෙදින් තැවි හොල්වැරොල්වූ ලොවක් නි

8 වං (වටප)ළැවිදැකිද වලාදළලම්බි පැවාසි නිල් ම

9 ගමෙයක්සෙයින් පිරිතැස් ගිම්හ් අඳුන් තෙ

10 දිළිඳ් මනතලා පුරා කුලුණ් මගමෙයින් නන් රුවන් පි

11 රි කුලුණු රජදන් වහරෙ වැස්වූ උද මහයා පින්සි

12 රිසර්තුමා තුනුරුවන්හි පතල දළ සදැහැ සි

13 යල් දියව් පළකොට් පැමෙකින් තමා හුත කි

14 සස්බො ඇපාහුද් තමාද් නැම්හ් තම්දි කැරැ අ

15 පිස් සතොස් සලෙ ඇ පුත් වියත් ගුණ අඹරණින්

16 සැදි කපාරමුල වැ වැවෙන පුවරම වෙහෙරින් අවුද් වත් දි

17 තන්වැ වැඩැවසන සඟුන් දෙලොස් දෙනක්හට් සතර ප

18 ස පුවදැ කැර උද කිසස්බො පමු වත් දි තන්හි අබ

19 දිතාක් ගම් කිම් දස් මිනිහුන් රැක්මට් උවක් ඉලි(යෙ)

20 මිහ් ගැගැ නන් දෙස්හි නන් රුපු තිරිඤ් සෙන්හි දළ ද

21 ජ කිඤැ පුද් මුහුඳ්හි ගලා සිරි ලකට් යස කිත් පමු(රු)

22 අල තුමා සෙය් බලකැන්හි බැඳ් අබාසලමෙවන් මහර

23 දඟු සත්ලැඟු දෙලොස් වන හවු[රු] දුයෙහි ඇසෙළ්ස

24 ඳැ ඇසෙළමස්හි දසපක් දවස් තැබැවූ වත්සිරි

25 ති මෙහි අබදිතාක් ගම්කිමට් වැරි පෙරෙනාවවූ මෙලා

26 ට්සි නොවද්නා ඉසා ගම්ගොන් නො ගන්නා ඉසා කු(ස)

27 ලැ කොළිලැ බලත් රැහැණ් නො ගසනු ඉසා රදෙල

28 න් වැදැ තලන් මීවන් නො කපනු ඉසා සිවුර්ගම්

29 දූත් සඟුන් දෙලොප් දෙනකු වසනු ඉසා

30 මෙහි උනුතැනකට් සඟුන් එළ්(ව)ත් තනැ සන්වත්හිමි

31 යනව් කස්සකැ වතැ කියෙන වත්ගිමියන් ගෙනෙ

32 රින් ගන්හා ඉසා මෙයින් වෙහෙරැ ගොස් විසියැපි ස

33 ග් කෙහෙක්නව් සහක් නො වැ ගන්නා ඉසා මෙ තැබැවූ

34 සිරිනව් ගිහිමිනිස් සහුන් වැසියන් විසින් ක

35 රණ වියවුලක් ඇත මහයාගෙ බැලැතුන් දඬස (ඇ)

36 ත්තන්විසින් දුනු නො තබාපිටැ ප(විගෙ)හුත් වැ

37 පාරයනට සාහා දෙනු ඉසා මෙකුන් තමන්විසි
38 ත් නො සැඹුණ් දැයක් ඇත රද්ගෙහි බැලය
39 ව ද් කියා සාහාදෙනු ඉසා දැයකු වසඟ නො පි
40 රිහෙලා දෙනු ඉසා මෙ පැ(වි)ගෙණි දැයක තමට දස්
41 වා දුන් **සක්** මගඇමැති **සහල්නාවස්** ඉසා
42 මොවුන් දරු මුනුම්බුරවුන් ඉසා මෙන්නට (අනදර)
43 සම්දරුවන්විසින් සඟුන්විසින් වූ ආකුලය
44 න් ඇත මහයාගෙහි බැලැතුන් දහස සාහා දෙනු ඉසා

TRANSCRIPT.

1 Siribara Käta-kula kot Okāvas parapuren ba-
2 -ṭ sav guṇa muḷin uturat **Mihind** Mahayā siri-
3 -sarahu piṇisä vimal guvanhi pāḷa nava ba(gḷa)
4 sand-leyak bandu kulen sama-dā **Kitā** räjna kusi-
5 -n dänä dunū säṇähi me āpā yuva-rad bisev tanā
6 pämäṇä si-pärākmen väjämbā siyal rupu dap bi-
7 -ndā rivi-tik-tedin tävī ho(ḷ)väroḷvū lovak ni-
8 -vä (vaṭa pa)ḷä vidäkida valādala[1] lamb pāvāsi, nil ma-
9 -ha-meyak-seyin piritäs gimin adan ne-
10 diḷind mana-taḷā purā kuluṇ maha-meyin nan ruvan pi-
11 -ri kuluṇu raja-dan-vahare väsvū **Udā** Mahayā pin-si-
12 -ri-sar tumā tunu-ruvanhi pataḷa daḷa sadähä si-
13 -yal diyaṭ paḷakoṭ pāmekin tamā suta **Ki-**
14 **-t-agbo** Āpāhu-d tamā-d nämin nam dī kärā a-
15 -pis satos sale ā yut viyat guṇa ambaraṇin[2]
16 sädi **Kapärā-muḷa** vä väṭena **Puvaram**-veherin avud vat dī
17 tanvä väḍā vasana saṅgun doḷos denak-haṭ satara pa-
18 -sa suvadā-kära **Udā-Kitagbo-pavu** vat dī tanhi aba-
19 -di-täk gam bim das minisun räkmaṭ uvak ili(ye)-
20 -min häňgä nan deshi nan rupu-nirind-senhi daḷa-da-
21 -p bindä yud muhund-hi galā siri Lakaṭ yasa kit paňḍuru

[1] *vidu-kiňdu valādala?* [2] Read *abaraṇin.*

Puliyaṉkuḷam Slab (c/B) of Udā Mahayā.

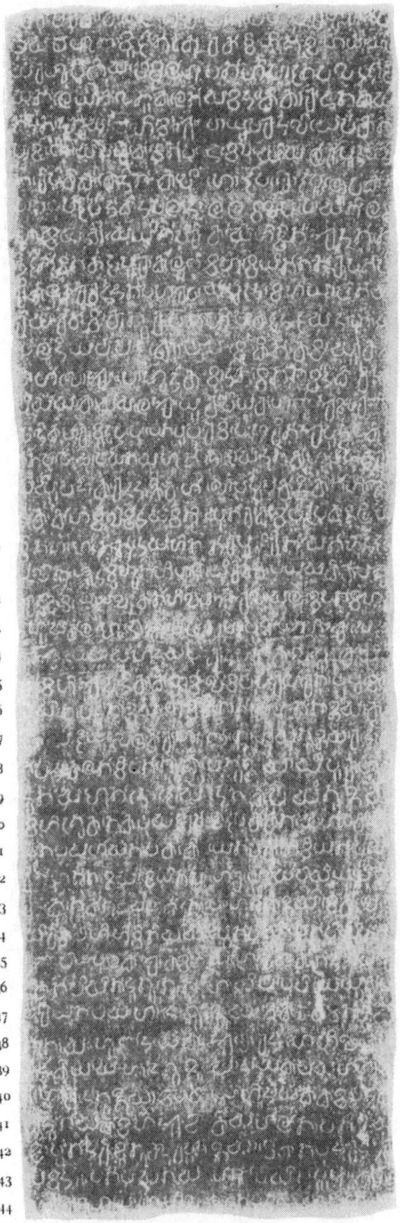

From an ink-impression supplied by the Archaeological Commissioner, Ceylon.
Scale about 2¾ inches to 1 foot.

22 a(ḷa)[1] tumā sey baḷa känhi bänd **Abā Salamevan** maha-ra-
23 -dahu sat-läṅgū doḷos-vana havu[ru]duyehi Äseḷ-sa-
24 -ndä Äseḷa-mashi dasa-pak davas täbävū vat-siri-
25 -ti mehi abaditäk gam-bimaṭ väri perenāṭṭu melā-
26 -ṭsi no vadnā isā gam-gon no gannā isā **Tu(sa)**-
27 **-yä Soḷiyā** balat rähäṇ no gasanu isā radola-
28 -n vädä talan mīvan no kapanu isā sivur gam
29 dun saṅgun doḷos denaku vasanu isā
30 mehi unu tänakaṭ saṅgun eḷ(va)t[2] tanä saṅg-vat-himi-
31 -yanaṭ **Saṅgsanä**[3] vatā kiyena vat-himiyan vehe-
32 -rin gannā isā meyin veherä gos visiyäṭi sa-
33 -ṅg-keneknaṭ sahak no vā gannā isā me täbävū
34 siritaṭ gihi-minis sasun väsiyan-visin ka-
35 -raṇa viyavulak äta Mahayā-ge bälätun[4] dahasa (ä-)
36 -ttan-visin dunu no naṅgā siṭā pa(viye) yut vä-
37 -pārayanaṭ sāhā denu isā mekun taman-visi-
38 -n no sāhuṇ däyak äta rad-gehi bälaya-
39 -ṭa-d kiyā sāhā denu isā dāyaku vasaga no pi-
40 -riheḷā denu isā me pä(vi)yehi däyaka-kamaṭ dak-
41 -vā dun **Sak**-maha-ämäti **Saṅgal-nävan** isā
42 movun daru munumburavun isā meknaṭa (anadara)
43 samdaruvan-visin saṅgun-visin vū ākulaya-
44 -k äta Mahayā-gehi bälätun[4] dahasa sāhā denu isā

TRANSLATION.

[Lines 1–5] His Virtuous and Illustrious Excellency[5], the Chief Governor[6] **Udā**[7] was born unto His Illustrious Excellency, the Chief Governor **Mihind**[8]

[1] This may also be read *aḷu*.

[2] *eḷpat* as an alternative reading.

[3] Probably for *Saṅg-senā*.

[4] Or *bälā tun*.

[5] *Pin-siri-sar tumā* (lines 11–12) = Skt. *puṇya-śrī-sāra* + *uttama*. Here *tumā* is a contracted form of *utumā*, the Sinh. nom. sing. masc. of Skt. *uttama*. *Tumā* or *tamā* is also a derivative of Skt. *ātmā* (P. *atumā*), see lines 13–14.

[6] *Mahayā* = P. *mahā-pāda*, same as *mahā-di-pāda* (*Mv.* li. 91). A comparison of the following references makes it quite clear that this is a ministerial title higher in rank than that of *āpā* (P. *ādipāda*, *Mv.* li. 94).—(*a*) *āpā mahayā siri vindā* (above, pp. 26, note 4, and 98, note 5), (*b*) *āpā mahapā* (*A. I. C.* 148 c, line 19), and (*c*) *Udā mahayā . . . tamā suta Kitagbo āpā* (ll. 11, 13, 14 of the present inscription).

[7] P. *Udaya*.

[8] P. *Mahinda*.

who abounds in a multitude of all virtuous qualities, and is descended from the [royal] line of the Okkāka dynasty, the pinnacle of the illustrious Kṣatriya race. [He was born] from the womb of the queen[1] **Kitā** of equal birth[2] [as her consort], in the race[3] which is like unto the crescent moon of the early . . . , shining in a clear sky.

[Lines 5–12] At the very instant of his birth[4] he received[5] the unction of governor and heir-apparent, and, flourishing with the prowess of a lion, he crushed the arrogance of all enemies.

Just as a great dark rain cloud, cooling[6] a world that has become parched up[7] by the heat[8] of the fierce rays of the sun, pours down torrents of rain accompanied by widespread sheets of lightning and thunder[9], so His Excellency caused showers[10] of gracious royal gifts, full of various gems, to pour down from the great rain cloud of compassion, filling the pond-like mind of many a poor man oppressed with the heat of [continual] begging[11].

[Lines 12–18] As an act of displaying publicly to the whole world his deep widespread faith in the 'Triple Gem,' His Excellency established [the monastery] **Udā-Kitagbo-pavu**, naming it after himself and his son **Kitagbo** *āpā*. He then graciously bestowed the four priestly requisites upon the twelve monks who are adorned with ornaments of distinctive virtues such as moderation in desires[12], contentment[13], and religious austerity[14], and who have come from the **Puvaram-vehera**[15] of the **Kapārā** fraternity and have taken up their residence [at this monastery Udā-Kitagbo-pavu], performing the religious duties [attached thereto].

---

[1] *Rājna* = Skt. *rājñī*, P. *rājinī*. See above, pp. 26, note 9, and 49, note 7.

[2] *Sama-dā* = P. *sama-jātika*. Cf. *eme kulen samajāy* in the Mihintale tablet (A, l. 2, above, p. 91).

[3] If *sand-leyak bandu* is taken as an attribute of *Kitā*, then the translation would run 'who is of equal birth [as her consort] in race and who is like unto the crescent moon,' &c.

[4] *Dunu sănāhi me*. See above, p. 26, notes 6–7.

[5] *Āpā-yuvarad-bisev-lanā pămāṇā*, lit. 'having attained to the position of being anointed as *āpā* and *yuva-rad*.' See above, p. 50, notes 18 and 20.

[6] *Nivā*, lit. 'having quenched,' gerund of *nivanavā*, 'to extinguish, to put out,' Skt. *nir* + √*vā*.

[7] *Hoḷvăroḷvū*. The above meaning is offered tentatively. *Hoḷa* is given in the *Piyummala* (p. 22) as a synonym for 'distress' or 'grief.' Cf. Marāṭhī, *hōḷapaṇēm*, 'to singe, parch;' *hōḷā*, 'a huge blazing fire:' Malayālam, *vaṛaḷ*, *vaṛaḷuga*, 'to grow parched;' *vaṛaḷḷuga*, 'to grill.'

[8] *Tăvī*, lit. 'having become heated,' gerund of *tăvenavā* (Pkt. *tavaī*, Skt. √*tap*).

[9] I am not absolutely sure of the perfect accuracy of the translation of this portion of the sentence.

[10] Cf. *satnaṭ ruvan-vaharē vasvamin* (*Amāvatura*, p. 5).

[11] Cf. *khinnā pubbassa rājassa kālē dīpamhi pāṇinō | nibbutā taṁ samāgamma ghammā viya valāhakaṁ ||* (*Mv.* li. 51).

[12] *Apis* = P. *appiccho*.

[13] *Satos* = P. *saṁtōsa*.

[14] *Sale* = P. *sallēkhō*.

[15] P. *Pubbārāma-vihāra*.

[Lines 18–24] He, moreover, searched for and ascertained means for the protection of villages, lands, serfs, and people belonging to the monastery. And accordingly on the tenth day [of the waning moon (?)] in the month of *Äseḷa* in the *Äseḷa* season[1] of the twelfth year after the canopy [of sovereignty] was raised by **Abā Salamevan,** the great king who has crushed the overweening arrogance of various hosts of hostile kings in divers countries, and who, plunging into the sea of war, has brought to this auspicious Laṅkā fame, glory, and tributes with which he decorated[2] his army of champion warriors, His Excellency instituted the [following] rules and observances[3] :—

[Lines 25–33] Labourers[4], *perenāṭṭu*[5], and *melāṭsi*[6] shall not enter the villages and lands appertaining to this [monastery]. Village oxen shall not be appropriated. The Guardians[7] at **Tusaya** and **Soliya** shall not throw or set ropes with nooses to catch cattle[8]. Royal officers[9] shall not enter [the monastic lands] and cut down *tal* and *mī* trees[10]. There shall reside twelve monks who have been allowed villages[11] that supply robes to the priesthood. Whenever monks are required for any place here deficient [in the right number], the master of priestly duties[12] [of this establishment] shall obtain them from the Vihāra of the master of ceremonies, who indicates

---

[1] This refers probably to the season of *Vassa*, which begins in Ceylon on the day of full moon in the month of *Äseḷa* (Skt. *Āṣāḍha*, June–July). The tenth day in the Vassa season must, therefore, be the tenth day after the full moon.

[2] *Bänd*, past rel. part. of *baňdinavā*, 'to bind, tie on.'

[3] *Vat-sirit* = Skt. *vṛtta-cāritra*.

[4] *Väri* may also mean 'hostile,' but see above, p. 53, note 7.

[5] Probably a tribe of rustics. In the inscription on the east wall of the Sōmanāthēśvara Temple at Paḍavēḍu (Paḍaiviḍu), *nāṭṭavar* means 'inhabitants' of a kingdom (*S. I. I.* vol. i. p. 111). Cf. also *pere-nāṭṭiyam*, above, p. 53, note 15.

[6] See above, p. 53, note 10.

[7] *Balat* = P. *balattha*.

[8] The phrase *rāhäṇ-gasanavā* or *rän-gahanavā* has several significations in modern Sinhalese :—(*a*) to throw or set ropes with nooses to catch cattle, (*b*) to draw strings or cords across a passage to obstruct egress, and (*c*) to put brand-marks on cattle (Clough's *Sinh. Dict.* s. v.).

[9] *Radola*, probably from *rāja-kula*, through the intermediate forms *rad-kola* and **raddola*. Cf. the modern term *radala* applied to a Kandyan chief.

[10] See Mihintale tablet (A, line 50, above, pp. 93, 106, notes 1 and 2). *Tal* = Skt. *tāla*, 'the borassus palm;' *mī* = Skt. *madhu*, 'bassia latifolia'?

[11] *Sivur-gama* (pl. *-gam*) = Skt. *cīvara-grāma*. The above meaning is quite clear from the passage *cīvara-navakarmaṇi niyuktāṁś ca grāmān samyag-ālōcya* in the Jētavanārāma Sanskrit inscription, ll. 4–5, above, pp. 4 and 6.

[12] *Saṅg-rat-himi* = Skt. *saṅgha-vṛtta-svāmin*.

the duties at the **Saṅg-sana**[1] [monastery]. And no indulgence shall be shown to any one of the monks from amongst them, who wishes to go and reside outside.

[Lines 33–44] Should there be any confusion caused by the laity or by the clergy in respect of the duties thus laid down, then those belonging to the thousand retainers of the house of the *Mahayā*[2] shall settle it for the employees at the [monastery Udā-Kitagbo-]pavu, without raising agitation[3]. Should there [still] exist matter which has not been settled by them, they shall settle it in consultation with the retainers also of the palace. Stewards[4] shall grant the allowance[5] without stinting[6]. Should a dispute be caused by unfriendly monks or lords [of the country] in respect of **Saṅgalnāvo** [entitled] *Sak-maha-ämäti*[7] who has been duly installed in the office of steward of this [monastery Udā-Kitagbo-]pavu, or in respect of his sons or grandsons, then the thousand retainers[8] of the house of the *Mahayā* shall settle it.

---

[1] Probably for *Saṅg-sena* = P. *Saṅgha-sēna*, the monastery built by Sēna I (*Mv.* l. 70), or that built by Saṅghā, Queen Consort of Sēna II (*Ibid.* li. 86).

[2] *Mahayā-ge bälätun dahasa ätlan-visin.* Here *Mahayā* obviously refers to Udā Mahayā, above, l. 11. *Bälätun* is the plural of *balatā*, P. *balattha*: but *bälā*, more correctly *bāḷā* or *bāḷa*, means 'a hired servant' (*Jay*, and *E. S.* s.v.) and *tun dahasa* 'three thousand.' Hence this clause can also be rendered 'by the members of the three thousand retainers of the house of the *Mahayā*.' I am not at all sure, however, that the word *dahasa* means here 'thousand.'

[3] *Dunu no naṅgā silā.* The meaning of this clause is somewhat obscure. *Dunu* = (*a*) pl. of *dunna* (Skt. *dhanu*), 'bow' (*E. S.* p. 41); (*b*) Skt. *janus*, 'birth.' Cf. *dunu sāṇdhi*, above, line 5; (*c*) P. *dinna*, 'given' (*E. S.* p. 41); (*d*) Skt. *dhūni*, 'agitation;' (*e*) 'victory' (fr. $\sqrt{ji}$); and (*f*) 'sharpness' (Clough, s. v.). *Naṅgā* or *nagā* = gerund of *naganavā*, 'to raise,' fr. Skt. $\sqrt{laṅgh}$.

[4] *Dāyaku* (lit. donors), 'monastic officials who look after the proper distribution of food, &c., in a monastery.'

[5] *Vasaga.* See above, p. 28, note 5.

[6] *Piriheḷā*, gerund, and *pirihеḷīma*, verbal noun of *pirihеḷanavā*, which, according to Sinhalese dictionaries, means 'to scorn, or contemn.' If so, *no pirihеḷā* may be rendered 'without showing condescension.' The context, however, both here and in the Mihintale tablet (A, lines 14–15, above, pp. 91 and 100), suggests the rendering I have given above, connecting it with Skt. *pari* + $\sqrt{hṛ}$. Compare also the meaning of *pirihеḷīma* in the clause *pāviddan labana lābhayen pirihеḷīma*, 'the deprivation of the benefits which the monks receive' (*Heraṇasika*, Colombo edition, 1897, pp. 2–3), this being the Sinhalese explanation of the passage *bhikkhūnam alābhāya parisakkati*, 'he goes about for the purpose of [causing] loss to monks,' in *Aṅguttara-Nikāya*, lxxxvii. 2.

[7] *Sak-maha-ämäti* = P. *Sakka-mahā-amacco*, evidently the same as *Sakka-sēnāpati* (*Mv.* lii. 52). The reference here is probably to the grandson of Kassapa V (*Ibid.* lii. 79).

[8] See above, note 2.

No. 16. BUDDHANNEHĀLA PILLAR-INSCRIPTION

THIS stone pillar, measuring 6 ft. 4 in. by 9 in. square, was discovered by me on October 9, 1891, while on a tour of exploration in Kuñcuṭṭu Kōrale of the North-Central Province with the Archaeological Commissioner, Mr. H. C. P. Bell. After we had inspected the ruins of Padaviya, some forty miles distant, NNE. of Anurādhapura, I went with a number of coolies to Buddhannehāla, about seven miles further north, to examine and report upon the ancient sites there, preliminary to the Archaeological Commissioner's personal inspection. These sites consist of five caves and a dāgaba. It was in Cave No. 3[1] that I found the inscribed pillar, evidently brought there from elsewhere and placed upside down to serve as a door-jamb of a Śaiva shrine of about the eleventh or early twelfth century A. D.

The inscription is in fairly good preservation. It covers the four sides of the pillar. Side A has 32 lines surmounted by a large ශ්‍රී *śrī* with an emblem of the sun or the lotus above it. The last two lines on this side are not at all legible. Side B has 34 lines, C 33, and D 26 lines, with the figures of a crow and a dog cut underneath to indicate that whosoever transgresses the rules enjoined therein shall be born in the future as a crow or a dog.

The **akṣaras**[2] are from half to three-quarters of an inch in height. They represent the alphabet of the latter half of the tenth century, and resemble

---

[1] The following are my notes on this cave, extracted from Mr. Bell's Report (*A. S. C. Seventh Progress Report*, 1891, p. 30):—

West of Cave No. 2 and adjoining it is a slab rock. Forty-three steps are cut in it leading to Cave No. 3. This cave, which faces south-west, is formed by a large [overhanging] boulder, 51 ft. by 16 ft. and 35 ft. high, lying on the large flat rock as if dropped there by some *yódaya* (giant). The summit is inaccessible, except with the aid of a long ladder. The mound of bricks on the summit was probably once a dāgaba. The cave is 16 ft. deep, 16 ft. wide, and 8 ft. high. The *kaṭāraya* is high. Within the cave is a brick building, seemingly a Piḷḷāiyár *kóvil*. The porched entrance and vestibule, which extends outside the cave, is 27 ft. long, 12 ft. wide. Brick wall, 1 ft. 4 in. thick and 7 ft. 9 in. high (outer wall), and 3 ft. (inner wall). The basement of the building has the usual brickmoulding.

The *liṅgam* (with *yōni*) is placed near the back wall. Pieces of a broken Piḷḷāiyár are found on the slab rock close by the *kóvil*. Bricks of the *kóvil*, 10 in. by 7 in. by 2 in. and 10 in. by 5 in. by 2 in.: pillars, some dressed, 8 in. square, 4 ft. high.

Within the porch I found a square pillar 9 in. square by 6 ft. 4 in., fitted with tennon and mortice for a door-post. It is covered with a long inscription on the four sides, and had been put in upside down. The pillar evidently belongs to some other ruin. A few rock-cut letters were also found near the boulder.

Close to the *kóvil* in a *gal-wala*, or rock-pool, was found a stone [*yantra-gala*] 2 ft. 2 in. by 1 ft. 7 in., perforated with five square holes.

[2] See accompanying Plate 25.

more the characters in the Kiribat-vehera pillar of the 14th regnal year of Kassapa IV (*circa* 963–980 A. D.), and in the slab-inscription of the sixth year of his successor, Kassapa V (*circa* 980–990 A. D.), than those in the Vessagiri slab of the second year of Dappula V (*circa* 991–1003 A. D.), while, on the whole, their type is distinctly later than that of the Īripinniyāva and Raṁbāva pillars, and older than that of the Mihintale tablets of Mahinda IV[1]. Further, as this record shows a greater tendency to advanced forms of letters than the Kiribat-vehera pillar, it is reasonable to suppose that its date in the third year of Abhā Salamevan is later than that of the latter in the fourteenth year of Kassapa IV. Hence the king Abhā Salamevan of our inscription can be no other than the successor of Kassapa IV, namely, Kassapa V, especially as Abhā Salamevan was one of his *birudas*[2]; and accordingly the period intervening between the two records can only be six years.

The **contents** give us no historical information of any consequence. The expression *abhiṣekayen daru*[3] (B, ll. 7–8), 'son by sacred sprinkling,' however, connotes the prevalence of certain Brahmaṇic or more likely northern Buddhist (*Mahāyāna*) rites not sanctioned by the southern Buddhist Church. The Vinaya rules, it is true, state that the preceptor (*upajjhāya*) ought to consider the pupil (*saddhivihārika*) as a son[4], but, so far as I know, there are no rites to be performed in connexion with the initiation of a pupil. The only formality that has to be observed is for the pupil to approach a senior monk, make his obeisance, and beg him three times to be his preceptor. If the latter express his consent by word or gesture the agreement is complete and binding[5]. Among the Mahāyānists, on the other hand, the initiation of a neophyte is accompanied by a solemn ceremony lasting for about three days. One of the rites connected therewith is the *kalaśi* or *udaka abhiṣēka*, at which the con-

---

[1] Cf. Īripinniyāva and Raṁbāva pillars (Nos. 12 and 13 above), කු *ku*, ම *ma*, රු *ru*; Kiribat-vehera pillar (above No. 11), කු *ku*, ම *ma*, රු *ru*; Buddhannehāla pillar (i.e. the present record), කු *ku*, ම *ma*, රු *ru*; Slab-inscription of Kassapa V (above No. 4), කු *ku*, ම *ma*, රු *ru*; Slab-inscription of Dappula V (above No. 2, iii), කු *ku*, ම *ma*, රු *ru*; Mihintale tablets (above No. 7), කු *ku*, ම *ma*, රු *ru*.

[2] See above, p. 24.

[3] Skt. *abhiṣēkēna dārakaḥ*.

[4] Upajjhāyō bhikkhavē saddhivihārikamhi puttacittaṁ upaṭṭhāpessati, saddhivihārikō upajjhāyamhi pitucittaṁ upaṭṭhāpessati (*Mahāvagga* i. 25. 6).

[5] Evañ ca pana bhikkhavē upajjhāyo gahētabbo: ekaṁsaṁ uttarāsaṅgaṁ karitvā pādē vanditvā ukkuṭikaṁ nisīditvā añjaliṁ paggahetvā evam assa vacanīyo: upajjhāyō mē bhantē hōhi, upajjhāyō mē bhantē hōhi, upajjhāyō mē bhantē hōhīti. Sāhū 'ti vā, lahū 'ti vā, ōpāyikan ti vā paṭirūpan ti vā, pāsādikēna sampādēhīti vā kāyēna viññāpēti, vācāya viññāpēti, kāyēna vācāya viññāpēti, gahitō hōti upajjhāyo (*Ibid.* i. 25. 7).

secrated water from the *kalaśi* or pot is sprinkled by the *guru* on the pupil's head, and prayers repeated over him [1].

Regarding the names of officials in the record, we have in some previous instances found it difficult to differentiate with certainty those belonging to one person from those of another, but no such difficulty exists here. If we compare the first two sets of names indicated by the conjunction *isā* (side C, lines 29–33, D, 1–6), we see that the adjectival clause *Mekāppar-Vädārum Vijuragu-varä van* is repeated in each case. And as it occupies the position which a family or *gē* name does in Sinhalese names, we may be justified in suggesting that this clause represents here the family or *gē* name of both *Saṅg-pa-him* [2] and *Kaḍusu-vadurim*, especially as similar family names are to be found in the pillar-inscriptions at Kiribat-vehera [3], Īripinniyāva [4], and Raṁbāva. *Mekāppar-Vädārum* is obviously an official title like *senevirad* (Skt. *sēnāpati-rāja*) in the Īripinniyāva record [5]. We know *mekāppar* is a Tamil title and it means 'body-guard [6],' but the form *vädārum* of the verb *vadāraṇavā* (Skt. *ava* + √*dhṛ*) 'to declare' or 'order' is puzzling. The verbal noun *vädāruma* (pl. *vädārum*) does not suit the grammatical construction, unless we take *mēkāp-par-vädārum* [7] as a *bahu-vrīhi* compound meaning 'he who possesses the commanding of the body-guard,' in other words 'commander of the body-guard.' *Vijuragu* or *Viduragu* cannot, we think, be identified with *Viduragga*, the commander of the army of king Udaya III (1015–1023 A. D.), as the present inscription belongs palaeographically to a much earlier period. We are, therefore, inclined to take *Vijuragu* as a Sinhalese form of Pāli *Vajiragga*, the name of the captain whom king Udaya I (952–963 A. D.) sent with prince Mahinda to quell a rebellion raised by Kittaggabōdhi [8]. The literal meaning of the next word *varä* (loc. of *var* or *vara*) is not altogether clear. The context suggests 'lineage.' If so, it may have the same etymology as Tamil *vari*, 'line,' *variçai*, 'row;'

---

[1] For a full account of this ceremony, see Hodgson's *Essays on the Language, Literature, and Religion of Nepāl and Tibet*, 139 ff.; Prof. Valée Poussin's *Bouddhisme*, 208 ff.; and Prof. F. W. Thomas's article on *abhiṣēka* in the *Encyclopaedia of Religion and Ethics*, as well as the *Agnipurāṇa* (chap. 90) and the Mahāyānist manual *Abhiṣēka-vidhi*.

[2] Skt. *Saṅgha-pā-svāmin*, 'Lord guardian of the Priesthood.' Cf. P. *Saṅghapāla-sāmi* or *-thēro*. *Him* or *svāmi* is purely an honorific here.

[3] *Pāṇḍirad Dāpuḷa-varä* (side A, lines 8–10, above, p. 159).

[4] *Senevirad Kuṭṭhā-varä van* (side D, lines 9–11, above, p. 169).

[5] Cf. also *Mekāppar-Vädārum Bamba-Senevi Lōkanātha* (Vessagiri slab, No. 2, ll. 32–33, above, p. 34).

[6] See above, p. 38, note 2.

[7] Cf. P. *dāna-saṁvidhānaṁ*, Sinh. *danhi vädārum* (*Dampiyā-aṭuvā-gäṭapada*, p. 144).

[8] *Mv.* li. 94–127.

Telugu *varasa* or *varusa*, 'line, relationship;' Malayālam *vara* and *vari*, as in *variśāsanam*, 'a perpetual assignment of land.' The other possible derivations are P. *ghara* (Skt. *gṛha*), as in *mehenī-vara*[1] (P. *samanī-ghara*), above, p. 53, n. 2, and the Sanskrit *vara*, often added to nouns honorifically as *guru-vara*, but hardly ever to proper names. The last word *van* is the same as *vana* on side B, l. 15. It is the relative participle, present, of *vanavā* or *venavā* (from Skt. √*bhū*), the past being *vū* (side B, l. 2). Thus the full name *Mekāppar-Vädärum Vijuragu varū van Mekāppar Sang-pa-kim* means '*Sangha-pā-sāmī* of the "body-guard", who is of the lineage of Vajiragga, the commander of the "body-guard".' The remaining names follow the same principle of arrangement. They will all be useful, not only in grouping together correctly the names of officials we may find in other inscriptions, but also in establishing a certain relationship between them, as in the case of the first two names in the present record.

In the preparation of the following text and translation I had before me an ink-estampage supplied to me by the Archaeological Commissioner (Mr. H. C. P. Bell), my own notes, and the text and translation published in the *Seventh Progress Report* of the Archaeological Survey.

TEXT.

A.

ශ්‍රී

1 අභා සලමෙව
2 න් මපුරුමුකා තු
3 න් වත්නෙ පොසො
4 නෑ පුර් දසවස්
5 දවස් වත්ගි
6 මියන් වගත්
7 සෙ වදෑලෙපින්
8 (දු)ඝොදක්දරම්
9 අවු ඝොන්ගරු
10 ගැම්ගි වෙවා
11 ස කිරිය ඉසා
12 වෙ කුමබුර්ගි අ
13 වූ අපුත්බද
14 වත්නා ඉසා බො
15 වත්නා ඉසාං ප
16 (ර්)දෙවුනෑ(මැ) වත්
17 නා ඉසා එන්දි
18 ගිනෑමැ වත්නා
19 ඉසා (නෑ)ඇළි(සා)
20 නා නෑමැ වත්නා
21 ඉසා නෙනතිලෙ
22 වත්නා ඉසා වෙ
23 ගි මැ අවූ ගෙමි
24 මි පිටකිමි ඉසා
25 මිවන් සිතිබල
26 න් ඉසා සොහු (පු)
27 (වා)පල උවරුක්
28 ඇතුළ්කොට් වෙ
29 තුවාස් නැන් ඝෑ
30 කිරිඝෑ මඩුළු
31 .. ..
32 .. ..

---

[1] In the names *Mehenavara Vīrabāhu* (*Nik.* p. 24) and *Mēnavaravaṁśābhijāta Sēnālaṁkādhikāra Senevirad* (*Ibid.* p. 22), the appellation *Mehenavara* or *Mēnavara* is undoubtedly a *gē* or family name. I am indebted to Mr. D. B. Jayatilaka for these two references.

B.

1 ගා බැඳෑ කා(ණී)
2 පී(ණෑ) වැඩැවූ (ණ)
3 (ර්සෙ)ණෙන් වහත්
4 සෙ වැළැඳෑ අත
5 ත්තරයෙන් මෙ
6 කුන්වගන්සෙ
7 අභිෂෙකයෙ
8 න් දරු මුඹම්
9 කණු ආවාසිය
10 යන්වහන්සෙ
11 වළඳෑනූ කොට් ඉ
12 සා එක්බිත්
13 තෙන් කෑණිපි
14 ණෑ ගලෑ වැ
15 ඩැවන ආවා
16 සියන්වහ
17 න්සෙ සන්ව
18 ත්තෑ ගිඳෑ ව
19 දළ එක්තෙහෙ
20 කුත් කාණිපි(ණ)
21 ලෑ ගිඳෑ වළඳෑ
22 නූ කොට් ඉසා
23 මෙ සකිර්යෙ
24 ගි කැබැලි නො
25 ගන්නා කොට්
26 ඉසා වෙහෙර්
27 කැබැලි නො ග
28 න්නා කොට් ඉ
29 සා දිය බෙදු
30 මී නො ගන්නා
31 කොට් ඉසා මෙ
32 රවිගි යෙදු
33 ණවුයත් මෙ කු
34 මබුරව පෙත්

C.

1 සමකොට් දි
2 ය පාතා කොට්
3 ඉසා මෙහි අවූ
4 වත්තෙහි කැබෑ
5 ලි නො ගන්නා
6 කොට් ඉසා ගෙ
7 කිඹිගි පිටිකි
8 මිගි ද කැබැලි
9 නො ගන්නා කො
10 ට් ඉසා වෙල්වැ
11 ජ්සත් නො ව
12 ද්නා කොට් ඉ
13 සා ගැල් ගො
14 න් නො ගන්නා
15 කොට් ඉසා උල්
16 (වාඩු) පෙරර (නාවු)
17 නො වද්නා කොට්
18 ඉසා (තුඩිසෙ)
19 නො වද්නා කො
20 ට් ඉසා වැරිය
21 න් නො ගන්නා
22 කොට් වදුළෙ
23 න් මෙය තුවා
24 ක් තැත් මෙ නී
25 යමෙත් වැළෑ
26 (ඇ)නූ කොට්
27 පගණේ යි
28 ඳ්වත්තව්
29 අ මෙකාප්ප
30 ර් වැදෑරුම් මි
31 ජුරඟුවරු [ව]
32 න් මෙකාප්ප
33 ර් (ගන්සක්)

D.

1 (ම) ඉසා මෙකාප්
2 පර් වැදෑරුම්
3 මිදුරඟුවරු
4 වත් මෙකාප්
5 පර් ක(ඹු)සු
6 වදුපිම් ඉසා

7 **නාවිනිකින්**
8 **ලනාවත්වරු**
9 වත් **කිලිග්**
10 **ගොලොබැග**
11 **ම බහමුශි**
12 **විම් ඉසා කි**
13 **න්සෙන් රක්**
14 **සමණන්ව**
15 රුවත් **කුඩ**
16 **සලා මිකිඳ්**
17 ඇතුළුවැ අ
18 පමෙයතුවා
19 ක් දෙනා අවු
20 ද් වත්ගිම්ය
21 න්වහන්සෙ
22 වදාළ එක්නැ
23 න්සම්යෙන්
24 මෙ සම්වතා
25 පහණ ගි
26 ඳ්වතු ලදී

TRANSCRIPT.

A.

Śrī.

1 **Abhā Salameva-**
2 **-n** mapurumukā tu-
3 -n vanne Poso-
4 -nä pur dasavak
5 davas vat-hi-
6 -miyan vahan-
7 -se vadāḷeyin
8 **(Da)nādakdarahi**
9 āvū **Nānnar(u)**[1]
10 gämhi veṭya
11 sa kiriya isā
12 me kumburhi ā-
13 -vū Asunbada-[2]
14 -vatta isā Bo-
15 -vatta isā Pa-[3]
16 -(ri)devu-nä(mä)[4] vat-
17 -ta isā Endi-[5]
18 -hi-nämä vatta
19 isā (Nä)ndaḷi(sā)-
20 -(tā) nämä[6] vatta
21 isā Neṇanile[7]
22 vatta isā me-
23 -hi mä āvū ge-bi-
24 -m piṭi-bim isā
25 mivan[8] sinibala-
26 -n[9] isā sesu (pu-)[10]
27 (-vā)-pala[11] uva-ruk
28 ätuḷu-[12]koṭ me-
29 -tuvāk tän **Sä-**
30 **-giriyä maṇḍulu**
31 .. ..
32 .. ..

B.

1 -gā bändä **Nā-(gi-)**[13]
2 **-ri(yä)** väḍävū **(Ha-)**
3 **(-rse)yan**[14] -vahan-
4 -se väḷändu ana-
5 -ntarayen me-
6 -kun-vahanse
7 abhiṣekaye-[15]
8 -n daru **Buddha-mi-**
9 **-ttra** ācāryya-
10 -yan-vahanse
11 vaḷandanu koṭ i-

---

[1] Bt. °*naru*. [2] Bt. *asunbada*. [3] Bt. *Va-*. [4] Bt. *-nume*. [5] Bt. *Enādihiname*. [6] Bt. *-lanāmā*. [7] Bt. °*nilu*. [8] Bt. *mivani*. [9] Bt. °*na*. [10] Bt. *vu*. [11] Bt. *popala*. [12] Bt. *ätuḷā*. [13] Bt. *nāgariyā*. [14] Bt. *-rārayan*. [15] Bt. *abhikṣakayen*.

Buddhannehäla Pillar-Inscription.

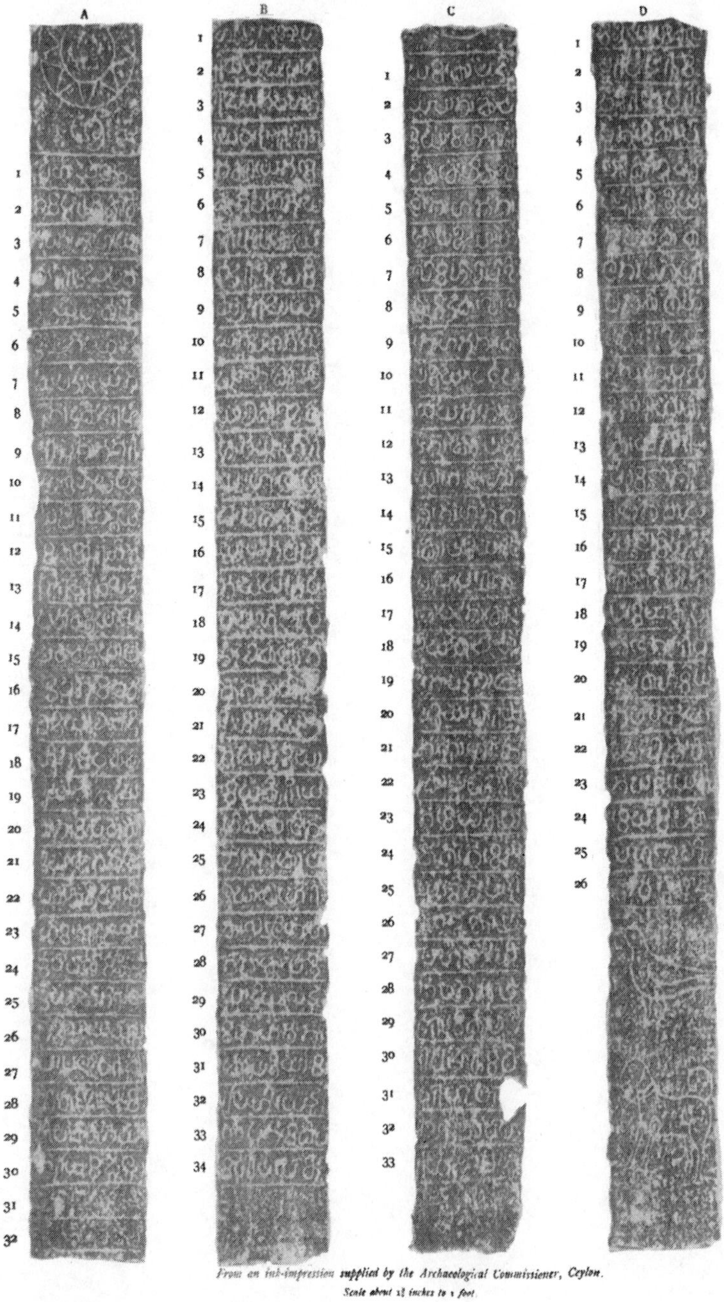

From an ink-impression supplied by the Archaeological Commissioner, Ceylon.

Scale about 1½ inches to 1 foot.

12 -sā ekbit-
13 -ten **Sāgiri-**
14 -**yä** galä vä-
15 -ḍä vana ăcā-
16 -ryyayan-vaha-
17 -nse **Saṅg-va-**
18 -**ttä**[1] hindä va-
19 -dāḷa ekkene-[2]
20 -kun **Nāgiri-(ga)-**
21 -**lä** hindä[3] vaḷanda-[4]
22 -nu koṭ isā
23 me sa-kiriye-
24 -hi käbäli no
25 gannā koṭ
26 isā veher
27 käbäli no ga-
28 -nnā koṭ i-
29 -sā diya bedu-
30 -m no gannā
31 koṭ isā me
32 ṙaṭ-hi yedu-
33 -ṇavun me ku-
34 -mburaṭ pet

11 -ssan no va-
12 -dnā koṭ i-
13 -sā gäl go-
14 -n no gannā
15 koṭ isā ul-
16 -(vāḍu) pere-(nāṭu)[6]
17 no vadnā koṭ
18 isā tuḍise[7]
19 no vadnā ko-
20 -ṭ isā väriya-
21 -n no gannā
22 koṭ vadāḷe-
23 -n meya-tuvā-
24 -k tän me ni-
25 -yamen[8] väḷä-
26 -(nda)nu koṭ
27 pahaṇ[9] hi-
28 -nd-vannaṭ
29 ā Mekāppa-
30 -r-Vädārum **Vi-**
31 -**juragu**-varä [va-]
32 -n Mekāppa-
33 -r (**Saṅgpa-hi**)[10]

C.

1 sama[5]koṭ di-
2 -ya pānā koṭ
3 isā mehi āvū
4 vattehi käbä-
5 -li no gannā
6 koṭ isā ge-
7 bimhi piṭi-bi-
8 -mhi da käbäli
9 no gannā ko-
10 -ṭ isā vel-vä-

D.

1 (-**m**) isā Mekāp-
2 -par-Vädārum
3 **Viduragu**-varä
4 vaṇ Mekāp-
5 -par **Ka(ḍu)su-**
6 -**vadurim** isā
7 **Nāvini**[11]-**Kit-**
8 -**lanāvan**-varä
9 van **Kiliṅg**
10 **Goḷobä-ga-**

[1] Bt. °*tk*. [2] Bt. °*na*. [3] Bt. *hind*. [4] Bt. *vāḷāudunu*. [5] Bt. *samā*. [6] Bt. *perenu*. [7] Bt. *tuḍās*. [8] Bt. °*yumin*. [9] Bt. °*ṇā*. [10] Bt. *Siṅgasubha*. [11] Bt. *Nāvinī*.

11 -**ma Bahaṭu-si-**
12 -(**vi**)**m** isā **Ki-** [1]
13 -**t-sen Ra**(**k**)-
14 -**samaṇan**-va-
15 rä van **Kuḍa-**
16 -**salā Mihind**
17 ätuḷu-vä a- [2]
18 -pa meya-tuvā-
19 -k denā avu-
20 -d [3] vat-himiya-
21 -n-vahanse
22 vadāḷa ek-tä-
23 -n-samiyen
24 me samvatā
25 pahaṇa hi-
26 -nd-vanu ladi

TRANSLATION.

[Side A] Hail! On the tenth day of the waxing [moon] of [the month of] Poson [4] in the third year of [the reign of] His Majesty **Abhā Salamevan**.

Whereas, touching the tract of field [5], six *kiriyas* [6] [in sowing extent] in the village **Nännaru** of [the district] of (**Da**)**nādakdara**, as well as the gardens Asunbada-vatta, Bo-vatta, Paridevu-vatta [7], Endihi-vatta, (Nä)ndaḷi-(sātā-)vatta, and Nenanile-vatta, belonging to this [tract of] field, together with the grounds [8] attached to houses and the lands outside [9] appertaining thereto, including *mī* [10] trees, tamarind [11] trees, and the remaining minor [12] trees bearing

---

[1] Bt. *Kit Senā Raka-*. [2] Bt. *ā-*. [3] Bt. *-da*.

[4] May–June. The Sinhalese names for the twelve months are *Bak*, *Vesak*, *Poson*, *Ăsaḷa*, *Nikiṇi*, *Biṇara*, *Vap*, *Hil* or *Il*, *Uňduvap*, *Durutu*, *Navan*, and *Mādindina*. They follow the same order as Sanskrit *Caitra*, *Vaiśākha*, &c. As to the division of the year into six seasons of two months in each, as *Hēmanta*, snow season (*Uňduvap* and *Durutu*, Nov.–Jan.), *Śiśira*, *Vasanta*, *Grīṣma*, *Varṣā*, and *Śarada*, the Pāli and the Sinhalese *nighaṇṭus* have merely copied *Amarakōṣa*, heedless of the fact that such seasons are not quite applicable to Ceylon or South India.

[5] *Veṭya*. The etymology of this word is not clear. It may be connected with either √*veṭ* or √*vṛt*, but compare Tamil வெட்ட *veṭṭa*, 'clear, open,' as *veṭṭa-veḷi*, 'an open plain,' *veṭṭāntarāi*, 'dry ground,' and *veṭṭāi*, [prov.] 'wild land without vegetation' (Winslow).

[6] See above, p. 3, n. 4.

[7] *Paridevu-nămā vatta*, lit. 'the garden having the name Paridevu.'

[8] *Ge-bim* = P. *geha-bhūmi*.

[9] *Piṭi-bim* = P. *piṭṭhi-bhūmi*.

[10] See above, p. 106, note 2.

[11] *Sinibalan*, cf. *siniṁbalā* (in *Ruvanmala*, p. 31), and the modern form *siyaṁbalā*.

[12] Cf. *talan*, *mīvan āy pala-ruk* (Mihintale tablets A, l. 50, above, p. 93); *bulat doḍam kel kos sesu upo pala* (Mahinda's inscription near the stone-canoe, l. 28, above, p. 117).

flowers and fruits, the Lord of Property[1] has declared that, soon after the reverend **Ha(rse)**[2], who built . . . in the Sāgiri[3] district [side B] and was the incumbent at **Nāgiri,** had enjoyed all this property[4], his son by sacred sprinkling, [namely,] the reverend teacher **Buddhamitra** shall enjoy the same. Thereafter one whom the reverend teacher, the incumbent at **Sāgiri** residing at **Saṅgvatta,** has elected[5], shall enjoy [the property] by living at **Nāgiri-gala.** The allotments[6] in these [aforesaid] six *kiriyas* shall not be appropriated; the allotments of the Vihāra [premises][7] shall not be appropriated, and the distribution of water[8] shall not be appropriated. Employees in this district[9] shall level the beds[10] (of fields) and [side C] lead[11] the waters to this [aforesaid] field. Allotments in the garden appertaining thereto, as well as in the grounds attached to the houses and in the lands outside, shall not be appropriated. Field-dwellers shall not enter. Carts and oxen shall not be appropriated. *Ulvāḍu*[12], *perenāḷu*, and (*tuḍise*) shall not enter. Farm labourers[13] shall not be appropriated.

It being [so] declared, we all of us[14], including Mekāppar **Saṅg-(pa-him)**[15]

---

[1] *Vat-himiyan-vahanse* (ll. 5–6). See above, p. 35, note 7. In inscriptions and books of the tenth to fourteenth centuries, this title is applied, as a rule, in the sense of *Vṛttasvāmin*, to a Buddhist monk who had the management of ecclesiastical duties and ceremonies of a monastery, e.g. *maha-saṅg-vat-himiyan* (above, p. 33, l. 12), *vat-teru* (*Nikāyasaṅgraha*, ed. 1907, p. 12). In the present record, however, it refers to the king, apparently as *vastu-svāmin*, 'lord of property,' and we know it is so used in the *Nikāyasaṅgraha* and in the *Kurunāgalavistaraya*, e.g. *Vijaya Bāhu Vat-himi* (*Nik.* p. 20), *Vat-himi Bhuvanaika Bāhu* (*Ibid.* p. 21), and *Vastu-himi kumāraya* (*J.C.B.R.A.S.* 1890, vol. xi. p. 388).

[2] Probably a corrupt form of Harṣa.

[3] P. *Cētiya-giri*, see above, pp. 75 and 80.

[4] *Me tuvāk tän* (A, ll. 28–29), lit. 'these places.'

[5] *Vadāḷa*, lit. 'declared.'

[6] *Kābāli*, see above, p. 37, note 5.

[7] *Veher kābāli.* Cf. the sentence *veherā kābāli gannā* (*aṭasiyā*) *sat hā ätulu*(*koṭ*) *hoyin e terā me terā vehera avaṭā kābāli no gannā isā* (Vessagiri slab-inscription, No. 2, A, ll. 23–24, above, p. 33).

[8] *Diya-bedum* = P. *daka-bhēdanam*, referring to the distribution of water from a tank for irrigation and other purposes. Cf. *Kaṇā-vävā diya van tāk tanhi pere Demeḷ kalā pere sirit diya-bedum me veheraṭ me galā yuṭu isā* (Mihintale tablets B, ll. 55–56, above, p. 97). See, however, above, p. 170, note 1.

[9] *Me raṭ-hi yeḍuṇavun* (B, ll. 31–33), probably referring to 'district superintendents of irrigation.' Cf., however, *raṭ-ladu* and *pas-ladu*, above, p. 170, notes 8–9, and below, p. 206, notes 7–8.

[10] *Pet*, probably same as modern Sinh. and Tamil *pätti*; but *pet* in the Moragoḍa inscription below, No. 17 (side B, line 3), is clearly a derivative of Skt. *paṅkti*.

[11] *Pānā*, probably a derivative of Skt. *pra* + *ā* + √*nī*.

[12] These seem to be the names of certain low-caste communities. *Ulvāḍu* probably same as *hulvaḍu*, basket-makers (*Ruvanmala*, p. 59).

[13] *Väriyan*, see above, p. 53, note 7.

[14] *Apa meya-tuvāk denā* (D, ll. 17–19), lit. 'we these individuals.'

[15] Skt. *Saṅgha-pā-svāmin*?

of the family of Mekāppar-Vädārum **Vijuragu** [side D] and Mekāppar **Kaḍusuvadurim** of the family of Mekāppar-Vädārum **Viduragu**; [as well as] **Kiliṅg-Goḷobā-gama**[1] **Bahaṭusivim** of the family of **Nāvini Kitlanāvan,** and **Kuḍasalā Mihind** of the family of **Kitsen Raksamaṇa**[2], who were deputed[3] to set up the stone-[pillar] to the effect that all the [above-mentioned] lands should be enjoyed in accordance with these regulations, have [now] come [together] and set up this edictal[4] stone-[pillar] in pursuance of the Mandate delivered by the Lord of Property.

No. 17. MORAGOḌA PILLAR-INSCRIPTION OF KASSAPA IV

IN his report on the Padaviya Tank[5], Mr. H. Parker mentions the discovery of this pillar-inscription 'in the forest below the embankment, at the site of an ancient town which is now called Moragoḍa.' It was still there, 'lying prone amidst the ruins,' in October, 1891[6], when the Archaeological Commissioner (Mr. H. C. P. Bell) and I visited the spot. It is a monolithic pillar with a vase-shaped or *kalasa* capital, measuring 6 ft. 2 in. in height by 1 ft. 1 in. square. The inscription covers all its four sides: A, 24 lines; B, 21, with sun and moon[7] symbols cut at the bottom in low relief; C, 24 lines; and D, 22 lines, with the figures of crow and dog carved at the bottom one above the other as on side B.

The **letters**[8] are cut moderately deep, and are legible with the exception of those on side B, lines 9–14, and on side D, lines 9–10, as well as a few others

---

[1] *Kāliṅga Gōṭhābhaya-gāma!*

[2] P. *Kittisēna Rakkhasamaṇa.*

[3] *Pahaṇ hindvannaṭ ā* (C, ll. 27–29), lit. 'who came to set up the stone.'

[4] *Sam-vatā-pahaṇa.* Cf. *vavasthā-pahaṇa*, above, p. 36, n. 1; *attāṇi-kaṇu*, above, p. 161, note 8.

[5] Ceylon *Sessional Paper*, xxiii, 1886, pp. 1–2. Padaviya is situated in the north-eastern corner of the North-Central Province, about forty miles from Anurādhapura. 'It is surrounded by a wide tract of dense forest which, except in its south-eastern part, is totally uninhabited. The middle of its embankment is only fifteen miles, in a direct line, from Viḷāṅkuḷam, in the Northern Province, and it is approached by four different footpaths. From the same spot in the embankment to the nearest point on the eastern coast, the Bay of Kokkiḷay, the distance in a direct line is twenty-three miles.' See *A. S. C. Seventh Progress Report*, 1891, pp. 28–31 and 35–43.

[6] For our account of the Moragoḍa ruins, see *op. cit.*, pp. 41–43.

[7] According to Mr. Bell, this represents a *dā-kätta*, 'sickle,' but I have not as yet come across this symbol as an auspicious sign on inscriptions. Possibly the crescent is badly carved on the stone.

[8] See accompanying Plate 26.

enclosed in round brackets in the text below. They vary from one to two inches in size, and represent the type of the alphabet in use during the tenth century, resembling as they do the akṣaras of the Īripinniyāva and Raṁbāva pillars. The inscription is dated in the sixteenth regnal year of king **Kasub Sirisaṅgbo**, who was no other than **Kassapa IV** (*circa* 963–980 A.D.), as will be shown presently. Now the Kiribat-vehera pillar-inscription[1] of this king is dated in the fourteenth year of his reign. It is, therefore, earlier than the present one by two years, and yet its alphabet represents quite a later type. This is an anomaly which may be accounted for by supposing that either the scribe or the engraver of the Moragoḍa inscription belonged to the older generation, and, therefore, followed the earlier form of writing.

The **language** of the record calls for no special remarks, save that its style is somewhat wanting in perspicuity, and that the phrase *Ruhuṇu-danavū Malamaṇḍulu eka ānnä koḷ tamahaḷ siri bhoga kaḷa*, which is used here in connexion with king **Udā Abhay** (Udaya I), is almost word for word the same as that applied to his elder brother king Abhā Sirisaṅgbo (Sēna II) in the Elle-väva pillar-inscription[2].

The **contents** tell us that in the sixteenth regnal year of **Kasub Sirisaṅgbo**, brother of the great king **Udā Abhay**, the two ministers **Ataragalu-Kottā** and **Mulavaḍā-Sakarā**, (both) of the family of **Mekāppar-Vädārum Seneviraju Vadurā**, came together under the order of His Majesty in Council and set up the present pillar-edict proclaiming the grant of certain immunities to lands irrigated by the waters of the **Padonnaru** tank—these lands being the property of **Vädārā Pirivena**, which was attached to **Magul**[3] **Pirivena** situated at **Abhayagiri-vihāra** in the range of [*pariveṇas* known as] **Kukuḷ-giri**.

Mr. H. C. P. Bell's identification of **Kasub Sirisaṅgbo** with **Kassapa IV**[4] (*circa* 963–980 A.D.) is quite correct. No other Kassapa reigned for sixteen years in the tenth century[5], to which the inscription palaeographically belongs. Moreover the *Mahāvaṁsa* itself corroborates the statement in our record that Kassapa was the brother and successor of Udaya[6].

---

[1] See above, p. 154. [2] *A. I. C.* No. 116; *A. S. C. Seventh Progress Report*, 1891, p. 45.

[3] Skt. *Maṅgala*. [4] See *A. S. C. Seventh Progress Report*, 1891, p. 60.

[5] According to the Sinhalese chronicles only two kings bearing the name of Kassapa reigned for more than sixteen years. They were Kassapa I (*circa* 479–497 A.D.), and Kassapa IV, mentioned here. See above, p. 156, as regards the date of the latter king's reign.

[6] Cf. the variant reading *saka-bhātaraṁ* of the text of the *Mahāvaṁsa*, li. 91, in the Colombo edition of 1877, which agrees with that of the MS. of this work in the Indian Institute, Oxford.

Of Kassapa's two officials, **Mulavadā-Sakarā** and **Ataragalu-Kottā**, nothing is known. The head of their family, Mekāppar-Vädārum[1] **Seneviraju Vadurā**, may, however, be identified with Vajira[2], a minister of Sēna I, who built, at the Abhayagiri-vihāra, the Vajira-Sēna-āvāsa, probably the Vädārā-pirivena of the present inscription[3].

Kukuḷ-giri-peta is the Sinhalese equivalent of Pāli **Kukkuṭa-giri-panti**, which latter is the name given to a range of *pariveṇas* which Kaniṭṭha Tissa (229–247 A. D.) erected, encroaching upon the bounds of the Mahāvihāra[4].

Padonnaru is apparently the Sinhalese equivalent of P. Padī-nagara[5], the capital of Padī-raṭṭha[6]. The ruins at Moragoḍa perhaps indicate where the town was. The tank is mentioned in the *Mahāvaṁsa* only as Padī-vāpi[7] in the list of irrigation works repaired by Parākrama Bāhu I (1153–1180 A. D.)[8]. It is not referred to by name even in the inscription on the beautifully carved pillar slab[9] which stands, to this day, on the top of the huge embankment, as a fitting memorial to this king's works of public utility there.

In preparing the following text and translation of the inscription I have utilized the ink-estampage supplied to me by the Archaeological Commissioner, as well as the text and notes published in his *Seventh Progress Report* for 1891.

TEXT.

A.

1 සිරි ලක්දිව්
2 ශි ඔගිපි සිරි
3 (ම)[10]ඬ යස ඉසි
4 (ර) රුහුණුදන
5 වූ මලවඩුසු
6 එක අත්නෑ කො
7 ට තමගට සි
8 රි ගොහ කල ඊදෑ
9 [අ]කේ මහර
10 ජ්හු සොහොවුර්
11 කලුව සිරිස
12 ගේගා මපුර්මු
13 කා සොළොස් වත්
14 ගෙ පොහොනෑ පුර

---

1 Regarding this title, see above, p. 193.

2 Mr. Bell suggests Vajiragga, the chief captain of Udaya I (*Mv.* li. 105).

3 *Ibid.* l. 84.

4 Mahāvihāra-sīmantaṁ madditvā tattha kārayi |
Kukkuṭagiri-pariveṇa-pantiṁ sakkacca bhūpati || *Mv.* xxxvi. 10.

5 See below, p. 206, note 4.

6 *Mv.* lxxxiii. 16.

7 *Mv.* lxxix. 34.

8 See above, p. 123.

9 For a full account of this record, see *A. S. C. Seventh Progress Report*, 1891, pp. 62–63.

10 'ම' යැපුත් ගත හැකි

15 තියැ වැ[1]කැ වජා
16 ලෙයින් එස්තැ
17 ත්සම්යෙන් ආ
18 මෙකාප්පර් වැ
19 දෑරුම් සෙනෙවි
20 රජු වදුරවරු
21 මුලවඩාසක
22 ණ් ඉසා අසර
23 ගඳුකොත්තා ඉ
24 සා මෙතුවාත් [එක්]

B.

1 සෙ වැ අකාගිරි
2 වෙහෙර්ණි (කුකු)
3 (ළ්)ගිරි පෙතැ පි
4 ගිරි මඟුල් පි
5 පිවෙනව් බහාලු
6 වැඳෑ(ණ) පිරිවෙ
7 නැ බද් ෂ(ඳො)ණ්[2]
8 නරුකුළියෙණි
9 (රඤනා දිය දැරු)
10 (ආවත්නාවෙගි)
11 (රු සත .. .. සි)
12 .. ..
13 .. මා යෙගි අව
14 මහා (සථාන ?) යව
15 ඈතුලැවූතාක්
16 තැනව් කුලී මෙ
17 ලාක්සින් නො
18 වද්නා කොව් ඉ
19 සා රව්ලදු ප
20 ස්ලදුවන් නො
21 වළඤනු කො

C.

1 ව් ඉසා දිගෙ බෙ
2 දුම් නො ගත්නා
3 කොව් ඉසා වෙල්
4 කැම් වෙල්බැදි පි
5 යො වජාරතුව
6 ත් නො වද්නා කො
7 ව් ඉසා පෙරෙනා
8 වටුවම් නො වද්
9 නා කොව් ඉසා
10 දුඃහු පාබල(ය)
11 ත් නො වද්නා කො
12 ව් ඉසා රද කම්
13 තැන් දෙරුව[ත්]
14 නො වද්නා කො[ව්]
15 ඉසා ගැල් නො
16 ත් මිවුන් වැරි
17 යත් නො ගත්නා
18 කොව් ඉසා ම
19 ස්දිව පෙදි[ව්]
20 නො ගත්නා කො[ව්]
21 ඉසා පෙරෙ ම
22 භූ(ගි)[3]මිත් පිට
23 ත් කො(ප)ල වළ
24 (ඤනු)තාක් තැ

D.

1 ත් ඈතුළත් කර
2 නු ඉසා මෙ ගැ
3 මිගි කොටු (කො)හෙ
4 කුත් ඈත ගැමි
5 ත් පිටත් කර
6 නු ඉසා කොවා ව

---

[1] 'පැ' යනුත් ගත හැකි
[2] 'පැදුන්' යනුත් ගත හැකි
[3] 'ශි' යනුත් ගත හැකි

7 ත්නාවුන් වැදෑ නොං
8 [ගත්]නා ඉසා මෙගි
9 .. .. .. ර් වැසි
10 .. .. ත් (බැහැර)
11 (නොය)තූ ඉසා
12 ශිය පිවතෑ අෑ
13 ත්තන් නො ලා ග
14 ත්නා ඉසා මෙතුවා
15 ස් පැරහැර් දී වද
16 ළෙඩින් මෙ අත්තා
17 ණී කණු ගිඳ් වන
18 ලදි මෙ අත්නෑ
19 උලහණ් කළ
20 කොණෙහස් ඇත්
21 නම් කවුඩු
22 බලු වෙත්වා

TRANSCRIPT.

A.

1 Siri Lak-div-
2 -hi pihiṭi siri-
3 (pi)[1]ḍ yasa isi-
4 -(ra) Ruhuṇu-dana-
5 -vū Mala-maňḍulu
6 eka ānnä ko-
7 -ṭ tamahaṭ si-
8 -ri bhoga kaḷa **Udā**
9 **[A]bhay** maha-ra-
10 -j-hu sohovur
11 **Kasub Siri-sa-**
12 **-ňgbo** mapurmu-
13 -kā soḷos van-
14 -ne Posonā pura
15 tiyä väkä[2] vajā-
16 -ḷeyin ek-tä-
17 -n-samiyen ā
18 Mekāppar-Vä-
19 -dārum **Senevi-**
20 **-raju Vadurā**-varā
21 **Mulavaḍāsaka-**
22 **-ra** isā **Atara-**
23 **-galukottā** i-
24 -sā metuvāk [ek]

B.

1 -se vä **Abhāgiri**
2 **Veherhi (Kuku)-**
3 (-ḷ-)**giri** petä pi-
4 -hiṭi **Maňgul-Pi-**
5 **-rivenaṭ** bahālu
6 **Vādā(rā)-Pirive-**
7 **-nä** bad **Pa(do)n-**[3]
8 **-naru-kuḷiyehi**
9 (randanā diya dārä)
10 (āvannāvehi)
11 (rä sata .. .. si)
12 .. ..
13 .. mā yehi aṭ
14 mahā (sthāna ?) -yaṭ
15 ätuḷävūtāk
16 tänaṭ kulī me-
17 -läksīn no
18 vadnā koṭ i-
19 -sā raṭ-ladu pa-
20 -s-laduvan no
21 vaḷandanu ko-

---

[1] *Vi* may be suggested as an alternative reading.

[2] This may also be read *pākā*.

[3] Bt. *Paḷonnuru*.

Moragoḍa Pillar-Inscription.

A B C D

From an ink-impression supplied by the Archaeological Commissioner, Ceylon.

Scale about 1½ inches to 1 foot.

C.

1 -ṭ isā diye be-
2 -dum no gannā
3 koṭ isā vel-
4 -kāmi vel-bädi pi-
5 -yo vajāranuva-
6 -n no vadnā ko-
7 -ṭ isā pere-nā-
8 -ṭṭuvam no vad-
9 -nā koṭ isā
10 dunu pābala(ya-)
11 -n no vadnā ko-
12 -ṭ isā de-kam-
13 -tän deruva[n]
14 no vadnā ko[ṭ]
15 isā gäl go-
16 -n mīvun väri-
17 -yan no gannā
18 koṭ isā ma-
19 -ňg-div pe-di[v]
20 no gannā ko[ṭ]
21 isā pere ma-
22 -ňgu (hi)[1]min piṭa-
23 -t ko(pa)la vaḷa-
24 (-ndanu-)tak tä-

D.

1 -n ätuḷat kara-
2 -nu isā me gä-
3 -mhi keṭū (ke)ne-
4 -kun äta gämi-
5 -n piṭat kara-
6 -nu isā koṭā va-
7 -nnavun vädā no
8 [gan]nā isā mehi
9 .. .. .. -r väsi
10 .. .. .-n (bähära)
11 (noya)nu isā
12 giya piṭatā ä-
13 -ttan no lā ga-
14 -nnā isā me-tuvā-
15 -k pärahär dī vadā-
16 -ḷeyin me attā-
17 -ṇi kaṇu hind vana
18 ladi me ännā
19 ulaghaṇa kaḷa
20 kenek ät-
21 nam kavuḍu
22 balu vetvā

TRANSLATION.

[Side A] Whereas, on the third day of the waxing moon of [the month of] Posōn[2] in the sixteenth [regnal] year of His Majesty **Kasub Sirisaṅgbo**[3], brother of the great king **Udā Abhay**[4], who having brought under one rule the Ruhuṇu Province and the Mala[5] District, secured for himself the enjoyment

[1] This may also be read as *gi*.

[2] May-June, see above, p. 198, note 4.

[3] P. *Kassapa Siri-Saṅghabodhi*.

[4] P. *Udaya Abhaya*.

[5] *Mala* stands for *Malayu* 'the hilly district.'

of the combined wealth, glory, and prosperity that prevailed[1] in the beautiful Island of Laṅkā, it was [so] declared[2] [by His Majesty], there came together by Order of the Supreme Council[2], **Mulavaḍā-Sakarā** and **Ataragalu-Kottā**, [both] of the family of **Mekāppar-Vādārum Senevi-raju Vadurā**.

[Side B] And whereas, in regard to the grounds contained within the precincts of the eight sacred places (in the tract of land irrigated by the flow of waters stored up)[3] in the tank **Padonnaru-kuḷiya**[4], belonging to the **Vādārā-Pirivena**, which was attached to the **Maṅgul-Pirivena** situated at the Abhayagiri-vihāra, in the range of [*pariveṇas* called] **Kukuḷgiri**, all these immunities were declared and granted[5], namely:—Coolies and *melākSī*[6] shall not enter. Heads of Districts[7] or keepers of (district) record-books[8] shall not enjoy [this property].

[Side C] The distribution of water-supply shall not be appropriated.

---

[1] The word *pihiṭi* admits of two interpretations. It may be either the p. p. p. of *pihiṭanavā* (fr. Skt. *pra* + √*sthā*, *E. S.* p. 55), or the name of the northern division of the Island. Ceylon was in ancient times divided into three principalities:—*Pihiṭi-raṭa* in the north, *Mayā-raṭa* in the centre, and *Ruhuṇu-raṭa* in the south.

[2] *Vajāḷeyin ek-tān samiyen ā* (A, ll. 15–17). In other records where this phrase occurs the form *vajāḷa* or *vadāḷa* is found in place of *vajāḷeyin*. Cf. *vadāḷa ek-tān samiyen āvā* in the Vessagiri Slab, No. 2, A, l. 32 (above, p. 34). See also above, p. 35, note 12. *Ek-tān* may be a derivative of Skt. *ēka* + *āsthāna* 'the one (or supreme) assembly' as distinct from other assemblies. Cf. *āsthāna-maṇḍapa* 'assembly-hall' built in honour of Viṣṇu (*Ep. Ind.* vol. iv. No. 4).

[3] The text on side B, ll. 9–14 being more or less illegible, the translation may admit of improvement. Regarding the phrase *Padonnaru-kuḷiyehi randanā diya-dārā*, compare *Bāndā ni gaṅga vāvu | Siri Lakā da keṭ karavā || siyal diya randavā | Pārākum-Bā nirindu keḷe me ||* (*A. S. C. Seventh Progress Report*, 1891, p. 63.)

[4] *Padonnaru* probably the Sinhalese form of P. *Padī-nagara*. Cf. *Polonnaru* for P. *Pulatthi-nagara*; *Kalunnaru* for P. *Kālaka-nagara*. *Kuḷiya* may be a Sinhalese corruption of Tamil *kuḷam* 'tank.'

[5] *Pārahār dī* (D, l. 15), lit. 'having given the immunities.' *Pārahār* = Skt. *parihāra*. See above, p. 161, note 8, and p. 170, note 5.

[6] This word is also spelt *melāṭsī* and *melātsī*. See above, p. 53, note 10, and p. 168, note 1.

[7] *Raṭ-ladu* = P. *raṭṭha-laddho*. See above, p. 111, note 4, and p. 170, note 8. Cf. also *gam-ladu* as the Sinhalese interpretation of P. *gāma-bhōjaka* in the *Dampiyā-aṭuvā-gāṭapada*, ed. 1891, p. 65.

[8] *Pas-ladu* is no doubt the designation of an officer like *raṭ-ladu*, but perhaps of lower standing. Professor Geiger in his *E. S.* (p. 51) gives nearly all the recognized etymologies of *pas*, but none of them seem to suit the context. There is, however, another derivation which the Professor has overlooked. The word *pas* in the compound *pas-pot* is used in the Mihintale tablets (A, l. 54) as a Sinhalese equivalent of Skt. *pañjikā* or *pañcikā* 'a register.' See above, p. 106, note 14. Possibly *pas-ladu* may here mean an officer who kept the village records, the *likam-miṭiya* of later times.

Field-workers, field-serfs, or enforcers of customary practices[1] shall not enter. *Perenāṭṭuvam*[2] shall not enter. Archers or foot-soldiers shall not enter. Holders (?) of [the management of] two places of business[3] shall not enter. Carts, oxen, buffaloes, or labourers[4] shall not be appropriated. Those who live by highway robbery or by vagrant habits shall not be admitted[5]. All the places outside (the bounds) on the front road, (the fruits whereof) are being enjoyed, shall be included [in this property].

[Side D] If there be any one in this village who has committed[6] a murder, he shall be expelled from the village. Those who have entered [the village] after committing a murder shall not be harboured. Residents . . . . . . here shall not go away (from the place). Should they go, the inhabitants outside shall not give them refuge.

This pillar of Council Warranty was set up conjointly [by the above-named officials].

Should there be any persons who transgress this order, may they become crows or dogs [in their future births].

---

[1] *Piyo-vajāranuvan.* The above is offered tentatively in place of Mudaliyar Guṇasēkara's rendering, 'those of crafty speech,' which does not seem to suit the context. *Piyo* = Skt. *prayōga*; and *vajāranuvan* is a derivative of Skt. √*dhṛ* with prefix *ava*.

[2] Probably a class of low-caste people, but see above, p. 53, note 15.

[3] *De-kam-tān deruvan.* In the Vessagiri Slab, No. 2, A, l. 25: *deruvānā de-kam-tān vāssan.* See above, p. 37, note 7, and p. 161, note 7. The meaning of *kam-tān* as an office where business is transacted seems to be clear from its use in the Mihintale tablets A, ll. 22, 24, 50, and 54; B, l. 43 (above, p. 102, note 7, p. 106, notes 3 and 12, and p. 111, note 9). Cf. *dharmasthāna*, which would in Sinhalese be *daham-* or *dam-tān*, 'the office where all business relating to justice, spiritual matters, and charities is transacted,' in Chammak Copperplate Grant, l. 24 (*A. S. W. I.* vol. iv. p. 123, note 6). Cf. also *pasagaṇa-tān*, *puṅgul-tān*, *ąya-tān*, *piriven-tān*, *dasa-mē-tān*, *par-mē-tān* in the *Pūjāvaliya Extract* (edited by Mudaliyar Guṇasēkara, Colombo, 1893, p. 38).

[4] *Vāriyan*, see above, p. 53, note 7, and p. 105, note 3.

[5] *No gannā* (side C, l. 20) stands for *vādā no gannā* as on side D, ll. 7–8.

[6] *Keṭū* for *minī keṭū* as in the Slab-Inscription of Kassapa V, l. 18 (above, p. 47).

No. 18. PĀLU MĀKICCĀVA ROCK-INSCRIPTION OF GAJA BĀHU I (*circa* 177–199 A.D.)

PĀLU MĀKICCĀVA is the present name of an abandoned tank in the jungle, about 120 yards off the high road to Trincomalee, at a distance of sixteen miles from Anurādhapura.

The inscription is on a rock at the *vāṇa* or 'spill-water' of this tank. Dr. Müller gives an account of it, with a transcript, an English translation, and a lithographic plate in his *Ancient Inscriptions in Ceylon* [1]; but Mr. Bell's examination of it resulted in the publication of a revised text and translation in his *Seventh Progress Report* for 1891. The present article is based on a good estampage and an eye-copy, with which he has since supplied me.

It will be seen from the accompanying facsimile (Plate 27) that, as Mr. Bell has already said, the inscription is in a well-preserved state. It is engraved in six lines, covering an area of $3\frac{1}{2}$ by 8 feet of the surface of the rock. The letters, with the exception of the fifth, sixth, and seventh in the first line, are quite clear. Their size varies from 4 to 7 in. in height, and $2\frac{1}{2}$ to 5 in. in breadth. They belong to the Southern Brāhmī alphabet of the latter part of the second century A.D., exhibiting, as they do, nearly all the graphic peculiarities of the script of the Nāsik, Kuḍā, and Junnār inscriptions of about the same period. There is besides a complete agreement in the admixture of types, old and young, in the same record. Those most noticeable in the present one are:—(*a*) the angular *ja* and the 'archaistic' round *ja* in ll. 4 and 2; (*b*) the cerebral *ḍ* in *vaḍamanaka* of l. 4, which differs but little from the shape of the cerebral *ṇ* in l. 5, appears to belong to the alphabet of the Northern Kṣatrapas [2]; (*c*) *ti* with the fully developed loop as on some Andhra coins [3], and in Nāsik, No. 17 [4], *ti* with the lower end of the vertical stroke ending in a curve to the left, which is most likely the precursor of the looped form: these two, both in the second line, are the only variations from the usual type of *ta* with the broad and more or less round side-limb; and (*d*) the forms of *ba* with the left side of the quadrangle slanting outward either concavely as in (l. 1) and (l. 5), or with an angular bend as in (l. 3) and (l. 5).

---

[1] See No. 10, pp. 28, 74, and 110.

[2] See, for example, the form of the akṣara *ḍa* in Śoḍāsa's record at Mathurā (*Ep. Ind.* vol. ii. p. 199, No. 2, Plate).

[3] For examples, see Rapson's *Catalogue of the Coins of the Andhra Dynasty in the British Museum*.

[4] See *Ep. Ind.* vol. viii. p. 90, Plate viii.

If we now carefully compare these various types in the Pālu Mäkiccāva inscription under discussion with those in the rock records of Perumäiyankuḷam and Maharatmale, dealt with above at pp. 58–74, we shall be constrained on palaeographic grounds to regard the Perumäiyankuḷam record as the oldest of the three. That at Pālu Mäkiccāva comes next, as the majority of its letters is in type distinctly older than the more ornamental forms with longer curves noticeable in the script of the Maharatmale rock. The **contents** too of these three inscriptions give us the same age, for the first, i.e. the Perumäiyankuḷam, record belongs to the reign of king **Vahaba** (P. *Vasabha*, 130–174 A.D.), the Pālu Mäkiccāva inscription to that of his grandson king **Gamiṇi Abaya** (P. *Gajabāhuka Gāmaṇī Abhaya*, 177–199 A.D.), and the Maharatmale one to the time of king **Naka** (P. *Mahallaka Nāga*, 199–205 A.D.).

The next point to be considered is the four-inch square symbol ⊞ engraved just below the akṣaras *va* and *ṇa* of the word *kahāvaṇa* at the end of the fourth line. It is subdivided into four equal squares, and resembles at first sight the conventional representation of the railed enclosure of the sacred Bōdhi tree, so often found side by side with other religious or auspicious symbols on ancient Buddhist coins, seals, and inscriptions[1]. But whether this is an instance of the railed enclosure alone without the tree being used as a Buddhist emblem or not we cannot decide until other examples are brought to light. There is also no ground to suppose that it is a Ceylon variation of the rounded figure ⊕ for 90 occurring on Kṣatrapa coins of the second and third centuries A.D.[2] In view, however, of its isolated position immediately under the name of the coin, Mr. Bell's suggestion[3] that 'it may denote the standard by which the value or weight of the *kārṣāpaṇa* was reckoned, i.e. by *pādas* or quarters,' seems quite plausible. The symbol may further signify that the coin in question was the silver *kārṣāpaṇa*, which had its half and its quarter size, *pādika* or *pāda*[4].

As regards the words in the text, the following remarks may be offered:—

The form *Vahabaya* (l. 1) for *Vasaba* or *Vahaba*[5] (P. *Vasabha*) is uncommon,

---

[1] See, for instance, the Sohgaura plate (*J. R. A. S.*, 1907, p. 510).

[2] See Rapson's *Indian Coins*, pp. 144 ff.

[3] *A. S. C. Seventh Progress Report*, p. 44.

[4] See Cunningham's *Coins of Ancient India*, p. 47; Rapson's *Indian Coins*, pp. clxxxiii ff., and Rhys Davids' *Ancient Coins and Measures of Ceylon*, p. 13.

[5] See above, p. 60.

though it occurs once or twice in the Habaraṇa inscription [1]. Possibly the later Sinhalese form *Vähäp* with modified *a*-sound is a derivative of it [2]. *Maṇumaraka* (l. 2) is also spelt *marumakane*. See above, p. 63. *Puti* and *maharaji* (ll. 2–3) have the Māgadhī nominative in *i* [3]. *Upala-vibajaka* (l. 3) is probably identical with *Upala-bijaka* of Tammännekanda record [4]. *Upala* may be either the Skt. *upala*, a stone or rock, or a derivative of Skt. *utpala*, P. *uppala*, the blue-lotus, often used as a personal name [5]. *Vibajaka* is Skt. *vibhājaka*. The form *paca* (l. 4) for Skt. and Pkt. *pañca*, Sinh. *pasa*, *paha*, occurs also in Indian inscriptions of about the second century A. D.[6] *Kahāvaṇa* is Skt. *kārṣāpaṇa*, Pkt. *kāhāpaṇa*, *kāhāvaṇa*, P. *kahāpaṇa*, Sinh. *kahavaṇa*. Hence *paca-sahasi-kahāvaṇa* (l. 4) is P. *pañca-sahassī-kahāpaṇā* [7]. *Dariya* and *kaṇavaya* are derivatives of gerunds in *ya* [8] from the causatives of Skt. *dhṛ* and *khan*. Their equivalents in Pāli would be *dhāriya* and *khanāpiya*, the Sinhalese causative sign *-va* being derived from Skt. *-paya* (P. *-paya*, *-pē*, Pkt. *-ve*) [9]. *Tubaraba* is no doubt a Sinhalese form of Thūpārāma as suggested by Mudaliyar Guṇasēkara [10]. *Buka* [11]*-sagahaṭaya* (l. 5) is P. *bhikkhu-saṅghassa atthāya*.

The inscription contains nothing historically important. It confirms the Ruvanväli Dāgaba [12] and Maharatmale [3] records as regards king **Gamiṇi Abaya** being the son of king **Tisa** and grandson of king **Vahaba**. It further states that he spent 5,000 *kārṣāpaṇas* on the excavation of the Vaḍamanaka Tank in the Upala district, which he then granted to the Buddhist priesthood at

---

[1] *A. I. C.* No. 61, l. 10. Cf. also *Tisaya* for *Tisa* (*op. cit.* No. 2).

[2] Compare, however, *vähäp* in *E. S.* p. 85.

[3] See Pischel's *Gram. der Pkt. Sprachen*, p. 249.

[4] See *A. S. C. Seventh Progress Report*, p. 47, and *A. I. C.* No. 55. Cf. also Upaladonika-vavi in *A. I. C.* No. 11.

[5] As Uppalo, the father of Ummāda Phussadēva (*Mv.* xxiii. 82).

[6] See, for example, Nāsik, Nos. 1 and 5 (*Ep. Ind.* vol. viii. pp. 59 and 73), and Bharhut, No. 144 (*Z. D. M. G.* xl. p. 75).

[7] Cf. P. *dasa-sahassī-lōkadhātu*.

[8] Prākrit dialects hardly make any distinction in the use of the suffixes *tvā* and *ya* to form gerunds. They are added indiscriminately to simple roots as well as to those with prepositional prefixes (Pischel, *op. cit.* § 581). For some examples of gerunds in *ya* from simple roots, see Whitney's *Skt. Gram.* § 990 a.

[9] Cf. also the Tamil causative in *-pi* or *-vi*.

[10] *A. S. C. Seventh Progress Report*, p. 44, note 8. Cf. *ohu Mahabō vända dā vaňdanaṭa Tuṁbarup yannāhu* (*Dharmapradīpikā*, p. 324).

[11] For the forms *bika* and *buka*, see above, p. 73. For examples of the change of original *i* to *u* and vice versa, see Pischel's *Gram. der Pkt. Spr.* §§ 117 and 124, and Geiger's *Litt. u. Spr. der Sinh.* § 12 (2).

[12] *A. I. C.* No. 5.

[13] See above, p. 62.

Palu Makiccāva Rock-Inscription of Gaja Bahu I.

From an ink-impression supplied by the Archaeological Commissioner, Ceylon.

Scale about 1½ inches to 1 foot.

Tubaraba (Thūpārāma). An account of these three kings is given at p. 60, above. Gamiṇi Abaya, or Gajabāhuka Gāmaṇī Abhaya, reigned twenty-two years (177–199 A. D.)[1]. The chronicles, though they speak of the large sums he spent on religious undertakings, make no special reference to the Vaḍamanaka (P. *Vaḍḍhamānaka*) Tank. Possibly he did not form a new tank, but only had an old one dredged or deepened[2]. If this be the case, the tank in question may be the Abhivaḍḍhamānaka-vāpi[3] constructed by his grandfather, king Vasabha.

TRANSCRIPT.

1 Maharaja(ha Vaha)bayaha[4]
2 maṇumaraka Tisa-maharajaha puti[5]
3 maharaji Gamiṇi[6]-Abeya[7] Upala-viba-
4 -jakahi Vaḍamanaka[8]-vavi paca-saha(si)[9] kahāvaṇa
5 dariya[10] kaṇavaya Tubaraba[11] buka[12]-saga- ⊞
6 -haṭaya catiri[13] paceṇi[14] pari [bujanaka koṭu diṇi][15]

TRANSLATION.

The great king **Gamiṇi Abaya**, son of the great king **Tisa** [and] grandson of the great king **Vahaba**, having borne [the expense of] five thousand *kahāvaṇas*, and having caused the Vaḍamanaka Tank in the Upala division to be dug, [granted the same] to the community of monks at **Tubaraba**, [and thereby secured for them the enjoyment] of the four priestly requisites.

---

[1] See the genealogical table on leaf facing p. 142 above. [2] *koṇavaya* (l. 5).

[3] *Mv.* xxxv. 95. Aggivaḍḍhamānaka in Prof. Geiger's edition. The *Ṭīkā*, however, supports the above reading.

[4] Mt. *maharajaha Wahabaya pu* . . .; Mp. °*raja(ha)pahabayahu*; Bt. *maharajaha* [*Vaha*]*baya*.

[5] Mt. Mp. *puta*; Bt. *puti*.

[6] Mt. *Gamini Abayaḷa*; Mp. *Gamiṇi Abaya*; Bt. *Gamaṇi Abeya*.

[7] Read *Abaya*. [8] Mt. *Wana manaka wawi*; Mp. *Vaṇamaṇaka-vavi*; Bt. *Vaḍamanakavavi*.

[9] Mt. *saha*[*sa*] *kahawana*; Bt. *sahase kahavaṇa*. [10] Mt. Mp. *jaraya*; Bt. *dariya*.

[11] Mt. Mp. *tā baraba*; Bt. *taba Raba*. [12] Bt. *bhuka*.

[13] Mt. *catari*; Mp. Bt. *catiri*. [14] Mt. *paceni*; Mp. Bt. *pacaṇi*.

[15] The inscription ends abruptly after *pari*, but the above words were undoubtedly meant to be engraved to complete the sentence. Cf. the closing words on the Ruvanvāli Dāgaba Slab now in the Colombo Museum (*A. I. C.* No. 5).

No. 19. JĒTAVANĀRĀMA SLAB-INSCRIPTION (No. 1) OF MAHINDA IV (*circa* 1026–1042 A.D.)

THIS slab lies in the Jētavanārāma area, not far from the 'stone-canoe' or trough on the outer circular road in Anurādhapura. It was examined by the Archaeological Commissioner (Mr. H. C. P. Bell) in 1890[1].

The inscription, which covers an area of 6 ft. 2 in. by 3 ft. 11 in. of its smoothed side, is engraved in 55 lines, each within a ruled space, 1¼ in. wide. Owing to the worn and damaged state of the stone a good portion of the text from the nineteenth line to the end is wholly illegible, as may be seen from the accompanying facsimile (Plate 28).

The **akṣaras** belong to the alphabet of the tenth and early eleventh centuries A.D. Their size varies from ¼ to 1 inch each, and their type[2] is that of the Vessagiri slab of Mahinda IV. The unsettled **orthography** too indicates its age, for example, the gerund of *upadinavā* is spelt *upädä* in the present inscription, *ipäjä* in the following one, and *ipädä* in the Mihintale tablet. Similarly, *biso* and *bisev*; *Abhā*, *Abahay*, and *Abā*; *eme kulen sama-jäy* and *emä kulen sama-dǟ*; *bimb* and *bib*; *ṭamb* and *ṭämb*; *pāmili* and *piyamili*.

The **language** is poetical, and teems with similes and metaphors, one jostling the other, which require a fair knowledge of Indian mythology to comprehend their full signification and the aptness of their application in ornate prose composition.

The inscription is one of **Mahinda IV**, referred to here, as in most of his other records, by the *biruda* title **Siri Saṅgbo Abā** (P. *Siri Saṅgha-bōdhi Abhaya*). The names of his parents too are given as **Siri Saṅgbo Abā** Maharaja and **Dev Gon** Biso-räjna. In the Mayilagastoṭa pillar-inscription[3], and in the Mihintale tablets[4], as well as in the following Jētavanārāma slab[5], No. 2, his father is called **Abhā (Abahay** or **Abay) Salamevan**, whilst the Vēvälkäṭiya record[6] agrees with ours in naming him **Siri Saṅgbo Abhā** (or **Abā**). This shows that Mahinda's father was known by both these *birudas*. The question regarding his identity with Dappula V, who bore the same title Abhā Salamevan, as advanced above at page 79, is still not settled. Some indirect evidence may, however, be derived from the present inscription in support of the suggestion.

---

[1] *A. S. C. Annual Report for* 1890, p. 9.

[2] See remarks on p. 242, below.

[3] *A. I. C.* 120. See above, p. 78, note 2.

[4] Above, p. 91.

[5] Below, p. 231.

[6] Below, pp. 243 and 248.

It is stated in lines 21 and 29 that Mahinda's grandfather, the great king (*miti-maha-rad*) resolved to build **Miṇimevulā-maha-pahā** (P. *Maṇimēkhalā-mahā-pāsāda*), and that he had the book **Dhammasaṅgaṇi** copied. The *Pūjāvaliya*[1] ascribes the former act to Sēna I, while the *Mahāvaṁsa* says that his successor Sēna II (*circa* 917–952 A.D.) put an image of the Bōdhisatta and one of the Buddha himself with its pavilion in the Maṇimēkhalāpāsāda[2]. The truth may be that he built the temple also before he became king, when he was Mahādipāda. He may, moreover, have had the Dhammasaṅgaṇi transcribed along with the **Ratanasutta**[3]; for his son Kassapa V 'caused the Abhidhamma Piṭaka to be written on plates of gold, and embellished the book Dhammasaṅgaṇi with divers jewels, and built for it a house in the midst of the city[4].' These notices tend to show that the king referred to by *miti-maha-rad* ('the grandfather, the great king') in the present inscription was possibly no other than Sēna II, the father of Kassapa V and Dappula V, both of whom had the *biruda* Abhā or Abahay Salamevan[5]. Hence Mahinda IV may have been the son of one of these two kings.

Further, it is stated in line 27 that the building of the **Huligam-piriven**[6] was half completed by the great king, his brother. This temple may be identified with the *parivēṇa*, built by Mahinda's predecessor, Sēna IV, at Sitthāgāma, especially because the qualifying phrase 'where he himself had dwelt' occurs in reference to this place both in the *Mahāvaṁsa* (liv. 6) and in the present inscription (l. 26). If this identification be correct, Sēna IV must have been a brother of Mahinda IV, in which case they were the sons of Kassapa V or Dappula V.

The **date** of the inscription is given in lines 43 and 44, but the portion containing the name of the king and the number of the regnal year is in great part obliterated. What remains tells us that the record was promulgated on the tenth day of the waxing moon in the month of *Poson* (May–June). The regnal year of [Siri] Saṅgbo Abā may be the eighth, the same as that of his second inscription at this spot[7].

The **contents** of the record give an account of the **Abhayagiri-vihāra** and

---

[1] See Guṇasēkara Mudaliyar's edition (1895) of Extract from the *Pūjāvaliya*, p. 27.

[2] *Mv.* li. 77. [3] l.c. 79.

[4] *Mv.* lii. 50–51. See also the slab-inscription of Kassapa V, line 10 (above, p. 46).

[5] See above, p. 24.

[6] This must not be confounded with Helagam-piriveṇa (*P. Hēligāma-parivēṇa*) built by Kassapa III more than two centuries before Mahinda IV. See *Mv.* xlviii. 24, and *Pūjāvaliya* Extract, p. 27.

[7] See below, p. 231.

a general survey of the charitable acts which Mahinda IV performed, as well as the religious monuments he erected and repaired. They agree in the main with what is related of him in the Ceylon chronicles, and afford us ample proof of his just and liberal principles. The policy of the 'open door,' which draws so much attention in modern politics, is tersely expressed in the phrase that he made Laṅkā 'a common stage for peoples of diverse appearances from diverse countries[1].' The statement in the fifth line that he drove away the Dravidian foe may have reference to the crushing defeat which the army of the Cōla king, Vallabha, sustained at the hands of Sēna, the chief captain of Mahinda's forces[2].

Maha-dämi (P. *Mahā-dhammika*, line 12) may perhaps have been the popular designation of Dhammamitta, the elder of Sitthagāma, whom Mahinda employed to expound the Abhidhamma[3]. This Thēra probably belonged to the **Dhammaruci Nikāya**[4], whose members residing in the Abhayagiri-vihāra are so highly praised in lines 8 to 12. The edifice **Ruvan-maha-pahā** (P. *Ratana-mahā-pāsāda*), referred to in line 8, was evidently the one which king Kaniṭṭha-Tissa (229–247 A.D.) built at the Abhayagiri-vihāra for Mahānāga Thēra of Bhūtārāma[5]. Mahinda II (838–858 A.D.) rebuilt it at a cost of three hundred thousand pieces of gold, and made it an exceedingly beautiful palace with several floors[6]. For its maintenance Mahinda III (863–867 A.D.) dedicated

---

[1] See line 38. [2] *Mv.* liv. 12–16. [3] l. c. 35.

[4] The *Nikāyasaṅgraha* gives the following account of the origin of this Buddhist sect:—'Now it happened that the high priest Tissa, who had received the Abhayagiri-vihāra [from king Vaṭṭa-Gāmaṇī Abhaya 28–16 B.C.], but was living at Kemgalla, was credited by general repute with living in domestic intercourse. Thereupon the pious priests of the Mahā-vihāra assembled, and were interdicting him, when one of his pupils who was among the assembly, by name Mahadāḷiyā-Tissa (P. *Mahādāṭhika Tissa*), obstructed them, saying, "Do not act thus by our High Priest." The priests then held the obstructor guilty of mixing in misconduct, and expelled him the Order.

'He then, burning with resentment, left with about five hundred priests, and breaking from the Thēriya Nikāya [i.e. the orthodox sect], went and lived at Abhayagiri-vihāra. There came to him the disciples of Dharmaruci Ācārya of Vajjiputta Nikāya before mentioned, who had found their way into this country from Pallārāma of Daṁbadiva (India); and he accepting their doctrines joined them and settled down under the title of Dharmaruci Ācārya. From that time those belonging to the Abhayagiri were known as the Dharmaruci Nikāya. Thus a Nikāya called Dharmaruci, of a body of men separated from the Thēriya Nikāya, was established in Bhagiri-vehera [the Abhayagiri-vihāra], in the fifteenth year of the reign of Vaḷagam Abhā (Vaṭṭa-Gāmaṇī Abhaya) and 454 years after the death of Buddha' (C. M. Fernando's English translation, pp. 11-12). The history of the sect is continued in the succeeding pages of the *Nikāyasaṅgraha*. See also Rhys Davids on 'the Sects of the Buddhists' (*J. R. A. S.* 1891. pp. 409–422).

[5] *Mv.* xxxvi. 7. [6] *Ibid.*, xlviii. 136

the water-course called Geṭṭhumba[1]. In the reign of Udaya II (1003–1006 A.D.) it was the scene of a great rising of people against the king and his ministers for violating the right of refuge in the Tapōvana[2]. The rebels ascended the Ratanapāsāda, terrified the king and cut off the heads of the ministers who took part in the unlawful act. We see from our inscription (l. 23) that another building of the same name was in existence in the tenth or early eleventh century A.D., attached to the Mahāmēghavana-mahāvihāra, the headquarters of the orthodox Buddhist sect[3].

The **Abayaturā-maha-sā** (P. *Abhayuttara-mahā-cētiya*, line 9) was another name for the Abhayagiri Thūpa. King Gajabāhu (177–199 A.D.) had it raised to a greater height, and caused arches (? *ādi-mukha*) to be built at the four gates thereof[4]. Mahānāga (617–620 A.D.) renewed its plaster-work[5]. Sēna III (1006–1015 A.D.) had its ground paved with stones at an expense of forty thousand *kahāpaṇas*[6], and Parākrama-Bāhu I (1153–1186 A.D.) had it repaired and raised to a height of 140 cubits[7].

The **Kasub-rad-maha-pahā** (P. *Kassapa-rāja-mahā-pāsāda*, line 15) was most likely the *pāsāda* which Kassapa IV (963–980 A.D.) built at the Abhayagiri-vihāra and called after his own name[8]. It may not be the same as the Kasub-raj-maha-vehera mentioned in the slab-inscription of Kassapa V as one of the temples he built[9].

The **Udā-Agbo** and the **Mas-toṭu** monasteries (line 16) may be identified with the Udayaggabōdhi-parivēṇa of Aggabōdhi VIII[10] (867–878 A.D.) and the Maccha-tittha-vihāra of Khattiya Kassapa[11] (783–789 A.D.). The **Kasub-giri** (line 16) was probably the Kassapa-giri-vihāra to which king Jeṭṭha-Tissa (*circa* 679 A.D.) dedicated the village Ambilāpika[12] and king Hatthadāṭha (715–724 A.D.) the village Sēna[12]. This Vihāra may be the same as the one built by Kassapa I (535–553 A.D.) and mentioned as Isurameṇu-Bo-Upulvan-Kasub-giri-rad-maha-vehera in the Vessagiri inscription[13] of Mahinda IV (1026–1042 A.D.). The *upōsatha* hall **Diyasen** (P. *Jayasēna*, line 17) seems to be one of the later additions to the **Denā-vehera** (P. *Jētavana-vihāra*, line 16) built by Mahāsēna[14] (331–358 A.D.). It should not be confounded with the rock-cut temple *Jayasēna*, which Sēnā, the queen of Dappula II (858–863 A.D.), erected at the *Cētiyapabbata*[15].

---

[1] *Mv.* xlix. 41. [2] *Ibid.*, liii. 17. [3] See Wijēsiṃha's translation of the *Mahāvaṃsa*, p. 255, note. [4] *Mv.* xxxv. 119. See also below, p. 253. [5] *Ibid.*, xli. 95. [6] *Ibid.*, liii. 33. [7] *Ibid.*, lxxviii, 101. [8] *Ibid.*, lii. 13. [9] See above, p. 51. [10] *Mv.* xlix. 45. Cf. also *Udā-Kitagbo-pavu*, above, p. 188. [11] *Mv.* xlviii. 24. [12] *Mv.* xliv. 98, xlv. 27, and xlviii. 24. [13] See above, pp. 29–39. [14] *Mv.* xxxvii. 33. [15] *Mv.* xlix. 23–24.

The **Viḷuvana-veher** (line 22), the **Maha-Mevnā-Maha-veher** (line 23), the **Isurmaṇu-veher** (line 27), the **Mirisiviṭi-veher** (line 28), and the **Sihigiri-maha-sā** (line 28) are historical monuments too well known to need drawing attention here. The Pāli forms of these names, as well as of those of other buildings referred to in the record, will be given as foot-notes to the translation.

The stone statue of the Buddha mentioned in lines 9 and 18, was probably the one which king Dēvānampiya Tissa (247–207 B.C.) set up at the Thūpārāma. King Jeṭṭha-Tissa removed it to Pācīnatissapabbata [1]. King Mahāsēna (331–358 A.D.) removed it from there and set it up at Abhayagiri in an image-house built for it [2]. King Dhātusēna (517–535 A.D.) also erected an edifice with an open hall for it, and 'caused its eyes to be set with two excellent jewels; also the halo, the crest, and the curled hair to be thickly studded with blue sapphires. He made offerings also of an excellent band of gold, an *uṇṇalōma* ornament (representing the curled hair on the forehead of the Buddha), a golden robe, a network for the feet, a lotus, an excellent lamp, and clothes of divers colours [3].'

Silāmēghavaṇṇa (670–679 A.D.) in his turn made offerings to the statue, renewed its old house, adorned it with divers gems, and dedicated to it the Kōlavāpi tank. He gave also to it all manner of protection, and always held the festivals connected with it with great pomp [4]. Saṅghā, the queen of Sēna II (917–952 A.D.), 'made a crest of blue (*nīla-cūḷāmaṇi*) for it, and offered daily offerings to it with all marks of honour [5].'

The stone statue of Mahinda Thēra (line 14) was probably the one set up by king Dhātusēna at the place where the Thēra's body was cremated, close by the Mahāthūpa in Anurādhapura [6]. About a century or so later, in the reign of Aggabōdhi I, there existed a statue of Mahinda Thēra on the bund of Mahindataṭa-vāpi at Mihintale [7], but this might have been another one.

In bringing out the following edition of this important record I have utilized four ink-impressions and a good eye-copy supplied by the Archaeological Commissioner. When collating them I often found one estampage remedied the defects of another. But for this fact, it would not have been possible to produce a satisfactory reading of that portion of the text where the letters are not clear.

I have also to acknowledge my indebtedness to Mr. D. B. Jayatilaka for the valuable help he so readily rendered me in the task.

[1] *Mv.* xxxvi. 128–129. [2] *Mv.* xxxvii. 14.
[3] *Mv.* xxxviii. 61–64. See also Wijēsiṇha's translation, p. 1, note.
[4] *Mv.* xliv. 68–69. [5] *Mv.* li. 87 [6] *Mv.* xx. 42–44 and xxxviii. 58. [7] *Mv.* xlii. 29.

TEXT.

1 ශ්‍රී සිරිවත් අපිරියත් ගුණමුළින් උතරත්ව(ා) බුළු අඹබදිවගි අත් කැනඹුල පාමිලිකළු ඔකාවස් ර(ජ්)

2 පරපුරෙන් බට කැත් උසබ **සිරිසඟබො අබා** මිහරජ්හට එමැ කුලෙන් සමදැ **දෙවගොණ් කිසො** රජ්

3 න කුසැ උපැදැ ඈපා මහයා සිරි විඳැ පිළිවෙළ් සෙ රදවැ මිණිදුම්ගනන් පැහැයූ සිය මුඤ්ගෙන්[1] ලො උතුරු කිසෙව්ගෙන් කි

4 සෙස් වැ තුමා සිරින් ලක්දිව් පහයා නන් දෙඅසත් රදුන් වඩිනා අස්හි පබුරෙන් දවහ පිරෙන රද්ඟග දෑර්ගි දියනාවන් පැ

5 රැකුම් සිරින් සිරි ලකට් යස එළවූ තෙදිනහිර් උදා ඉගිමැ ළක් අඹුරෙන් **දෙමෙළ්** රුපු අසුර් හැරැ ලො එක්ගෙළි කැරැ සොමි

6 යෙන් නිසපුර්වැ ගැඹුරෙන් සපුර්වැ නුහවුර්නෙන් මෙර්වැ දෙගෙන් දිනිසුර්වැ ගුණව (අඩු)ර්වැ දසරද්දගමට් නෙවෙ

7 ස්වැ තුඹුරුවන් රුවනට් මැනෙඳාස්වැ මුනි සස්නට් එක්වහල් වැමඛවැ හැමැ සිරිව් සිරිසෙවැ දියව් පගිටවැ

8 පියවර් වර් පිරිවෙන් කුලගල්[2] මැඳගි **රුවන් මහපසා** රුවන් සුනෙර් තෙව්න සතර් මුළ් සතර් මහදිව්බවන අවටගි මුනි

9 ඤ් පිළිකිබ් විමන් රුවන්පව් පැහැන් පහයන **අබයහුරු මහසෑ** ගිමගල් සොරබාන මහගුන් උරක් පෙලව් නුවණි පියා

10 (විගි)දෑ වියත් ගුරිළ් මුළ් ඛමන දහම්දරන් දහම් විසක්ගන ගුමන් ගුගුමන සත්දනන් රුවන් අරෙන් වොරෙදන අපිස් ස

11 තොස් සලෙ සැහැ මහණගණ පබිළ ලිය ඉළ් රඳන විගිගුම් පඬෙර පඩුර් තරන් වදඹන මුනිඳ් පුද උදම්මන නය් ඈඳුර(ා)

12 පාවන් තිමි තිමිඟුල් මන මස් සරන **දහම්රුසි** පවර මුනුඳ් මරු පුය්හු රක්න **මහදැමි** වසුදෙව්හු පර්වැඩ .. ..

13 අරඹ් අනත් යහනක්ගි වැඩැ දහම් සිර්වම්ය සිගො සිරි විඳුන සිරිගෙ සිරි ඉසිඳු **අබාගිරි වෙහෙරැ** කරවූ සැ

14 ගි රුවන් දිවක් බඳු ගෙනාල් නවකම්ගෙන් හොබවා පිරිවර් ගෙ (යැ)ළින් කර **මිහිඳුමහ සල්පිළිමෙ** තුල් (දැහි)මිණින් ඇස් නබවා (ර)

15 න්මුවා පාද දළ කරා පන්හිස්හන් **කසුබ රද් මහපසා** සි(ය)න් නවකම් කර **පුසර්බා පහා** කරා මහසඟ්නට් පස් (පිළියෙ)

16 ළ්ගි බද් **සම බැහිල්හි**[3] මහහල් කරා **උදා අශ්බො මස්සොබු මි(හි) කසුබගිරි** නවකම් කරා සිරිවත් **(දෙකා) වෙහෙරැ** (ම්ර) .. ..

17 (ව ගි)මන්ගි මුනිරද්හව් පිළිසන් සිරි අළ **දිසෙසන් මහසොගෙ** යැළින් කරා නන් දෑරුවනින් නොවනා රන් මෙර්මෙන් (ද) .. ..

18 කම්ගෙන් (හුවා) කළ පින් පෙළෙන් තුමා අන(ව) දුවන රුවන්සක්මෙ(න්)

---

[1] 'සිය මුඤ්ගෙ' දෙවෙනි ලේඛනයෙහි 5 වෙනිපෙළේ (232 වෙනිපිටබලනු)

[2] 'කුළුගල්' වියයුතුයි

[3] 'සටබැහිල්දන්' සිද කියවිය හැකිසි

ගිරි මඩුලු කර උදගිරි ගිස්හි තෙවනා රිවී කි(ම්බ) [මෙන් මුනිඳ් පිළිබි]

19 මඩ මුඳුන් රන් සතින් රඳ්වා තමා සිථු දිව් පිංගාදුතු පල තෙද් රැඳි සිරින් සිථු කත් ගෙම්බුවා කොතුර් වැම්බින් ම .. ..

20 සද **සිද්දගම** කත්මුවා කර හුදින්පත් සැපැත්මෙන් මහ විරියෙන් සෙන්(වතුසෙ) **කසුබරද්** පිරිවෙණ් සත් .. ..

21 ළින් කල ෂ්ඩාසස් සිහක්සෙයින් **මිණිමෙවුලා මහපහා** කරනුයෙහි සනිව්හන්වූ මිහිමහරද්හු න(ව) .. ..

22 කර **විළුවන වෙහෙර්හි** පහා ගැළින් කර **හිල්පහාණ** බොසත් පිළිබිඹ් කත්මුවා කර (හැමැ) .. ..

23 (ළි) පෙල්හි බද් සතුර්හල් කර **මහමෙව්නා මහවෙහෙර්හි** රුවන්(**පහාණ** තමබු තමා) .. .. .. ය් එක්(සෙ) .. ..

24 දියටමබ්මෙන් දදවම්බි හුවා මිහිගිර්දෙව්හු පිළිබිඹ්බඳු ගිර්මඬලෙන් (සි) .. .. මුහුණ් .. ..

25 ත් සිථුසගරවත්මෙන් ගෙම්බුවා කොතුර් වැමිහින් සිථු කන් සද දලවුලත්තෙන්[1] සිථු මුඳුන් (පිළිබිඹ්) .. .. [සි]

26 රි ඉසිලූ අපූණ් මහසල පිළිමෙ දැරන් මිණිහින් ඇස් තබවා තමා ඇපා සිරි වි(ඇ) වූසු මිහි .. ..

27 බැ මහරද්හු අඩාලා කල **හුලිගම** පිරිවෙණ් කර **ඉසුර්මණුවෙහෙර් මහපහා** කර (**මහසැ**) .. ..

28 ත් සුලබ්වනු වව් **මාරහල්** කර **මිරිසිවිතිවෙහෙර්හි** ලවෙහෙර්හිමි **සිහිගිපිමහ(සැණ)** .. .. [මි]

29 ත් මහරද්හු ලියවන ලද් **දහම්සඟුණි** (ද)කරවූ කත්මුවා කර (කැරු) **රුවන් දගබ** (ගැළින්) .. ..

30 (හි) **අනුරාපුර** වූවුන් සැදූ සිල්මිණිමෙන් මුහිරද්හු වර **දළදගෙරවූ** කර **සුතුර් ස(හගි)** .. ..

31 සුපිරු මහනැව් ගව්යෙන් දගෙ කර තමා කලහං විසිතුර් පිත් රැස් රැස් කර (නූ) .. ..

32 **සුර්මාලා මහපෙල්** කර ගැළින් මෙහෙණි මහපෙල් කර නිමව් ගිලන් පුහක්නු දුව .. ..

33 මා මූල්තැන් වෙද්හල් කර අසරණ මෙහෙණිගණ වෙංහෙණිවර් නවකම් කර (ගෙ) .. ..

34 .. **උණිලොම්දරුවනව** වඬෙආස් බඳු **රන්සැගෙ** කර හැමැ[2] මහතුමබ නව[කම්කර] .. ..

35 (මු)ල්[3] **අතුලා) වෙහෙර්හි** සුවන් මූවං තමා ප(ලහි) මුනිඳ් පිළිබිඹ් කර ස .. ..

36 ලකල සහ වූවුනැ තමා බරණින් තුලං අග් අර කිර දන් (ගෙය) .. ..

---

[1] 'දලපුලත්තෙන්' සිද කියවිය හැකිසි [2] 'සැමැ' සිද කියවිය හැකිසි

[3] 'සූල්' සිද කියවිය හැකිසි

37 සිරි සඟබො විජයබා ජුත් සතර් සස් දත් (සද)ගැ වනම්ස්සග්නාව .. ..
.. .. [නො]

38 එක්වෙස් ‍නො එක්දෙසින් අ නො එක්දනනාව සිරි ලක එක්රන් කර .. ..
.. ..

39 ණේ සානදුන්වත් දැරැ තිළින් වහරෙනෙත් ලොය් සැනැහු පිරිසුද් .. ..
.. ..

40 සු පළිපත් මහසඟ්හි .. වූ තමා සඟ වූවනා නිරිඤ් බ .. ..
.. ..

41 සඟ වූවනා නිරඤ් අම්බරණින් සැදූ දත් ද (තොය)ත් පුහු(ණේ) .. ..
.. ..

42 (ව)ත් පුත්නාව උවසර් (ව්)පුත්නාව සඟර දහමව පුද සි .. ..
.. ..

43 ති නුවණ් හැමැ මනා හැමැ කුසල් තමහට එක් අත්සරු (කා)ල [සිරි සඟ]මෙ අබා මහරජ්හු සත් ලැහු .. .. [තව]

44 රුදුයෙහි පොසොනැ පුර දසපක් දවසැ මිහිඳු මහ (ගි) .. ..
.. ..

45 දූ සසුන් කර දළ් සදහැයෙත් පිනා පගත් නුවණින් .. ..
.. ..

46 සඟ්නාව තමන් තිළින් මහ රිස්හි ගත් (පෙලගැවිය) .. ..
.. ..

47 (මෙ)ත් පැහු කෙලෙසස්සෙපින් හැම(කල්හි නො හැ) .. ..
.. ..

48 (මෙකි)යත් බුදුරද්හු දහම්සැක්(ගි පගත්) .. ..
.. ..

49 මඟුල් මහ ඇතුපිවිහි තබා නුවර් පැද්[කුණ් කරවා] .. ..
.. ..

50 (ව)නු ලද් මනො වාස් .. ..
.. ..

51 සසු මහතාම් පස්සලෙලා .. ..
.. ..

52 ණම තු .. සා .. ..
.. ..

53 ල සි .. සාමිසා .. .. තට .. ..
.. ..

54 .. .. .. පාලො සා .. ..
.. ..

55 .. සා .. .. .. ඛ .. ..
.. ..

Jētavanārāma Slab-Inscription
(No. 1) of Mahinda IV

From an ink-impression supplied by the Archæological Commissioner, Ceylon.

Scale about 1⅓ inches to 1 foot.

TRANSCRIPT.

1 Śrī siri-vat apiriyat guṇa-muḷin uturat-v(ä) muḷu Damb-divhi an Kät-kula pāmili-kaḷa Okā-vas ra(j)-

2 parapuren baṭ Kät-usab **Siri Saṅgbo Abā** maha-raj-haṭ ema kulen sama-dā **Dev Gon** biso-räj-

3 -na kusä upädā äpā mahayā siri vindä piḷiveḷ-se rada-vä miṇi-vuṭnen pähäyū siya mundnen[1] lo-uturā-bisevnen bi-

4 -ses-vä tumā sirin Lak-div pahayā nan desen radun vaṭna asiri paṅḍuren davaha pirena rad-ge-dorhi diya-nāvan-pä-

5 -räkum-sirin siri-Lakaṭ yasa eḷvū tedin hir-udā-ihimā Lak-amburen **Demeḷ**-rupu-andur härä lo ek-heḷi-kärä somi-

6 -yen nisayur-vä gämburen sayur-vä tahavurnen mer-vä denen dinisur-vä guṇaṭ (avu)r-vä dasa-rad-dahamaṭ neve-

7 -s-vä Tunu-ruvan-ruvanaṭ mändos-vä Muni-sasnaṭ ek-vahal-ṭāmba-vä hämä-siriṭ siri-se-vä diyaṭ pihiṭa-vä

8 pirivar var piriven kula[2]-gal mänd-hi **Ruvan-maha-pahā** ruvan-Suner tevna satar muḷ satar maha-div-bavana avaṭahi Muni-

9 -nd-piḷibib-viman ruvan-pav-pähän pahayana **Abayaturā-maha-sä** hima-gal sobona maha-gat urak peḷaṭ nuvaṇ piyā

10 (vihi-)dā viyat guriḷ-muḷ bamana daham-daran daham-viyak-hana-guman gugumana sat-danan ruvan-ären vorodana apis sa-

11 -tos sale Sähä-mahaṇa-gaṇa pabḷa liya iḷ randna vihigum paṅḍera pavur taraṅg vadambana munind puda udammana nan ädur(u)-

12 pāvan Timi Timiṅgul maha-mas sarana **Dahamrusi** pavara muhund maru-put-hu rakna **Maha-dämi** Vasudevhu parväḍ .. ..

13 arab Anat yahanak-hi väḍä daham siri-vamiya siyo siri vinduta Siri-ge siri isilu **Abägiri-veherä** karavū sä-

14 -hi ruvan-divak bandu ganoḷ nava-kamnen hobavā pirivar-ge (yä)ḷin karā **Mihind-maha-sal-piḷime** tul (däti)-miṇin äs tabavā (ra-)

15 -n-muvā päda-dāla karā pan-tis hat **Kasub-rad-maha-pahā** si(ya)n nava-kam karā **Pusarbā-pahā** karā maha-saṅgnaṭ pas (piḷiye-)

16 -ḷhi bad **Yaṭabähilhi**[3] maha-hal karā **Udā-Agbo Mas-toṭu Mi**(ti)-**Kasub-giri** nava-kam karā sirivat (**Denā**)-**veherhi** (mara) .. ..

17 (-ṭ gi)manhi Muni-rad-haṭ pilisat siri aḷa **Diyasen-maha-po-ge** yäḷin karā nan dā-ruvanin tevnā ran-Mer-men (da) .. ..

---

[1] *Mundne* in slab No. 2, line 5 (below, p. 234). [2] Read *kuḷa-gal*. [3] This can also be read *yaṭa bähil dan*.

18 kamnen (huvā) kaḷa pin-pelen tumā ata(ṭ) duvana ruvan-sakme(n) hiri-maṇḍulu karā Udāgiri-hishi tevnā rivi-bi(mb)-[men Munind-piḷibi-]

19 -mb mundun ran-satin randvā tamā siyu div piyodunu paḷa ted rändi sirin siyu kan hem-muvā kotur-ṭämbin ma .. ..

20 sadā **Sid-dāgab** kan-muvā karā hudin-pat säpätmen maha viriyen sen(vatuse) **Kasub-rad-piriven** saṅg .. ..

21 -ḷin kaḷa Bo-sat sitak-seyin **Miṇimevulā-maha-pahā** karanuyehi saniṭ-hanvū miti maharad-hu na(va) .. ..

22 karā **Viḷuvana-veherhi** pahā yäḷin karā **Nilpahāhi** Bosat-piḷibib kan-muvā karā (hämä) .. ..

23 (-ḷi) peḷhi bad sakur-hal karā **Maha-Mevnā-Maha-veherhi Ruvan-(pahāhi** tambu tamā) .. .. .. n ek(se) .. ..

24 diya-ṭamb-men dada-ṭamb huvā miti-hir-devhu piḷibib baṅdu hir maṇḍlen (si) .. .. muhuṇ .. ..

25 -n siyu-saṅgarā-vat-men hem-muvā kotur-ṭämbin siyu kan sadā dalavulatnen[1] siyu Budun-(piḷibib) .. .. [si-]

26 -ri isilū apuṇ Maha-sala-piḷime dāraṅg-miṇin äs tabavā tamā āpā siri vi(ndä) vusū Mihi .. ..

27 bā maha-rad-hu aḍāḷā kaḷa **Huligam-piriven** karā **Isurmaṇu-veher-maha-pahā** karā (**Maha-sā**) .. ..

28 -t sulab-vanuvaṭ **Mārā-hal** karā **Mirisiviṭi-veherhi** veher-himi **Sihigiri-maha-(sāhi)** .. .. [mi-]

29 -ti maharad-hu liyavana-lad **Daham-saṅguṇ** (dā)-karaṇḍu kan-muvā karā (käru) **Ruvan-dāgab** (yäḷin) .. ..

30 (-hi) **Anurāpura** vuṭun sädu siḷ-miṇi-men muni-rad-hu vara **Daḷadā-karaṇḍu** karā **Sutur-sa(ṅgarā)** .. ..

31 supiru maha-näv haviyen dāge karā tamā kaḷa-tā visitur pin-räs räs-karā (nu) .. ..

32 **Purimālā-maha-peḷ** karā yäḷin meheṇi-maha-peḷ karā nimav gilan putak-hu duṭa .. ..

33 mā muḷtän ved-hal karā asaraṇa meheṇi-gaṇā meheṇivar nava-kam karā (he-) .. ..

34 .. **Uṇ-lom-dā-ruvanaṭ** mandos bandu **Rak-sā-ge** karā hāmä[2] maha-tumba nava-[kam karā] .. ..

---

[1] This can also be read *dalapulatnen*.

[2] This can also be read *sāmä*.

35 -(bu)ḷ[1] **Atuḷā-veherhi** suvan-muvá tamá pa(laṅgi) Munind-piḷibib karā sa .. ..

36 lakaḷa saha vuṭunä tamá baraṇin tula ag ara kira dan (heya) .. ..

37 **Kir-bimb-viharhi** yut satar sas dat (sada)hä maha-bik-saṅgnaṭ .. .. [no-]

38 -ek-ves no-ek-desin ā no-ek-dana-haṭ siri Laka ek-raṅg karā .. ..

39 -ṇi kahavun-vat därä tiḷiṇ vaharenen loy sänähū pirisud .. ..

40 su-piḷipan maha-saṅg-hi .. vū tamā saha vu(ṭ)nā nirind ba .. ..

41 saha vuṭnā nirind ambaraṇin sädū dan dī (teya)n puhu(ṇ) .. ..

42 (va)t yutnaṭ uvasar (vi)yutnaṭ saṅgrā dahamaṭ puda si .. ..

43 -ti nuvaṇ hämä manā hämä kusal tamahaṭ ek atsaru (ka)ḷa [**Siri-Saṅg**]bo **Abā** maharaj-hu sat läṅgū .. .. [hav-]

44 -ruduyehi Posonā pura dasa-pak davasā **Mihind** maha (hi-) .. ..

45 -dū sasun karā daḷ sadahäyen pinā pahan nuvaṇin .. ..

46 saṅgnaṭ taman tiḷin maha rik-hi gat (pelayä-viya) .. ..

47 (-ḷe)n pähū kelesak-seyin häma(-kalhi no hä-) .. ..

48 (meki-)yan Budu-rad-hu **Daham-sāk**-(hi pahan) .. ..

49 maṅgul maha ätu-piṭ-hi tabā nuvar päda[kuṇ karavā] .. ..

50 (-va)nu ladi mano vāk .. ..

51 -ssu mahatam passallo .. ..

---

[1] This can also be read *sūḷ*.

52 -ṇām tu .. hā .. ..

53 -la si .. kāmikā .. .. ttha .. ..

54 .. .. .. pālo sā .. ..

55 .. ka .. .. .. ṇḍa .. ..

TRANSLATION.

[Lines 1-5.] Hail! The great king [**Siri Saṅg**]**bo Abā**[1] was born[2] unto the great king **Siri Saṅgbo Abā**, the Kṣatriya Lord, descended from the royal line of the Okkāka dynasty, which abounds in a multitude of boundless[3] and benignant virtues, and which has [thereby] caused other Kṣatriya dynasties of the whole of Ḍaṁbadiva to render homage[4], [he was born] in the womb

[1] See line 43.

[2] *Upādā*, 'having been born,' same as *ipādā*, above, p. 91, and *ipājā*, below, p. 234, the gerund of *upadinavā* (Skt. *ud*+ √*pad*).

[3] *Sirivat apiriyat guṇa-muḷin uturatvā.* In the following inscription (No. 2) of this king, as well as in later ones such as the Devanagala record of Parākrama Bāhu I (*A. S. C. Report on the Kegalla District*, p. 75), and the Ḍaṁbulla rock-inscription of Kīrti Niśśaṅka Malla (above, p. 130), we find the words *lo* or *lo ikut* inserted between *apiriyat* and *guṇa*. This makes it clear that *apiriyat* and *lo ikut* are two attributes of *guṇa-muḷin*.

The translation of this phrase at p. 132 should be amended accordingly. As regards *sirivat*, we are not sure whether it qualifies *guṇa* or *Okāvas*.

[4] *Pāmili* is the same as *piyamili* in the following inscription (p. 234, below). Both point phonetically to a Sanskrit original *pādamūlika* or *-mūlaka*. In the phrase *an-Kät-kula pā-mili kaḷa Okā-vas-raj-parapuren* the past passive participle *kaḷa* (Skt. *kṛta*) is used in an active sense, governing *an-Kät-kula* (Skt. *anya-Kṣatriya-kulāni*) and *pā-mili* (Skt. *pāda-mūlikāni*) in the accusative case. Instances of the active use of the past passive participle of certain verbs are to be found in Sanskrit also. See Kāle's *Higher Sanskrit Grammar*, pars. 705 and 900, and Apte's *Sanskrit Composition*, par. 152. In Tamil the relative participle of the past tense, which is really equivalent to the past passive participle of Sanskrit, can have an object in the accusative as well as a subject in the nominative, e.g. *kāṭṭile ceyda velai*, the work (which was) done in the wood; *nāṉ ceyda vēlai*, the work I did; *vēlai ceyda paiyaṉ*, the boy who did the work. Sinhalese grammarians on the other hand would consider the subject or agent as a noun in the instrumental case and the object as one in the accusative, e.g. *mā kaḷa vāḍa*, the work done by me, and *vāḍa kaḷa daruvā*, the child who did the work. Possibly just as the preterite stem of Sinhalese verbs is derived from the Sanskrit passive participle, so the endings த் *t* (*d*), த்த் *tt* or ந்த் *nt* (*nd*), and இன் *iṉ* of the preterite stem of Tamil verbs may have some connexion with the Sanskrit endings *ta* and *na* of the past passive participle.

of the anointed queen[1] **Dev Gon,** of equal birth and descent[2]. After enjoying the dignities of governor and chief-governor[3], he in due course became king, and was anointed on his head, resplendent with the bejewelled crown, with the unction of world supremacy. With his glory he illumined the Island of Laṅkā; with the prowess of victorious lords[4], displayed in the precincts[5] of the Palace constantly filled with the wonderful presents offered by kings of various lands, he brought glory upon prosperous Laṅkā. With [the rise of] his majestic power he drove away from Laṅkā the Dravidian foe, just as the rising sun dispels darkness from the sky[6], and sheds lustre upon the world.

[Lines 5–7.] In gentleness he was like the moon, in depth [of character] the ocean, in firmness the mount Mēru, in wealth the Lord of Riches (Kubēra); he was a mine of good qualities, an abode of the ten kingly virtues[7], a jewel casket for the 'Triple Gem,' the supporting pillar for the religion of the Sage, the goddess[8] Śrī for every prosperity, and the mainstay of the world[9].

[Lines 8–13.] The **Abāgiri Vehera**[10], which displays the grace of the abode of Śrī at the moment when **Mahadāmi**[11] residing in . . . Ārāma [experiences the joy of association] with the Dharma, just as Vāsudēva enjoys the bliss

---

1 *Bisō-rājṇa*, same as *bisev-rājna*. See above, p. 49, note 7, and p. 78.

2 *Emā kulen sama-dā*. Cf. *eme kulen sama-jāy*, above, p. 91.

3 *Āpa mahaya*. See above, pp. 26, note 4, 98, note 5, and 187, note 6.

4 *Diya-nāvan*, the plural oblique stem of *diyanā*. This word can be equivalent to Skt. (1) *jagan-natha* or *-nāga*, 'world-lord,' an epithet of the Buddha (or the Bōdhisattva as in *Kāvyaśēkhara*, vi. 54), also of Viṣṇu or Kṛṣṇa; (2) *jaya-nātha* or *-nāga* or *-nayaka*, 'lord of victory;' (3) *udaka-nātha*, 'lord of water;' and (4) *udake snātvā*, 'having bathed in the water.' Cf. *Kāvyaśēkhara*, iii. 46:—

Ahas-gaṅga Yamunā
ekvū tānehi sobanā
Payāgaya diya nā
giman sānalū kumaru diyana.

'The world-lord (*diya-na*) prince having bathed in the waters (*diya nā*) of the beautiful Payāga (Skt. *Prayaga*, modern Allāhābād) at the confluence of the Ganges (*Ahas-gaṅga*, Skt. *Ākāśa-gaṅgā*) and *Yamunā*, assuaged the heat (of his journey).'

5 *Rad-ge-dorhi* = P. *rāja-geha-dvāramhi*, 'at the gate of the Palace.'

6 In this and in the following passages the metaphors of the text have been converted into similes for the sake of clearness

7 See above, p. 181, note 7.

8 The comparison of a king to a goddess is unusual.

9 For a similar string of comparisons, see the Devanagala inscription of Parākrama Bāhu I (*A. S. C. Report on the Kegalla District*, p. 75).

10 P. *Abhayagiri Vihāra*, see line 13.

11 P. *Mahādhammī* or *-dhammika*.

of union with Śrikanta on the couch of [the serpent] Ananta[1]; in which (Vihāra) there rises in splendour the **Ruvan-maha-pahā**[2] surrounded by the noble Pariveṇas, like unto the golden Mēru[3] centred by the Kuḷa-gal[4]; where around [the residences of] the four fraternities is shed the effulgence of the shrine of the image of the Lord of Sages[5], like the lustre of the Ruvan-pav[6] around the abodes of the four regent gods; where dwell bands of scholars directing their wisdom to great literary works and adorning the **Abayaturā-maha-sā**[7], just as a flight of *garuḍas* hovers with widespread wing over rows of serpents on the Himālayan range; which resounds with the voice of those versed in the scriptures[8], expounding the Dharma; which is adorned by virtuous men as by mines of gems; where flourish like unto an assemblage of coral tendrils numbers of *Śakya śramaṇas* (Buddhist monks) endowed with the virtues of temperance, contentment, and religious austerity[9]; whose broad and white ramparts rise aloft like the waves (of the ocean); which waxes with the offerings to the Lord of Sages[5]; where frequent various teachers of eminence, as the great fishes *Timi* and *Timiṅgala*[10] [gambol in the sea]; and over which [Abhayagiri-vihāra] presides the Head of the *Dhammaruci* [fraternity], just as the sea-god [over the sea].

[Lines 14-20.] Of the *cetiya* built [in this Vihāra] his Majesty renewed the brickwork and made it shine like a golden islet[11]; he rebuilt the edifices

[1] This seems, according to the Indian myth, to refer to a time after the churning of the ocean when the goddess Śrī rose from the waves, and not to the interval of creation during which Viṣṇu sleeps on the serpent *Śēṣa* or *Ananta*.

[2] P. *Ratana-Mahā-pāsāda*, 'the great Ratanapāsāda.' See line 8.

[3] *Ruvan-sumr* = P. *Ratana-Sumēru*. In Sinhalese *ruvan* means 'gem' as well as 'gold.' See below, p. 238, note 1. For an account of the golden Mēru mountain, see *Viṣṇupurāṇa*, ii. 2, and Wilson's notes to his translation.

[4] The seven concentric circles of rocks (*sapta-kūṭa-parvata*) in Hindu cosmology. For an account of the universe derived from Buddhist works, see Hardy's *Manual of Buddhism*. For illustrations, see Bastian's *Die Welt in ihren Spiegelungen unter dem Wandel des Völkergedankes*.

[5] i.e. the Buddha. *Munind-piḷibib-viman* = Skt. *munīndra-pratibimba-vimāna*.

[6] *Ruvan-pav* = P. *Ratana-pabbata*, the *Ratna-sānu* or *Mēru* mountain. Cf. *Ruvan-giri* in *Kāvya-śekhara*, viii. 40.

[7] P. *Abhayuttara-mahā-cētiya*. See *Mv.* xxxv. 119, li. 86.

[8] *Dahamdara* = P. *dhamma-dhara*.

[9] See above, p. 188, notes 12-14.

[10] *Timi*, *Timinda*, *Timiṅgala*, *Timiraṗiṅgala*, *Maha-Timi*, *Ananda*, and *Ajjharōha* are the names of certain mythical fishes of enormous size haunting the oceans between the seven concentric circles of mountains (*Kūṭa-pabbatas*) which surround mount Mēru. See Hardy's *Manual of Buddhism*, p. 13. See also *Mahāsutasōma-jātaka* (Fausböll, No. 537).

[11] *Ruvan-diva* = P. *ratana-dīpa*, 'a jewel-island' (Skt. *ratna-dvīpa*), or 'a jewel-lamp' (*ratna-dīpa*).

surrounding it, set the eyes of the great stone statue of Mahinda[1] with large brilliant rubies, and made a network of gold for the feet. He repaired the roof, thirty-five cubits [in length], of **Kasub-rad-maha-pahā**[2] (the great edifice of king Kasub), built the monument **Pusarbā-pahā**, erected the great alms-hall at **Yaṭabähila**, which was set apart for providing the requisites for the great community of monks, and repaired the **Udā-Agbo**[3], **Mastoṭu**[4] **Mi(ti)-Kasub-giri**[5] [Vihāras]. He built anew the great *upōsatha* hall [named] **Diya-sen**[6], which displayed the grace of *pilisat*[7] to the Lord of Sages in summer . . . in the beautiful **Donā-vehera**[8]. [Like] the golden Mēru shining with gems of various kinds . . . he raised . . . with . . . work. He made an orb of the sun like unto a wheel of gems[9], which rolls to his hands as the fruit of his meritorious work. With a golden parasol[10] like the orb of the sun shining on the Orient Mount, he adorned the head of the image [of the Lord of Sages], and with golden capital-topped[11] pillars at the four corners, which displayed the splendour of his majesty widespread over the four continents, he made . . .

[Lines 20–25.] He gilded tho **Sid-dāgab** (white[12] *dāgaba*). Like wealth acquired by virtuous men and as . . . with great exertion, the community of monks of the **Kasub-rad-piriven**[13] . . .

By the great king, his grandfather who had decided upon the building of the great monument **Miṇimevulā-maha-pahā**[14], like the determination of a Bōdhisatta, repairs were [effected] . . . He rebuilt the *pāsāda* at the **Viḷuvana-**

---

[1] The great Thera Mahinda, son of Asōka.

[2] *Kasub-rad-maha-pahā* = P. *Kassapa-rāja-mahā-pāsāda*. Cf. *Kasub-raj-maha-vehar*, above, p. 51.

[3] Cf. *Udā-Kitagbo-paṇu*, above, p. 188.

[4] P. *Maccha-tittha* (*Mv.* xlviii. 24).

[5] P. *Kassapa-giri*, above, p. 31.

[6] P. *Jaya-sēna*, above, p. 82.

[7] I do not know the meaning of this word. Taken as *piḷi-sat*, it can, however, mean 'a silk umbrella.' Skt. *paṭṭa-chatra*.

[8] P. *Jētavana-vihāra*.

[9] *Ruvan-sak* = P. *ratana-cakka*, 'wheel of gems.'

[10] *Ran-satin* = P. *hirañña-chattāna*.

[11] *Kotur-ṭāmba*; *ṭāmba* = Pkt. *thambha* and *ṭhambha*, Skt. *stambha*. I do not know the exact meaning of the architectural term *kotur*. It occurs in the *Kāvyalēkhara*, viii. 18, as follows:—

Nana miṇi ṭām koturu
dāva pēhaḍin piyakaru
liya-mal-kam soñduru
maḍuva sārasū sudam-saba-yuru.

[12] *Sid-dāgab* = Skt. *śvita-dhātu-garbha*. This may also be equivalent to P. *citta-dhātu-gabbha*.

[13] *Kasub-rad-piriven* = P. *Kassapa-rāja-pariveṇa*.

[14] P. *Maṇimēkhalā-mahā-pāsāda* (*Mv.* li. 77).

vehera [1]; he gilded the statue of the Bōdhisatta in the **Nil-pahā** [2]; all . . . he erected the guest-hall attached to the . . .; [he . . .] the bronze (work) in the **Ruvan-pahā** [3] **of the Mahamevnā-maha-vehera** [4]; he set up flag-posts like columns of victory; . . . faces (adorned with) solar orbs which were like unto the reflection of the sun-god **Mitra**. He adorned the four corners with golden capital-topped pillars like the four cardinal attributes of royalty, and . . . the statues of the four Buddhas with *dalavulatna* [5].

[Lines 26–30.] He caused to be set with rubies [6] the eyes of the incomplete colossal statue in stone [of the Buddha], which displayed the grace of . . . He completed the **Huligam-piriven**, which had been half finished by the great king, his brother, [and is situated at] **Mihi** . . ., where he had resided enjoying the dignity of governor (*āpā*). He built a great edifice (*mahā-pāsāda*) at **Isurmaṇu-veher** [7], and erected the **Mārā** hall for the abundant supply of . . . at the **Maha-sā** [8]. The warden of the monastery at **Mirisiviṭi-veher** [9] . . . at **Sihigiri-maha-(sā)** [10]. He gilded the relic casket for the (book) **Daham-saṅguṇ** [11] which the great king, his grandfather, had caused to be written . . . The **Ruvan-dāgab** [12] . . . He made a noble casket for the tooth relic of the King of Sages [13], like unto the crest jewel on the crown of **Anurāpura** [14] . . . **Sutursa-(-ṅgarā)** [15] . . .

[Lines 31–35.] He built a relic-house like unto a big ship well filled with . . . and heaping up the manifold and diverse meritorious deeds he had performed . . . He established the great alms-hall [16] **Purimālā**, and also the great alms-hall [16] for the nuns. Whenever a motherless sick child is seen . . . He established kitchens and medical halls, and repaired the nunneries belonging to communities of helpless nuns . . . He built the **Rak-sā-ge** [17] like unto

---

[1] P. *Vīhuvana-vihāra*, built by Aggabōdhi II and dedicated to the Sāgali Order (*Mv.* xlii. 43).

[2] P. *Nīla-pāsāda*. Cf. *Nīlageha-pariccheda* (*Mv.* xlii. 39).

[3] P. *Ratana-pāsāda*.

[4] P. *Mahāmēghavana-mahā-vihāra*, the Headquarters of the orthodox Buddhist sect in Ceylon.

[5] I cannot make out the meaning of this word.

[6] *Dīrang-miṇi* = Skt. *jāti-raṅga-maṇi*.

[7] P. *Issarasamaṇaka Vihāra*. See above, pp. 12, 31, 60, note 1, and p. 68.

[8] P. *Mahācētiya*, the Ruvanväli-dāgaba.

[9] P. *Maricavaṭṭi-vihāra*. See above, p. 51, note 3.

[10] P. *Sīhagiri-mahā-cētiya*.

[11] P. *Dhammasaṅgaṇi*, a book of the Abhidhamma Piṭaka of the Buddhist canon. See Müller's edition of 1885 in P.T.S. and Mrs. Rhys Davids' translation, 1900.

[12] Probably *Ruvanväli-dāgaba*.

[13] *Muni-rad*, an epithet of the Buddha, like *Munind* (*munīndra*.)

[14] i.e. Anurādhapura.

[15] Skt. *Sūtra-saṅgraha*, P. *Sutta-saṅgaha*.

[16] *Mahapuḷ* = P. *mahāpāli*.

[17] P. *Ārakkha-cētiya-gēha*.

a casket for the jewel of the **Urṇa**[1] hair relic, and repaired all the great stūpas . . . In the **Atulā Vihāra** he made a golden image of the Lord of Sages of his own size . . .

[Lines 36–45.] Wearing the insignia (of royalty), including the beautiful crowṇ, he mounted the scale pans and weighed himself and the bridge (?) of alms . . . to the great community of pious mendicants in the **Kir-bimb-vehera**[2], who are well versed in the four (noble) truths[3] . . . He made the prosperous Laṅkā a common ground for various peoples of various appearances who came from diverse countries . . . The holy (ones) who, wearing the saffron-coloured robes, satisfied the world with showers of bountifulness . . . In the well-conducted community of monks . . . the king with his crown . . . Having given [to the priesthood] gifts composed of royal ornaments including the crown (he promoted charity) . . . Kindly services to those engaged in religious observances, patronage to the learned, offerings to the Dharma . . . He made all wisdom and all good deeds his own treasure. In the . . . year after this great king [**Siri-Saṅg**]bo **Abā** [who has done all these acts] raised the canopy of dominion, on the tenth day of the waxing moon in the month of *Poson* (May–June), the chief of the monks, **Mahinda**, . . . filled with great faith in the Buddhist religion . . . and [endowed] with clear intelligence . . .

[Lines 46–49.] Like the fruits which the great tree of his [i.e. the king's] liberality bore to the Saṅgha . . . Like a passion burnt out of his heart he always . . . pleased with the **Daham-säk**[4] of the Lord Buddha . . . he placed (it) on the back of the state-elephant and caused (it) to be taken round the city[5].

---

[1] *Uṇ-lom-dā-ruvana* = P. *Uṇṇa-lōma-dhātu-ratana*. See *Mv.* xlii. 62.

[2] P. *Khīra-bimba-vihāra*.

[3] *Satar-sas* = P. *catussacca*.

[4] P. *Dhamma-cakka*, probably a copy of the *Dhammacakkappavattana-sutta*.

[5] The text beyond this is in verse, and, with the exception of a letter here and there, is illegible.

No. 20. JĒTAVANĀRĀMA SLAB-INSCRIPTION (No. 2) OF MAHINDA IV (*circa* 1026–1042 A.D.)

THIS slab lies close by No. 1 described above. The inscription which it contains is engraved in sixty lines on the side prepared for the purpose, and covers an area of 8 ft. by 3 ft. 3 in., of which the middle portion is now so much worn and damaged that a considerable part of the text from lines 6 to 39 is illegible, as may be seen from the accompanying facsimile (Plate 29).

The **script** and the size of the letters are similar to those in No. 1. In **orthography**, too, one would expect a complete uniformity, for the two records are more or less like the first and second sections of a single charter in respect of the Abhayagiri-vihāra. But this is not the case. We find quite a number of variant spellings. Compare, for example, *Damb-div*, *pämili*, *sama-dā*, *upädä*, *ūpā*, *mahayā*, and *rad* in the first slab with *Jamb-div*, *piyamili sama-jāy*, *ipäjä*, *ayi-paya*, *maha-paya*, and *raj* in the present one.

The style of the **language** in the two slabs is practically the same, though the second is not so rich in figures of speech as the first. Both begin alike, and in both the same words and phrases occur[1].

The **contents** of our record deal principally with the regulations which Mahinda IV instituted at the Abhayagiri-vihāra soon after completing the reparation of the dāgaba and other buildings attached to the monastery. These rules are similar in character to those in his Mihintale tablet A, and in the Jētavanārāma Sanskrit inscription, as well as in the slab-record of Kassapa V near the 'stone canopy[2].' They afford ample proof of the care which this king bestowed on the proper administration of monasteries.

Touching the stone statue of the Buddha (*maha-sala-piḷima*) mentioned in line 45, I have gathered in a former page (217) most of the historical references found in the *Mahāvaṁsa*. I now wish to draw attention to the possibility that this image might have been the same as the one which the Chinese pilgrim Fâ-hien saw at the Abhayagiri-vihāra when he visited Ceylon in the fifth century A.D.[3]

[1] Cf. lines 1–6, 14–16, with lines 1–5 of No. 1.

[2] See above, pp. 6–9, 40–57, and 98–113.

[3] Fâ-hien's account runs :—'By the side of the tope he [i.e. the king of Ceylon] further built a monastery called the Abhayagiri, where there are (now) five thousand monks. There is in it a hall

The introductory portion of the record (lines 1–19) gives a short account of Mahinda himself and his charitable works. As shown above (p. 213), his father bore two *birudas*, namely, Siri Saṅghabōdhi Abhaya and Abhaya Silāmēghavaṇṇa. In the first slab he is referred to by the former title and in the present one by the latter.

The **date** is given in lines 19 and 20, but the text here is so much damaged that the reading of the regnal year, eight, is doubtful. The name and the day of the lunar month are quite obliterated. So, too, is the first portion of the name of the king. But on comparing the subject-matter of the slab No. 1, described above, with that of the present slab, which we call No. 2 for purposes of identification, it will be apparent that the first forms as it were an introduction to the second. Both deal with the **Abhayagiri-vihāra.** The first confines itself to an eulogistic account of Mahinda IV, a poetic description of the Abhayagiri Monastery and a general survey of the charitable acts he performed and of the religious monuments he built or repaired. All this may be taken as introductory to what follows in the second slab, namely, the repairs he effected at the monastery in question and the rules which he instituted for its good government. Even if we regard the two records as unconnected with each other, still there is sufficient evidence, both in their phraseology and in their contents, to infer that the second inscription, that is the one now under discussion, must have been promulgated soon after the first, namely, about the end of the eighth year after the coronation of Mahinda IV (1034 A.D.?).

In deciphering this record, I have had before me four ink-estampages and an eye-copy supplied by the Archaeological Commissioner. But for this ample supply of material I would not have been able to make out so much of the damaged text as I have done below.

---

of Buddha adorned with carved and inlaid work of gold and silver, and rich in the seven precious substances, in which there is an image (of Buddha) in green jade, more than twenty cubits in height, glittering all over with those substances, and having an appearance of solemn dignity which words cannot express. In the palm of the right hand there is a priceless pearl. Several years had now elapsed since Fâ-hien left the land of Han; the men with whom he had been in intercourse had all been of regions strange to him . . . Suddenly (one day), when by the side of this image of jade, he saw a merchant presenting as his offering a fan of white silk; and the tears of sorrow involuntarily filled his eyes and fell down.' Legge's Translation of *The Travels of Fâ-hien*, pp. 102–103.

TEXT.

1 (ශ්‍රී) සිරිවත් අපිරියත් ලොව් ඉකුත් ගුණඹුලින් උතුරත්වැ මුළු ජම්බුදිවහි අ
2 ත් කැත්කුල පියම්ලි කළ ඔකාවස්රජ්පරපුරෙන් බට් කැත උසබ් අබහ්
3 සලමෙවණ මහරජ්හට් එමෙ කුලෙන් සම්ජැය් දෙව් ගොන් කිසො රැජ්න කුසැ ඉ
4 පැජැ අසිපය මහපය සිරි විඳැ පිළිවෙල්සෙ රජ්වැ මිණිඩුවනෙත් පැගැලූ සි
5 ය බුඤ්ජෙන ලොව් උතුරු කිංසම්නෙන් තිසෙස්වැ යසස් තෙජින් දස අත්හි පැතිරැ
6 තුමා සිරින් ලක්දිව් පහයා .. .. යැ තුන් මහසලපිළිම බුදු
7 ත් නත් රුවන් මිගි .. ගන [කුළු] .. .. ඉඤුසැව්ලෙසින් සතින් සජය්
8 .. .. මහ .. .. ගුය් බුද් පිරිබොය්
මිණිපය්
9 .. .. (රුවන්සත්මහපෙර) .. .. දුවෙහෙරට් ලකර්
මගුල් පි
10 පිවෙණ් (කරය්) .. .. ව් .. .. විහිගුම් දගෙ නත්වය් බමු
11 ණු .. .. කොට් බද් ගන්කඬ බඳ්ව
12 ය් නව්(බුත්) .. .. (පැ)වැත්වූ දියගත්
ගෙල්දිවැ දුබි
13 ක් [නිවය්] .. .. [දන්]වතුරෙන්
ගලවත් උපුල්විය්
14 .. .. (දෙය) .. .. (මහණ කරය්) ජම්බුදිවසි (නත් රදු)න් වචින අසිරි
පඩුරෙ
15 න් දවත පිරෙන රජ්ගෙදෙර්හි දියනාවන් පැරැකුම්සිරින් සිරි ලකට යස
16 එළ්වූ තුනුරුවනට් පුජ අ(ජ)ර .. .. .. (වචින සත්)නට් (හි)ඩුර් වියත්නට
17 (සගරු සියනට තුගරු) .. .. තුව .. ව් සව් සත්නට් කු
18 ලුණුවත් සබැවජනුවනට් .. .. කොට් .. .. තොප් සනහන සොම් ඉගිමැ
19 .. .. (තව්)මි .. .. [සිරිසඟ්බො] අබහ් මහරජ්හු
තුමා සක්
20 ලැගූ (අච්වන) හඳුරුදුනෙය(හි) .. .. (ස) .. ස පස් දවස්
අබහය්
21 සිරි සැණි .. .. කරය් (තු)න්
සරවනෙන්
22 (සිර්) .. .. පවත්නා කොට්
තුබූ සිරින්
23 අබහය්ගිරිවෙහෙරැ (අව) .. .. [ඈතුළ්] බැහැර් ගණසතු පුගුල්
සතු ලා
24 (හගෙහි) ඉසා සත්වත් ගිම් .. .. අවසැ බද් (ග)ම් කිම් කවරිපරියාගෙ
25 න් .. .. ඉසා .. .. (ස) කොට් නො වලඤ්වනු ඉසා
පෙරෙ නො පැ

26 .. .. (නාක සඟි) .. .. ව .. .. ඉසා
ඝුනුවන් දෙස්

27 (යවතු ඉසා) .. .. (ගම් කම් අවසව) .. .. වත්වා දෙනු ව

28 සා මේ .. .. සැ ගිගිම්නිස්වැ නො වළඳනු
ඉසා ම

29 .. .. ඥ .. රක්නාවුත් ගි[ෆ්]ම්නිසුත් ගස්

30 .. .. ඉසා (ගිම්සුරන්) .. .. .. (ස)හුන් පමණින් පොවාරණ
කරනු ව

31 සා පොහෝරණ ලත .. .. අවසැ
සන්නව

32 .. .. (ගි) වැසැ වළඳනු කොව .. .. ඉසා (ලාන) පිළි(පසි)න[1] මිසැ
ලාභයෙහි

33 .. .. (කම් කිම්) .. .. නො පිළි(පසි)නු[2] ඉසා ගම් කම් .. .. (රළ ක)රත් වැඩි
ලාභයක්

34 .. .. (නො කරනු) ඉසා (ල) .. (ස)පයා අතුසස් නො ගන්නා ඉසා ලාභ

35 .. .. නිසි .. .. (කා)රය මිසැ දසකැරැ නො
දෙනු ව

36 සා මෙ වෙහෙර් බ(ද්) .. .. නො දෙ[නු] ඉ[සා
ඝුනු]වත් දෙස් ය

37 විනු ඉසා ගතුවන් නො ගිම් වනු ඉසා බ(දා)ව(ස) .. .. .. ගිබද(ව) .. .. .. ගිඤැ
වළඤ

38 නු මිසැ මුල් අවස්ගි ගිඤැ නො විළඳනු ඉ[සා] .. .. .. (ණ්) වන අවසැ වියැ
සුතු තු

39 .. .. ලාභයෙහි වසනු ඉසා .. .. [කළ] වරජක් ඇත නිසි

40 යත් (සිඤැ දඬකම්) කරන් මිසැ ලාභ රදෙල්කො[ව් නො] ගන්නා ඉසා කම්
නවාමැ බ

41 (ද් ගම්) කඩැපිඩැ නො බැඳැ කම්නවාම් කරවනු [ඉසා] කම්නවාමැ බද්
ගම් නැති

42 (සැඤැ) පෙරෙ සිරිය් කඩපිඩිත් ඉහිරි ගෙනැ කම්නවාම් කරවනු ඉසා කඩපිඩි

43 න් ඉහිරිවනු (නැත[3]) කඩැ බද් අයින් භාගයක් (ගෙ)නැ කම්නවාම් කරවනු ඉසා

44 මෙසෙ නො කළ ගිම්යන් අවසින් පිටත් කරනු ඉසා මෙ (කක) .. ..
වෙහෙර්හි ව

45 සා (මහ) සලපිළිමගෙහි ඉසා රුවන්පහාහි ඉසා අබයගු(රාමහසැ)ගෙහි ඉසා

46 .. .. .. බොගෙහි ඉසා සැගිරිහි ඉසා (සැමැගිරි)ගෙහි[4] ඉසා .. .. (න්)
කම්නවා

[1] 'පිළිවැසිය්' යිද කියවිය හැකිපි

[2] 'පිළිවැසිනු' පිද කියවිය හැකිපි

[3] 'දැගි' පිද කියවිය හැකිපි

[4] 'නාවෙහෙරගෙහි' පිද කියවිය හැකිපි

47 මින් ඉනිරි ගරුබඩි කොට් තබත් ඊසැ ගනු ගැති නො දෙනු ඉසා මෙතුවාස් තැන්හි

48 අයකලංසෙ ඉසා වියකලංසෙ ඉසා දස්නාට නිම් දුත්සෙ ඉසා දසකැරු දුත් සෙ

49 ඉසා හඩුරුදුපතා සාවසැ සඟුන් පිඩි කො[ට්] .. .. .. මැ .. .. .. කැම් වෙහෙර් කැමියන්

50 ලෙකම් අස්වනු ඉසා මෙහි උපන් විවාදය[ක් ඇත] .. .. .. (හාගෙය)[1] සම්දරුවන් ශිඥැ

51 විවාද ගර්නා කොට් මෙ තුබුනාස් සිරින් අග් .. .. කුලැදැනිය කැරු පිරි

52 ල(ස්ගි) නො බොසත්නු නො රජ්වන්හටි සැඟැකුල කොප් සවැනියමුනිරජ්නු ..

53 .. (මියාරණි) ලද් තුමා පස් සිවුර් රස්(නුව)ස් මහසඞ්නු පිළිමැසූ රජ්සි

54 රි පැමිණෑ සැණෑ කීසෙට් විඥන (ද)වස් මහ[ස]ඞ්ගට් මෙහෙයට් උවසර්වස්

55 (සෙවෙළ්) බඳුන අප පරපුරෙන් (බස්න) බුද් බැහි කැත්උසබ්නවිසින් (නිර)

56 (තුර් ඇඳුර්) ඇතියාවැනු රුකියැ පුතු **නුගහල් කඩ** මැඳෑ ජල්නා කප්ජල් ක

57 (ලම්බ්) බඳු (ල)වගඳැ පැනිරෙත්[2] සොර කෙනෙකුනු (තුළ්) නො සිඳැ දොහො අත්ගි බද් නු

58 නුසුවූ පැලැ නො සිඳ්න පැමැණි අඬුසාප්අවද්ගි කියදසුවැ පෙවෙත් දැහැප්

59 සඟුන් මෙ රස්නා සිකකැමි මහණ සලෙ අවජන් ඇති දහම් මන් නො ඉස්මෙ

60 න දහම්දැසි ඇප්පුරාලෙහි මහසඞ්නුවිසිනුප් මෙ සිරිය් වැටියැ පුතු

TRANSCRIPT.

1 (Śrī) siri-vat apiriyat lov ikut guṇa-muḷin uturat-vä muḷu Jamb-divhi a-

2 -n Kät-kula piya-mili kaḷa Okāvas-raj-parapuren baṭ, Kät-usab **Abay**

3 **Salamevan** maharaj-haṭ eme kulen sama-jāy **Dev Gon** biso räjna kusä i-

4 -päjä ayi-paya maha-paya siri vindä piḷi-veḷ-se raj-vä miṇi-vuṭnen pähäyū si-

5 -ya mundne lov uturā bisevnen bisesvä yasas tejin dasa at-hi pätirā

6 tumā sirin Lak-div pahayā .. .. -yä tun maha-sala-piḷima-Budu-

7 -n nan ruvan vihi- .. gana [kuḷu] .. .. indu-säv-lesin satin sajay

8 .. .. maha .. .. -gut Bud piriboy miṇi-pay

9 .. .. (ruvan-sat-maha-pera) .. .. -dū-veheraṭ lakar **Mañgul-pi-**

[1] 'හාගෙ' සිද කියවිය හැකිසි

[2] 'වැනිරෙත්' සිද කියවිය හැකිසි

Jētavanārāma Slab-Inscription (No. 2) of Mahinda IV

Scale about $1\frac{1}{16}$ inches to 1 foot.

Vēvälkätiya Slab-Inscription of Mahinda IV

Scale about $1\frac{1}{4}$ inches to 1 foot.

From ink-impressions supplied by the Archæological Commissioner, Ceylon.

10 **-riven** (karay) .. .. ṭ .. .. vihigum dā-ge naṅgvay Bamu-
11 -ṇu .. .. koṭ bad gaṅg-kaḍ band-va-
12 -y naṭ(bun) .. .. (pä)vät-vū diyen Heḷ-divä dubi-
13 -k [nivay] .. .. [dan]-vaturen levan upulvay
14 .. .. (deya) .. .. (mahaṇa karay) Jamb-divhi (nan radu)n vaṭna asiri paṅḍure-
15 -n davaha pirena raj-ge-dorhi diya-nävan pärākum-sirin siri Lakaṭa yasa
16 eḷvū tunu-ruvanaṭ puja a(ja)ra .. .. .. (vaṭna-saṅg)-naṭ (hi)vur viyatnaṭ
17 (saṅgarā siyanaṭa-nugarā) .. .. nuva .. -ṭ sav satnaṭ ku-
18 -luṇu-vat sabā-vajanuvanaṭ .. .. koṭ .. .. tej sanahana somi ihimä
19 .. .. (taṭ)mi .. .. [**Siri Saṅg-bo**] **Abay** maharaj-hu tumā sat
20 läṅgū (aṭ-vana) havuruduye(hi) .. .. (sa) .. -sa pak davas **Abahay-**
21 **-giri-sähi** .. .. karay (tu)n saravanen
22 (sir) .. .. pavatnā koṭ tubū siriti
23 **Abahaygiri-veherä** (ava) .. .. [ätuḷ] bähäri gaṇa-satu pugul-satu lā-
24 (-bhayehi) isā saṅg-vat-himi .. .. avasä bad (ga)m bim kavari-pariyāye-
25 -n .. .. isā .. .. (sa) koṭ no vaḷand-vanu isā pere no pä-
26 .. .. (naka saṅgi) .. .. ṭ .. .. isā dunuvan des
27 (yavanu isā) .. .. (gam bim avasaṭ) .. .. vatvā denu i-
28 sā me .. .. -sā gihi-minis-vä no vaḷandanu isā ma-
29 .. .. mi .. raknā-mut gi[hi]-minisun gas [1]
30 .. .. isā (himisuran) .. .. .. (sa)sun pamaṇin povoraṇa karanu i-

[1] This clause probably runs *gas-kol no kapanu isā*. See above, p. 93, line 50.

31 -sä povorana lat .. .. avasä saṅgnaṭ
32 .. .. (-hi) väsä vaḷandanu koṭ .. .. isā (lābha) piḷi(pasi)t[1] misä lābhayehi
33 .. .. (gam bim) .. .. no piḷi(pasi)nu[1] isā gam bim .. .. (-raḷi ka)rat väḍi lābhayak
34 .. .. (no karanu) isā (la-) .. (sa)payā anusas no gannā isā lābha
35 .. .. nisi .. .. (ka)rat misä dasakärä no denu i-
36 -sā me veher ba(d) .. .. no de[nu] i[sā dunu]van des ya-
37 -vanu isā gatuvan no himi vanu isā ba(d-a)va(sa) .. .. .. -hi bada(va) .. .. .. hindä vaḷanda-
38 -nu misä mul-avas-hi hindä no vaḷandanu i[sā] .. .. .. (-ṅg) vana avasä viyä yutu tu-
39 .. .. lābhayehi vasanu isā .. .. [kaḷa] varajak äta nisi-
40 -yan (hindä daṇḍ-kam) karat misä lābha radol-ko[ṭ no] gannā isā kam-navāmä ba-
41 (-d gam) kaṇḍä-piṇḍä no bändä kam-navām karavanu [isā] kam-navāmä bad gam näti
42 (sändä) pere sirit kaṇḍ-piṇḍin itiri genä kam-navām kara-vanu isā kaṇḍ-piṇḍi-
43 -n itiri-vanu (näta)[2] kaṇḍä bad ayin bhāgayak (ge)nä kam-navām karavanu isā
44 mese no kaḷa himiyan avasin piṭat karanu isā me (**Naka**) .. .. -veherhi i-
45 -sā (**Maha**)**-sala-piḷima-gehi** isā **Ruvan-pahāhi** isā **Abayatu**(**rā-maha-sä**-) **-yehi** isā
46 .. .. .. **Bo-gehi** isā **Sā-girihi** isā (**Näṭä-giri**)**yehi**[3] isā .. .. (-n) kam-navā-
47 -min itiri garu-baṇḍ koṭ tabat misä gatu gäti no denu isā metuvāk tänhi
48 aya-kaḷa-se isā viya-kaḷa-se isā dasnaṭ nimi dun-se isā dasa-kärä dun-se
49 isā havurudu-patā sāvasā saṅgun piṇḍ ko[ṭ] .. .. .. mä .. .. .. kämi veher-kämiyan

[1] *Piḷi-väyil* and *piḷiväyinu* may be suggested as alternative readings. See below, line 53.
[2] This can also be read '*dähi*'.
[3] This can also be read '*Nä-veherayehi*'.

50 lekam asvanu isā mehi upan vivādaya[k äta] .. .. .. (-bhāye)[1] samdaruvan hindä

51 vivāda harnā koṭ me tubūtāk sirit at .. .. kulädätiya kärä siri

52 La(k-hi) no bosat-hu no raj-vanhayi Sähä-kula kot Saväniya-muni-raj-hu ..

53 .. (viyāraṇ) lad tumā pay sivur rak(nu-va)s maha-saṅg-hu piḷiväyū raj-si-

54 -ri päminä säṇä bisev vindna (da)vas maha-[sa]ṅg-haṭ meheyaṭ uvasar-vas

55 (seveḷ) bandna apa parapuren (basna) Bud bäti Kät-usabna-visin (nira)-

56 (-tur ädur) ätiyā-vänu räkiyä yutu **Nuṅgahal-kaṇḍ** mändä jalna kap-jal ka-

57 (-lamb) bandu (ḷa)vahandä pätiret[2] sora kenekunu (tuḷ) no sindä doho-at-hi bad nu-

58 -husu-vū pälä no sindna pämäṇi aṇu-säj-avad-hi biya-dasu-vä pevet dähäj

59 sasun me rakna sika-kämi mahaṇa sale avajan äti daham maṅg no ikme-

60 -na daham-däsi äjurolehi maha-saṅg-hu-visin-uj me sirit väṭiyä yutu

TRANSLATION.

[Lines 1–6] Hail! The great king [**Siri Saṅgbo**] **Abay**[3] was born[4] unto the great king **Abay Salamevan**, the Kṣatriya lord, descended from the royal line of the Okkāka dynasty which, abounding in an assemblage of benignant, boundless, and transcendental[5] virtues, has caused other Kṣatriya dynasties of the whole of Jambudvīpa to render it homage[6]: [he was born] in the womb of the anointed queen **Dev Gon** of equal birth and descent[7]. After enjoying the dignities of Governor and Chief Governor[8], he, in due course, became king and was anointed on his head, resplendent with the bejewelled crown, with the unction of world supremacy. With the effulgence of his fame he filled the ten directions, and with his glory he illumined the Island of Laṅkā.

[Lines 6–14] He adorned the three great stone statues of the Buddha at . . . . with parasols (diffusing [the glitter of] various gems) like rainbows (on rain clouds) . . . . the gem-set bowl used by the Buddha . . . .

---

[1] This may also be read '*hāye*'. [2] This may also be read '*väliret*'.

[3] See line 19. [4] *Ipäjä*, same as *upädä* in the foregoing record (p. 221).

[5] *Lo ikut*, 'ultra-mundane.' Regarding these adjectives, see above, p. 224, note 3.

[6] *Piyamili*. See above, p. 224, note 4.

[7] *Eme kulen sama-jāy*, see above, p. 225, note 2.

[8] *Ayi-paya maha-paya* = P. *ādi-pāda mahā-pāda*. See above, pp. 26, note 4, 98, note 5, and 187, note 6.

(the great festival of the golden[1] parasol) . . . . ; (he built) the beautiful **Mañgul-piriven**[2] for the monastery at [**Vahadū** ?] . . . . . ; he built a lofty relic-house; **Bamuṇu**[3] . . . . . . ; he made . . . . and dammed the rivers and channels connected [therewith]; [he repaired] the dilapidated [tanks and ponds] and by means of the water thus supplied he [put an end to] scarcity of food in the Island of Ceylon[4]. He made the people float on the flood of his gifts . . . . . . (and caused . . . . to enter the Order).

[Lines 14–18] With the prowess of victorious lords, displayed in the precincts of the Palace, constantly filled with the wonderful presents offered by various kings of Jambudvīpa[5], he brought glory upon prosperous Laṅkā. [He bestowed] reverential offerings on the 'Triple Gem[6],' robes on monks who observe . . . . . (patronage) on the learned[7], (help on his kindred,) . . . . sympathy on all beings, and . . . . . . on truth-tellers. With the gentleness that assuages the majesty . . . . . .

[Lines 19–30] On the . . . day . . . . in (the eighth) year after this great king [Siri Saṅgbo] Abay raised the canopy of dominion, His Majesty having effected [improvements] at the **Abhayagiri-cētiya** . . . . enacted the [following] regulations :—

In the **Abhayagiri-vihāra**, both inside and outside, the villages and lands connected with the incomes accruing to the clergy in common[8] or to individual monks, as well as those connected with the . . . . . *āvāsa* (residence) of the Director of Religious Ceremonies of the Order shall in no wise be . . . . or be enjoyed . . . . Those who have transferred [lands] shall be deported[9] . . . . In the capacity of laymen [these lands] shall not be enjoyed . . . . shall protect, but laymen [shall not cut down] trees [and plants][10].

[Lines 30–40] Monks shall be invited [for religious ceremonies] in accordance with the Buddhist code. Those who have received invitations . . . .

---

[1] *Ruvan-sat* = P. *ratana-chatta*. In Vedic Sanskrit and Pāli *ratana* means 'a precious mineral,' such as gold, silver, pearl, gems, &c. Hence in Sinhalese *ruvan* is often used as a synonym for *suvan* (P. *suvaṇṇa*). *Ruvan-sat* may, therefore, mean either 'golden' or 'gem-set parasol.' Cf. *ruvan-suner*, above, p. 226, note 3.

[2] P. *Maṅgala-pariveṇa*. [3] Skt. *Brāhmaṇa*. [4] *Heḷ-div* = Skt. *Siṁhala-dvīpa*.

[5] In the foregoing inscription (line 4) this phrase runs 'the wonderful presents offered by kings of various lands.'

[6] Cf. *Mv*. liv. 39. [7] See line 42 of the foregoing inscription.

[8] *Gaṇa-satu pugul-satu*. See above, p. 53, notes 3–4.

[9] See Mihintale tablet B, line 58 (above, p. 97).

[10] See Mihintale tablet A, line 50 (above, p. 93).

. . . . to the monks in the *āvāsa* (residence) . . . . . They shall enjoy whilst residing . . . . . . They shall claim[1] the income, but they shall not claim . . . . of the villages and lands connected with the income. When lands (are cultivated ?) they shall not be (cultivated) for excessive profit . . . . . but they shall not be given [for cultivation] on tithe tenure[2]. [Lands] attached to this Vihāra shall not be given . . . . The grantors shall be deported, while the grantees shall have no proprietary right. [Monks] shall enjoy [the income accruing] to the attached residences while living in them, but they shall not enjoy [the same] while dwelling in the chief residence . . . . it shall be in the residence . . . . . They shall reside in [conformity with] the income . . . . . should there be any commission of wrong, competent persons shall sit [in session] and award punishment, but the income [from endowments] shall not be appropriated to the State.

[Lines 40–51] [The income of] the villages set apart for repairs[3] [of buildings] shall not be devoted to [the provision of] food and raiment[4] [to monks], but shall be utilized for repairs. When there are no villages set apart for repairs, the surplus [of the revenue] that remains after providing food and raiment, according to ancient usage, shall be used for effecting repairs. Should there be no surplus remaining after providing food and raiment, half of the income on account of raiment shall be spent on repairs. The wardens who have not acted in this manner shall be sent away from residence. Whatever remains after repairs have been effected at (**Naka . . . .**) Vihāra, at the shrine of the great stone statue [of the Buddha], at the **Ruvan-pahā**[5], at the **Abayaturā-maha-sā**[6] . . . . at the shrine of the sacred Bo-tree, at **Sā-giri**[7] and at (**Nāṭā-giri**)[8] shall be kept as communal property[9], but shall not be allowed to be appropriated by those having the handling of it[10].

---

[1] The reading *piḷipasit*, *piḷipasinu* is doubtful. If it be correct, the two words may be etymologically connected with Skt. *prati* + √*prach*. If, however, the correct reading be *piḷivāyit*, *piḷivāyinu*, derivatives of Skt. *prati* + √*pad*, the translation would perhaps be, 'they shall spend the income, but they shall not spend . . . . of the villages and lands connected with the income.'

[2] *Dasa-kārā*, see below, p. 240, note 1. [3] *Kam-navām*, see above, p. 57, note 6.

[4] *Kaṇḍā piṇḍā*, see above, p. 39, note 5, and p. 91, transcript, line 12.

[5] P. *Ratana-pāsāda*, see above, p. 215. [6] P. *Abhayuttara-mahā-cetiya*.

[7] P. *Cetiya-giri*, i.e. Mihintale. [8] Cf. *Nāṭeviya-maha-sā*, above, p. 97.

[9] *Garu-baṇḍ* = P. *garubhaṇḍa*, 'property held in common by a community of priests, as lands, tanks, crockery,' opposed to *parikkhāro*, 'personal requisites,' (Childers' *Pāli Dict.*, p. 144.)

[10] *Gatu gāti no denu.* The exact meaning of this clause is not clear to me. *Gatu* may be the same as modern Sinh. *gat* or *gatta*, the past relative participle of *gannavā* (Skt. √*grah*). Cf. *gāt-* or *gatu-deya*, 'received thing;' *gatuvan*, 'recipients' (line 37, and above, p. 48, line 39). *Gāti* commonly means 'a servant;' but the *Amāvatura* (pt. ii, p. 10) uses it as a Sinhalese rendering of P. *santaka* in

Every year the monks of the six *āvāsas* shall be convened, and (before them) there shall be read out the records kept by the temple officials . . . . in connexion with the income derived and the expenses incurred at the aforementioned places, as well as in connexion with lands given to serfs on *nimi* tenure [1] and *dasa-kärä* tenure. Should any dispute arise in regard to these matters, the royal officers [of the 'Curia Regis'?] . . . . shall hold session and settle the dispute.

[Lines 51–56] The regulations thus enacted should always be maintained with due regard by the descendants of our dynasty, the Kṣatriya lords devoted to the Buddha, who [of yore] have received the assurance [2] [made by] the omniscient Lord of Sages, the pinnacle of the Śākya race, that none but the Bōdhisattas would become kings of prosperous Laṅkā; who are wont to wear the white scarf [3] to serve and attend on the great community of monks on the very day they celebrate the coronation festival after attaining to the dignity of kingship, bestowed [4] by the great community of monks for the purpose of defending 'the bowl and the robe [5]' of the Buddha.

---

the sentence *tamā gäti dā viyadam koḷa mahadan deyi*, the Pāli original in the *Sumaṅgala-vilāsini* (p. 301) being *attano santakaṁ ēva nīharitvā mahādānaṁ dēti*. It seems *gäti* has this signification in the present inscription. If *gatugäti* be a technical term opposed to *garubaṇḍ*, the translation should run 'but shall not be given away as *gatugäti* goods.'

[1] *Nimi.* This word ordinarily means 'finished,' probably from Skt. *nirmita*, Pkt. *nimmia*, as suggested by Professors Müller and Geiger, but its signification as a term of land tenure is not known. The context, however, when compared with that of lines 46 and 47 of the slab-record of Kassapa V (above, p. 49) where the terms *dasa-kārā* ('tenth part') and *pamaṇu* ('transfer') occur in connexion with similar regulations, seems to indicate that it is a form of tenure under which the grantee has the exclusive possession of the land without payment of a tenth (*dasa-kārā*) or any part of the revenue, probably same as Tamil *nindam*, 'exemption from claim by others' (Winslow), *nindakkāṇi*, Sinh. *ninda-gam*. In regard to these terms, Dr. A. B. Keith has favoured me with an interesting note, in which he suggests that *nimi* might have been used to distinguish a tenure which was *definite* in its incidence as opposed to vague or undefined services, while *dasa-kārā* might mean a 'servile tenure' in view of the existence of the term *dasa-gam*. See below, p. 243.

[2] Probably referring to the injunction supposed to have been addressed to Sakka by the Buddha on his death-bed as related in the *Mahāvaṁsa*, vii. 1–6.

[3] *Se-veḷ* = Skt. *śvēta-vēṣṭa* or *śvēta-paṭṭa*, probably a turban of silk cloth. Cf.

Gata sav-baraṇa sädi
Balamin isa seveḷu-*bäňdi*
Kiruḷa da tama pälaňdi
Tabā ohu mudunatehi siri-räňdi—(*Kāvyaśēkhara*, xiv. 64).

[4] *Piḷivāyū* = Skt. *pratipādita*, P. *paṭi-pādita*.

[5] *Pay-sivur* = P. *patta-cīvara*, 'the bowl and the robe,' i. e. 'the priesthood.' Cf. the royal title, 'defender of the faith.'

[Lines 56–60] These regulations should also be observed by the great community of monks belonging to the line of teachers, the servants of the Dharma, who do not transgress the Path of the Law, whose thoughts are bent upon the observation of the precepts and the elimination of passion, who preserve the Buddhist religion even though [in so doing] they sacrifice their life, realizing cause for fear even in faults of a trivial nature (so much as the plucking off of disagreable (?) plants caught in the two hands . . . . whilst there flourish young monks who are like unto flames of fire at the end of the world cycle and who shine in the midst of **Nuṅgahal-kaṇḍ**)[1].

No. 21. VĒVÄLKÄṬIYA SLAB-INSCRIPTION OF MAHINDA IV (*circa* 1026–1042 A.D.)

VĒVÄLKÄṬIYA is a small village in Pahalà Kăndă Tulăna in Kăndă Kōrale, about twenty-one miles to the north-east of Anurādhapura. Dr. Goldschmidt, who visited the place in 1875, was apparently the first to bring to notice the existence of the inscription[2]. It was subsequently examined by Dr. Müller, who in 1883 published a rough transcript with a short introductory note, but no translation[3]. Mr. Bell, on inspecting the slab in 1891, found it 'inscribed on one side only and considerably worn[4].'

The **writing**, however, is tolerably clear on the ink-estampage before me. It consists of forty-five lines, covering a ruled space of 6 ft. by 1 ft. $6\frac{1}{2}$ in. See Plate 29. The **characters** belong to the Sinhalese alphabet of the tenth and early eleventh centuries. Their size varies from $\frac{3}{10}$ to $\frac{4}{5}$ in. each, and their type is the same as that of the Mihintale tablets[5] of Mahinda IV. In regard to the formation of the

---

[1] I am unable to make out satisfactorily the meaning of the text in lines 56–58, beginning from *Nuṅgahal-kaṇḍ*. The above is offered tentatively.

[2] See *Ceylon Sessional Papers*, xxiv, p. 1.

[3] See *A. I. C.*, No. 122, pp. 58, 85, and 86. The introduction runs:—'Wewelkæṭiya, eleven miles from Madawacci on the Horowapotāna road. Inscription on both sides of a large slab, tolerably well preserved, but some letters are doubtful, and the whole is difficult to translate, as it contains many words which are not known from elsewhere. The king calls himself Siri Sangbo Abahay, the son of Siri Sangbo: this does not agree exactly with any of the kings mentioned in the previous inscriptions, but as the language, and especially the beginning, is exactly the same as at Ambasthala, I have ascribed this inscription also to Mahinda III.'

[4] *A. S. C. Annual Report*, 1891, p. 7.

[5] See above, Plates 14–15.

akṣaras *a*, *ra*, and the medial vowel *u*, it will be seen on following their development from the original Brāhma signs that, of the two vertical strokes the one on the left is only the result of the gradual elongation of the lower end of the other which in its intermediate cursive stage is curved upwards to the left[1]. In the Vessagiri and the Jētavanārāma inscriptions of Mahinda IV[2] (*circa* 1026–1042 A. D.) we find the two verticals engraved in one continuous line, although the more cursive and later style of writing them separately with their lower ends quite apart was in vogue at the time. We see this from the advanced type used in the Mihintale tablets and in the present record of the same king Mahinda IV, as well as in some of the earlier inscriptions of Kassapa V and Dappula V[3]. Attention should also be drawn to the akṣara ෙයෝ, *yō*, at the beginning of the third line. It is doubtless the precursor of the modern form යෝ. The upward stroke attached to the sign of the medial vowel *o* to lengthen it is no other than the final circular stroke ౕ in Telugu, e. g. కే *kē* and కో *kō*. In South Indian alphabets a loop or an extra curved stroke attached to a short vowel is the common sign used to denote that it is long. In Sinhalese the curved stroke seems to have been confounded with the vertical *virāma* sign[4], owing perhaps to their resemblance to each other. Otherwise it is difficult to account for the use of the *virāma* signs ් and ් in modern Sinhalese to indicate the long vowels *ē* and *ō*[5]. Besides, the marking of these two vowels long is in itself an innovation. I have not yet come across a single instance in early Sinhalese inscriptions. The present one is unusual and is the earliest case I know of a medial *o* marked long.

As regards **orthography** and the style of the **language**, our record hardly differs from the other inscriptions of Mahinda IV dealt with in this volume; but, as Dr. Müller has already stated, it contains many words and phrases of which the exact meaning is still somewhat obscure. Such forms as *kuhivaku* (l. 9) obviously for *kisivaku*, 'any one,' *kasilä* (l. 27) for *kisilleki*, 'in the armpit,' and the expressions *kaňda palā sora-kam kaḷa* (l. 10), *elvanu koṭ* (l. 14), *div-milä* (l. 18), &c., are quite new to me. These and other technical terms will be discussed in the notes to the translation.

---

[1] See Bühler's *Indische Palaeographie*, p. 69.

[2] See above, Plates 9, 28, and 29.

[3] See above, Plates 8 and 12.

[4] For examples of the vertical *virāma*, see Bühler's *Indische Palaeographie*, Plates VII and VIII; Burnell's *South Indian Palaeography*, Plates VI to VIII; and the modern Grantha, Malayālam, and Sinhalese alphabets.

[5] See Mendis Guṇasēkara's *Sinhalese Grammar*, p. 7.

The inscription is one of king **Siri Sañgbo Abhay** [1], and he can be no other than Mahinda IV. Apart from palaeographical and linguistic considerations, a comparison of the *birudas* alone, by which this king and his parents are referred to in his Mayilagastoṭa inscription [2], the Mihintale tablets [3], the Vessagiri slab [4] No. 2, the slab near the 'stone-canoe [5],' the two foregoing Jêtavanārāma inscriptions and in the present record will make this fact quite clear. Mahinda's full name was **Siri Sañgbo Abhā** [6] **Mihindu,** his mother's was **Dev Gon Biso-räjna,** and his father was known by the two *biruda* titles **Abhā** [6] **Salamevan** and **Siri Sañgbo Abhā** [7].

The two akṣaras, in line 4, which give the number of the regnal year in which this Vēvälkäṭiya record was incised are unfortunately not very clear. They look exceedingly like *na* and *va*. If this be the correct reading, the wording of the **date** would be *Siri Sañgbo Abhay Maharaj-hu sat läñgū* (*nava*) *vana havuruduyehi Undvap sand pere aḍ mashi dasa pak davas*, 'on the tenth day of the first half of the (lunar) month of Undvap (Nov.–Dec.) in the (ninth) year after the great king Siri Sañgbo Abhay raised the canopy of dominion.' This is word for word the same as that in the Vessagiri record of Mahinda IV (*circa* 1026–1042 A.D.), with the exception of the name of the month of Binera (Aug.–Sept.). Our inscription, therefore, is probably later only by three months.

The **subject-matter** is the administration of criminal justice in the *dasa-gama* of Kibi-nilam district in Amgam-kuḷiya in the Northern Quarter. As such it is an important epigraphical document. It furnishes us with some definite information concerning the Sinhalese law relating to 'crimes and wrongs,' *crimina* and *delicta*, and also concerning the administrative methods that must have prevailed in the Island during the tenth and eleventh centuries A.D. At the outset we are confronted with the technical term *dasa-gama*, of which the meaning is ambiguous. We know that *gama* is Skt. *grāma*, 'village.' But whether *dasa* should in the present instance be connected with P. *dasa*, 'ten,' or with *dāsa*, 'a slave,' it is difficult to decide. The fact, however, that the *dasa-gämä ättan*, 'inhabitants of *dasa-gama*,' seem from the context to belong to a class higher in the social scale than that of the ordinary serfs with hardly any proprietary rights, as well as the expression *dasa-gamaṭ ekeka nāyakayan*, 'each chief of the *dasa-gama*,' suggests the possibility of the existence of a system of dividing the country for administrative purposes into groups of ten villages

---

[1] Skt. *Śrī Saṅghabōdhi Abhaya*

[2] *A. I. C.*, No. 120.

[3] Above, pp. 75–113.

[4] Above, pp. 29–38.

[5] Above, pp. 113–120.

[6] Variously spelt *Abhay*, *Abhā*, *Abahay*, *Abay*, *Abā* (Skt. P. *Abhaya*).

[7] See also above, pp. 213–214.

as prescribed in the Hindu Law Books of Manu, Viṣṇu, and others[1]. Compare also the term *dāśa-grāmika* in the Khālimpūr Plate of the Buddhist king Dharma-pāla-dēva[2]. According to the late Professor Kielhorn, it probably means 'an officer in charge of a group of ten villages.' On the other hand, the absence of any reference to such a system in Sinhalese literature so far as we know, and the occurrence of terms such as *sivur-gam* (Skt. *cīvara-grāma*), 'villages that supply robes to the priesthood[3],' *gabaḍā-gam*, 'royal villages,' and *ninda-gam*, 'villages assigned for the exclusive use of the grantee,' lead us to think that *dasa-gama* may after all be nothing more than a village occupied by the serfs attached to a temple. Whatever the actual significance of this term may be, we learn from the inscription that within the *dasa-gama* justice was administered by means of a Communal Court composed of headmen and responsible householders subject to the authority of the King in Council, 'the Curia Regis.' In its democratical character, this tribunal differs from the Courts prescribed in the Hindu Law Books[4] unless the judicial assemblies mentioned by Nārada include such an institution. This village court was empowered to carry into effect the laws enacted by the King in Council and promulgated by his ministers. It could, for example, investigate cases of murder and robbery, exact the prescribed fines from law-breakers, and in certain cases even inflict the punishment of death. Moreover, the collective responsibility[5] which lay upon the inhabitants of the *dasa-gama* for producing offenders within a limited time, the fines imposed upon the whole community in case of failure, the system of compensation for offences, and the surety required for good behaviour as stated in lines 15–19, 35–37 remind us strongly of certain administrative features of the Saxon and Norman periods in English history, such as the institutions of tithing and frank-pledge and the *bôt* and *wite*. Another point of resemblance to early English administrative methods is to be seen in the references both here and in other tenth and eleventh century inscriptions[6] to royal officers who, like the itinerant justices or members of the Curia Regis of the Norman kings, went on yearly circuits in the country not only to settle important disputes but also to promulgate new laws and to see that the Government dues were properly collected.

---

[1] *Manu*, vii. 115; *Viṣṇu*, iii. 8.

[2] *Ep. Ind.* iv, No. 34.

[3] Above, p. 189, note 11.

[4] Cf. *Manu*, viii. 9–11; *Viṣṇu*, iii. 71–74; *Nārada*, i. 7.

[5] For a general sketch of the primitive conditions of society involving such communal responsibility, see Marett's *Anthropology*, ch. vii.

[6] See above, p. 47, transcript, lines 22–23.

In the present inscription we read in lines 41–45 that the measures for the administration of criminal justice in *dasa-gama* which were enacted by the King in Council were promulgated by the following four members of his Curia :—**Goḷuggamu Raksāim Kuḍāsenu, Meykāppar Kuburgamu Lokohi, Kätiri Agbohi,** and **Kuṇḍasalā Arayan.**

In the preparation of the following text and translation I had before me an ink-estampage supplied by the Archaeological Commissioner (Mr. H. C. P. Bell) and the faulty transcript published in the *A.I.C.*

TEXT.

1 ශ්‍රී: සිරිබර් කැත්කුල කොත් ඔකාවස් රජ්පරපුරෙ
2 න් බට් කැත්ලසබිනාට් අග්මෙහෙසුන්වූ ලක්දිව්පොළො
3 යෝන පරපුරෙන් ගිම්වූ **සිරිසඟ්බො අභා** මහරජ්හු
4 පුත් **සිරි සඟ්බො අභය්** මහරජ්හු සත් ලැගූ (නව)ව
5 න හවුරුදුයෙහි උඳුවප් සඳ් පෙරෙ අඬ (ම)ස්හි ද(ස)
6 පක් දවස් උතුරු පසැ අම්ගම්කුළියෙහි කිබි(නිල)
7 මිහි දෙමෙළ්වෙහෙර් පමණියෙන් දසගමට් එකෙක
8 නායකයන් කිබිගම් ඈපැ දුන් නායකයන් කුඩි
9 න් මෙහි ඈතුලත්තාක් තැනැ කුඟිවකු මරා කෙ(ටුව)
10 කඩ පළා සොරකම් කළ තිරැ කොට් ගෙනැ දසගැමැ ඈ
11 ත්තන් ගිඬැ විචාරා උපන් දැයට් පැ හැකිසෙ ලියා
12 තබා මැරුවෙහු මරා පච්චනු කොට් ඉසා කඩපළා සොරැ
13 න් ගත් අයතියෙන් නියතකළාක් අයතිය (ගි)මි
14 ගට් ගෙන දි එල්වනු කොට් ඉසා තිරැ නො කළ දසගැ
15 මැ ඈත්තන් පන්සාලිස දවසෙකින් සොයා ගෙනැ පච්
16 වනු කොට් ඉසා සොයා නො ගත දසගැමින් එක්
17 සිය පස්විසි කළඳක් රන් රදෙලට් දෙනු කොට් ඉසා
18 නො මරා කෙටුව දිව්මිලැ පනාස් කළඳක් රන් ගන්නා
19 කොට් ඉසා නො පොහොත් ගෙදඬ ගන්නා කොට් ඉසා තිරැ
20 නො කළ දසගැමින් පනාස් කළඳක් රන් රදෙලට් දෙනු කො
21 ට් ඉසා අත්පාවහලට් ගියාකුගෙන් දඩැ පනාස් කළ
22 ඳක් රන් ගන්නා කොට් ඉසා නො පොහොත් (ගෙ)දඬ ගන්නා කො
23 ට් ඉසා ගෙදඬ නැත අත් කපා පච්චනු කොට් ඉසා ..
24 වූ දඬ සිඟින් දඬ පෙරෙසිරිත්සෙ ගම්ලද්දන් පමණු
25 (ලද්දන් බෙදා) ගන්නා කොට් ඉසා මිවූන් හෙරිගොන් එළි
26 වන් මැරුවන් මරා පච්චනු කොට් ඉසා නො මරා සොරා
27 ගෙනැ ගිය නියත කොට් ඔවුන් ඔවුන් කසිලැ සත්ල
28 කුණ් ඔබා හර්නා කොට් ඉසා තිරැ නො වත් කොටා පච්ච

29 තු කොට් ඉසා බැහැරින් ඈ.ර් වික්‍ණිත මිදුන් ගෙයි
30 කොත් එළුවන් හැඤ්නැ ඇපැ ගෙනැ ගත්තා කොට් ඉසා
31 අණ මැකූවන් රක්කල යමරවැෆි(ෙ)ය සිටිවනු නො
32 ව් ඉසා මෙ දසගැ(මැ කුඩි)ත් තමත් තම්න් කුලෙගි (වැ
33 ටෙ)න මඟුලවමඟුල වලඤ්නා [1]. පැරනැර නො ඉක්මැ
34 වැනෙවනු කොට් ඉසා මෙ දසගමට (වැවස්ථා)කල තැනි
35 න් (එකොක) අවුද් (වුන්) [2] කු(ෂ්)ෙකනෙනකුන් ඇත හැඤ්නැ ඇ
36 (පැ) ගෙනැ ගිඤ්වනු කොට් ඉසා නො යෙදෙන්නක් කොට් ව
37 න් කොෙනකුන් ඇත ඇපැ ගතදැ පලමුවු ගැමැ ඇ(ත්ත
38 න්) පවිවන්නට් හර්නා කොට් ඉසා මෙ දසගැමැ ඇ
39 ත්තන් මෙ නි තාක් දැපින් ඉක්මැ වැවුණ හවුරුදු
40 නවුරුදු පතා ඉල්ලත්නට් ගිය රජ්කොල් සම්ද(රු
41 වන් කෙ .. කැව)ත්නා කොට් වජාල එක්තැන් සභියෙ
42 න් අ රජ්සභායෙ ගිඤ්නා **කොළංගමු ර(ක්)ස(ඉම්)**
43 **කු(ඩා)** [3] **සෙනු** ඉසා **මෙක්නාජපය් කුඹුර්ගමු ලොකො(ා)**
44 **ෂි** ඉසා **කැතිරි** [4] **අග්බොධි** ඉසා **කුඩසලා අර(ණ)**
45 ඇතුළැවැ මෙතුවාක් සම්දරුවන්විසින් මෙ වැවස්ථා කරනු ලදී

TRANSCRIPT.

1 Śrī: siri-bar Kät[5]-kula kot Okā-vas raj[6]-parapure-
2 -n baṭ Kät-usabnaṭ ag-mehesun-vū Lak-div-poḷo-
3 yōna[7]-parapuren himi-vū **Siri-Saṅgbo Abhā**[8] maha-raj-hu
4 put[9] **Siri-Saṅgbo Abhay** maha-raj-hu sat läṅgū (nava-)[10]va-
5 -na havuruduyehi Undvap sand pere-aḍ-(ma)s-hi da(sa)-[11]
6 pak davas uturu pasä Amgam-kuḷiyehi Kibi-(nila)-[12]
7 -mhi **Demeḷ-veher** pamaṇiyen dasa-gamaṭ ekeka[13]
8 nāyakayan Kibi-gam äpä dun nāyakayan kuḍī-
9 -n mehi ätuḷattāk tänä kuhivaku marā ke(ṭuva)

[1] 'පලඤ්නා' යිද කියවිය හැකියි
[2] 'වන්' යිද කියවිය හැකියි
[3] 'කසා' යිද කියවිය හැකියි
[4] 'කැතිරි' යිද කියවිය හැකියි

[5] Mt. *siri bara Käta.* [6] Mt. *raja.* [7] Mt. *you.* [8] Mt. *aga.*
[9] Mt. *puta* (omitting *maha-raj-hu*). [10] This may also be read as *de* or *tun*. Mt. *tun.*
[11] Müller's text here and further on differs considerably from that of mine.
[12] *Kabāna-gamhi* or *Kibina-gamhi* may be suggested as alternative readings; Mt. *kamānak.*
[13] Or *ekeku.*

10 kaňḍa paḷā sora-kam kaḷa tirā koṭ genä dasa-gämä ä-
11 -ttan hindä vicārā upan däyaṭ pā häki-se liyā
12 tabā märuvehu marā paṭvanu koṭ isā kaňḍa-paḷā soru-
13 -n gat ayatiyen niyata-kaḷāk ayatiya (hi)mi-
14 -haṭ gena dī elvanu koṭ isā tirā no kaḷa dasa-gä-
15 -mä ättan pansālisa davasekin soyā genä paṭ-[1]
16 -vanu koṭ isā soyā no gata[2] dasa-gämin ek-
17 siya pas-visi kaḷandak ran radolaṭ denu koṭ isā
18 no marā keṭuva div-milä panās[3] kaḷandak ran gannā
19 koṭ isā no pohot ge-daḍ gannā koṭ isā tirā
20 no kaḷa dasa-gämin panās kaḷandak ran radolaṭ denu ko-
21 -ṭ isā at-pā-vahalaṭ giyākugen daḍä panās kaḷa-
22 -ndak ran gannā koṭ isā no pohot (ge)-daḍ gannā ko-
23 -ṭ isā ge-daḍ näta at kapā paṭ-vanu koṭ isā ..
24 -vū daḍ sihin daḍ pere-sirit-se gam-laddan pamaṇu-
25 (laddan bedā) gannā koṭ isā mīvun geri-gon eḷu-
26 -van märuvan marā paṭvanu koṭ isā no marā sorā-
27 genä giya niyata koṭ ovun ovun kasilä san-la-
28 -kuṇ obā harnā koṭ isā tirā no vat koṭā paṭva-
29 -nu koṭ isā bähärin[4] ärä vikuṇana mīvun geri-
30 -gon eḷuvan händinä äpā genä gannā koṭ isā
31 aṇa mäkuvan rat-kaḷa ya-maraväḍiy(e)[5] siṭvanu ko-
32 -ṭ isā me dasa-gä(mä kuḍī)n taman taman kulehi (vä-
33 -ṭe)na maňgul-avamaňgula valandnā[6] pärahära no ikmä
34 väṭenu koṭ isā me dasa-gamaṭ (vävasthā[7])-kaḷa täni-
35 -n (ekeka) avud (vun)[8] ku(ḍi)-kenekun äta händinä ä-
36 (-pä) genä hindvanu koṭ isā no yedennak koṭ va-
37 -n kenekun äta äpä[9] gata-dä paḷamu-vū gämä ä(tta-
38 -n) paṭvannaṭ harnā koṭ isā me dasa-gämä ä-
39 -ttan me kī tāk däyin ikmä väṭuṇa havurudu
40 havurudu patā illannaṭ giya raj-kol sam-da(ru-
41 van ke .. käva)tnā koṭ vajāḷa ek-tän samiye-
42 -n ā raj-sabhāye hindnā **Goḷuggamu**[10] **Ra(k)sā(im)**

---

[1] Or *pen*.
[2] Mt. *gat*.
[3] Mt. also *panās*.
[4] Mt. *ḍähärin ara pikaṇala*.
[5] Mt. *samar paḍiya*.
[6] This may also be read as *palandnā*.
[7] Read *vyavasthā*.
[8] Or *van*.
[9] Mt. *äpa gena di paḷamuva hämä aṇa*.
[10] Mt. *hoḷaggam*.

43 **Ku(ḍā)-senu** isā **Meykāppar Kuburgamu Lok(o)-** [1]
44 **-hi** isā **Kätiri** [2] **Agbohi** isā **Kuṇḍasalā Ara(yan)**
45 ätuḷävä metuvāk sam-daruvan-visin me vävasthā [3] karanu ladi

TRANSLATION.

[Lines 1–6] Prosperity! On the tenth day of the first half of the (lunar) month of *Undvap* (Nov.–Dec.) [4] in the (ninth) [5] year, after the canopy of dominion was raised by the great king [6] **Siri Saṅgbo Abhay,** son of the great king **Siri Saṅgbo Abhā**, lord by lineal succession of the lords of the soil of the Island of Laṅkā, which has become [as it were] the chief queen [7] unto the

---

[1] Mt. *mega kap para kamur me loke.* [2] Or *Kākiri.* [3] Read *vyavasthā.*

[4] See above, p. 198, note 4.

[5] *Nava-vana* = ninth; the readings *de-vana, tun-vana* = second, third respectively. See above, p. 246, note 10.

[6] *Maha-raj.* See Dr. Fleet's interesting note on the title *mahārāja* in his *Gupta Inscriptions,* p. 15, note 4.

[7] *Kät-usabnaṭ ag-mehesun vū Lak-div-poḷo-yōna-parapuren himi-vū.* The above rendering of this passage is founded on the meaning assigned to the similar expressions *Lak-div-poḷo-mehesana-parapuren himi* and *Lak-poḷo-mehesanaṭ talā-ṭik bandu* occurring in the Vessagiri slabs of Dappula V and of Mahinda IV (above, pp. 25 and 32), and in the slab-record of Kassapa V (above, p. 46). Compare also the expressions *Rāṣṭrakūṭēśvarāṇāṁ vaṁśa* and *Rāṣṭrakūṭa-kula-tilaka* (*Ep. Ind.* vii. p. 217). In my note on the subject (above, p. 26, note 10), I derived *mehesana* from Skt. *mahēśāna* (*mahā* + *īśāna*), and suggested that the forms *yohon, yōna,* and *yon* found in other inscriptions might possibly be derivatives of *īśāna* without *mahā*, but in combination with *poḷo* (Skt. *pṛthivī*, P. *paṭhavī*, Pkt. *puḍhavī, puhavī, puhai*; Sinh. *poḷova* and *poḷō*), which accounts for the vowel changes and the insertion of *y*. As for the change of Skt. *ś* into Pkt. and Sinh. *h*, see Pischel's *Pkt. Gram.*, par. 262, and Geiger's *L. S. S.*, par. 21. The compound *Lak-div-poḷo-yōna* may, however, admit of another interpretation. In Sinhalese poetry, the Island of Laṅkā is invariably compared to a maiden, as, for example, *sulakaḷa puvaḷa Lak-aṅgana*, 'the fair, proud dame Laṅkā' (*Sälalihiṇi-sandēsa*, v. 9). And *yōna, yona* or *yon* (from Skt. *yuvan*) means in Sinhalese 'a maiden,' e. g. *pura-yōnan*, 'city maidens' (*Kavsiḷumina*, v. 14), and *nava-yōnan*, 'young maidens' (*Sasadāvata*, v. 169). See also *Nāmāvaliya*, v. 150. The phrase *Kät-usabnaṭ ag-mehesun-vū Lak-div-poḷo-yōna-parapuren himi* may therefore be rendered 'lord, by hereditary succession, of the soil of the Island of Laṅkā, [which is like unto] a maiden that has [always] been [as it were] the chief queen unto the Kṣatriya princes.' The occurrence of the compound *poḷo-nava-yon*, in the Nāmbākaḍa pillar (*A. S. C. Seventh Progress Report*, p. 66), lends support to this interpretation, whilst the form *yohon* in the Devanagala slab of Parākrama Bāhu I (*A. S. C. Report on the Kegalla District*, p. 75), and the use of *yona*, independent of *Lak-div-poḷo*, in the Galpota record of Niśśaṅka Malla (*A. I. C.*, No. 148, A. 5), seem to militate against this view. I have as yet no grounds to suppose that the word *yona* or *yon* in Ceylon inscriptions may possibly refer to the *Yavanas* or *yonas* as applied to the ancient Arabian traders and their descendants in Ceylon.

Kṣatriya princes descended from the royal line of the Okkāka dynasty, the pinnacle of the very illustrious Kṣatriya race.

[Lines 6–14] Touching the *dasa-gam*[1] from amongst the endowments to **Demeḷ-vehera** (Tamil monastery) at Kibi-nilam[2] in Amgam-kuḷiya[3] in the Northern Quarter, each headman [of these villages], as well as those headmen and householders who have given security[4] for Kibi-gam, shall ascertain [the facts], when in any spot within this [district] murder[5] or robbery with violence[6] has been committed. Thereafter they shall sit in session[7] and inquire of the inhabitants of the *dasa-gam* [in regard to these crimes]. The proceedings [of the inquiry] having been so recorded that the same may be produced [thereafter], they shall have the murderer punished with death[8]. Out of the property taken by thieves by violence, they shall have such things as have

---

[1] See my explanation of this technical term above, p. 243. Compare also the phrase *vehera avaḷā ävū tāk tanaṭ . . . . . . vāri*, (*pere*) *nāṣṭiyam dasa-gam no vadnā isā* in the Vessagiri slab, No. 2, side A, lines 24–26, above, p. 33; *perenāṣṭiyam* is the correct reading. Here *dasa-gam* obviously stands for *dasa-gammu*, 'the inhabitants of *dasa-gam*.' My translation at p. 37 should, therefore, run 'nor shall *vāri* (labourers), *perenāṣṭiyam* (same as *pere-nāṭṭiyam* and *pere-nāṭṭu*) or inhabitants of *dasa-gam* enter.'

[2] *Kibi*, probably from P. *kumbhiko*, 'containing a measure of ten ammaṇas in sowing extent,' and Tamil *nilam*, 'ground.' Compare, however, the reading *Kibina-gam* (p. 246, note 12), and *Kibi-gam* in line 8: both obviously refer to the same locality and may have a technical meaning. Cf. also *Kubigamika* in the Jētavanārāma inscription of Maḷu-Tisa, line 8, below, p. 255.

[3] Cf. *Padonnaru-kuḷiya*, above, p. 206, note 4. Also *Pankuḷiya*, a hamlet near Anurādhapura.

[4] *Kibigam äpā dun nāyakayan kuḍin.* Cf. *ätuḷ bähäri aya-vijchi yut kämiyan näsūvāk denuvaṭ nisi kuḍīn äpā genā*, 'for the purpose of compensating for whatever may be destroyed by those engaged in matters relating to receipts and disbursements, both inside and outside (the Vihāra), security having been taken from suitable householders' (Mihintale record of the same king Mahinda IV, above, p. 92, lines 23–24). Compare also the principle of pledges in Saxon and Norman times of English history.

[5] *Marā*, lit. 'having killed;' *keṭuva*, from *koṭanavā*, 'to beat with a club.' Cf. *vī koṭanavā*, 'to pound paddy.' The compound *marā koṭanavā* has, therefore, the signification 'to beat to death.' Cf. *no marā keṭuva* in line 18, *minī keṭū kenekun*, 'those who have committed murder' (above, p. 47, line 18), *minī maraṇavā*, 'to murder.'

[6] *Kaṇḍa-paḷā sora-kam kaḷa.* I am not sure of the exact signification of this expression. The above is given tentatively. *Kaṇḍa* may be a derivative of Skt. *kāṇḍa* or *khaṇḍa*, 'section' or 'fragment;' *kāḍa* has also the significations 'privacy, vile, low.' *Paḷā* can be the gerund of *paḷanavā*, 'to tear asunder' (from Skt. √*sphaṭ* or *sphuṭ*). Cf. also P. *khaṇḍa-phullam*, 'breakage.' *Sora-kam* = P. *cōra-kamma*. Mr. Bell's rendering of *kaṇḍa-paḷā* is 'by breaking into boutiques' (*A. S. C. Seventh Progress Report*, 1891, p. 53).

[7] *Hindā*, lit. 'having sat in session.' Cf. *meluvāk janā . . . Ätveherhi hindā*, 'all these persons having held sessions in the Ätvehera' (Mihintale tablet A, lines 21–22, above, pp. 92, 101). Dr. Keith informs me that the ancient Indian *sabhā* held judicial sittings; cf. Macdonell and Keith, *Vedic Index*, s.v. *sabhā*.

[8] Cf. *Viṣṇu*, v. 1–11; *Nārada*, xiv. 8.

been [duly] identified, restored to the respective owners, and have [the thieves] hanged[1].

[Lines 14–18] If [offenders] are not detected, the inhabitants of the *dasa-gam* shall find them and have them punished within forty-five days. Should they not find them, then the *dasa-gam* shall be made to pay [a fine of] 125 *kaḷaňdas*[2] [weight] of gold to the State[3].

[Lines 18–20] If [the case] be an aggravated assault and not murder, [a fine of] 50 *kaḷaňdas* [weight] of gold shall be exacted as [penalty for] damage to life[4]. Should this not be feasible, *ge-daḍ*[5] shall be exacted. If [however, the assailants] are not detected, the *dasa-gam* shall be made to pay [a fine of] 50 *kaḷaňdas* [weight] of gold to the State.

[Lines 21–25.] From those who went out to do menial work, a fine of 50 *kaḷaňdas* [weight] of gold shall be exacted. Should this not be feasible, *ge-daḍ* shall be levied. Should there be no *ge-daḍ*, they shall be punished by having their hands cut off. Holders of villages[6] and of *pamaṇu* lands[7] shall divide among themselves in accordance with former usage the proceeds of (the ....) fines and the minor (?) fines.

[Lines 25–30] Those who have slaughtered buffaloes, oxen, and goats shall be punished with death. Should [the cattle] be stolen but not slaughtered, after due determination [thereof], each [offender] shall be branded under the armpit.

[1] *Elvanu*. This word is used in the sense of 'suspending' both in the modern language and in an ancient Sinhalese tract called *Sikhakaraṇī* (above, p. 99, note 5). The context, too, seems to support the above rendering, for it provides punishment in the case of theft, just as in that of murder. But I have not yet come across 'hanging' mentioned as a form of capital punishment in Sinhalese literature. Besides, if death penalty was meant, we should expect the phrase *marā paļvanu koļ* repeated. It is true that in the *Dēśavaļamai*, 'hanging' is referred to as one of the forms of death punishment, but this Tamil work is a compilation of the eighteenth century founded on the laws and customs prevailing in Jaffna during the Dutch period. Regarding the restoration of stolen goods, see *Manu*, viii. 40; *Viṣṇu*, iii. 66.

[2] Compare in this connexion the statutes of William the Conqueror (Stubbs's *Charters*, pp. 83–85).

[3] *Radolaṭ*, lit. 'to the royal family.' Cf. the forms *raj-kol* and *rad-kol*, above, pp. 47. 54 note 1, 55 note 2, 161 note 5, 189 note 9.

[4] *Div-milā*, lit. 'life-price.' It is not clear from the context whether this is a *bōt* or a *wite*. Cf. Taswell-Langmead's *English Constitutional History*, p. 32, *Manu*, viii. 287, and *Viṣṇu*, v. 60–75. Cf. also the old Indian term *vaira* in Macdonell and Keith, *Vedic Index*, ii. 331. 332.

[5] Probably a fine imposed on each household. Skt. *gṛha-daṇḍa*. See above, pp. 54 note 3, 103 note 12.

[6] *Gam-laddan*, lit. 'recipients of villages.' Same as P. *gāma-bhōjaka* (above, p. 206, note 7, and below, p. 259). Compare in this connexion the official title *bhōgika* so often occurring in Indian inscriptions. *Bhōgika* may also mean 'a village proprietor.' See *Ep. Ind.* v. p. 39.

[7] *Pamaṇu-laddan*. Cf. *pamaṇu-laduvan*, *kabali-laduvan*, and *pamaṇu-gam*, above, p. 117.

If [the nature of the offence][1] be not determined, [the culprits] shall be beaten. The buffaloes, oxen, and goats which are brought from outside for sale, shall only be bought after due identification of them and on security being given.

[Lines 31–36] Those who have effaced brand-marks[2] shall be made to stand on red-hot iron sandals. The inhabitants of these *dasa-gam* shall observe without transgression the privileges they enjoy[3] on [occasions of] rejoicing and mourning that occur in their respective families. If there be a villager who has come from (outside ?)[4] the limits prescribed for these *dasa-gam*, [he] shall be [duly] identified, and after taking security, shall be allowed to remain [in the *dasa-gam*].

[Lines 36–41] If there be one who has entered [these villages] after having committed an improper act, though security is taken, the inhabitants of the village in which the party at first resided, shall be permitted to impose [punishment on him].

Should the inhabitants of these *dasa-gam* villages have transgressed any of the rules stated [above], the Royal Officials who go[5] annually [on circuit] to administer justice[6] [in the country] shall . . . . . .[7].

[Lines 41–45] **Goḷuggamu Ra(k)sā(im) Ku(ḍā)-senu, Meykāppar Kuburgamu Lok(o)hi,** and **Kätiri Agbohi,** as well as **Kuṇḍasalā Ara(yan)**: all these lords who sit in the Royal Council, and who have come [together] in accordance with the mandate delivered [by the King in Council] have promulgated[8] these regulations.

[1] That is to say, whether the crime is one of cattle-slaughtering or of cattle-lifting.

[2] Probably the brand-marks on cattle.

[3] If the reading '*palandnā*' is adopted, the translation would run 'privileges in respect of dress on occasions of rejoicing and mourning.'

[4] The text here not being clear, I cannot be quite certain of my interpretation.

[5] *Giya* (line 40), lit. 'went.'

[6] *Illannaṭ* (line 40), modern Sinh. 'to claim or demand.' The full expression should be *raṭ illannaṭ*. Compare the two decrees *dede havurudden gos raj-kol-sam-daruvan raṭ illā pas mahā sīvaddā-varaj illaṭ-mut sesu varad no illanu isā . . . . . . raṭ paṭavannaṭ giya raj-kol-sam-daruvan gat daṇḍā giṅgiriyak äla sam-daruvan daṇḍa-nāyakayan hindā vicāra-koṭ häriyā yuṭuvak harnā isā* in the slab-inscription of Kassapa V (lines 19–20, and 22–24, above, p. 47). *Raṭ illannaṭ* and *raṭ paṭavannaṭ* are both technical official terms. The first seems to signify the administration of justice in the country, the second the imposing of punishment. See above, p. 53, note 13, and p. 54, note 1. In the *Dampiyā-aṭuvā-gäṭapada* (p. 92) *iliyannem* is given as the translation of P. *anvēsaṁ*, the present participle of *anvēsati* (Skt. *anu* + √*iṣ*), 'seek, search, or investigate.' Possibly this has the same etymology as our word *illanavā*, as it certainly has the same meaning in all the tenth and eleventh century inscriptions known to us.

[7] I am unable to make out this word owing to the indistinctness of some of the letters.

[8] Lit. 'these regulations were made by the lords.'

No. 22. JĒTAVANĀRĀMA INSCRIPTION OF MAḶU-TISA
(*circa* 229–247 A. D.)

THIS inscription was discovered by the Archaeological Commissioner of Ceylon (Mr. H. C. P. Bell) in 1910. It consists of 16 lines, covering an area of 6 ft. 10 in. by 4 ft. 8 in. of the top side of a slab now forming one of the flag-stones of the pavement at the south altar of the so-called Jētavanārāma Dāgaba.

The **letters** are boldly engraved and are quite clear, with the exception of those at places where the stone is worn or damaged. Their size varies from $1\frac{1}{2}$ to $2\frac{1}{2}$ in. each, and they belong to the Southern Brāhmī alphabet of the latter part of the second or the first half of the third century A. D. Their type, however, indicates a certain 'archaic' or retrograde tendency. The elongated vertical strokes, as a rule curved at the end, of *a*, *ka*, *ra*, and *la*, which are some of the characteristic features of the Southern Brāhmī alphabet of this period both here and in India, are entirely wanting. In other respects the letters have undergone normal development, as will be seen on a comparison of the accompanying facsimile (Plate 30) with those of the earlier inscriptions at Perumāiyankulam, Pālu-Mākiccāva, and Maha-Ratmale (above, Plates 13 and 27). Attention should be drawn to the *svastika* in lines 9, 12, and 14. It is used here perhaps to serve both as an auspicious symbol and as a mark of punctuation.

The **language** is ancient Sinhalese, which in style and phraseology resembles so much the Prākrit dialects employed in the earliest inscriptions of India.

The **orthography** seems to be faultless with the exception of *gari* in line 10, which is obviously a clerical error for *giri*, as given in line 13. The **grammar** too is regular. We see the nominative singular in *-i*, the genitive in *-ha*, the locative in *-hi*, the dative in *-haṭaya*, and the gerund in *-ṭu* and *-ya*, e. g. *koṭu*, *kaḍaya*, and *karavaya*. We find also the crude form of the noun used for the nominative, as is sometimes the case in Prākrit. All these have already been noticed and in part explained elsewhere in the present volume [1].

Regarding the etymology and the meaning of uncommon words and phrases in the text, the reader is referred to the remarks which immediately follow the translation.

The inscription is one of king **Maḷu-Tisa**, son of king **Naka**. His identity

[1] See the Index for references.

with **Kaniṭṭha-Tissa** (*circa* 229–247 A.D.), son of **Mahallaka-Nāga**, was first established by Dr. Müller[1]. It records that at **Utara-maha-ċeta**, he effected repairs, built four gateways and a 'sitting-hall' (*asana-hala*), and granted the income derived from certain tanks and 'anicuts' for the maintenance of the monks of the Abhayagiri-vihāra and for expenses connected with the repairs of its buildings, the 'Great Refection,' and the supply of oil and offerings. The **Utara-maha-ċeta** may be identified with the **Abhayuttara-mahā-cētiya** of the **Abhayagiri-vihāra**, mentioned both in the *Mahāvaṁsa* and in the two foregoing inscriptions[2] of Mahinda IV from the same locality as the present one. In lines 5, 12, and 15 we are told that Maḷu-Tisa caused the construction of four *ayikas* ('gateways'?) to this *Mahā-cetiya*, the **Gamiṇi-Tisa** tank, and a 'sitting-hall.' The *Mahāvaṁsa*[3], however, ascribes the erection of *ādimukhas* ('arches'?) at the four gates of the same *cetiya*, the formation of the Gāmaṇī-Tissa tank, and the building of the *Mahā-āsana*[4] hall in the capital to king Gajabāhu, who reigned some thirty years before Maḷu-Tisa.

Finally, seeing that the present slab and the two foregoing ones of Mahinda IV as well as the slab-inscription of Kassapa V (above, No. 4) exclusively deal with the Abhayagiri Monastery, we would naturally expect to find them set up in the vicinity, if not within the precincts of the monastery in question. But they were discovered within the area of the so-called Jētavanārāma. Hence arises the question whether the stones were in their original position when they were found, or they have been brought to Jētavanārāma in later times from the Abhayagiri. If the former be the case, doubts may be entertained as to the correctness of the accepted identification of the Jētavanārāma ruins, especially as this monastery was only built in the reign of Mahāsēna, some eighty-four years after king Maḷu-Tisa. It may, in view of these facts, be possible that these ruins belong to another monastery attached to the Abhayagiri fraternity, if they are not of the Abhayagiri-vihāra itself.

As to the places mentioned in the record, **Upala-ketaka** (Skt. *Utpala-kṣētraka*) may have been a tract of field in **Upala-vibajaka** or **-bijaka** referred to in the inscriptions of Pālu-Mākiccāva and Tammännä-kanda[5]. I take

---

[1] *A. I. C.*, p. 29. [2] See above, p. 216. [3] Ch. xxxv. 119–122.

[4] It is unfortunate that the letters immediately preceding the word *asana-hala* are so indistinct in the inscription; else they would probably help us to determine whether the building in question was a temple dedicated to the *yakkha* named *Mahīja* (*Mv. Ṭ.* xvii. 30), or *Mahejjā* (Professor Geiger's edition), that is to say, whether it was called *Mahējāsanasālā*, as the Burmese recension of the *Mahāvaṁsa* gives, or was simply an *āsana-sālā* of the congregation of monks, as the Sinhalese recension seems to indicate.

[5] See above, p. 210.

Majata-gamaṇa as a proper name with *kiriye*, loc. of *kiriya* (P. *karīsa*) added to it. In the Habaraṇa record[1] Dr. Müller reads *mujita gamaṇa keriyahi*, which he translates 'on account of the inundated villages,' deriving *mujita* from the p.p.p. of √*majj* and *keriya* from P. *kāriya*. The **Kubigamika-vavi** may have been a tank in Kibi-gama mentioned in line 8 of the Vēvälkäṭiya inscription[2]. The district **Vihira-bijaka**, where the tank **Visaḷa-gamika-vavi** (line 11) was, may be identical with the one named in the Maha-Ratmale and the Galkövila inscriptions[3], and in *Mv.* xvii. 59.

The following edition of the record is based on two ink-estampages and two eye-copies supplied by the Archaeological Commissioner of Ceylon.

TEXT.

1 [සිධ- **නකමහරජහ පුත ම**]**ළ(ති)සමහරජි උතරමහචෙතහි** .. ..
(චත) ..

2 .. .. (වග පව) .. .. [ස](කල)
සම(තෙ)ය කර කඩය දිනි ඒ [නක මහ

3 රජ]හ පුත මළතිසමහරජි උපල[4]කෙත(කහි) .. .. (රගණකගලි)ගෙහි
අට ක(රිහි) .. ..

4 .. .. (උතර)මහ(චෙ)තහි තෙල ච (හුති) ච මුලකොටු දිනි .. ..
.. ..

5 [උතරමහ](චෙත)හි චතර අයික කරවය ජිණ පටිසතිර්ය කරනක කොටු (ච)
.. ..

6 මහබිකුසන[හටය] (ම)හපක(ච)වහ උවණික කොටු ච මජතගමණ[5]කිරි(ගෙ)
හිය (කො)මත(ළුමහවවි ච)

7 (සුමිතමහවවි ච) .. .. (වවි) ච නිපිලවිපියවවි (ච) නළි(බි)අවියවවි ච
(තමළ)වයිව(වි) [ච] .. .. ..

8 .. (වවි ච උතර)වවි ච .. .. කවවි ච කුබිගමිකවවි
ච මහබපි(දන)ව

9 පි ච (මහනිළදරක අවරණ ච මිචතකිවවි) .. .. (අව)රණෙහ[6] ච දකපති කර
කඩය මහරජි දිනි ඒ [නකමහ]

10 (රජහ) පුත (මළ)තිසමහරජි අබයගරි[7]මහවිහර .. .. (න කඩ)ගරි
.. .. ය .. ..

11 හවය ච බුකුසගහවය ච විහිරබිජකිහි විස(ළ)ගමිකවවි .. .. [ක]

12 ර කඩය දිනි ඒ නකමහරජහ පුත මළතිසමහරජි තිලරජිය ගමිණිතිස
.. .. .. [ක]

---

[1] *A. I. C.*, No. 61.

[2] See above, p. 246.

[3] See above, p. 61.

[4] 'උපලි' සිද කියවිය හැකිය

[5] 'ගමතෙ' යිද කියවිය හැකිය

[6] මෙය 'අවරණහ' විය හැකිය

[7] මෙය 'ගිරි' විය යුතුය

13 රවය දකපතිය ච බො(ජී)යපතිය ච කර කඩය අබයගිර්මහවිහරහි මහ
14 මහපකවටහ (උවන)ක කොටු දිනි 卐 නකමහරජහ පුත මළුතිසමහරජි
15 චත(ර)ගි(ණි)කිල (අ)ස(වක) අසනගල කරවය ජිණ පටිසතිරිය කර(න)ක කොටු (මහ
16 ලෙකෙතකගි) දෙළස කරිගි (ච) .. යගි දෙළස කරිගි ච දෙපති ච (උ)ත කුබර කර කඩය (දිනි)

TRANSCRIPT.

1 [Sidha- **Naka**-maha-rajaha puta **Ma**]ḷu-(**Ti**)**sa**-maha-raji **Utara-maha-cetahi** .. .. (cata) ..
2 .. .. (-vaya pava) .. .. [sa](ka-la)-sama(te)ya kara kaḍaya dini 卐 [Naka-maha-
3 raja]ha puta Maḷu-Tisa-maha-raji Upala[1]-keta(kahi .. .. (rahaṇaka-gaḷi)yehi aṭa ka(rihi) .. ..
4 .. .. (Utara-)maha-(ce)tahi tela ca (huti) ca mula-koṭu dini .. ..
5 [Utara-maha-](ceta)hi catara ayika karavaya jiṇa paṭisatiriya karanaka koṭu (ca) .. ..
6 maha-biku-saga-[haṭaya] (ma)hapaka-(va)ṭaha uvaṇaka koṭu ca Majata-gamaṇa[2]-kiri(ye) hiya (Ko)mata(ḷa-maha-vavi ca)
7 (Sumita-maha-vavi ca) .. .. (-vavi) ca Niṭilaviṭiya-vavi (ca) Naḷi(bi)-aviya-vavi ca (Tamaḷa)-vari-va(vi) [ca] .. .. ..
8 .. (-vavi ca Utara-)vavi ca .. .. -ka-vavi ca Kubi-gamika-vavi ca Mahabaṭi-(dana-)va-
9 -vi ca (Mahaniḷadaraka avaraṇa ca Micataki-vavi) .. .. (ava)raṇeha[3] ca da-ka-pati kara kaḍaya maharaji dini 卐 [Naka-maha-]
10 (-rajaha) puta (Maḷu)-Tisa-maharaji Abayagari[4]-maha-vihara .. .. (na kaḍa)-gari .. .. ya .. ..
11 -haṭaya ca buku-sagahaṭaya ca Vihira-bijakihi Visa(ḷa)-gamika-vavi .. .. [ka]
12 -ra kaḍaya dini 卐 Naka-maha-rajaha puta Maḷu-Tisa-maha-raji Nilaraji--ya Gamiṇi-Tisa .. .. .. [ka-]
13 -ravaya dakapatiya ca bo(ji)ya-patiya ca kara kaḍaya Abayagiri-maha-viha--rahi maha

---

[1] Or *upali*.

[2] This may also be read *gamane*.

[3] Probably for *avaraṇaha*.

[4] Read *-giri*.

14 maha-paka-vaṭaha (uvana)ka koṭu dini Naka-maha-rajaha puta Maḷu-Tisa-maha-raji

15 cata(ra)hi(ṇi)kila (a)sa(vaka) asanahala karavaya jiṇa paṭisatiriya kara(na)-ka koṭu (Maha-

16 -le-ketakahi) doḷasa-karihi (ca) .. -yahi doḷasa-karihi ca do-pati ca (u)ta kubara kara kaḍaya (dini)

TRANSLATION.

[Lines 1–2] [Hail!] The great king **Maḷu-Tisa**, [son of the great king **Naka**] . . . . at **Utara-maha-ceta** granted . . . . exempting [the same] from all recognized taxes.

[Lines 2–4] The great king Maḷu-Tisa, son of [the great king Naka] granted . . . . in the tract of field [called] Upala, and eight *karīsas* in . . . . . (-rahaṇaka-gaḷiya)[1] . . . . . providing [thereby] money for oil and (offerings) at the Utara-maha-ceta.

[Lines 5–9] The great king causing four gateways (?) to be built at the [Utara-maha-]ceta, dedicated free of tax the income derived from the waters of the great tanks (Ko)mata(ḷa) and (Sumita) situated in Majata-gamaṇa-kiriya, the tank . . . . the tank Niṭilaviṭiya, the tank Naḷi(bi)-aviya, the tank (Tamaḷa)-vari, the tank . . . . . the tank Utara, the tank . . . . the tank Kubigamika, the supplying tank Mahabaṭi, (the 'anicut' Mahaniḷada-raka, and the 'anicut' . . . . the tank Micataki) for the purpose of effecting repairs of dilapidated [buildings] . . . . and as an endowment for the maintenance of the 'Great Refection' for the great congregation of monks at . . . .

[Lines 9–12] The great king (Maḷu-)Tisa, son [of the great king Naka] granted free of tax [the income derived from the waters of] the tank Visaḷa-gamika in Vihira-bijaki unto the congregation of monks and unto . . . . at the Abhayagiri-mahā-vihāra.

[Lines 12–14] The great king Maḷu-Tisa, son of the great king Naka, causing the construction of Nilarajiya and Gamiṇi-Tisa . . . . . granted free of tax the income derived from water and the income enjoyed by the *bhōjika* as an endowment for the maintenance of the 'Great Refection' at the great Abhayagiri Monastery.

---

[1] Cf. *Palanagala*, above, p. 70.

Jetavanārāma inscription of Malu-Tisa (*circa* 229–247 A.D.)

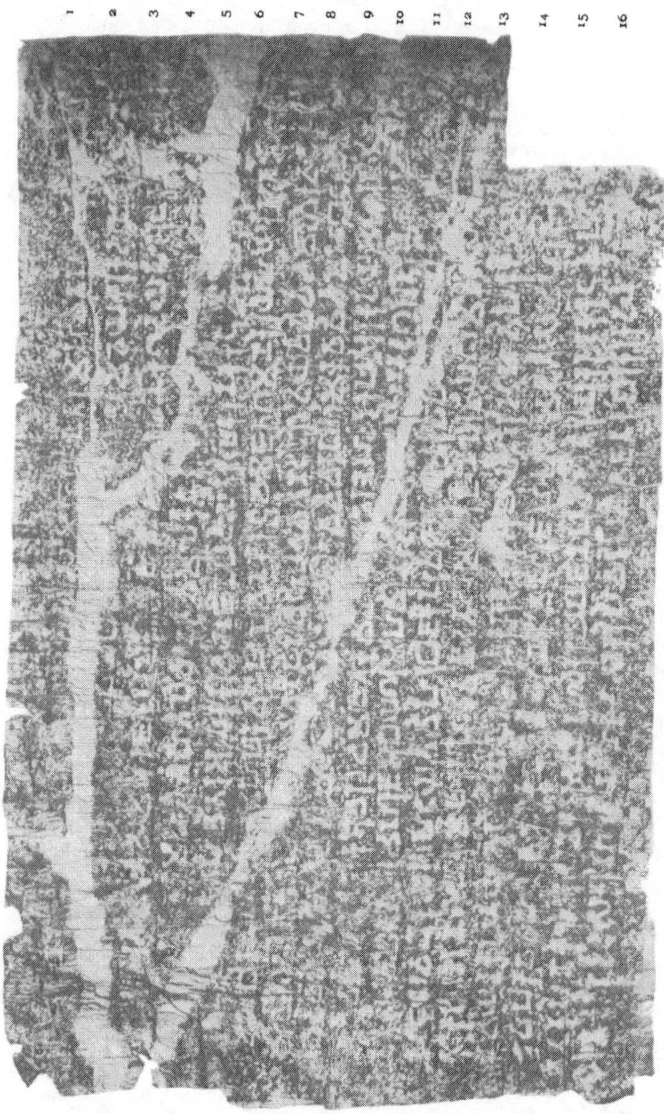

From an ink-impression supplied by the Archaeological Commission, Ceylon.
Scale about 1¼ inches to 1 foot.

[Lines 14–16] The great king Maḷu-Tisa, son of the great king Naka, causing to be built a 'sitting-hall' . . . . at the four . . . . granted free of the *uta* grain-tax, twelve *karīsas* [sowing extent] of (Mahale-ketaka) and twelve *karīsas* [sowing extent] of . . . . . . , as well as the two [kinds of] income [1] for the purpose of effecting repairs of dilapidated [buildings].

REMARKS.

The above translation is offered tentatively. Its accuracy depends much on the correctness of the following interpretation of the obscure words and phrases in the text:—

Sakala samateya kara kaḍaya = Skt. *sakalaṁ sammatikaṁ karaṁ kaṇḍayitvā* (or *kāḍayitvā*), 'having removed every recognized tax [2].' Compare, for example, (*a*) *daka-pata sakala samata dini* [3], 'the water-income recognized by all was given;' (*b*) *sakala samatuya catara* [*Chuna*] *mahapati*, *Baka-maha-patika Gije-pava-koḷasa Kaḍavaka-koḷasa* [4], 'the four which are recognized by all [namely] the revenues of [Chuna] and Baka, and the shares at Gije-pava and Kaḍavaka.' The expression *kara kaḍaya* occurs also in the sense given above in the inscriptions of Habarana [5], Galkōvila [6], and Tammännä-kanda [7]. Compare also *dasa-kärä*, above, p. 103, note 12, and p. 240, note 1.

Tela ca huti ca mula koḷu (line 4). I take this to be equivalent to P. *tēla-mūlañ* [8] *ca huti-mūlañ ca katvā*. Dr. Müller, however, reads in the Habarana inscription *tela huta mala koḷu*, which he renders 'having made offerings of oil and flowers [9].'

---

[1] Namely, *daka-pati* and *bojiya-pati*.

[2] If we, however, take *sakala samateya* as one compound word *sakala-sammatikaṁ*, the translation would run 'having remitted the taxes accepted by all.'

[3] *A. I. C.*, No. 16. Here *pata* is probably an incorrect reading for *pati*. Dr. Müller's rendering of the passage is 'after having seen he gave it over altogether.' With this I cannot agree for reasons advanced on p. 72.

[4] *A. S. C. Seventh Progress Report*, 1891, p. 54. *Samatuya* probably incorrectly for *samatiya*. Mudaliyar Guṇasēkara renders this passage 'all these in common to the four . . . Chuna-maha-pati,' &c.

[5] *A. I. C.*, No. 61, where the causative *kaḍavaya* is wrongly transcribed and translated as *karakaḷa waya*, and *karakaṭa wawiya*, 'the Karakaḷa tank.'

[6] *Ibid.*, No. 98, where also erroneously *bojiya pati karakaṭaya*, 'having assigned the Karakaṭa field.'

[7] *A. S. C. Seventh Progress Report*, 1891, p. 47, Inscr. No. 2.

[8] Cf. P. *diguṇaṁ pupphamūlaṁ*, 'twice the amount of money for flowers;' *mūlaṁ karōti*, 'he provides money.'

[9] Cf. also *tela mala* in his transcript of the Galkōvila record (*A. I. C.*, No. 98).

Catara ayika (line 5) = P. *cattārō agghikāyō*, Sinh. *satara ägā*. The Pāli form *agghikā* is not in Childers' *Pāli Dictionary*, but Clough, in his *Sinhalese Dictionary*, gives *ägā* with the meaning 'festoon work.' This does not seem to be correct, judging from its use in the following verse from the *Kāvyaśēkhara* (i. 102):—

Ras-udula rat palasa
vasan'ev ran ägā-pasa
nuga-pala-van sakasa
perava malu sivura risiyena-lesa.

'Having put on well and satisfactorily the robe which is of the colour of the fruit of the banyan tree (*nyagrōdha-phala*), just as one covers the side of a golden *ägā* with a brilliantly shining red mantle.' The *sanne* to this verse explains *ran-ägā-pasa* by *svarṇa-maya agghikā-pārśvayak*. As mentioned above, the *Mahāvaṁsa* records the building of *ādimukhas* at the four gates of the Abhayuttara-mahā-thūpa by king Gajabāhu, some thirty years before king Maḷu-Tisa of the present inscription. Whether *ādimukha*, which Wijēsiṇha renders 'arches,' is only another word for *agghikā*, and whether the two statements refer to one and the same event or not I am not sure.

Jiṇa paṭisatiriya karanaka koṭu (lines 5 and 15), see above, p. 71.

Maha-paka-vaṭaha (line 6) = P. *mahā-pāka-vaṭṭassa*. *Mahā-pāka*, 'the great cooking,' was probably a technical name like *mahāpāli*[1], given either to the common refection or to the kitchen of a great monastery, otherwise it is difficult to understand why *pāka-vaṭṭāya* in *Mv.* xxxv. 120 is explained in the Ṭīkā by *mahā-pāka-vaṭṭatthāya*. The expression *maha maha-paka-vaṭaha*, in lines 13 and 14, also supports this supposition. Here the first *maha* simply qualifies *maha-paka* as a single word having a special meaning.

Uvanaka koṭu = P. *uppannakaṁ katvā*, 'having caused the arising.' Similarly, *avanaka* in dates such as *sata avanaka vasahi*, 'in the seventh year,' is derived from Skt. P. *āpanna* + *ka*, as Mudaliyar Guṇasēkara has already pointed out[2]. The forms *vana*, *veni*, *väni*, and *vanna* now added to cardinals to convert them to ordinals are obviously derivatives of *āpannaka* or *āpannika*. I do not think they can be connected with *vana* or *vena*, the relative participle, present of *vanavā* or *venavā* (from Skt. √*bhū*).

Hiya. See above, p. 71.

---

[1] See above, p. 228, note 16.

[2] *A. S. C. Seventh Progress Report*, 1891, p. 48, note 9.

Dana-vavi (line 8) = P. *dāna-vāpi*. See above, p. 36, note 8.

Avaraṇa (line 9) = Skt. *āvaraṇa*. Cf. Sinh. *avura*, *avuraṇavā*, from Skt. *ā* + √*vṛ*.

Daka-pati (line 9) = P. *daka-patti*. See above, pp. 71–72.

Daka-patiya = *daka-pattika*. Compare the intermediate form *patika* in the Aminicciya inscription [1].

Karavaya (line 13) = modern *karavā*, probably derived from a form **kārāpay-ya*, the gerund in *ya* added to the full causative stem, as *tvā* in *kārāpayitvā* or *ya* in *-kramayya*. Cf. Whitney's *Sanskrit Grammar*, par. 1051. d., and Geiger's *Litt. und Spr. der Singhalesen*, par. 65. 2.

Bojiya-patiya = Skt. *bhōjika-prāptika*, 'the income accruing to the *gāma-bhōjaka*, 'village headman,' or one who enjoys certain proprietary rights in a village. See above, p. 206, notes 7 and 8; p. 250, note 6. The term *bojiya-pati* or *-patiya* occurs in other records of the third century A. D. Dr. Müller translates it 'after having made serve,' 'after having assigned.'

Karihi is a difficult form. It is not clear whether this is the locative singular of *kari* (Skt. *khāri*) [2], or is simply another spelling of *kariha*, *kiriya* (P. *karīsa*), the singular being in both cases used for the plural in a collective sense, or whether we have here a plural ending in *i*.

Do-pati = Skt. *dvi-prāpti*, referring to the two (kinds) of income, namely, *daka-pati* and *bojiya-pati*.

Uta kubara kara. I take *kubara-kara* to mean 'a grain-tax.' *Uta* describes the special nature of the tax. This word is most probably the same as the modern agricultural term *otta* or *otu*, which Clough renders as 'tax, tithe, duty;' *otu*-duty is one-tenth of anything.

---

[1] *A. S. C. Seventh Progress Report*, 1891, p. 54.

[2] *A. I. C.*, Nos. 18, 61, 97 (*b*), 98.

INDEX

The following is a complete index of words and proper names occurring in the first volume of the Epigraphia Zeylanica.